Dr Rudolf Steiner

RUDOLF STEINER: Herald of a New Epoch

Stewart C. Easton

Anthroposophic Press

Copyright © 1980 Anthroposophic Press, Inc.

Published by Anthroposophic Press
RR4 Box 94-A1, Hudson, NY 12534

Library of Congress Catalog Card No. 80-67026

ISBN 0-910142-93-9

10 9 8 7 6 5 4 3 2

Printed in the United States of America

CONTENTS

ACKNOWLEDGMENTS

I have again to thank Paul Marshall Allen for having carefully reviewed the entire manuscript of this biography, as a result of which he made numerous suggestions, almost all of which I have followed. I owe a special debt to Joan DeRis Allen for her suggestions and corrections, without which I should have made several important errors in my account in Chapter 8 of the building of the First Goetheanum. Joan Allen is one of the consulting architects for the Camphill Movement, and a life-long student of both Goetheanums. I wish to thank also Susan Stern and Hilary Williams for much help in the translation of documents available only in German used for Chapter 5. Dr. Gilbert Church, managing director of the Anthroposophic Press, also made a number of important suggestions following his first reading of the manuscript, as well as seeing the finished book through to publication. Lastly, Benedict Wood proposed some changes in my sections on eurythmy and education in the course of his reading of the entire manuscript, and these have been incorporated into the text to its great improvement.

Stewart C. Easton

Chapter 1

INTRODUCTORY

When Rudolf Steiner was born in 1861 near the confines of the Austrian Empire, the dominant aspect of Western thought was its materialism, the denial by so many thinkers not only of the truths of traditional Christianity, but of any divine activity whatever in earthly affairs. In that year Charles Darwin's masterpiece *The Origin of Species*, which purported to explain mankind's evolution in wholly material terms, was beginning its meteoric success, while Karl Marx's teachings seemed to offer a convincing and satisfying explanation of mankind's history without having to resort to any hypothesis of divine purpose or intervention. Auguste Comte's philosophy of positivism, which attempted to show how man had thrown off old superstitions in order to arrive at an enlightened understanding of the world and man in material terms without the aid of religion, was making new converts every day among mid-nineteenth century philosophers and scientists. Artur Schopenhauer, deeply pessimistic, had published his epoch-making work *The World as Will and Idea*, in which he tried to demonstrate the meaninglessness of human evolution, a philosophy soon to be adopted as the point of departure for his own work by Friedrich Nietzsche, a battler, as Rudolf Steiner was later to call him, against his time. Nietzsche's whole life work, indeed, was a long cry of anguish against the ideas of his day, which he was not able to refute but could not accept with equanimity—his anguish leading him ever more deeply into a kind of nihilism, and above all into that

1

opposition to Christianity that was characteristic of his latest work.

Such was the cultural and intellectual atmosphere of Europe when Rudolf Steiner was born. But from his earliest childhood he was aware of the reality of the invisible or spiritual world, and it was for that reason impossible for him to share the skepticism, agnosticism and materialism of his age. He *knew* that all reality was not encompassed within the visible earthly world and thus never experienced an anguish comparable to Nietzsche's. His problem lay elsewhere. Once he had discovered that other men did not possess his spiritual vision he might have conceived it to be his task to convey to others what he himself perceived in the world of spirit, leaving it to those others to convince themselves as best they could of his veracity, and make what they could of his revelations. The revelations themselves they would in effect have been required to accept on faith, or reject because they could not bring themselves to believe them. In essence this was the path taken by seers of earlier epochs, men like Jacob Boehme or Emanuel Swedenborg, who spoke or wrote directly of their spiritual experiences and "revealed" what they had perceived in the spiritual worlds hidden from the rest of mankind.

Steiner set himself a more difficult task. Recognizing at an early age that the human capacity for thinking is not simply a bodily process carried out by the brain, but is a supersensible activity of the human spirit which uses the brain as its instrument, he made it his task never to speak of any of his spiritual experiences unless he had first clothed them in a conceptual form that could be grasped by other men when they too had activated their thinking. For many years he was known only as a philosopher, and none of those who read his original works on philosophy or his studies of Goethe, which by the end of the nineteenth century had won him a modest acclaim in the cultural world of Wilhelmine Germany, would have been able to detect the spiritual experience that lay behind his philosophical expositions. Only later, at a time when he was speaking openly about Theosophy or Anthroposophy, did he point out to his new audiences how everything that he said later had

2

already been provided with its philosophical basis in his earlier works. He then explained that he could have spoken, even before the end of the nineteenth century, of the spiritual truths that he had apprehended through his supersensible faculties. For example, he could have explained how the activity of the higher self of man is made possible only through man's permeation by the Christ Impulse. But if he had revealed this truth in his major philosophical work, *The Philosophy of Freedom*, published in 1894, the disclosure would have been premature. It could not have been accepted and would therefore have been meaningless. Not until after he had spoken of the Christ Impulse for many years and from many points of view did he draw the attention of his hearers to what he had said in 1894, telling of what lay behind the carefully worded statements of the earlier epoch. It seems clear that at no time in his life did Steiner ever say anything *gratuitously*. It was a part of his genius that he neither said anything for the sake of effect, nor before at least some of his hearers had acquired the basis for understanding what he said.

Thus his life falls naturally into two parts, his philosophical period until 1900, culminating in the completion of his book *Conceptions of the World and of Life in the Nineteenth Century*, and his theosophical and anthroposophical period, when he devoted the greater part of his books and lectures to revealing numerous truths that derived from his direct experience of the spiritual worlds. He was able to do this after 1900 for three major reasons: he believed, as we shall see, that with the turn of the century the time had become propitious for making such revelations; an audience had now been found that was eager and willing to hear what he had to say; and last, but for him by no means the least important consideration, he felt that he could now put into intelligible concepts what had always been for him a matter of direct experience, the truths of the spiritual world concealed from almost all his contemporaries because they had neither been endowed with the faculties that had been his from birth, nor had they as yet acquired them by their own efforts—as he assured his hearers was possible if they followed the path he was to indicate for them.

3

Throughout his life Steiner spoke, often in considerable detail, of what he called "mystery knowledge," knowledge dating from much earlier periods in mankind's history when all human beings had been clairvoyant and could see into the spiritual worlds. As men began to perceive the external world more clearly and grew to understand some aspects of it, they gradually lost their primitive clairvoyance, and the earth became more real to them than the world of spirit. The knowledge of the course that evolution would take in later epochs was known to some spiritual leaders of mankind. For this reason in almost all parts of the world preparations were made so that knowledge of the spiritual worlds would not disappear from the earth even though direct vision would so largely be lost. This knowledge was therefore preserved in "mystery centers," where after due preparation and undergoing certain trials under the direction of their elders, candidates for intiation were instructed in the wisdom preserved from antiquity. In due course they themselves became "initiates," with the task of transmitting the wisdom to a new generation of those who had proved themselves worthy to receive it.

Although almost all peoples had established these mystery centers, most of them by the time of the founding of Christianity had become decadent. According to Steiner the old knowledge was dying out or becoming distorted, and no new spritiual knowledge was as yet available. For more than a millennium after the turn of the Christian era it was necessary for men to nourish their souls by *contemplating* the truths of Christianity without truly *understanding* them. This, according to Steiner, was the true reason why it was necessary to have an "age of faith," which continued until the high Middle Ages, to merge in the fullness of time into an age when men would acquire knowledge and understanding of the world. In that newer age men would at last begin to take their own future in hand, and accept the responsibility for earthly evolution, a responsibility that had formerly belonged exclusively to divine powers. From the beginning of time divine beings had willed that man should be free, but only gradually could they yield up to him those capacities and powers that would enable him to be free, and to take over those responsibilities hitherto exercised by themselves. If man had been endowed prematurely with the scientific knowledge he was to acquire later he would not, *could* not, have known how to use it—and indeed it can certainly be contended that he still does not know how to use it. But it is no longer *impossible*, as it was in earlier ages, for him to learn how to use his powers responsibly. The higher beings who watch over man's evolution have had to take the risk that he will so misuse the powers entrusted to him that he will not be able to reach his goal. But if man were ever to be free, thus becoming a being unique in the whole universe, as it was planned that he should be, the risk had necessarily to be taken.

During the quarter of a century spent in teaching the science of spirit Steiner constantly stressed this theme of man's task and man's responsibilities; and he tried to show *why* it was necessary for him to lose all direct knowledge of the spiritual worlds it he were to be truly free. As it is necessary for evil to exist in the world if man is to be able to make a choice between good and evil, so is it necessary for him to be able to *deny* the existence of divine powers, and for those powers to be hidden from his vision if he is truly to believe in his own freedom, and not feel himself coerced by beings wiser and more powerful than himself. It is necessary for darkness to exist if light is to be valued at its true worth, and if man is to be able to choose to follow the light and not bog down in the darkness. But Steiner also held that man's spiritual helpers had not lost interest in him, and had no intention of allowing him to struggle on alone toward the light without aid. However, they too must be willing to respect his freedom, and in no circumstances to coerce him, even for his own good. When therefore men had reached the point of totally disbelieving in the very existence of the spirit, when knowledge of the soul had become vague and only knowledge of the body seemed real, and the body itself was seen to dissolve into its component elements at death, the moment came when it was necessary that they should again be given some true knowledge drawn from the spiritual worlds. It was no longer possible to breathe new life into old religious

5

teachings, however effectively these had nourished the soul in earlier epochs, nor should men be introduced once more to the old mystery knowledge preserved by occultists through the centuries. Such knowledge must now be given in such a form that men could accept or reject it through their own capacity for thinking, and by exercising their own power of judgment. Men must in future feel the *need* for this knowledge and seek it. Steiner taught that divine powers indeed wished man to have this knowledge so that on the one hand he could fulfill his responsibilities toward the earth and its non-human inhabitants, and on the other could give back to these divine beings from his own freedom what he alone, as a free being, could give—his love.

Such, in essence, was the picture of man and his destiny consistently taught by Rudolf Steiner. But it would be impossible to find such a summary as the foregoing in any of his works. It has always been necessary for the student of his teachings to work hard at every sentence Steiner wrote or spoke, trying to enliven his own thinking by rethinking for himself the often packed concepts that may at first reading appear dry, though never abstract. In order to determine whether they "make sense" it is almost always necessary to relate them to other concepts that have been slowly and gradually made one's own, sometimes through years of study. Indeed, it is a curious but well attested fact, familiar to almost all anthroposophists, that every time they return to a book or lecture of Steiner that they had thought was entirely familiar to them, much, if not all of it seems totally new as if they had never read it before. Students of anthroposophy may admiringly refer to the "more than six thousand" lectures given by Rudolf Steiner, as if numerous university professors had not given far more than six thousand in a lifetime of teaching. What is so extraordinary about Steiner's lectures is the concentrated thought that went into them and the concentrated thought that is necessary if they are to be grasped by today's readers. This is, as might be expected, even more true of his books which he worked over again whenever new editions became necessary.

For many years before 1900 Steiner tells us that he was waiting for some kind of indication from the spiritual worlds that the time had become ripe, and that he could begin to speak openly of all that he knew. He was never entirely sure that he would *ever* be permitted to speak, and time and again he put to himself the question: Must I forever keep silent? Meanwhile he continued to make himself as familiar as he could with all the concepts and ideas accepted by the science and philosophy of his day. Having long recognized that no one else appeared to have the same kind of knowledge as he, and believing, as he did, that mankind needed that knowledge, it was natural for him to suppose that some day he would be given a task to perform. But he was not willing to begin that task without spiritual guidance whose validity he could not doubt. With his knowledge of history and his understanding of the predominant thought of his day, it was clear to him that he would be required to give to mankind something truly *new*, something that if it were used properly would make man's future different from what it had been in the past. It could not be a question of making minor changes, slight deviations from the path man was now following. A totally new orientation would be essential. Without abandoning any of the scientific advances of the last centuries, recognizing them for what they were, one of the most stupendous achievements in the history of mankind— spiritual achievements, as Rudolf Steiner did not hesitate to call them—it was nevertheless necessary to make clear that the material world does not comprise the whole of reality. Indeed, in Steiner's view the material visible world itself cannot be understood without taking into consideration *also* the immaterial invisible world that enfolds it. The invisible world existed before the material world, solid matter being a very late development in world evolution. It will exist long after the material world has disappeared; man must begin to rediscover it if he is to move onwards toward his goal.

It is impossible to guess what the experience was that convinced Steiner at last that the time had arrived for him to speak. In the autobiography that he left unfinished at his death he was reticent on the subject, even though he did refer clearly enough to some external factors that were present after the turn

7

of the century that had been missing before. From the choice of subjects for his books and his lectures prior to the War it can be inferred that he wished first to lay the foundations of the science of spirit, or Anthroposophy, as solidly as he could before he gave the courses full of practical advice that were characteristic of the postwar years. All his artistic innovations had been inaugurated before the War, though they were perfected afterwards, whereas the scientific work that stems from Anthroposophy belongs almost exclusively to this later period. He had given some lectures on social problems as early as 1905 and 1906, and he had hinted in a lecture on the education of children that he had first given in 1907, that he stood ready to aid in the establishment of a school based on entirely different principles from those in vogue at the time. It was not until almost the end of the War that he proposed detailed changes in the social order, and not before 1919 did he head a movement looking toward the establishment of such a new order. Directly linked with that movement was the first Waldorf School founded in Stuttgart in 1919, followed by a small handful of similar schools during Steiner's own lifetime. Today more than a hundred and fifty schools throughout the world call themselves either Steiner or Waldorf schools, and all endeavor to follow the principles explained by Steiner in the course of several lecture cycles given between 1919 and 1924. The curative education inaugurated by Rudolf Steiner and biodynamic farming which stems also from his insights both resulted from courses given in June, 1924. Now in 1980 there are more than a hundred curative homes based on his indications, and at least as many biodynamic farms in operation throughout the world. The General Anthroposophical Society, with its center at the Goetheanum in Dornach, Switzerland, and the much wider Anthroposophical Movement appear to be solidly established, and are certainly gaining new members, even if the membership is modest by comparison with that of movements which make less exacting demands upon their members. By every external standard of comparison Anthroposophy is clearly a more influential movement than it was at Steiner's death in 1925. Such progress has surely been possible only because its

8

newer adherents have continued to find his indications either fruitful in their own lives, or both in their lives and in their work.

Nevertheless it might well seem presumptuous to call Rudolf Steiner the herald of a new epoch if all there was to show for his life work was the influence he has exercised and is still exercising over an almost infinitesimal percentage of present day humanity. Such men and women are no doubt entitled to think of him as such a herald, and at the same time to think of the twentieth century as a new epoch precisely because it was at the beginning of the century that Steiner began his public work. But have others who have thus far not been influenced by Rudolf Steiner any reason to think of this century as a new epoch? Does a person born in the late twentieth century differ in any significant respect from his predecessor born a century ago? Is the cultural, even the religious climate of our epoch different from that of the 1880's?

From whatever point of view we look at the past century it seems impossible to doubt that we are living in a totally different world from that of our grandparents. Nothing is even remotely similar to what it was even in 1900. Although there are without doubt numerous materialists alive today, they no longer set the fashion. Nor are materialistic scientists—and numerous scientists are no longer materialists—listened to with awe and respect as they once were. It is no longer fashionable to deride even traditional Western religion, while the urge to seek for enlightenment in non-Western religions and philosophies has never been stronger than now. Whatever name they give to these experiences countless thousands are trying to gain direct experience of the supersensible worlds. Meditation in one form or another has become fashionable, every small town has its specialists in yoga, men and women who a century ago would have thought of themselves as agnostics engage in practices such as that of "transcendental meditation" in order to enlarge their consciousness and even help them solve their daily problems. Indeed, in our day it is difficult to discover any old fashioned skeptics, however hard one looks.

None of these practices has stemmed from Rudolf Steiner's

work. Nevertheless the world has changed since his time, whatever explanation or combination of explanations we may offer for the phenomenon. And it has changed almost entirely without being in any way influenced, much less guided, by Rudolf Steiner. But he certainly foresaw the changes that were to come in this century, and he perceived the spiritual causes that lay behind them. For this reason as early as 1904 he was already instructing his pupils how to find their true path to the spiritual worlds for themselves; and all his life he was constantly warning against false paths, especially paths that required the dimming of human consciousness. It was an essential part of his teaching that all spiritual knowledge must be acquired, as it must also be checked in full consciousness.

Steiner therefore can be a guide for those who wish to understand our epoch, and for those who wish to play an active part in it, in accordance with the needs of the time. Although he died more than fifty years ago, because his teachings were so much in advance of his time they have not become outdated. On the contrary, still very few of them have been made as yet truly fruitful either in the lives or the work of men and women born in this century. Even his social ideas, put forward as they were for a specific purpose at a definite time in history—the end of World War I—are by no means necessarily archaic. They have never been put into effect, and so may yet be rethought out and applied in the quite different social conditions of a later epoch. So it may properly be contended that he could still be a guide for the end of this century if enough persons occupy themselves with his work, reactivating their thinking and transforming their inner lives as he insisted was necessary, and in the end coming to an understanding of the relationship between the material and spiritual worlds that constitutes the essence of Anthroposophy.

If it is admitted that his work is still worthy of study, why should we also study his life? The life of this modern initiate-teacher, unlike that of some other modern spiritual teachers, seems to have been a truly admirable, even an exemplary one. We do not know much about his inner life after 1906, the year he had reached in his autobiography at the time of his death;

10

and even the years of his youth and young manhood are not at all well documented. Personal information is only too often lacking. So it is necessary when writing a biography of Rudolf Steiner to deal mainly with his work in relation to his life, offering only occasional glimpses of the man as others saw him. But it is nevertheless hoped that out of this material that may sometimes seem dry and factual his essential humanity will shine forth—and that those who read the book will come to feel at the end that they have after all come to know with some intimacy a remarkable man. They may perhaps even feel that he was indeed, as the title calls him, the herald—an exemplary herald—of a new epoch.

Chapter 2.

CHILDHOOD AND YOUTH

In the last chapter of Rudolf Steiner's fundamental work on social questions, *The Threefold Commonwealth*, or *The Threefold Social Order*, first published in 1919, there appears a short passage devoted to the old Austro-Hungarian Empire, which came to an end in 1918: "The fact that many nationalities went to compose the fabric of her state might well seem to have made it Austria-Hungary's mission in the world's history to lead the way in evolving a healthy form of social order. The mission was not recognized; and this sin against the spirit of the world's historic life drove Austria-Hungary into war."

Such a remark as this was undoubtedly based on Steiner's own experiences as a boy and young man. The Austrian Empire was still a powerful state when he was born in 1861, but its foundations were beginning to crumble, even though Vienna, its capital, was still comparable only with Paris on the European continent as a center of culture. In 1849 the Habsburg rulers of the Empire had only with great difficulty and with the aid of the Russian Tsar been able to suppress an unexpected rebellion by their Hungarian subjects, while the numerous other minorities in the Empire were no less restive, and had taken the opportunity of the Hungarian rebellion to voice their own demands. All the minorities resented the dominance of the German-speaking Austrians, who after 1849 had been able to hold the Empire together only by force, accompanied by a policy of enforced "Germanization."

12

The Empire was scarcely more secure in the West. Throughout the nineteenth century Prussia had been pursuing a policy of trying to unify the numerous princedoms and kingdoms of Germany into an effective economic union, with the evident hope of some day unifying them politically also. The south German kingdoms of Bavaria and Württemberg regarded Austria as their natural ally, and resisted the blandishments of the Prussians, but they proved no match for Otto Von Bismarck's unscrupulous policies once he had been appointed chancellor the year after Steiner's birth. In 1866 he and his master William I succeeded in provoking Austria into declaring war on Prussia, which resulted in a calamitous defeat for the aging Empire. Thereafter Austria's only option was to try to strengthen her ties with her eastern provinces—a policy that required her to take Hungary into partnership as co-ruler of the largely Slavic Empire. Thus in 1861 began the so-called Dual Monarchy of Austria-Hungary, which survived until 1918.

Rudolf Steiner was born at Kraljevec, on the border between Hungary and Croatia, the most westernized of the eastern Slavic provinces. His birthplace is now in Yugoslavia. Both his parents, however, came from Lower Austria, and were German speaking, belonging therefore to the ruling power in the area. His father, who had started his career as a gamekeeper in private employment, had learned telegraphy and thus been able to obtain employment with the Austrian Southern Railway. A year after Rudolf's birth he was transferred to Moedling, not far from Vienna, but a few months later he received a real promotion and was transferred to Pottschach in Lower Austria as stationmaster, and thereafter he had full charge of a series of stations on the railway. Even so the job was scarcely an exalted one, and Steiner's autobiography makes it clear that money was in short supply in the family, which included a brother and sister in addition to Rudolf. For the boy the natural beauty of his surroundings, especially at Pottschach, clearly compensated for the lack of money, to which he alludes only in passing, as when he refers to the pleasure experienced by the children when they could gather wild berries to add to the otherwise monotonous evening meal.

13

In 1868, a year after the establishment of the Dual Monarchy, Johann Steiner became stationmaster at Neudörfl, over the border in Hungary, and though German had been the language in general use in this part of the Empire, as it was in all the regions bordering Lower Austria, an attempt was now made by Hungarian patriots to revive the old Magyar language. Hungarian literature and history could now be taught in the Hungarian part of the Empire, with the result that German literature and history were slighted. Steiner in his autobiography speaks of a Hungarian patriot-priest who gave religious instruction in the village school at Neudörfl that he attended, and his favorite teacher was another such patriot. Fortunately for the young Rudolf Neudörfl was too small to support a resident medical doctor, and an Austrian doctor from Wiener-Neustadt, a much larger town the other side of the border in Austria, came over regularly to take care of the medical needs of the people of Neudörfl. This doctor was a lover of German literature and found a willing listener in Rudolf Steiner, who caught his enthusiasm. So when from 1872 onwards it was necessary for him to cross the border every day to go to his secondary school in Wiener-Neustadt, he was well prepared to continue his studies in German language and literature in his new school.

Thus Steiner as a boy experienced in his own person not only the division between east and west, but more particularly the clash of cultures in the Austro-Hungarian empire. In Neudörfl, as the son of Austrians, he was regarded as a foreigner who had, as he tells us, no "right" to any nuts that were harvested from the village nut trees until all the local children had taken their shares. If he had attended the Neudörfl school before the establishment of the Dual Monarchy in 1867 the political discussions in which his father loved to participate might well have been acrimonious since the Hungarians, especially after the suppression of their rebellion in 1849, regarded themselves as oppressed by the Austrians and resented being forced to speak a language they detested.

The "healthy social order" to which Rudolf Steiner referred in 1919 would have permitted the small national entities of

14

Europe to be self-governing in certain respects as well as enjoying a free cultural life, without becoming separate national
states as they did after the First World War. If the Austrians had
granted all the minorities in their country the right to use their
native languages and given them a measure of self-government, instead of merely taking the single Hungarian minority
into partnership, they might well have been able to keep the
country together as a free union, with all the economic and
other advantages accruing to a multinational state. This state
might have survived intact even after losing the war. This is
clearly what the mature Rudolf Steiner had in mind when he
made his remark quoted at the beginning of this chapter. As it
was, the Slavic minorities looked to their fellow Slavs beyond
the imperial borders for support, both independent Serbia and
the huge Russian empire, and it was a clash of nationalities on
the eastern and south-eastern fringes of Austria-Hungary that
led to the murder of the Austrian archduke Francis Ferdinand
in June, 1914, an event which precipitated the war.

Although Steiner's autobiography does not emphasize the
matter, his birth and upbringing in the middle of these clashes
of nationality undoubtedly contributed to the total absence of
any chauvinism in his make up, while the movement he founded is world wide and cosmopolitan, rather than Germanic.
Steiner himself always spoke German with a slight Austrian
intonation, and all his life he possessed to a marked degree
certain typical Austrian traits, especially a general good nature
and sociability as well as a characteristic Austrian sense of
humor. But once his higher education had been completed in
Vienna he never again lived in Austria. In early manhood and
until the war he lectured extensively in every Western European country, and much of the theosophical and anthroposophical work was centered in three of the German capital
cities, Berlin, the capital of Prussia, Munich, capital of Bavaria, and Stuttgart, capital of Württemberg. During the war
he established himself in Switzerland, at Dornach, near Basel,
where the Goetheanum was built. Here he was only a few miles
from both the French and German frontiers, and for much of
the war the sounds of battle could be heard, mingling with the

sounds of hammering, as the first Goetheanum was taking shape. The building itself was constructed by anthroposophists from seventeen different countries.

Thus by his destiny Steiner was, on the one side, a "world-man," or at least an "all-European" man, and on the other side he was also what we call a "self-made" man in that he was born into a family that lived on a subsistence level and could afford no special advantages of any kind for him. His parents helped him as best they could, as, for example, when Johann Steiner moved to the neighborhood of Vienna and accepted an inferior job in less attractive surroundings in order to provide his son with a home when Rudolf first moved to Vienna to study at the age of eighteen. Once he was there he supported himself entirely by his own efforts, and all his later positions he secured as the result of his own work.

A few significant remarks may be cited from his autobiography that throw light on his psychological and spiritual development and how he was prepared by destiny for the life he was eventually to lead and the mission he was to undertake.

In the first school to which he was sent, in the village of Pottschach, the teacher had little interest in his job, and was able to excite no interest in his pupils. As a result Johann Steiner, after a sharp quarrel with the man, took over his son's education himself, trying to teach him how to read and write. Young Rudolf, however, was not especially interested in learning these arts, but preferred to amuse himself in playing with the writing sand, which at that time was used for drying the ink. He liked also to watch the letters being formed, and how the feather pens were prepared for writing. In short, at that early age he learned by imitation and experimentation, spurred on by his interest in the mechanics of human activity—how the railway station was managed, how the local flour mill operated, and the like. One day when the train pulled into the station with one of its cars on fire, he wanted to know how and why this had happened, and, as usual with children, he received no answers that satisfied him. In such respects Steiner followed the usual pattern of childhood, gradually becoming aware of the physical world and asking questions about it. But, not being able to learn to read and write by simple imitation, Rudolf did not take easily to reading and writing, and if in fact he did learn to read well at a fairly early age this was because he was vitally interested in the content of the books that fell into his hands, whereas according to him his ability to write was a by-product of his interest in the sand used to dry it. Only much later, and with great difficulty, did he learn to spell correctly, and he detested grammar. Not for many years was he able to write without making many mistakes in spelling.

Such details would be of little interest were it not for the fact that from very early childhood he was clairvoyant. He tells us, indeed, that the spiritual worlds were fully open to him as far back as he could remember. But for a long time he was unaware that they were not equally perceived by others who lacked his faculties, and it was many years before he became fully convinced of his uniqueness in this respect—unique, that is, among his friends and playmates. He was never at any time afraid of anything he perceived through his clairvoyance, taking it entirely for granted. What he perceived was, if anything, more real to him than anything he saw in the material world. For example, when he was eight years old a woman appeared to him as he was sitting in a waiting room. Indeed he saw her open the door and come toward him, and heard her ask him "to do everything he could for her now and later." At the same time he was well aware that she was not present in her earthly body. By this time he had learned not to speak to anyone about such experiences. But he was neither surprised nor frightened when he heard later that a near relative of his parents had committed suicide on the day the woman had appeared to him.

Such experiences are indeed not at all uncommon with children and, as a rule, such early clairvoyance tends to disappear from puberty onward. For example, I well remember meeting a charming child of eleven, daughter of a Dutch father and a partly Mexican-Indian mother, almost all of whose female relatives were in some degree clairvoyant, and several were mediums. Little Alexandrina used to prattle on about the dead, what they were doing, where they were, when she had seen

17

them before, all in the most natural manner in the world. Part of what she said could be confirmed, and the perfectly correct facts that she gave she could not have learned in any other way. The young Rudolf was also very well aware of the nature spirits with whom, indeed, he held converse, again not unlike many other children, especially in such unspoiled areas as those in which he passed his childhood. As a rule children tend to keep quiet about such experiences, and often forget them, or even try to explain them away in later life, supposing them to have been figments of their imagination. Steiner, however, continued to be fully aware of such beings all his life, but could find no one who shared his experiences, as far as he knew, until at the age of eighteen he became acquainted with a part-time herb gatherer named Felix Koguski, who used to take the same train to Vienna, and with whom he became friends. In his autobiography Steiner speaks of Felix (who formed the basis for one of the characters in his Mystery Dramas under the name of Felix Balde) as a man full of devotion but without schooling, who owned and had read a number of mystical books which did not satisfy him, trying, as he was, to "find in others what he already knew for himself." Steiner could not at first understand what Felix said, but later grew to appreciate him, recognizing that he had an instinctive knowledge of the spiritual worlds such as had been common in earlier ages. This contact was of the greatest importance to the young university student because it was "possible to talk about the spiritual world as with one who had his own experience of this world." He commented in his autobiography that "if anyone possesses the perception of the spiritual world in himself very deep glimpses can be obtained into this world through someone else who has a firm footing in it."[1]

The kind of instinctive clairvoyance possessed by Felix, and by Steiner himself from early childhood, could not possibly have sufficed for the kind of spiritual work to which Steiner was to devote his life, which in effect consisted of translating his spiritual vision into a conceptual form capable of being transmitted to others in thoughts and images. For this his spiritual vision had to be developed through the appropriate

18

methods, which he was to describe later in his basic books and elaborate in numerous lectures. Steiner also felt it necessary to come to terms with the scientific conceptions of his age, in this respect differing from either such predecessors as Jakob Boehme, or from medieval and modern mystics as well as from Oriental sages. Steiner wished, indeed, to reconcile his perceptions of the spiritual worlds with modern scientific notions. This forced him to reject some of the latter, for example, Darwinism as it had been taught by Darwin and his orthodox followers. Even the work of Ernst Haeckel, the most distinguished exponent of the theory of evolution at the turn of the century, had to be rejected, at least in its theoretical part. Nevertheless Steiner did not deny the facts of evolution; but the conclusions then being drawn from the facts were in direct contradiction with his own *vision* of the spiritual origin of man. These thoughts simmered in Steiner's mind in the 1870's and 1880's as he attended his scientific courses in school and university, but even when he was studying at Vienna he did not as yet feel justified in putting forward, *even to himself*, the criticisms he could have formulated against the prevalent currents of thought. This criticism "had to be suppressed within me to await a time when more comprehensive sources and ways of knowledge would give me greater assurance."[2]

These words were, of course, written by Rudolf Steiner very much later in his life, but there is no reason to doubt that they express very clearly his peculiar state of mind as he was nearing the end of his formal education, when he had been very thoroughly exposed to all the currents of thought of his age, both in science and philosophy. If we think these preoccupations extraordinary for a young man in his early twenties, or not as yet even twenty, we should perhaps try to imagine the special difficulties he had always encountered in his mental life, the contrast between what he knew from his spiritual vision, and what he was taught and was expected to learn—how, for example, he could perceive the nature spirits, but at the same time could not always be certain of just what his ordinary senses were telling him. If he had been simply a dreamy boy, nothing of this would have mattered. He could have contentedly enjoyed his dreams. But from the beginning his thoughts were always impelling him to *understand,* to explain to himself, to reconcile his vision and his learning, while at the same time until he met Felix he never received any confirmation that anyone else in the world had the same kind of vision as himself.

Such experiences naturally accentuated his loneliness since it was impossible for him to share this part of his life with his friends. Indeed when he made the attempt to talk about them he was invariably met with a total failure to understand what he was saying. However, in all other respects he did share the life of his companions, and, as we have noted, he was throughout his life a man of great sociability. He was also fortunate in having a considerable number of teachers who were, in their different ways, very helpful to him; and some of the subjects he studied filled him with joy because it became clear from these studies that a non-material world did in fact exist, even though it is not usually recognized as such. This world is that of mathematics, which deals with something that is inaccessible to the senses, and the young Steiner first entered this world when his assistant teacher in his elementary school at Neudörfl allowed him to borrow a book on geometry, into which, as he tells us, he "plunged with enthusiasm. For weeks at a time my mind was filled with the coincidence, the similarity, of triangles, squares, polygons. I racked my brain over the question: Where do parallel lines actually meet? The theorem of Pythagoras fascinated me. That one can live within the mind in the shaping of forms perceived only within oneself, entirely without impression upon the external senses, became for me the deepest satisfaction. I found in this a solace for the unhappiness which my unanswered questions had caused me. To be able to lay hold upon something in the spirit alone brought me an inner joy. I am sure that I learned through geometry to know happiness for the first time."[3]

In relation to this early experience Steiner tells us in his autobiography that such thoughts lived "more or less unconsciously" within him during his childhood, but took on a definite and fully conscious form when he was about nineteen.

He felt that one "must carry knowledge of the spiritual world within oneself after the manner of geometry." The next paragraph is worth quoting in full for the light it throws on his particular way of perceiving and thinking, as well as on the tremendous struggle that went on unceasingly throughout his life, the struggle to bring together his spiritual vision and his ordinary perception through the senses, how to reconcile them and how to explain them to others.

"For the reality," he writes, "of the spiritual world was to me as certain as that of the physical. I felt the need, however, for a justification of this assumption. I wished to be able to say to myself that the experience of the spiritual world is just as little an illusion as is that of the physical world. With regard to geometry, I said to myself: 'Here one *is permitted* to know something which the mind alone through its own power experiences.' In this feeling I found the justification for speaking of the spiritual world that I experienced in the same way that I could speak of the physical. And I did speak of it in this way. I had two conceptions which were, naturally, undefined, but which played a great role in my mental life even before my eighth year. I distinguished things and beings which 'are seen' and those which are 'not seen'.". . ."But it is just because I know how little I have later followed my personal inclination in the description of a spiritual world—having, on the contrary, followed only the inner necessity of the matter—that I myself can look back quite objectively upon the childlike, awkward way in which I confirmed for myself, by means of geometry, the feeling that I must speak of a world 'which is not seen.' Only, I must say also that I loved to live in that world. For I should have been forced to feel the physical world as a sort of spiritual darkness if it had not received light from that side."[4]

The same assistant teacher who lent him the geometry book also played the piano and violin, and taught the young Rudolf to draw, at first with charcoal, making copies of the pictures that were in his house. A little later, the priest who came regularly to the school in Neudörfl began to teach elements of the Copernican system of astronomy to a select group of

21

youngsters. Rudolf naturally formed part of the group, and immediately began to make numerous drawings showing the various revolutions of the planets, although he still could not, as he tells us, write without making mistakes in spelling and grammar, his difficulties now arising from the fact that he spoke a Lower Austrian dialect, and expected the words to be written according to their sounds—whereas the dialect was markedly different from the written German language. So it was far from impossible that he might be rejected when he applied for entrance into one of the higher schools in Wiener-Neustadt.

The immediate choice was between a higher elementary school where he could spend a further year studying the subjects learned at Neudörfl in preparation for entrance into the *Gymnasium,* which laid emphasis on the humanities, or going at once to the *Realschule,* or technical high school, where he could study to be a civil engineer, the career his father had planned for him. Steiner himself at this time had no particular preference, and he took both entrance exams, passing into the higher elementary school with distinction, largely on the basis of the astronomical drawings that he submitted. He passed the other exam less brilliantly, but well enough to be admitted, though at first he had difficulty in keeping up with his schoolmates because of the insufficiency of his education in the village school at Neudörfl. By the end of his second year in the school, when he was twelve years old he was regarded as a good student.

It was during his first year at the school that he came upon an article written by his principal, Heinrich Schramm, which constituted a considerable challenge to him, though at first he could understand almost none of it. The article was entitled "Attraction Considered as an Effect of Motion," and some parts of it could be fitted within the framework of physics that he had learned at Neudörfl. But as a sketch it was too tantalizing, and it soon became necessary for him to buy a book already published by Schramm, entitled *The General Motion of Matter as the Fundamental Cause of All the Phenomena of Nature,* in which the principal's full theory was put forward. In order to buy this work Steiner had to save up his pocket money, but once he had it in his possession he certainly had his money's worth out of it, for it accompanied him throughout his school career, while he gradually mastered its content, with the aid of the mental and mathematical tools he acquired during those years.

The author was trying to explain the universal attraction or repulsion between bodies without using the notion of forces acting at a distance, which he regarded as an unjustified "mystical" hypothesis. Attraction, he insisted, was not any special force but only an "effect of motion." "Out of the motions occurring between the small and the great parts of matter, the author undertook," so Steiner explains, "to derive all physical and chemical occurrences in nature."

The eleven year-old boy was now faced with a dilemma. "I had," he tells us, "nothing within me that inclined me in any way to accept such a view, but I had the feeling that it would be very important for me if I could understand what was expressed in this way." So he "set to work over and over again to read the paper and the book," using whatever works in mathematics and physics he could find—not expecting to be convinced by what he read but to understand the point of view and the arguments put forward by the principal, even though they contradicted his own inner experience, in so far as this was as yet conscious in him.

Meanwhile he found two excellent teachers, one of mathematics and physics, and the other an expert in geometry, especially geometrical drawing, a subject that always fascinated him because it seemed to him that the forms he drew were derived directly from the world of spirit that was known to him. Later also he was helped by a highly gifted teacher of chemistry. But it was through home study that he acquired the mathematics necessary to come to a fuller comprehension of Dr. Schramm's work, since he was too impatient to wait until he reached calculus in the regular course of his studies. Indeed this work on motion seems to have represented for him a kind of obstacle course which had to be overcome, even though, or perhaps particularly because, its ideas were so uncongenial to him.

In the course of these studies the question as to what actual!y goes on in nature became of vital importance for him. "My feeling," he tells us, "was that I must grapple with nature in order to acquire a point of view with regard to the world of spirit which was directly visible to me. I said to myself that it is possible after all to come to an understanding of the experience of the spiritual world through one's soul only if one's process of thinking has itself reached such a form that it can attain to the reality of being which is in the phenomena of nature."[5] In a lecture given in England (Torquay) in the last year of his life, Steiner was to sum up the kind of difficulties he experienced during these years when he was studying the world as it was presented to him by modern science: "Conceptions of the reality of the spiritual world presented no difficulty to me at any age. What the spiritual world revealed penetrated into my soul, formed itself into ideas, into thoughts. On the other hand things that came easily to others were difficult for me. I was always able to grasp quickly the arguments of natural scientific thinking, but concrete facts would not remain in my memory, simply would not register there. I could without effort understand the wave-theory, the arguments of the mathematicians, physicists and chemists. On the other hand, unlike most others, I could not recognize a particular mineral if I had seen it only once or twice; I was obliged to look at it perhaps thirty or forty times before I could recognize it again. I found it difficult to retain concrete pictures of the things of the external, material world. It was not easy for me to come fully into the world of sense."[6]

In later life he was as competent with his hands as he was clear in his thinking. But both accomplishments were the fruit of a disciplined will, and could not be acquired as easily by him as by others, who become correctly oriented to the earthly world during childhood and adolescence, as a perfectly natural process.

In spite of his work in mathematics and his constant efforts to penetrate more deeply into the book written by his principal, the way of thinking of ordinary human beings was still somewhat alien to him, especially the process that most of us simply take for granted—the process of reasoning, particularly that kind of intellectual reasoning which is not concerned with the relations between earthly objects or the attempt to understand the given world, but is more or less self-sufficient, even metaphysical. This process is called in the German language *Vernunft*, and does not have an exact English equivalent. It was thus a moment of great excitement in young Rudolf Steiner's life when at the age of fourteen he saw in a bookshop window a cheap reprint edition of Immanuel Kant's masterpiece *Kritik der reinen Vernunft*, usually translated in English as *The Critique of Pure Reason*. At this time Steiner had never heard the name of Kant, still less did he know anything about his place in the history of philosophy. But the book presumably promised to enlighten the reader on the nature of human reason, a subject of surpassing importance to the boy. "In my boyish way," he tells us, "I was striving to understand what human reason might be able to achieve toward a real insight into the nature of things."

For anyone who, like Steiner even at this age, had a direct perception of the spiritual world, it would surely prove to be a striking experience to follow the logical but dry precision of a thinker such as Kant, who through pure thinking forced himself to the conclusion that the human mind could know nothing certain of the world outside the mind, either of the real nature of things in the earthly world, or of anything belonging to the spiritual world, which *a fortiori* was forever shut off from man. Always therefore aware that Kant's conclusions were false, Steiner nevertheless struggled mightily with his philosophy without being as yet overtly critical of it. His primary purpose was indeed to come to understand his own thinking, and to learn how to direct it. It was not in fact easy for him to find the opportunity to study Kant, occupied as he was in trying to perfect his geometrical drawing which fascinated him at this period, and occupied him on Sundays to the exclusion of everything else. Nor had he yet found the way to study while on the way to and from school, a journey that occupied three full hours of his day. However, he found the solution as a result of the laziness of his history teacher who preferred not to prepare his classes or give a lecture in the lower grades of the school, but simply to read from the text book. Steiner soon discovered this fact and read the book for himself at home, taking it each day to class. But instead of following what the teacher was reading he took the opportunity to study Kant, having cut up Kant's work into suitable sections and fastened them into the history text. It may be noted that no one was any the wiser and he had no difficulty in passing his history examinations, and indeed earned the highest grade in the class! The study of Kant was completed during his vacations, but perhaps it is not surprising that, as he tells us, he found it necessary to read some pages of Kant "more than twenty times in succession."

From his fifteenth year onward he began to earn some money to help his parents to pay the fees for his schooling in Wiener-Neustadt. He did this by tutoring other boys who were in his own grade or lower. In this he was encouraged by his teachers who were no doubt aware of his home circumstances and his need for money (especially for books!), and regarded him as a good student. Far from being a drudgery, as such work sometimes is, for Rudolf Steiner it proved to be especially helpful, for an unusual reason. In his work at the school, even though he excelled in it, he claims that at that time he was never fully awake and functioning in full consciousness. He was, as so many young people are at this stage of their lives, and on into late adolescence, extremely receptive to what he heard and read, and able to pass examinations without difficulty. But the knowledge he thus acquired, unlike what he had worked out for himself, was not fully his own. In Steiner's own case, this "condition of dreaming," as he calls it, was accentuated because of his dual consciousness. But when he was called upon to give this knowledge out again to the pupils he tutored, the effort to express it in suitable words made it, for the first time, fully his own. Thus, unexpectedly, he benefited in his own development from this work and in addition was able to learn more about how minds other than his own functioned, a knowledge that he could not acquire, as the rest of us do, from examination of his own thought processes, since they were unlike those of others.

One last item from his high school career is of significant interest. From his sixteenth year onward he was required to study Greek and Latin poetry in German translation. Apparently this use of translations so offended him that he made up his mind to study Greek and Latin for himself so as to be able to read Greek and Latin literature in the original. He felt for the first time how much he had missed by attending the *Realschule* instead of the *Gymnasium* where the ancient languages were studied. While he was engaged in this new study he entered into a closer relationship with the physician from Wiener-Neustadt who had earlier been the first to introduce him to German literature. This physician evidently took a great interest in the young man, and lent him as many books as he could absorb, thereafter questioning him on their contents. Largely through this association, and with the aid of his other extracurricular work, Steiner acquired a competence in the subjects studied at the *Gymnasium* as well as those required of him in the *Realschule,* a competence that was to stand him in good stead later when he was a student in Vienna. There he was able to tutor pupils who possessed both the *Gymnasium* and *Realschule* background, and thus actually earned his living from tutoring, in this way paying for that part of his education not covered by scholarship.

The tutoring he performed while still in high school enabled him to buy the books he needed in order to teach himself Latin and Greek. But it remained difficult for a time to find the time and place to study these subjects and to read his German literature. This problem was solved for him through the aid of the stationmaster of Wiener-Neustadt who no doubt admired the boy's thirst for learning and his persistence and enthusiasm. Because the train to Neudörfl went late in the evening the stationmaster opened a railway car specially for him and on most weekdays he was therefore able to pass several solitary hours studying in the train, leaving his precious time at home to be used for preparing his regular work and making his geometrical designs.

In the early summer of 1879 at the age of eighteen Steiner completed his studies at the *Realschule* in Wiener-Neustadt, winning his baccalaureat with honourable mention and earning a scholarship to the Technische-Hochschüle in Vienna.* At this time it was his intention to prepare himself to teach in a *Realschule.*

His father had already made arrangements with the railway company to let him move with his family nearer to the capital, in order to make it possible for his gifted son to follow his chosen career. The Steiner family therefore took up residence in an unlovely suburb called Inzersdorf, where Rudolf spent the first summer wrestling with philosophical problems before enrolling in the Institute of Technology. He was still engrossed in his efforts to understand human thinking as it presented itself in the works of others, and reconciling it with what he himself knew from direct experience of the problems expounded by the others. Of his inner life and his experiences he was still unable to speak to anyone; and it was not until his meeting with Felix, the herb-gatherer, while he was commuting to Vienna, that for the first time he was able to find someone with whom, as we have noted, he was able to share his experiences and who helped him indirectly toward the path in life that he was eventually, as a mature man, to follow.

---

*This was a kind of advanced technical institute at university level similar to the Massachusetts Institute of Technology and many European Polytechnic colleges. Its degrees were limited to certain scientific and technical subjects, but in other respects its standards were similar to those of the University of Vienna, and, as we shall see, Rudolf Steiner was permitted to attend courses also at the university while enrolled there. It will be translated here as the Vienna Institute of Technology, probably the nearest English equivalent.

Chapter 3

VIENNA AND THE DISCOVERY OF GOETHE

At the end of Chapter 1 a brief reference was made to Steiner's autobiography, and a few extended quotations from it form part of Chapter 2. It now becomes necessary to give some more detailed attention to this work, which is our main source for Steiner's life until after the turn of the twentieth century.

Steiner began the autobiography late in 1923 at a time when he had become an established teacher, and was well known, especially in central Europe, both as educator and as the founder of Anthroposophy. Soon after he had begun the book he assumed the presidency of the newly founded General Anthroposophical Society, with its center at the Goetheanum in Dornach, Switzerland, a Society which was world wide in scope. It was in the review published by this Society (*Das Goetheanum*) that instalments of the autobiography appeared every week until his death in March, 1925. In the very first instalment he explained that he was writing the book, which was to be called *Mein Lebensgang* (The Course of my Life) because he had often been accused of inconsistency. He wished to show that his ideas had not changed during the course of his life, but had evolved as he himself and his thought had gradually matured over the years. But he felt that it had become necessary to set the record straight, for the benefit especially of those who had recently come into the movement and were unacquainted with its history.

The book is therefore the work of a man in his sixties who was above all a thinker. It was never a part of his intention to

29

recount anecdotes of his youth or manhood simply because they happened and might be interesting to his readers; nor did he plan to write a real biography of himself. He wished especially to trace his thought and show how it had evolved in the course of the years; and indeed in no other of his works does he describe his thinking processes with such clarity and precision as he did in this last book of his lifetime. Nevertheless this is far from being all that he gives us. He also provided a picture, often a very vivid one, of a number of persons with whom he was in contact during these years and his feelings with regard to them—and it is especially noticeable with what charity, indeed loving kindness he describes even those with whom he evidently had little sympathy, while he makes clear also how much he loved his friends. In the course of these descriptions he naturally narrates some selected incidents in his life that he felt to be of significance.

Nevertheless, the book is not easy to use as a source for Steiner's actual life. It is sometimes difficult to follow the chronology, and it should never be forgotten that he was remembering and describing himself, his feelings, and his thoughts many decades after they had been experienced. He was also carefully choosing what he wished posterity to know about him. So it is of great importance to follow this selection process, and to try to imagine why he chose to record a particular episode or experience and to say nothing about others. It seems clear that he wrote nothing at this stage of his life that he had not made a positive decision to include because of its significance. When at the beginning of the autobiography he writes the sentence: "It has always been my endeavor so to order what I had to say and what I thought I ought to do according as the matter itself might demand, and not from personal considerations," we may believe him, and place a proper value on all that he does say even while we may regret that he omitted so many things we should have liked to hear from him. In short, the book is irreplaceable but incomplete, and even with the aid of such letters from the early part of his life as have been preserved and of material collected decades later by would-be biographers, it remains impossible to construct the kind of biography that can usually be written about personages as important, and who lived such public lives as Rudolf Steiner. So our account of these early years will in general follow Steiner's own procedure of describing the evolution of his thought and the development of his inner life as he described them, adding to these only those episodes and human contacts that seem to have been truly significant in his life and career, and leaving aside those of his recollections that were significant to him, but not to us who live and work so many years after his death.

When Rudolf Steiner moved to Vienna in 1879 the city was world renowned for its cultural life, and its cafés, in particular, were the resort of students from all classes, as well as of poets, artists and writers. It was not necessary to be rich to buy a cup of coffee in the Café Griensteidl and nurse it all the evening while engaging in animated conversations with one's fellow-students, or even to use the café as an accomodation address, as Steiner did. Until 1884 he had no choice but to live in cheap lodgings, while commuting from time to time to Inzersdorf where his parents lived, or, after 1882, to the pretty little suburb of Brunn am Gebirge where they finally settled. Here, in this village which was also a summer resort, Johann Steiner was able to obtain the job of manager of the freight department of the Southern Railway, remaining there until his retirement in the late 1890's. Steiner visited there quite frequently, and he occupied a tiny room in the fifteenth century house of his parents. It was there that he wrote most of his first major books. The house is now preserved as a memorial to Rudolf Steiner, who, according to local tradition, was much admired for his industry and intellect, and regarded with considerable awe by the villagers.

Steiner often spoke of himself as being an extremely sociable man, and it is certain that he was well provided with what the Austrians call *gemütlichkeit*, a kind of soul warmth that enabled him to make friends easily and keep them. In the restricted circumstances of his early life this quality had not had much chance to show itself, as it did now in the student society of Vienna, at an epoch when professors also showed great interest in their more gifted students and invited them regularly to their homes. Steiner's quite natural and not unusual interest in his fellow students was strengthened in his case by his own special aptitude for listening to others, and, if we are to believe his autobiography, for understanding them, including what they did not say. In a striking passage in his book *Knowledge of the Higher Worlds: How is it Attained?* (1904) he writes of the necessity for a student on the path of higher development to learn to listen to others while keeping his own inner self utterly quiet, to listen to the most contradictory views, while silencing within himself not only all adverse criticism but even assent. He can thus "train himself to listen to the words of others quite selflessly, completely shutting out his own person and his opinions and way of feeling." "Then he hears through the words into the soul of the other."

All through his life Steiner practiced this "exercise" to perfection; and it is clear from his autobiography and from testimony given about him by others, even in his university days, that he possessed this capacity to listen selflessly in a degree astonishing for one of his years. It is indeed difficult to escape the conclusion that, as he tells us, the soul of the other person was actually open to his perception; and throughout his autobiography it is especially striking to note how he speaks of everyone he knew at this time, describing in particular their configuration of soul as if indeed it were open to his gaze. An extant photograph of him in his early days in Vienna shows a young man with most beautiful and delicate features, almost feminine in appearance, with hair worn very long for that epoch, the eyes not yet so penetrating as his later photographs show them, but full of feeling and sympathy, which is also suggested by a mouth of great tenderness. Of this young man one can easily believe that he had numerous friends whom he loved, and by whom he was loved in return though they knew nothing of his inner life. Many of these friends were fated to endure lives of sadness and in some cases to commit suicide, for it seems that the young Steiner was especially drawn to such people. We can understand how he was invited everywhere because he could fit in anywhere, in the homes of his professors, at the salon of a noted young poetess, or at a café thronged with the cultural leaders of Vienna. He tells an amusing story of how he was elected president of the German Reading Hall at the Vienna Institute of Technology because of his well known impartiality. But after he had been in office a short time "the adherents of the various parties would come to me, and each would seek to convince me that his party alone was right. At the time I was elected every party had voted for me, for up to that time they had heard I had always supported what was justified. After I had been president for a half-year, all voted against me. They had then found that I could not decide as positively for any party as that party desired!"[7]

Happy as his relations were, and appreciatively as he writes of his fellow students and professors, it was of the women he knew during these years that he wrote most warmly. Indeed it seems clear that the feminine soul was at the time more open to what he had to give, even though, as far as we know, none of them had any greater knowledge of his own soul life and his exceptional spiritual gifts than had the men. Letters from such distinguished women as Rosa Mayreder, painter, writer and poet, long after he had left Vienna, show how great had been his influence, and especially his ability to enter into their intimate soul life without ever interfering with their freedom or making any demands upon them. Such men, especially as young as Steiner was during the Vienna period, are necessarily rare, and perhaps more appreciated in this respect by women than by men. Soon after he had left Vienna Rosa Mayreder wrote him a letter in which occurs the following passage:

"Every day, indeed every hour, I become more aware of the emptiness that our separation has left in my life, when innumerable subjects for thought awake in me uncertainty, doubt, error, and uneasiness, and make me long for the incomparable happiness that you gave me by your friendly help. The longer you remain away, my faithful friend, the more the thought that you will stay so far away seems unthinkable to me."[8]

Of this friend Rudolf Steiner wrote in his autobiography:

"This was the time when my *Philosophy of Freedom* was taking more and more definite shape in my mind. Rosa Mayreder is the person with whom I talked most about these forms at the time when my book was coming into existence. She relieved me of part of the inner loneliness in which I had lived . . . Often in later life has there risen before my mind in most grateful memory one or another picture from this experience—such, for example, as a walk through the noble Alpine forests, during which Rosa Mayreder and I discussed the true meaning of human freedom."

A friendship not unlike this one also occurred with another woman writer in Weimar, who later became famous, Gabrielle Reuter. But one Vienna relationship was clearly of quite a different nature. Until recently even the name of the girl was unknown, and it was only by an odd chance that letters written to her by Steiner were at last able to be matched with letters in the Rudolf Steiner Archives in Dornach. In essentials this correspondence merely confirms that the young Steiner was indeed in love with her, and the fact was known to all his friends who even teased him about the relationship. He was a regular visitor at her home, into which he had been introduced by her brother who was a fellow student at the university. The story could easily have been omitted altogether from the autobiography, but evidently Steiner, even in the last year of his life, felt that it was too important to omit. The girl's father was a recluse who never left his room, although he exercised a strong influence on his family, and indeed upon all visitors to the house. Steiner became deeply interested in the man after reading a number of his books, which were full of interesting notations, as well as from the information he was able to glean about him from members of his family. We do not know whether the younger daughter, Radegunde, with whom Steiner fell in love, recognized his supersensible gifts or not, but at least someone in the family circle must have become aware of the fact that he possessed a remarkable knowledge of this man, whom he had never seen. Otherwise it seems scarcely believable that he should have been asked to deliver the customary funeral address when the father died, in preference

34

to anyone who had actually known him in life, even though only members of the family and the elder sister's fiancé were present. The brother and sisters told him afterwards that he had given a true picture of the man, and "from the way in which they spoke and from their tears, I could not but feel that this was their real conviction."

In a later chapter of his autobiography Steiner returns to the subject of this man whom he had never met, and explains that he had indeed accompanied the man after death into the spiritual worlds. Indeed, it became clear to him afterwards that the main purpose of his intimacy with this family was because he had something to learn from the father he had never met, and not because of the daughter with whom he fell in love for the first, and, as far as we know, the only time in his life. The father, as Steiner already knew from his knowledge of the books he had studied, had been fully convinced by the scientific materialism of the age, and did not permit himself to entertain any ideas of the spiritual worlds of which he was totally ignorant. However, his materialistic ideas had never been allowed to affect his inner life or his actions. Thus when he died, and by so doing actually entered those spiritual worlds whose existence he had denied throughout his lifetime, Steiner was able to accompany him in spirit, and experienced the remarkable fact, which it seems he did not yet know and might never have learned had it not been for his experience, and perhaps would not even have suspected, that the man's intensive efforts to discover the true nature of the visible world bore good fruit for him in the afterlife even though in this earthly life they had resulted only in the conclusion that current scientific ideas were sufficient to explain the world. Steiner was able to perceive in the case of this man, (and later of another man who had devoted his life just as singlemindedly to the same search), that his denial of the spiritual worlds while he was alive in no way hindered his progress in the spiritual worlds after death. As soon as his earthly body fell away from him, and with it his earthly prejudices, his soul appeared to spiritually awakened sight as shiningly beautiful, thus revealing to Steiner that such ideas, so long as they do not result in actions of the kind that so often result from a crassly materialistic world view, are to be revered, and neither condemned nor despised— as they so often are by people who consider themselves to be superior beings because their outlook is so "spiritual," and because they devote themselves exclusively to "spiritual" pursuits, while making no attempt to appreciate at its just value the hard and patient work accomplished by serious scientists. The lesson was not lost on the young Steiner whose subsequent writings are full of admiring recognition of the "spiritual activity" engaged in, after their own manner, by scientists, who nevertheless deny the very existence of the spiritual.

In view of the importance of this relationship with the father of the girl he loved, the few words devoted by Steiner to his relationship with her take on an added poignancy. If he had married her, as it seems clear might well have happened if he had spoken of his feelings for her, there can be little doubt that his subsequent life-work could not have taken the form it did. Such a union must have diverted him from the work for which, if not yet perhaps quite consciously, he was preparing himself. Whether or not the twenty-four year old Steiner purposely denied himself this earthly happiness, it was in sad measured words that he wrote of it when he was sixty-three.

"Between the younger daughter and me there gradually came about a beautiful friendship. She really had in her something of the primal type of the German maiden. She bore within her nothing of an education acquired by routine, but manifested an original and charming naturalness together with a noble reserve. This reserve of hers caused a like reserve in me. We loved each other, and both of us were fully aware of this; but neither of us could overcome the diffidence which kept us from saying that we loved each other. Thus the love lived between the words we spoke to each other, and not in the words themselves. I experienced our relationship as an intimate soul-friendship, but it found no possibility of taking even a single step beyond what is of the soul.

"I was happy in this friendship; I felt my friend as a ray of sunshine in my life. Yet this life later parted us. In place of hours of happy companionship there remained only a short-lived correspondence, followed by the melancholy memory of a beautiful period of my past life—a memory, however, which through all my later life has arisen again and again from the depths of my soul."[9]

In 1884 Steiner was at last able to move from his lodgings when he became resident tutor with the Specht family, in which there were four boys, of whom Otto, the youngest, suffered from hydrocephalus and was both physically and mentally retarded. Ladislas Specht, the father, was a sales agent for Indian and American cotton, and was financially well off. As a result, for almost the first time in his life Rudolf Steiner had no financial troubles, and was in a position to give up his other tutoring. He could now spend his summer holidays with his employers in the beautiful Alpine country of Upper Austria, and he tells us that it was while living with this family that for the first time he learnt to play (and invent) games.

Although he does not discuss in any detail the educational work that he undertook with the Specht children, it is clear enough from what he says in his autobiography that we may trace to this time the genesis of what later became his curative educational work for children "in need of special care of the soul," as he was later to call such children as Otto Specht. His work with the normal members of the family was also to bear fruit in his educational work for normal children for which he became equally famous in later years, and for which he is now known. Although at the beginning he had no knowledge of the particular kind of pedagogy that would be needed for Otto, and was without any practical experience in this domain, his supersensible faculties were by this time sufficiently developed for him to be able to perceive how the boy's soul, as he puts it, did not "fit" his body, and he did not hesitate to use his insights to help the lad to awaken his "hidden mental faculties." Almost immediately he won the full confidence of the boy's parents, and was given full charge of his education. At that epoch, in the 1880's, almost nothing was done for such retarded children by orthodox medicine, so Steiner could have learned little or nothing from that source.

Steiner tells us that this experience was to him profoundly

37

satisfying, and it enabled him "to gain in a living way a knowledge of the nature of the human being which I do not believe I could have developed so vitally in any other way." Unfortunately he does not go into any detail as to how he succeeded in "awakening the soul" of the boy, but such detail as he gives enables us to trace how he arrived at the basic insights that later came to full fruition in the educational work of his mature years. The first necessity was to win the loving attachment of the boy, and then, when this was secure, to divise a method of instruction and a curriculum that would not be too great a strain on his delicate health. At the beginning it was impossible to spend more than fifteen minutes at a time on actual teaching without causing injury to his health, and the young tutor had never to lose sight of the very limited possibilities for improvement, and to observe every change with the utmost attention.

"Through the method of instruction that I had to employ," he tells us, "there was laid open to my view the association between the spirit-soul element and the bodily element in the human being. It was then that I went through my real course of study in physiology and psychology. I became aware that instructing and educating must become an art having its foundation in a genuine knowledge of the human being. . . . I frequently had to spend two hours in preparing half an hour's instruction in order to get the material for instruction into such a form that, in the least time and with the least strain upon the mental and physical powers of the child, I might reach his highest capacity for achievement. The order of the subjects of instruction had to be carefully considered; the division of the day into periods had to be properly determined. I had the satisfaction of seeing the child in the course of two years catch up in the work of the elementary school and successfully pass the entrance examination into the *Gymnasium*. Moreover his condition of health had materially improved. The existing hydrocephalic condition was markedly dimishing. . . . My young charge was successfully guided through the *Gymnasium*; I continued with him until the next to the last class. By that time he had made such progress that he no longer needed me."[10]

The erstwhile retarded child then entered the School of Medicine at Vienna and graduated as a doctor, practicing for many years as a successful physician until he was killed in action during the First World War.

While living in the Specht household Rudolf Steiner was for a short time the editor of a weekly periodical *Deutsche Wochenscrift*, and had among other duties to compose a weekly article on world events. He admits frankly that his life experience was as yet quite inadequate to fulfil such a task, and he was relieved when the journal suspended publication in a quarrel between the new and former owners over financial not editorial matters. The editorship gave him some new insights into Austrian racial struggles, but otherwise was not especially rewarding. Meanwhile he continued with his Goethe studies already begun in his first year at the Institute of Technology. These proved to be so important in his life that they merit detailed attention here.

As we saw in the last chapter Steiner already became acquainted with the work of Immanuel Kant while still in high school. In his last summer before going to the Vienna Institute of Technology he began to work with great intensity on the German idealist philosophers, having bought several volumes by Fichte, Hegel and Schelling from the proceeds of the sale of his school books. He was at first, and indeed for many years thereafter, especially interested in Johann Gottlieb Fichte and his philosophy of the Ego, since, as he tells us in his autobiography, it was a matter of direct perception for him that "the Ego is spirit and lives in a world of spirits." The German idealists had succeeded in achieving numerous insights solely through an intense activity of thought. But unlike Steiner, they had not actually penetrated into the spiritual world consciously, though Hegel, in particular, 'had experienced this world most intensely through his activity of thought. After studying most carefully what these men had to say Steiner came to conceive it as his task to "mould into the forms of thought the immediate perception of the spiritual world which I possessed."

This conclusion he had reached even before entering the

Institute of Technology, and it seems likely that he had already come also to the conviction, though perhaps a little less consciously, that it would become for him a spiritual necessity to oppose the prevalent materialistic conception of the world by formulating the spiritual conception which he held to be the true one, which alone was in conformity with what he perceived directly through his supersensible faculties. Pondering over these matters even while he was deeply engaged in his other studies, by the time he was twenty-one he had come to the conclusion, as he puts it, that "spiritual vision perceives spirit as the senses perceive nature," and recognized that this spiritual vision did not rest upon "obscure mystical feeling, but took its course rather in a spiritual activity which in its transparency might be compared completely with mathematical thinking." Thus, as he formulated it, he felt himself to be "approaching a state of mind in which I felt that I might consider that the perception of the spiritual world which I bore within me was justified also before the forum of natural scientific thinking."[11]

It will not therefore be difficult to see why for Steiner philosophy was scarcely at all a subject for academic study; and it seems that he took no courses at all in philosophy either at his secondary school or university, though he attended some lectures by practicing philosophers, mainly in order to see for himself *how* they thought, being very little interested in *what* they thought. His main concern was to discover to what realm philosophers penetrate when they think, a subject that was especially fascinating in the case of Hegel, whose tremendous capacity for thinking he always admired. Steiner felt that he knew the nature of Hegel's "living thought-world," but he could not help being disappointed that Hegel had never been able to penetrate into and perceive a world of concrete spirit. Indeed he goes so far as to say that this failure of Hegel "repelled" him, whereas the more he entered into the world of geometry, especially synthetic or projective geometry, the more sure he was that this was indeed a real world of spirit, totally unlike the world of sense perceptions in which we ordinarily live. To Steiner mathematical concepts were true, independent of any confirmation from the sense-perceptible world, and this was always a solace for him as he struggled with the concepts of other thinkers who lacked his own first hand experience. Thus he edged his way toward the theory of knowledge that as yet he did not dare to formulate, even to himself, a theory of knowledge that he never found in any of the philosophers whose works he studied, but that he was to find implicit in the work of Goethe, who was not even regarded as a philosopher at all by Steiner's contemporaries—and by few indeed of his successors.

When at high school Steiner had no knowledge at all of Goethe, but in the course of his studies at the Institute of Technology it became necessary for him to study German literature in a formal manner. Thus when he was only a freshman he made the acquaintance of the professor of German literature at the Institute, Karl Julius Schröer, who took a great interest in him and invited him frequently to his home. Schröer was at the time one of the leading experts on Goethe, and had recently published an edition of Part I of *Faust* for a series on German literature sponsored by the publishing house of Kürschner. Part II he was already preparing when Steiner made his acquaintance, and the young student at once began to share his enthusiasm. He tells us that he "listened with the utmost sympathy to everything that came from Schröer," commenting that his professor "lived so strongly in the spirit and work of Goethe that, with every sentiment or idea which entered his mind, he asked himself the question: Would Goethe have felt or thought this?"

Steiner soon discovered that Schröer had no interest at all in Goethe's scientific works, in this conforming to the general opinion of Goethe held in the late nineteenth century. These works were usually regarded as an interesting by-product of his poetic genius, and not at all as a substantial contribution to scientific knowledge—still less as a contribution to scientific method. Newton's theory of color continued to hold the field as it had in Goethe's own lifetime, and Goethe's thousands of experiments in the field of color recorded in his huge book on the subject were almost totally neglected. Even Goethe's small

41

book on the metamorphosis of plants which had won unstinted praise from the early nineteenth century British historian of science William Whewell (1839) was no longer read, much less taken seriously. Darwinism held the field in biology as Newton in physics. Goethe was classified as a poet and dramatist, among the greatest, if not the greatest in modern times. His proper, and sole, academic niche was in the specialty of German literature.

Steiner, quite independently of Goethe, had already come to the conclusion even before he left high school that Newton's theory of color was fundamentally wrong, and he was opposed also to what he knew of Newton's optics. So he began to make experiments as soon as he had the time and opportunity to make them, and could buy the simple equipment that he needed; and in his early days at the Institute he wrote a few simple papers on what he had discovered. These he showed to Schröer, but the professor was not at all interested. Indeed he never at any time showed much sympathy for Steiner's efforts to evolve for himself a personal philosophy, called by him at the time, for want of a better name, "objective realism." For Schröer ideas were simply "a propelling force in the creative work of nature and of man," a conventional viewpoint that was of no interest to his pupil, who held that "behind ideas were spiritual realities of which the ideas themselves were only the shadows."

The relationship between teacher and pupil might therefore never have made any further progress if Steiner had not one day come upon Goethe's *Farbenlehre* (Theory of Color) and discovered that Goethe had made similar experiments to his own, whereupon he proceeded to repeat as many as he could of Goethe's, always arriving at the same results, and reaching the same theoretical conclusions. When he told Schröer about this work, which now involved Goethe, the professor at once became interested and gave him every encouragement. Steiner then began to devour every scientific work of Goethe that he could find, and as he read his excitement grew. At last he had found someone who had worked in the same field as himself, appeared to have at least some of his own spiritual faculties,

42

and had used them in the field of science—precisely what he intended to do himself!

It may be imagined how much consolation Steiner derived from this discovery, and he tells us that he found inner release from the soul-depressing mood from which he suffered because of his necessary isolation from his companions that resulted from his unique spiritual perception, and he constantly re-read the conversation that Goethe had with his friend Friedrich Schiller after a meeting of the Society for Scientific Research in Jena. Goethe had told Schiller that he had actually *seen* what he called the *Urpflanze*, or archetypal plant, whereupon Schiller insisted that what he had seen was only an "idea." To which Goethe retorted that he was glad that he could perceive ideas *with his eyes*. "I derived comfort," Steiner tells us, "after a long struggle of the mind from what came to me out of the understanding of these words of Goethe to which I felt I had penetrated. Goethe's way of viewing nature appeared to me as in keeping with spirit. Impelled now by an inner necessity, I had to study in detail all of Goethe's scientific writings." Before leaving Vienna Steiner also had seen the *Urpflanze*, but, unlike Goethe, he was able to explain just what it was—a "sensible-supersensible form which is interposed, both for true natural vision and also for spiritual vision, between what the senses grasp and the spirit perceives." Goethe, he commented, " 'saw' the whole *spiritually* as he saw the group of details with his senses, and he admitted no difference in principle between the spiritual and the sensible perception, but only a transition from one to the other."[12]

In 1883 when Steiner was twenty-two years old an opportunity was presented to him of which he took full advantage. Schröer was, as we have seen, in the process of editing *Faust* for the publishing house of Kürschner, and he could also have had from the same house the task of editing Goethe's scientific writings. But, as we have seen, he had no interest in this work except in so far as everything written by Goethe fell within the domain of his interest. He therefore proposed to Kürschner that his young pupil should be entrusted with the editing, since he was already deeply interested in the work, and no other experts were easily to be found. Kürschner agreed to take the chance, although Steiner was completely unknown, and Steiner was appointed as the official editor of the scientific works of Goethe in the German National Literature series. By the following year he had prepared the first group of introductions, and these were immediately published. Three further groups were published in subsequent years.*

It is clear from these introductions that Steiner believed that the method to be used for observing the organic world must differ essentially from that used in observing and describing the inorganic. The first writings for which he provided the introductions include Goethe's work on the morphology of plants and that on animal morphology, in which the poet predicted the existence of the human intermaxillary jawbone, which had not yet been discovered anatomically. The apparent successes of Goethe's method aroused the utmost enthusiasm in the twenty-two year old Steiner. He had discovered a key that could be expected to open all doors. The passage in which Steiner predicts the glorious future awaiting scientific investigation through the use of the Goethean method is surely worth quoting in full:

"With what intensity the thought was alive in Goethe to set forth in a major work his ideas concerning nature becomes especially clear when we see that, with each new discovery which he succeeds in making, he cannot refrain from expressing emphatically to his friends the possibility of expanding his ideas to embrace the whole of nature. . . .

"We must regret that such a work was not produced by Goethe. In the light of all that is available, it would have been a creation far outdistancing everything of the kind achieved in modern times. It would have been a canon from which every undertaking in the natural-scientific field would have had to take its point of departure and in connection with which it would have been possible to test the spiritual substance of

---

*These introductions are available in English in a book entitled *Goethe the Scientist*, translated by Olin D. Wannamaker (New York: Anthroposophic Press, 1950). The extract quoted is from this edition.

44

every undertaking. The profoundest philosophical spirit—a characterization which only superficiality would deny to Goethe—would here have united with a loving absorption in what is presented to sense experience. Remote from any craving for a system supposed to embrace all beings in one universal scheme, here every individual entity would have come into its right. We should have had the work of a mind for which no single branch of human endeavor presses forward to the neglect of all others, but for which the totality of human existence always hovers in the background while it is dealing with a single field. Thus does every single activity acquire its appropriate place in connection with the whole. The objective absorption in the things under consideration causes the mind to enter completely into them, so that Goethe's theories appear not as something abstracted by a mind, which in its reflecting forgets itself. This inflexible objectivity would have made Goethe's production the most perfect work of natural science. It would have been an ideal which research scientists would have had to emulate. For the philosophers it would have been a typical model for the discovery of the laws of unbiased world-contemplation. One can assume that the theory of knowledge, which is now coming into view everywhere as a fundamental branch of philosophical knowledge, will be fruitful only when it takes as its point of departure Goethe's manner of observing and thinking. . . ."*

Steiner was to learn, painfully enough, in later years how deeply embedded scientific materialism was in the minds of men, especially at the end of the nineteenth century, and how difficult it would be to change their viewpoints. Nevertheless the sentiments expressed in this quotation remained his personal convictions for the rest of his life, and he would have had to change nothing if he had rewritten this introduction in 1924. But he did realize at once after writing it that it was a necessity for him to lay the philosophical foundations of the theory of knowledge he had discovered in Goethe's work, and that was to become, after a very thorough elaboration, his own.

Goethe the Scientist, page. 39.

Thus before he embarked upon his second introduction he set to work to sketch Goethe's theory of knowledge in a book whose title reveals exactly what Steiner believed he had found: *The Theory of Knowledge Implicit in Goethe's World Conception*. This book was completed at the end of April, 1886 and published before the end of the year. Steiner had just passed his twenty-fifth birthday. Again, it was not necessary for him to change anything of importance when he prepared a new edition of this work in 1924. It remains a bare, perfectly articulated but skeletal presentation of a theory of knowledge, which provides above all a method of studying the organic world that had been Goethe's special concern. Almost every theme developed later in Steiner's *Philosophy of Freedom* (1894) is to be found in this little book, and even today it is well worth reading and studying for itself, and not only because it marks a milestone in Steiner's thinking. His work on Goethe likewise reached its own climax in the 1890's with the publication in 1897 of his book *Goethe's Conception of the World*, of which a new edition appeared in 1918 at the same time as the second edition of *The Philosophy of Freedom*.

The discovery and study of Goethe—not only his scientific works but his poetry which he never tired of quoting throughout his life—played a part in Rudolf Steiner's life that it is difficult to overestimate. Nevertheless it is untrue to suggest or imply that his thinking was, even in the slightest degree, influenced by that of his great eighteenth century predecessor. It is, indeed, difficult, if not impossible, to find any real influence on his thinking exercised by *any* predecessor or contemporary. From his earliest youth he had read books to find if other men had ever thought what he himself was thinking. Hence the crucial importance to him of Goethe's work because he had at last found someone who had indeed thought along the same lines as himself; although Goethe had not himself attained supersensible perception, he had come very close to it, and on several occasions had clothed what he had perceived in marvellous poetic-imaginative form. This is especially true of his "fairy tale" of the *Green Snake and the Beautiful Lily* whose supersensible truth was at once recog-

46

nized by Steiner, who knew from it to what realm of the supersensible Goethe had penetrated. We have already alluded to Steiner's comments on the so-called "archetypal plant" which Goethe claimed to have been able to see, and which Steiner also declared to be a reality in the realm between the sensible and the supersensible.

In Chapter 12 of his autobiography he explains how he was "constantly driven from Goethe to the presentation of my own world view, and then back to him so that I could interpret his thoughts better in the light of my own thoughts. . . . I had to struggle for years to obtain a better understanding of Goethe so that I could present his ideas. Looking back on this struggle I realize that it is to this that I owe the development of my own spiritual experience of knowledge. This development proceeded far more slowly than would have been the case if the Goethe task had not been placed by destiny on the pathway of my life. I should then have pursued my spiritual experiences and set these forth just as they appeared before me. I should have been drawn into the spiritual world more quickly, but I should have had no inducement to struggle to penetrate into my own inner being."

Steiner then proceeds to emphasize how his work with Goethe served a most important purpose in his life work since the attempt to come to terms with him *slowed him up*, while forcing him to realize that whatever spiritual gifts a person has received as an "act of grace," he should never move too quickly, neither being in a hurry to develop his spiritual gifts further nor speaking prematurely of the knowledge resulting from these gifts. While his own mental impulses, as he tells us, were leading him to direct perception of the spiritual world, the "outer spiritual life of the world brought the Goethe work to me." These remarks seem to imply that without his struggle with the work of Goethe he might never have laid the philosophical groundwork which was essential for his later presentation of Anthroposophy.

Further light is thrown on Steiner's understanding of the role of Goethe in his life and work by a lecture given in 1918 to the members of the Anthroposophical Society in Dornach,

47

where the Goetheanum was nearing completion. Here he wished to explain why he had chosen to call the building that was to be the center of Anthroposophy after Goethe and why he was republishing his major work on Goethe for the first time since 1897. Goethe, Rudolf Steiner told his audience, always conceived of man as an integral part of the universe, and refused to look upon him as if he were an isolated being. Man is imbued, he said, "with the same wisdom that informs nature. . . . To pursue the path of Goetheanism is to open the doors to an anthroposophically oriented science of spirit. . . . In many ways the safest approach to spiritual science is to begin with the study of Goethe." With regard to the book *Goethe's Conception of the World* Steiner pointed out that it was "written specially in order to show that in the sphere of knowledge there are two streams today: a decadent stream which everyone admires, and another stream which contains the most fertile seeds for the future, and which everyone avoids."[13]

Throughout his life Steiner insisted that the world cannot be understood by the analytical methods of modern science which are competent to deal only with the inorganic world, and not fully even with that, for lack of the ability to perceive the spiritual behind the physical. Indeed analytical science must regard even the organic world as if it were dead if its methods are to be valid and yield any usable information. According to Steiner the only way to comprehend the living organic world is to develop a new kind of thinking that he calls "living thinking" or sometimes "imaginative thinking." Goethe had already begun to develop this kind of thinking for himself without ever having understood fully just what he was doing, and certainly without having ever conceptualized it.

The service Goethe performed for Steiner was to show him that his own kind of thinking was not unique, but that it had been developed by an eminent predecessor, even though it had not been thoroughly worked out by him. His work with Goethe also brought Steiner to the attention of other Goethe specialists, few if any of whom shared his view of Goethe's preeminent talents as thinker and experimenter. Steiner was treated by these men as an equal, although many of them later were to regard his anthroposophical work as a deplorable waste of his philosophical and scientific talent. Perhaps most important of all the consequences of his immersion in the work of Goethe was, as has been suggested, the fact that it held him back from premature disclosures in the field of Anthroposophy.

From early adolescence Steiner had been a voracious reader, and, as we have seen, he studied almost every subject offered both in the *Realschule* and the *Gymnasium*. At the end of his high school career he began to study German idealist philosophy in a concentrated manner, and he attended courses on the most varied subjects during his years at the Vienna Institute of Technology, including lectures given by leading specialists at the University of Vienna. What he needed by the time he was twenty-one was to concentrate his attention, and bring his talents to bear on some single field of study that it was really worth his while to grasp from all the angles he could. He found this field in his work with Goethe—not because he concentrated on Goethe himself so much as because through his study of Goethe he was able to create his own philosophy, almost as a byproduct. At all events it started as a byproduct when he discovered the need to write his *Theory of Knowledge Implicit in Goethe's World Conception* after he had written his first introductions to Goethe's scientific work. Thereafter, as we shall see in the next chapter, he went on to write an original philosophical work which was accepted as his doctoral dissertation at the University of Rostock, and he wrote his major philosophical work *The Philosophy of Freedom* published in 1894, completing this phase of his career in 1900 with a book on the philosophical thinkers of the nineteenth century.

Although we have stressed here Steiner's primary interest in Goethe as scientist he admired Goethe also not only as poet but as thinker in other realms than science. In 1888 he gave a lecture to the Goethean Society in Vienna on an aspect of Goethe's work that is rarely stressed, a lecture that was soon published and has been many times republished in the years since. The title given to the lecture was *Goethe as the Founder of a New Science of Aesthetics.* In it Steiner tried to show that Goethe held a coherent theory of beauty that differed in its essentials from the idea of beauty held by almost all the German idealist philosophers, who regarded beauty as the highest embodiment of the Idea. The lecture is sprinkled with numerous apt quotations from Goethe, including many that Steiner was to quote again and again in later life. It is quite possible that among the distinguished audience were some persons who were hearing him for the first time, and this fact may have played some part in the invitation that was extended to him in the following year, although the actual recommendation that Steiner be given the position certainly came from Schröer, who alone was able to vouch for his qualifications.

A new and complete edition of Goethe's works was in preparation under the sponsorship of the Grand Duchess Sophie of Saxony, who was a Dutch princess in her own right and was a devoted patroness of all forms of German culture. As a result of receiving a legacy from Goethe's grandson of all the extant manuscripts of his grandfather the Grand Duchess had decided to create the Goethe Archives in Weimar, and to invite the leading Goethe scholars of the day to edit the new volumes she proposed to publish. By the end of World War I when the work was completed there were 133 volumes in all, of which the scientific books were edited by Steiner.

The work had been in progress for some years when Bernard Suphan, director of the Archives, decided that the scientific work needed a qualified editor. He therefore after consulting Schröer invited Rudolf Steiner to pay a visit to Weimar to look over the scientific material in the Archives to see if he would be interested in collaborating in the new edition. Thus Steiner paid his very first visit to Germany, to a city which was one of the most important cultural centers of the country, as well as being the city of Goethe. Steiner's initial experience in Weimar seems to have been an overwhelming one, as evidenced by the many letters extant that date from that first visit. In addition to Goethe, Schiller had lived in Weimar, John Sebastian Bach had been court organist there, and in the mid-nineteenth century Franz Liszt had been its director of music. The first performance of Wagner's *Lohengrin* had been given there. So Steiner was full of enthusiasm at everything he saw and experienced and immediately made himself familiar with the old haunts of Goethe, who had not yet been dead sixty years. For him Weimar was saturated with memories of Goethe, and when he examined the scientific collection in the Archives he discovered numerous manuscripts that he knew would be of surpassing interest to him. No doubt his enthusiasm communicated itself to Suphan, who invited him to come to Weimar in due course to work with the Archives. On the way back to Vienna Steiner paid a call on the leading philosopher of the day, Eduard von Hartmann, who lived in Berlin, but was disappointed to find that they disagreed on fundamental philosophical matters. He also took the opportunity to visit art collections in Berlin and in Munich before spending the rest of his holidays in the Austrian Alps with the Specht family.

It was in the last months of his period in Vienna that he made the acquaintance of Rosa Mayreder, as well as with a number of theosophists, and he tells us that it was also during this time that *The Philosophy of Freedom*, which he discussed so often with Frau Mayreder, took final shape in his mind. In 1890 he felt he could safely leave Otto Specht who was now able to make progress on his own. For years he kept in touch with the boy's mother through correspondence, but there was no further need for his direct help. So in the autumn of 1890 he finally wound up his affairs in Vienna and moved to Weimar. The seven years he spent there were in some respects disappointing to him, but aside from the work he did in the Goethe Archives, he also completed his major philosophical works while he was living there, and accomplished a great deal of other writing, some of which will be mentioned in the next chapter. Most important of all, Weimar brought him into close contact with German culture at a time when imperial Germany in so many respects led the world. The rest of his life until the War was spent in Germany, and he was never again to live in Austria, the land of his birth.

Chapter 4.

AT THE GOETHE ARCHIVES IN WEIMAR
NIETZSCHE AND HAECKEL *

At the end of the last chapter it was mentioned that Rudolf
Steiner's seven year sojourn in Weimar was in some respects
disappointing to him in spite of his deep interest in the work
to which he had been assigned, and his initial enthusiasm
began to wane soon after his thirtieth birthday. The major reason for the disappointment was that he discovered a fundamental difference between his own attitude and that of the
majority of his fellow workers, whose approach to Goethe's
work was, to use Steiner's invariable word for it, "philo-
logical."

There can be no doubt that the attitude of these men was the
polar opposite of his own. There is a kind of learning that
became widespread for the first time in the nineteenth century
(especially, indeed, in Germany) that concentrates on the textual details of the work of great writers of past epochs, thus too
often failing to grasp the scope and true importance of the
writers themselves and their works. In present-day Shakespear-
ian studies, for example, especially as they are pursued in
institutions of learning, scholars become extraordinarily interested in tracing every image, every historical nuance, the
sources used by the master, even the smallest indications of
authorship and the tiniest wisp of evidence for his life and
activities other than his writing. Such material is the stuff of
which doctoral dissertations are composed. Already at the beginning of the 1890's Goethe was in the process of being

mummified by too many of the scholars now engaged in the work of editing his extant manuscripts. And these scholars, to Steiner's horror, seemed to be precisely those who now enjoyed the highest reputation and whose influence was becoming paramount at Weimar.

Steiner, by contrast, *loved* Goethe and his work. He entered imaginatively into Goethe's life and thought. Everything Goethe had written, whether classified as literature or science, was of vital importance to him. In Steiner's view Goethe's ideas were still alive and not ready to be embalmed. They should be made known to the entire world so that other men's thinking could become as alive as his. His scientific observations and experiments, his theory of color, above all his conception of the world implicit in all his work—these things were valued by Steiner but by few others in Weimar, and it was impossible to find anyone to whom he could really talk on these matters with the certainty of being understood. Not even to Hermann Grimm, an essayist of note, a sensitive historian of art, and author of a book on Goethe which was greatly appreciated by Steiner. Indeed, Steiner made frequent references to Hermann Grimm throughout his life, and his friendship with the older man (Grimm was born in 1828), both in Weimar and Berlin, evidently meant much to him.

Grimm was an important figure in German cultural life at the time, though he was not, strictly speaking an academic and was therefore looked down on by some German academic pedants as little better than a dilettante. Only when in mature life he was appointed professor of the history of art in the University of Berlin was he accepted as a member of the academic fraternity, though his many teaching innovations caused some academic eyebrows to rise. Many of his books eventually became classics and all are still in print in German. This was the man of whom Steiner wrote: "Whenever he appeared in Weimar and in the Archives one felt that hidden spiritual threads united Goethe with the place where his legacy now reposed." But even Grimm, friendly and helpful though he was to Steiner, could not follow him in his appreciation of Goethe as a seminal thinker, confining himself

53

to an appreciation of and understanding of his work in literature and poetry—much as Schröer had done in Vienna. But this, at least, was a refreshing change from the attitude of most of the "philologists," whose feeling for the poetry, if it had ever existed, had been long ago subordinated to their interest in the exact scholarship of textual criticism.

Although Steiner was active in the social life of Weimar, and made many friends, as he had in Vienna, his letters of the time make it clear that he suffered seriously from his isolation and the fact that to not one, not even to Gabrielle Reuter, the authoress referred to in the last chapter, nor to Hermann Grimm, who for all his insights was too much the child of his age, could he speak of what lay closest to his heart, including his spiritual experiences and the content of his inner life. But he was fortunately given the opportunity, as he had been in Vienna, to enjoy a home life because of his work with a family of children. Anna Eunike, a recent widow, asked him to supervise the education of her five young children. This position required him to make his home with the family, and he was given a part of the Eunike house where he could entertain his own friends. The move was a welcome change after the early period of his stay in Weimar when he had been compelled to rent unsatisfactory lodgings. Later when he moved to Berlin Frau Eunike again provided him with a home, and in 1899 she became his first wife.

Perhaps in part because of his relative isolation Steiner spent his seven year period in Weimar in completing, in all essential respects, his philosophical corpus. When he arrived in Weimar he had not yet earned his doctorate in philosophy, in spite of the fact that he had already written and published an important philosophical work on the theory of knowledge implicit in Goethe's world conception (1886) and had prepared a kind of sequel to that work that might be acceptable as a doctoral dissertation. From the point of view of the authorities in the University of Vienna Steiner's formal education had been deficient. Having attended only the *Realschüle* and not the *Gymnasium* he was not eligible to receive a doctorate in philosophy, however brilliant his dissertation. Similar regulations did not apply in Germany. All that was needed was for a recognized professor of philosophy to be willing to accept his dissertation and examine him orally on his general competence in philosophy as well as on the dissertation itself.

The work that Steiner proposed to submit was still concerned with the theory of knowledge, but no longer with Goethe. It was intended as a refutation of Kant's belief that there are necessary limits of knowledge, but this time Steiner took his departure from Johann Gottlieb Fichte's book *The Science of Knowledge*. Steiner's dissertation when it was eventually submitted bore the full title *The Fundamentals of a Theory of Cognition with Special Reference to Fichte's Scientific Teaching*. It was followed in 1894 by *The Philosophy of Freedom*, or *Philosophy of Spiritual Activity*, which placed the capstone on his work in epistemology, and showed how a theory of freedom could be derived from a theory of knowledge that places no limits on human cognition. The dissertation, later published under the simpler title of *Truth and Science* or *Truth and Knowledge* (*Wahrheit und Wissenschaft*) was thus a kind of half way point between the 1886 work on Goethe and the major work of 1894.

Early in his stay in Weimar Steiner came upon a three volume work on Plato, written by a certain Heinrich von Stein, professor of philosophy at the University of Rostock in northern Germany. Greatly impressed by this work on Plato Steiner thought it possible that von Stein might be willing to sponsor his dissertation. So he sent off the manuscript and in due course received word that it was acceptable, and instructing him to go to Rostock for his examination, which took place in May, 1891. To his disappointment the oral examination was concerned only with Kant, and not, as he had hoped, with Plato, whom he had in the meantime studied intensively. Kant, of course, presented no difficulties. As for the dissertation von Stein remarked drily that "one can see from it that you have not produced it under the guidance of a professor," adding at once, "but what it contains makes it possible that I can very gladly accept it."

So Rudolf Steiner earned his doctorate at the age of thirty

from a university he had never attended, and did not know, and from a professor whom he met only on this occasion, and who died shortly afterwards. The dissertation, only slightly revised, was published the following year.

Once this hurdle was out of the way, Steiner returned to work on the book that had been maturing in him since he first conceived it in 1881 when he was only twenty years old. But neither at this nor any other period in his life did he devote himself simply to one subject or one book. His bibliography for the seven year Weimar period consists of no fewer than 95 titles, including books and articles, of which his introductions to the works of Schopenhauer and Jean Paul in the Cotta World Literature library were by no means the least. While he was completing *The Philosophy of Freedom* he was studying Friedrich Nietzsche in an intensive way, having discovered him only the year before going to Weimar. A book on Nietzsche appeared from his pen in 1895, just a year after publishing *The Philosophy of Freedom*. Lastly he completed his introductions to the scientific work of Goethe for the Kürschner edition, and wrote his major work on Goethe which was published in 1897 (*Goethe's Conception of the World*).

The Philosophy of Freedom was referred to time and again by Rudolf Steiner in his later life, and it undoubtedly constitutes his most important philosophical work. In it Steiner believed he had laid the philosophical groundwork for everything he was to give out later as Anthroposophy, which he called the *science* of the spirit (*Geisteswissenschaft*). At this time he was trying to convince his fellow-philosophers and scientists that Kant's teachings on the limits of knowledge must be false. As yet he had said nothing publicly about his perceptions of the spiritual world. He had not yet found his audience for Anthroposophy, nor had he received the indication from the spiritual worlds that he should speak of these perceptions. He was, indeed, constantly asking himself if he should forever have to keep silent, and perhaps have no task to perform but to show through philosophical argument that thinking itself was a spiritual activity, in no way dependent on the senses, that when man thinks he is exercising a faculty that can truly be called *supersensible*.

As a result of his personal experience Steiner knew for certain that Kant's teaching must be untrue, and that all those philosophers who still followed him were mistaken. The spiritual knowledge that he himself possessed was as clear and conscious as any other kind of knowledge, yet it was not derived from the sense world. Therefore the world of spirit *did* exist, and it was accessible to man. What was therefore needed was a theory of knowledge that was capable of explaining his own actual *experience* that knowledge did indeed have no limits, and that the entire world of spirit could be explored by human thinking once this thinking had been developed to a higher stage than that normally attained by the average human being.

Steiner's attempt to disprove Kant and establish his own point of view is to be found in the first half of his *Philosophy of Freedom*, the second half being taken up by his discussion of the consequences for human freedom of the recognition that knowledge has no limits and that thinking is a supersensible activity. Steiner in later life insisted that the two parts of the books belong together and that only by experiencing the first part inwardly can one truly accept the second part of the book, which at first reading appears much more simple to follow. It seems clear that the book does not yield up all its riches at a first reading, and many of Steiner's followers in fact read it very frequently, perhaps as often as every year, always discovering new insights in it, and measuring their own progress by how much more of it they can understand and apply. It is difficult, indeed virtually impossible, to give any meaningful outline of the content of the book, clear though its arguments are. But an attempt can be made at least to show the kind of argument used to disprove Kant's thesis that there are necessary limits to knowledge.

Steiner succeeds first of all in demonstrating that *no* perception by means of the senses is possible unless *at the same time* a thinking element is present, that is to say, a concept. In actual life therefore concepts and percepts are inseparable. Thinking is therefore an essential element in perceiving, as the Greeks must have known since their original word for seeing was "noein," from which came later their word for mind, "nous."

Since all objects in the world possess both perceptual and conceptual elements, it is never possible simply to *perceive* an object without in some manner making use of our thinking capacity, if only to take notice of it or to recognize it. Aristotle, who developed a theory of knowledge similar to Steiner's, was well aware of the two elements present in all objects, and he named the conceptual element the *form*, while the perceptible element he called *substance*. Everything in the world was therefore made up of substance and form. For Aristotle as for Steiner the form was no less *real* than the substance. Both are equally real, though the form, as such, is never visible to the senses, and must be perceived by the thinking. For Steiner, therefore, thinking was in the truest sense of the word, a *super*-sensible capacity, since it was able to perceive (or conceive) that element in things that is forever imperceptible to the senses. When thinking is systematically developed through exercises described by Steiner in his later works, it is capable also of perceiving (or conceiving) the invisible, supersensible world.

Not only Aristotle but also his medieval successor Thomas Aquinas formulated theories of knowledge similar to Steiner's though there is no reason to suppose that Steiner was aware of the fact when he wrote his *Philosophy of Freedom*. In any event the great wealth of illustration and argument that he brings to the subject place Steiner's book in a different category from theirs. It is worth noting that the second half of the book concerning the reality of freedom and how it can be attained was a subject that had relatively little interest for his predecessors, though it is of surpassing interest for men and women of our present age.

At the beginning of the second part of his book Steiner after a brief digression on the subject of feeling and willing plunges into what must be regarded as the central chapter of the second half, in which he writes of the nature of freedom, and he succeeds in showing with great clarity how all free acts must be preceded by free thoughts. Freedom, for Steiner, was not something that was ever achieved, or enjoyed, but, as Goethe says in his *Faust*, "freedom must be conquered anew every day." Ordinary thoughts are not free, nor are the deeds that we perform in our ordinary life. A thought, for Steiner, can be free only when it has been created anew through the activity of the human spirit. If an act is performed simply out of habit, obedience to that habit prevents it from being a free act, in exactly the same way that an act is unfree if it follows the dictates of a Church, a government, an external authority of any kind, or even an ethical principle which one has accepted. All free acts are *individual* and *unique*, and therefore cannot be based on any general principle, however praiseworthy; they can be based only on thinking brought to bear on a specific situation uninfluenced by any previous situation of the same kind or by moral principles enunciated by others, or even by oneself on the basis of similar but essentially different cases in the past.

Since free acts are based, in the last analysis, on thinking, such thinking must be enlivened so that it becomes what we have already called "living" or imaginative thinking. Hence Steiner speaks of the quality that must be developed if free acts are to be performed as "moral imagination," which through inner development can eventually become "moral inspiration," and "moral intuition." All are the result of what Steiner calls "spiritual activity," and it was for this reason that he suggested that the word *Freiheit* in German, which does not have an exact English equivalent, should be translated in English as *Spiritual Activity*, making his book's exact title in English *The Philosophy of Spiritual Activity*. All editions prior to the current translation by Michael Wilson bore this title, but Wilson decided that *The Philosophy of Freedom* was less misleading for English speaking people, who, in his view, were inclined to think spiritual activity must be something to do with religion, and the philosophy of spiritual activity would be expected to offer a justification of religious practices. Since the book certainly does provide a philosophical basis for the existence of human freedom in the English sense of the word, describing, as it does, exactly what freedom consists of, as well as what it is not, the title *Philosophy of Freedom* is fully justified in itself, and it could well be preferable for an English or American audience. Since the English and American peoples believe themselves to be already free, and even that they possess and enjoy certain

59

"freedoms" guaranteed to them by their governments, it may be as well for them to give more consideration also to the true nature of freedom and perceive for themselves whether or not they enjoy it; if the book were to be called, as Steiner suggested, *The Philosophy of Spiritual Activity*, its relevance to the question of freedom might easily be overlooked.

For Steiner it was essential to link his demonstration of the spiritual nature of thinking to his discussion of the nature of and possibility of performing free acts, that is to say to link the first half of his book to the second. The moral philosophy that results he called "ethical individualism," a philosophy that may be found, more or less explicitly, in the work of Max Stirner, an anarchist philosopher whose book *Der Einziger und sein Eigentum*, variously translated as *The Ego and its Property*, *The Ego and his Own* and *The Only One and His Possession*, appeared in 1845. Steiner in his book on Nietzsche praised the book, and speculated what the consequences would have been for Nietzsche if he had become a disciple of Stirner rather than of Schopenhauer. Nietzsche himself, the best known living philosopher at the time of Steiner's stay in Weimar, although because of a mental breakdown he was no longer writing, had in numerous works insisted that the individual man must use his freedom to create his own ethical standards, and not rely on any one else to do his thinking for him. Although very few of Nietzsche's premises could be accepted by Rudolf Steiner, the ethics resulting from his philosophy was in some respects similar to his, though reached by quite different paths of thought. The similarity was surely responsible for Steiner's sudden interest in Nietzsche when he first came upon his work in 1889.

By contrast Eduard von Hartmann, a more traditional philosopher than Nietzsche, whose work was admired by Steiner, who had dedicated his earlier work *Truth and Science* to him, could not understand the true purpose of *The Philosophy of Freedom* as Steiner had expressed it, and in particuar could not grasp the relation between the first and second parts of the book. Though he read the whole with great care when he received from Steiner one of the first copies off the press, he remained unconvinced that Kant's work was now superseded. He himself was a Kantian type of thinker, though he went further than Kant in some important respects. Holding with Kant that the entire sense-perceptible world is "merely a subjective phenomenon existing in the mind," and that consequently reality can be known only by *inference*, von Hartmann evidently thought that Steiner by abandoning this position was wishing to return to a primitive pre-Kantian belief that the apparent world presented to the senses is a real one. Steiner in fact was quite willing to admit that sense impressions are only mental pictures, but was unwilling to adopt the Kantian position that the mind *infers* from its own mental pictures the true reality of what lies behind the pictures and this inferred reality is all that man can know. Von Hartmann could not see what Steiner was driving at in his discussion of the linkage between concepts and percepts, nor that it was in any way relevant to his arguments regarding freedom. And as he could not follow Steiner's arguments in the first half of his book, he regarded the discussions on ethical individualism as interesting in themselves but in no way a logical consequence of those arguments. Steiner, by contrast, believed that his moral philosophy was a necessary consequence of man's ability to enter the spiritual world through his thinking, and draw from it the concepts which would eventually unite with percepts and result in free human deeds.

It is scarcely surprising that *The Philosophy of Freedom* (published in an edition of only 1,000 copies) met with little success after its publication in 1894, and that a new edition was not required until 1918, by which time Steiner had been established as a spiritual teacher for many years, and had often drawn the attention of his hearers to the book. By that time also there had been a considerable evolution in men's thinking, and at least some anthroposophists were well able to follow the arguments and accept the conclusions of the *Philosophy of Freedom*. Even so, it still is true that the book requires a great effort from the reader, and almost no one can take in all that it has to give at a first reading; and the superficial reader will never make much progress with it.

It may be taken for granted that Steiner was deeply disappointed by the lack of understanding for his work shown by his contemporaries, and, as we shall see in the next chapter, for the last few years of the century he was unclear as to the way that he would take in the future. He was especially incensed by the initial success of the Ethical Culture Society founded by Felix Adler in 1876 that was now spreading to Europe. Adler and his followers wished to found their movement on the highest principles to which men could attain by their own unaided thinking. Steiner regarded this effort as doomed to certain failure because the movement paid no attention to the possiblity of basing its ethics on the perception of a spiritual moral world that actually existed, and to which man could have access through his developed thinking. Any ethics that took no account of this was to him worthless, and he said so. But he was unable to persuade any of his friends or associates to take what he said seriously. None of them could see why he was so wrought up about the Ethical Culture Society. As Hermann Grimm remarked with a magnificent obtuseness, the Society "included many amiable people among its members."

Remembering this difficult time thirty years later, Rudolf Steiner commented in his autobiography: "In truth no unknown lies behind the sense world, but within it lies the spiritual. . .the sense world is in truth spiritual and the human mind is in living union with this recognized spiritual world as it widens its consciousness to encompass it. The goal of the process of knowledge is the conscious *experience* of the spiritual world in the presence of which everything is resolved into spirit. . . .My endeavor to reach the spirit through the enlargement of consciousness was contrasted [by von Hartmann and others] with the view that "spirit exists solely in man's mental pictures. . .from these no path could be found leading to a real (objective) world of spirit. . . .

"In a certain sense *The Philosophy of Freedom* released from me and externalized what my destiny had led me to experience in the first chapter of my life, in the form of riddles of existence as natural science perceived them. The next step could now be nothing else than a struggle to arrive at idea-forms for the spiritual world itself. . . .The fact that I did not yet use the term "anthroposophical" was due to the circumstance that my mind always strives first to arrive at concepts, and scarcely concerns itself at all with terminology. I was now confronted by the task of forming ideas which could express the experience by the human mind of the spiritual world itself."*

Rudolf Steiner also had to face incomprehension from quite a different source when his friends criticized him for his insistence on the preeminence of thinking in the life of the soul. A good friend from Vienna days kept up a correspondence with him, in which everything *not* concerned with the life of spirit was discussed in the warmest possible manner. But Steiner and his friend were utterly opposed on this question, and the friend insisted that Steiner was alienating himself from all that was human, and "rationalizing the impulses of his soul" in working out his philosophy and expressing it in this fundamental book. The friend "had the impression that in me the life of feeling was changed into a life of mere thought, and this he sensed as a certain coldness proceeding from me. . . . I could not avoid seeing, indeed, that the warmth of his friendship at times diminished because he could not free himself of the belief that I must grow cold in relation to what is human since I consumed my soul life in the region of thought."

To such a criticism it was impossible for Steiner to reply. From his own actual experience he *knew* that when he was thinking in a living manner he was actually within the spiritual world, and it was not possible even to enter into that world without taking his "full humanity" with him. In other words the feeling life must be *enhanced* if one is to be able to function at all within the spiritual world. The friend, not unnaturally, could not see this at all. For him thinking was abstract thinking, for which Steiner had at least as much aversion as had his friend. "My friend saw that I moved in thought out of the physical world; but he failed to realize that at that very moment I stepped over into the spiritual. When I spoke, therefore, of the reality of

---

*The Course of my Life, Chapter 17. The entire chapter, which is concerned with von Hartmann's failure to understand the book, is of the utmost value for comprehending the essence of the *Philosophy of Freedom*, to which scant justice could be given in the few passages discussed and quoted in this chapter.

the spiritual, this was to him quite without real existence, and he perceived in my words merely a web of abstract thoughts. I was deeply grieved by the fact that, when I was uttering what had for me the profoundest import, my friend actually felt that I was speaking of a "nothing." Such was my relation to many persons."[14]

Although, as has been noted, it was in 1889, before he left Vienna, that Rudolf Steiner first became acquainted with the work of Nietzsche, it was in Weimar that he truly immersed himself in his writings, even winning a reputation as an expert on Nietzsche, especially after his book *Friedrich Nietzsche : a Battler against his Time* appeared in 1895.[15] Until the turn of the century he retained his interest and continued to write about him until Nietzsche's death in 1900. Thereafter references to him in Steiner's writings are much rarer, and in later life he was much more severely critical of him than he had been during his stay in Weimar and Berlin.

The first book of Nietzsche read by Steiner was *Beyond Good and Evil*, and it had the effect of exciting in him the desire to read everything else that Nietzsche had written—curiously enough exactly the same reaction that Nietzsche himself had had when reading Schopenhauer for the first time. The year 1889, as it happened, was the year when Nietzsche had his final mental breakdown, making it impossible for him to write any more, even though he lived until 1900. By 1889 his reputation was only just beginning to be established, mainly a result of an appreciation written the previous year by Georg Brandes, the Danish literary historian whose influence in European literary circles was at the time second to none. Nietzsche himself, though grateful to Brandes to whom he addressed his last extant letter, and aware of the importance of his support, never did know the extent of his own popularity, which was already very great at the time of his death, while the vogue for his work has continued in the twentieth century, and even now he may be read more than any other nineteenth century thinker.

For us the problem to be considered is why Steiner, an original thinker and philosopher in his own right, whose thought in essence is poles apart from that of Nietzsche, should have devoted so much attention to him, especially at a time when he was so fully engaged in other work. Even Steiner's book on him does not really provide the key, and it was perhaps the overwhelming impression he received when he was allowed to go into the room where Nietzsche, by that time in the throes of madness, was resting, that affected Steiner so deeply, coming as it did after five years of concentration on Nietzsche's writings. From lectures given in later years we know that Steiner became deeply interested in Nietzsche's destiny, and in the influences he investigated that played upon him from the spiritual world. Whether Steiner already knew these things in the 1890's we do not know, and there is certainly no indication of such knowledge in his book on Nietzsche published in 1895.

Nietzsche was not truly in the German philosophical tradition at all, nor was he in any sense an academic philosopher. Neither he nor Artur Schopenhauer, whose writings deeply affected him, were interested by the kind of problems that concerned most philosophers, including the theory of knowledge, which occupied Steiner as well as most of his recent predecessors. Both Schopenhauer and Nietzsche seemed to write their works out of their hearts' blood and not at all from abstract thinking, and both, according to Steiner, were, in a profound sense, victims of the age in which they were born, of which something more will be said in Chapter 9. Nietzsche, with his particular soul configuration, could scarcely breathe in the materialistic world into which he had been born. He therefore set himself in opposition to almost every feature of the culture of his own age—its professed Christianity (he himself was the son of a Protestant pastor and had been very devout in his early youth), its inability to inspire men to attempt to realize the possiblities inherent in human nature, its lack of freedom.

As Steiner was to explain later in his life, it was a necessary step in man's evolution that the materialistic world view should be accepted by mankind for a limited period, which included the second half of the nineteenth century and the first half of the twentieth. The darkest period of materialism was the second half of the twentieth century and man's immersion in this world conception was, according to Steiner, paralleled by certain events in the spiritual world. Nietzsche was born in 1841 at a period when an important struggle was beginning in the spiritual world, and all through his life his soul was profoundly influenced by the struggle and its earthly consequences, making it impossible for him to accept the culture into which he was born. Hence the subtitle of Steiner's book "A battler against his time."

Indian philosophy long ago gave a name to the period of five thousand years that came to an end in 1899. During this age, which the ancient Indians called Kali Yuga, or the Dark Age, it was held that man's spiritual faculties, including his clairvoyance, had gradually fallen into disuse, to such an extent that men, instead of being able to see into the spiritual worlds, even came to deny that they existed at all. According to traditional beliefs this age, which had begun about 3100 B.C. was due to come to an end in 1899 A.D., and it would be followed by a new Age of Light, during which man will acquire new faculties enabling him once more to see into the spiritual worlds. It was Nietzsche's destiny to be born in the darkest period of Kali Yuga, and within his inner being he felt that the age was one in which it was impossible for him to live as a normal human being. Thus when in 1889 his mind darkened, even this was a kind of protection for him, as his thought was growing ever more destructive, especially to himself. When Nietzsche's sister took Steiner into his bedroom five years after the onset of his madness he may well already have been able to recognize what he spoke of only many years later. At all events it is in the light of this recognition that we should certainly read his description of this meeting, written thirty years later.

"There on the lounge lay the one with benighted mind, with his beautiful forehead, artist's and thinker's forehead in one. It was early afternoon. Those eyes which, even in their dullness, yet worked with the permeating power of the soul, now merely mirrored a picture of the surroundings which could no longer find access to the mind. One stood there, and Nietzsche knew it not at all. And yet it might have been supposed, from that countenance permeated by the spirit, that this was the expres-

66

sion of a mind which had all the forenoon long been shaping thoughts within, and which now would fain rest a while. I could feel that the inner sense of shock which seized upon my soul was transformed into an understanding for the genius whose gaze, though directed towards me, yet failed to rest upon me. The very passivity of this gaze that rested on me for such a long time set free the comprehension in my own gaze, so that it could cause the soul force of my eye to work even while it was being met by no response from him. And so there appeared before my soul the soul of Nietzsche, as if hovering above his head, already boundless in its spiritual light, surrendered freely to spiritual worlds for which it had yearned before being benighted but which it had not found; but still chained to the body, which knew of the soul only so long as the world of spirit continued to be the object of yearning. Nietzsche's soul was still there, but only from without could it hold the body—that body which, so long as the soul remained within it, had offered resistance to the full unfolding of its light.

"I had before this *read* the Nietzsche who had written; now I *beheld* the Nietzsche who bore within his body ideas drawn from widely extended spiritual regions—ideas still sparkling in their beauty even though they had lost on the way the power to illumine that they had once had. A soul which bore within it from previous earthly lives a wealth of the gold of light, but which could not in this life cause all its light to shine. I had admired what Nietzsche wrote, but now I saw a brightly shining form behind what I had admired. In my thoughts I could only stammer about what I then beheld, and this stammering is the content of my book *Friedrich Nietzsche, a Fighter against his Age.* That the book is no more than a mere stammering conceals what is nevertheless true—that the image of Nietzsche himself inspired the book."[16]

For a relatively short time Steiner was in close touch with Nietzsche's sister, who made her brother's library available to him, and asked him to collaborate in establishing a Nietzsche archive in Weimar to set beside those of Goethe and Schiller. But soon difficulties arose between them and the brief collaboration came to an end. Meanwhile Steiner's book on Nietzsche had been published in which he seemed to identify himself with Nietzsche in a most extraordinary way. He was later to remark that such an "objective" book about Nietzsche was never written about him by anyone else, and in it he certainly wrote as if Nietzche's ideas had been his own. Today this capacity for identifying oneself with someone else is called "empathy," but the word had not yet come into general use. In an introduction to the second edition of his book *The Riddles of Philosophy* which appeared in 1923 Steiner explained why this particular kind of identification with others, especially with those writers whose works he appraised and criticized, was valuable for a man like himself who was pursuing the path of spiritual development. In this passage Steiner was referring to Haeckel, but what he says is surely equally applicable to his relationship with Nietzsche. He had been accused of having changed his ideas when he abandoned philosophy for Anthroposophy. Having at one time been regarded (obviously erroneously) as an "orthodox follower" of Haeckel, it was supposed that he had undergone "a complete transformation of spirit" when he wrote his later works on Anthroposophy. His comment on this matter is worth an extensive quotation:

"The question," he wrote, "is only seen in the right light if one remembers that my later works, which seem to contradict my earlier ones, are based on a spiritual intuitive insight into the spiritual world. Whoever intends to acquire or preserve for himself an intuition of this kind must develop the ability to suppress his own sympathies and antipathies and to surrender with perfect objectivity to the subject of his contemplations. He must really, in presenting Haeckel's [or Nietzsche's] mode of thinking, be capable of being completely absorbed by it. It is precisely from this power to surrender to the object that he derives spiritual intuition. My method of presentation of the various world conceptions has its origin in my orientation towards a spiritual intuition. . . . One must be capable of thinking idealistically with the idealist and materialistically with the materialist. For only thus will the faculty of the soul be awakened that can become active in spiritual intuition."[17]

In 1900 just after Nietzsche's death Steiner summarized his opinion of his work in a memorial address given in Berlin on September 13, 1900. In it he makes clear that he had understood very fully the nature of Nietzsche's struggle:

"From the most recent natural science he had acquired the idea that a worm evolves into a human being. He himself was never a scientist, and took the idea of evolution from others who simply thought it out intellectually, by contrast with Nietzsche, for whom it was a matter of the heart. While others were waging a spiritual battle against all old prejudices. Nietzsche asked himself how he could live with the new idea, and *this* battle took place within his own soul. Without his own idea of the superman into which one man evolves, he could not endure the scientific notion of man, and his sensitive spirit was compelled to overcome the natural science that he had absorbed. . . .

"Nietzsche produced no new ideas leading to a new world conception, and we must always recognize that his genius did not lie in this direction. He suffered deeply from the thinking of his epoch, and as a compensation for this suffering he achieved the exalted language of his *Zarathustra*. He became the *poet* of the new ideas of the world; his hymns of praise to the "Superman" are his *poetic* answer to the problems and findings of modern natural science. Nietzsche contributed nothing to the ideas of the nineteenth century, which would all have been produced without him. In future ages he will not be regarded as an original philosopher, nor as a founder of religion nor a prophet. He will be seen as a martyr of knowledge, who found words in poetry with which to express his suffering."[18]

After the publication of his book on Nietzsche Steiner was welcomed into social circles where Nietzsche was greatly revered, and a few sentences from his autobiography will form a fitting conclusion to this section on Nietzsche, showing as they do one kind of influence exercised by Nietzsche's works shortly before his death.

"The whole group stood, so to speak, under the banner of Nietzsche. They looked upon Nietzsche's view of life as being of the utmost importance. They surrendered themselves to the mood of soul manifest in Nietzsche, considering it as representing in a certain way the flowering of genuine and free humanness. . . My own attitude toward Nietzsche did not change at all in this circle. But the fact that I was the one questioned when there was a desire to know something about Nietzsche brought it about that the relation of the others to Nietzsche was assumed to be mine also. I must say, however, that just this circle looked up more understandingly to what Nietzsche believed he knew, and that they sought to express in their lives the substance of the Nietzschean ideals of life with greater understanding than was manifest in many other instances, where the qualities of the "superman" and where *Beyond Good and Evil* did not always bear the most desirable blossoms.

"For me the circle was important because of a strong and enthralling energy that swept one along with it. On the other hand, however, I found there the most responsive understanding for everything that I felt it possible to introduce into this group. The evenings, made brilliant by Ansorge's musical renditions, its hours filled with talk about Nietzsche interesting to all, in which far-reaching and weighty questions about the world and life formed, so to speak, a satisfying contrast, were indeed something to which I can look back with contentment as having given a beautiful character to the last part of my stay in Weimar."[19]

Ernst Haeckel, the other leading personality whose views were seemingly opposed to his, whom Rudolf Steiner defended against his critics, is no longer much read today. But in his own time he was without doubt the most famous scientist in Germany, for most of his life the center of controversy, a position he certainly enjoyed to the full. Professor at the University of Jena for more than forty years, writer of many books concerned with evolution, in Germany he was scarcely less renowned than his predecessor Charles Darwin, whose work he developed in a manner found shocking by more narrow specialists than he, as well as by theologians and others who for so long refused to accept the Darwinian theory of evolution. As a highly gifted and imaginative popularizer he has during the twentieth century suffered a decline in reputation, since

70

we are inclined to give more credit to specialists, while some of Haeckel's bolder guesses and suppositions have been falsified by later detailed research. Haeckel also ventured more daringly into the field of philosophy than had Charles Darwin, and for this, according to Steiner, he was very poorly equipped, even though Steiner was perfectly willing to admit that the logical conclusion drawn systematically by Haeckel that man is descended from the apes was firmly based upon his evolutionary material, as interpreted by him.

In an early lecture defending Haeckel, published under the title of *Haeckel and his Opponents*, Steiner indeed remarks that "it is characteristic of Haeckel's deeply philosophical nature that, after the appearance of Darwin's *Origin of Species*, he at once recognized the full significance for man's entire conception of the universe, of the principles therein established; and it speaks much for his philosophical enthusiasm that he boldly and tirelessly combated all the prejudices which arose against the acceptance of the new truth by the creed of modern thought. . . . What has been yielded by the remodelled doctrine of evolution and our present scientific knowledge towards the answering of the "question of questions," he has recently expounded in its broad lines in the address *On our Present Knowledge as to the Origin of Man*. Herein Haeckel handles afresh the conclusion, which for every logical thinker follows as a matter of course from Darwinism, that man has developed out of the lower vertebrates, and further, more immediately from the apes. It has, however, been this necessary conclusion which has summoned to battle all the old prejudices of theologians, philosophers, and all who are under their spell. Doubtless, people would have accepted the emergence of the single animal and plant forms from one another if only this assumption had not carried with it at once the recognition of the animal descent of man."[20] It may be noted that Haeckel was already drawing such conclusions well before Darwin himself did so in his book published in 1871, *The Descent of Man and Sexual Selection*, though the address referred to by Steiner was itself delivered in 1877 after the appearance of Darwin's book.

As a consequence of his work on evolution Haeckel came to the conclusion that the only possible conception was *monism*, the recognition that, in Steiner's formulation, "everything which is called for in the explanation of appearances must be sought within that same world. Opposed to this view stands *dualism*, which regards the operation of natural law as insufficient to explain appearances, and takes refuge in a reasoning being ruling over the appearances from above." The word translated here as *appearances* can also be translated by the more usual word *phenomena*. Two forms of monism are possible, the regarding of all material things as manifestations of spirit, and the reverse, which holds that what is usually called "spiritual" is in fact only another aspect of the material, as for example such intangible realities as energy. Steiner, of course, held the first view, and Haeckel was accused of holding the second, even though he hotly denied that he was a materialist in the ordinary sense of the word. In a book written in 1900 in which Steiner summed up his philosophical writing, entitled *Conceptions of the World and of Life in the Nineteenth Century*, which he dedicated to Haeckel, and in which appears a very sympathetic account of Haeckel's work, he quotes him as follows: "The spirit and soul of man are also nothing else but energies that are inseparably bound to the material substratum of our bodies. As the motion of our flesh is bound to the form elements of our muscles, so our mind's power of thinking is bound to the form elements of our brains. Our spiritual energies are simply bound to the form elements of our brains. Our spiritual energies are simply functions of these physical organs just as every energy is a function of a material body."[21]

For Steiner such ideas were greatly superior to those of the dualists who held that matter and spirit were two separate entities, leading to the notion of the creation of the material world and men by a higher being who could never be known by man because he was of a quite different nature. Such dualism requires that man should submit to ethical demands made on him by this totally different being, whereas, as we have seen, monism, in Steiner's words, "throws man wholly upon himself. He receives ethical standards from no external world-being, but only from the depths of his own being." Through moral imagination "man elevates the ethical instincts of his lower ancestors into moral action, as through his artistic imagination he reflects on a higher level in his works of art the forms and occurrences of Nature." Moreover moral ideals themselves are indeed evolved over the process of time, and there is nothing in Steiner's ethical individualism that is incompatible with the theory of evolution. As he himself says in *The Philosophy of Freedom*, this ethical individualism is "the crowning feature of the edifice that Darwin and Haeckel have striven to build for natural science. It is a spiritualized theory of evolution carried over into moral life."[22]

If Steiner had to choose between the Darwinian and Haeckelian theories of evolution as an explanation for the diversity of forms to be found in the world of nature, and the creationist views of traditional theologians, he was unhesitatingly prepared to espouse the former because in his view the facts discovered by the evolutionists must lead to conclusions similar to theirs, whereas the theologians simply paid no attention to the facts and made no real attempt to explain them—a way of proceeding quite out of accord with the spirit of the time which was nothing if not scientific, in the sense that all known facts were taken into consideration by all true scientists, and every effort was made to explain them. Although Steiner could not of course accept the monistic materialism of Haeckel he did not deny the facts that led him to adopt a materialistic viewpoint. It was not Haeckel's fault that he had an inadequate idea of spirit (as who had not?), nor that he vehemently affirmed the existence of "spirit" without knowing anything about it. Indeed Steiner in his autobiography reports a personal conversation with Haeckel about it, in which the great zoologist said to him: "People say that I deny the spirit. I wish they could see how substances take form through their forces; they could then perceive "spirit" in everything that happens in a retort. Everywhere there is spirit." To which Steiner appends the remark that "Haeckel, in fact, knew nothing whatever of real spirit. The very forces of nature were to him 'spirit'."

The paragraph that follows is most significant since it explains Steiner's entire attitude toward Haeckel and the evolutionists. "Such blindness to the spirit," he wrote (in the year 1924), "should not have been attacked at that time with philosophically dead concepts, but it would have become clear how far the age was removed from experience of the spirit, and the effort should have been made to strike the spiritual sparks out of the foundation which the age afforded— the biological interpretation of nature. Such was then my opinion. On that basis I wrote also my *Conceptions of the World and of Life in the Nineteenth Century.*"[23]

In other words the theories of evolution, not excluding even the notion that man himself had descended from the lower animals, could have been used as a kind of platform from which could have been launched Steiner's own teachings about the spiritual origin of man, teachings which, as later expressed in particular in *An Outline of Occult Science* (1910), took full account of all the factual data assembled by Haeckel and the other evolutionists. It was not yet possible, in Steiner's view, just before the end of Kali Yuga, to teach the spirit directly, as he was to do after the turn of the century. But such teachings could have been grafted on to the current theories of evolution. Indeed as Steiner was to say later, "there is no better scientific basis for occultism than the teachings of Haeckel, but Haeckel himself is the worst commentator of his own teachings." When he first came in contact with Haeckel himself and his work, as Steiner had written enthusiastically to Frau Specht from Weimar (1894), the idea had come to him of creating a "methodical monism," which would of course include his own personal knowledge of the reality of spirit: and he told his correspondent that soon this "younger sister" might be carrying on the combat by the side of her elder sister, the monism of the evolutionists! This letter was written just two months after the appearance of *The Philosophy of Freedom*, about whose prospects for wide circulation he must have harbored few illusions. But the union of what he had written in that book with what was being taught by Haeckel, especially in his pamphlet *Monism as a Link Between Religion and Science* which had appeared in 1892, could have truly had a real influence on the arid thinking of the day, in which only science was making progress and that science, unhappily, was heading toward ever greater depths of materialism.

After meeting Haeckel personally and exchanging correspondence with him it became clear to Steiner quickly enough that the kind of collaboration of which for a brief time he seems to have dreamed was impossible, and he pursued the path he had always pursued, of keeping his spiritual perceptions strictly to himself, and working along philosophical paths. But it is also true, as he revealed in his autobiography, that he could not as yet, even if he had wished to, have added the spiritual capstone to the work of the evolutionists for the excellent reason that he was not yet in possession of the spiritual facts. He knew enough by the end of the century to be sure that the ideas of evolution held by Darwin, Haeckel, and the others were incorrect but the full truth had not yet become clear to him. "Only later," he explains in his autobiography, "did I work through to imaginative perception [the first stage of higher knowledge, according to Steiner's formulation]. This perception first brought me the knowledge that something of the nature of real being different from the simplest organisms was present within spiritual reality in primeval times. That man, as a spiritual being, is older than all other beings. . .that man is a macrocosmic being who bore within him all the rest of the terrestrial world, and who has thus become a microcosm by eliminating all the rest—this was for me a knowledge to which I first attained in the earliest years of the new century."[24]

In a lecture of fundamental importance given to a public audience on October 5th, 1905 in Berlin Steiner explained with the utmost clarity why there was no contradiction between his defense of Haeckel and his own teachings on evolution that he was at that time engaged in expounding to the German Section of the Theosophical Society. This lecture, first published in 1935 in English, is worth reading in its entirety, but even the section on how his own teachings fitted the facts uncovered by the evolutionists is too long to be quoted here, and only a brief summary is possible. Theosophy, Rudolf Steiner told his audience, is not "antagonistic or contradictory to the facts advanced by natural science; only with the materialistic interpretations of these facts it can have nothing to do."

He then went on to explain that as far as the physical structure is concerned, there is a relationship between man and the higher mammals, especially the apes. But, even from a physical point of view, though both man and ape have a common ancestor, the ape has degenerated from that ancestor, while man has ascended. Man, however, also has a soul-ancestor, who was always present, even in the very earliest times, long before the ape had diverged from the genealogical tree whose most perfect descendant has been man. Animals, all animals, are "but deteriorated and degenerated forms occupying those lower stages through which the human soul has passed on its upward journey. Externally, therefore the resemblance between Haeckel's genealogical tree and that of Theosophy is sufficiently striking. . . Hence Haeckel's deductions are so eminently suited for the learning of sound elementary Theosophy. One need do no more than master, from the theosophical point of view, the facts he has elucidated in so masterly a manner and then raise his philosophy to a higher and nobler plane."[25]

It would seem that Steiner and Haeckel, who lived on until 1919, continued to have an amicable relationship, though they came no nearer to a common viewpoint. Steiner always speaks of him with respect, and he made frequent references to him in his lectures. In the very last years of his life when both Nietzsche and Haeckel were dead Steiner also investigated the previous earth lives of these two personalities who played such an important part in his own development during the period he spent at Weimar and the last years of the century; and much in their lives in the nineteenth and twentieth centuries is explained thereby. But a discussion of this part of Steiner's work lies outside the scope of this book.

In the circle which Rudolf Steiner found so congenial during the last part of his stay in Weimar, where Nietzsche was discussed with so much enthusiasm, there was also much criticism of Weimar and the culture associated with it. The work done in the Goethe and Schiller Archives was valuable in itself, and the artistic and cultural life of the small grand-ducal city was agreeable enough. But for those who took the future of German culture seriously it seemed to be a backwater, without any real influence on imperial Germany and its world capital of Berlin. Great events were happening in the world, and Kaiser Wilhelm II and his ministers were playing an active part in them—even if not as active as the Kaiser at least would have wished. German prestige in the world of science and learning, and German industrial development, were scarcely equalled anywhere else, even though the older capitals of London, Paris, and Vienna may have had a more active artistic life than was to be found in the nouveau-riche capital of imperial Germany.

There can be no doubt that Berlin was beginning to beckon to Rudolf Steiner during the last part of his sojourn in Weimar. It seemed to him that he was living in an atmosphere of a hothouse culture which had become cloying to him; and though his admiration for the cultural life of Berlin was far from wholehearted, and his regard for some of its leaders was slight, it was in Berlin that he could hope to find an audience for what was still in the process of gestation within him, for the mission that he believed he would be called upon to fulfill. He had been inwardly isolated in Weimar, as we have seen, but had nevertheless been able to lead an active social life. He had made many friends and had met personally a considerable number of leading personalities in the cultural life of the epoch. His work had been prodigious in its extent, and he had acquired a high reputation in the restricted circles in which it was known; and if he had wished, he could surely have found some congenial academic position in the growing university life of Germany. The men who were responsible for the work in the Goethe Archives were fully satisfied with what he had done, and gave him written recognition in their Annual Report when he left Weimar. "What was done here," it was stated, "by a useful common work and a positive and productive activity, has been found acceptable by all the researchers here. We must thank him for his selfless efforts, and for the many original indications, given as part of a systematic and unitary construction, which assure to Goethe as a man of science a greater and more universal value than had hitherto been accorded to him."

Some critics, however, were of the opinion that Steiner ought to have gone into much greater detail in his editorial work and in his introductions, that he might have made the effort to show how Goethe had anticipated the findings of some of his successors, and how some of his remarks had been proved and others disproved; his influence on geology, botany, zoology and the other specialized sciences could have been stressed, and the entire work handled in a more systematic manner, acceptable to academic researchers. Some of the errors pointed out by these critics in parts of Steiner's work could have been, and ought, in their opinion, to have been avoided. To all this Steiner replied that his purpose was known to those who invited him to come to Weimar, and that his intention had always been to present Goethe's world view, as he had done in his introductions to the Kürschner editions and in his book on Goethe's theory of knowledge published in 1886, and as he did once more in his last summation, *Goethe's Conception of the World*, published just as he left Weimar in 1897. His books and articles on Goethe were works of synthesis, and he had no wish to be a "philologist," like so many of his fellow workers in the Goethe Archives. The errors in most cases, he told his critics, he could easily have pointed out himself if he had made the effort. But he continued to consider his presentation of Goethe as something of great value for the world, especially the manner in which he had carried Goethe's views further to their logical conclusions, as Goethe had not done himself. In short he had performed a creative work which should not be judged in the same way as the work of the collators of Goethe's manuscripts, who attempted no explanations, still less a synthesis.

Steiner was also later to emphasize in his autobiography that at that time he actually *could* not have done some of the things his critics thought he ought to have done. "I have made it clear," he wrote, "in this account of the course of my life that, even in childhood, I lived in the spiritual world as that which was self-evident to me, but that I had to struggle hard in achieving everything pertaining to knowledge of the outer world. For this reason I have been a person slow in development as to this form of knowledge in all its aspects. The results *of this fact* appear in details of my Goethe editions."

A year before his departure from Weimar Steiner tells us that his inner life began to change, and that from this time onward he was able to orient himself in relation to the external world in a way that had not been possible before. This change again must have played its part in his decision to leave Weimar and begin a new life in Berlin. If he had wished, there can be little doubt that an appeal to his influential friend Hermann Grimm, who now held a chair at the University of Berlin, would have brought Steiner an academic position. But he preferred to follow an entirely different course, which brought him into a milieu the very reverse of the academic—a milieu that can best be described as "bohemian." He was given the chance of purchasing the editorship of a periodical that had been established in the year of Goethe's death, which in its varied career had known a considerable number of different editors. The former proprietor, however, was unwilling to sell it to Steiner without some kind of guarantee, the more so since the latter's experience of editorship was confined to a brief period in Vienna in the 1880's, and he was unable to offer any financial guarantees himself. The condition required of him was the acceptance of Otto Erich Hartleben, a well enough known man-about-town, who belonged to a circle of litterateurs, and who had the entrée to Berlin café society. In addition Hartleben was himself a writer of some reputation, a poet and dramatist, with a developed interest in all forms of art. This curiously enigmatic personage was familiar to Steiner from his many trips to Weimar, where, characteristically enough, he went in order to take part in meetings of the Goethe Society, which in the end he never bothered to attend, preferring to remain in bed at his hotel—where on occasion Steiner visited him. As might have been expected, Hartleben later absented himself from Germany for visits to Italy at times when his presence would have been welcomed in the editorial offices of the *Magazine for Literature* of which he was co-editor.

Although Steiner in later years sometimes permitted himself to write sharply about Hartleben and he must have been a sore trial to his conscientious co-editor, nevertheless this literary playboy was, at his best, an interesting, even congenial companion. Indeed he and a number of Steiner's other friends of this time were not those one would have expected Steiner to have had, if one had known him only during the period of his anthroposophical activity. The first years in Berlin were in all respects difficult ones for him, and, as he tells us, "so long as I edited the Magazine, it was a constant source of anxiety to me." But they were also years during which he "digested," as it were, the important experience which came to him in his thirty-sixth year, and while the process was going on, he could not have undertaken the work that he undertook after the turn of the century. The many trials of this period brought the two parts of his life into harmony for the first time, and contributed to the maturity and mastery he showed from his fortieth year onward. Even the friendships of those years, damaging as some of them may have been to his reputation, always held something fruitful in them for him. He recognized fully that they were brought to him by destiny, and "not to accept what I recognized clearly as forces of destiny would have been for me a sin against my experience of the spirit." Moreover the direct experience of the inner being of so many persons who were so very different from himself was enriching.

Speaking of these years, Steiner wrote later, "The thought then hovered before me that the turn of the century must bring a new spritual light to humanity. It seemed to me that the exclusion of the spiritual from human thinking and willing had reached a climax. A change in direction in the process of human evolution seemed a necessity . . . . "[26]

But as far as he himself was concerned, "A state of inner movement, which drove into billows and breakers all the forces of my soul, was at that time my inner experience."

Chapter 5.

THE TURN OF THE CENTURY

At the end of the last chapter brief reference was made to the inner experiences that in some respects reoriented Steiner's entire life. From his thirty-fifth year onwards, and indeed for almost seven years—perhaps right up to the watershed lecture given to the Giordano Bruno Bund in October, 1902—the changes taking place in his inner life were visibly reflected in his outer life, which seems to have been lacking in the clear sense of direction that was to be so noticeable from the end of 1902 onward, when the decision had at last been taken to "keep silent" no longer. Steiner speaks of this seven year period as one of severe testing, and this was as true of his outer as of his inner life. The chapters he devotes to this period in his autobiography are undoubtedly the most dense, the most compact, in the entire book. Written as they were when he was on his deathbed, on the one hand they constitute an altogether remarkable feat of the reliving of mental and spiritual experiences of the far from recent past. But at the same time they also represent Steiner's last word on the very nature of spiritual perception as he himself knew and experienced it. As such, these chapters, especially 22 and 23, should be read most carefully by anyone who is seriously interested in Steiner's own manner of thinking, the relation between thinking and perception, the different kinds of knowledge and how they are verified through spiritual experience—and above all how the external world, which comprises both the world of nature and man himself, can be comprehended in its sense-perceptible and non sense-perceptible aspects by the living thinking that it is now the primary task of man to develop, through his own intensive efforts. These chapters, rather naturally, do not reveal their secrets at once, nor necessarily at the tenth or twentieth reading. But especially those who are sceptical of Rudolf Steiner's exceptional powers may find it worth while making the effort to understand this distillation of the experience of one of the very few fully self-conscious seers of our epoch. Such a study ought especially to be undertaken by those who dismiss him as deluded or a charlatan without having ever given any serious consideration to his work.

In essence the beginning of this period was marked, as Steiner himself tells us, by his sudden ability to perceive the external world in a manner that he had found impossible hitherto. Though the spiritual worlds had always been open to him, the ordinary sense world was perceived through what amounted to a kind of veil, and not in the entirely clear manner experienced by most of us. Or, as he puts it himself with exquisite precision: "It was as if I had not been able to pour the soul's inner experience deeply enough into the sense-organs to bring the mind into union with the full content of what was experienced by the senses."[27]

Steiner recognized that this process of perceiving with clarity the external world open to the senses—a process ordinarily taken for granted even by psychologists, and defined here as passing "from the soul's weaving in the spiritual world to an experience of the physical"—as a rule occurs very early in the life of a child, so early that we are not aware of the change at all when we are children, and it is not ordinarily perceived by parents in their children from lack of having had knowledge of it in themselves. Now that Steiner experienced the change as a mature man it proved to be not only remarkable in itself but carried implications of the utmost importance for his life thereafter. This was because at the same time that he began to perceive the external world clearly he became aware that because of his developed spiritual faculties it could not be perceived as it truly is unless by an effort of will the self made itself, so to speak, *selfless*, thus allowing the external world to

82

reveal itself in its essence—not only as it appears to sense perception but with its spiritual counterpart behind, thus revealing to his selfless gaze both percept and concept at the same time. This possibility, of course, had been already *known* to him in his mind since it is the essential core of *The Philosophy of Freedom*, and constitutes his main argument for the existence of a spiritual, non-physical world. But this recognition in advance was very different indeed from what he now knew beyond any possibility of doubting from his own experience.

It is, indeed, an essential part of his experience of these years of testing that so much of what he had formerly known through his mental and spiritual development he was now able to *perceive*. This includes perception through his developed spiritual faculties in the worlds of spirit that are ordinarily imperceptible to man. And very much of what he was later to set down in writing soon after the turn of the century in his remarkable little book on the development of these faculties called *Knowledge of the Higher Worlds—How is it Attained?* was certainly experienced for himself in these years with an intensity neither possible nor necessary for him before the age of 35.

In our materialistic and generally sceptical age it is difficult for most people to take seriously the ancient teaching that there ever was a "fall" of man, as described in the Old Testament, though they may be willing to admit that the story embodies a powerful myth, presumably devised by some prehistoric or even historic religious genius, perhaps Moses himself. Still less are they willing to accept the notion of a real devil, the actual embodiment or personification of evil. When Christ was "tempted" in the "wilderness," as narrated in the New Testament, they believe that the temptation at most must have been in his own soul (or mind), not whispered to him by any devil or Satan. However, if a man develops those higher faculties which, in Steiner's words, "slumber within every human being," it becomes possible, indeed very early on the path of higher development, to recognize the existence in the spiritual worlds not only of those beings belonging to hier-

83

archies above man (such as the angels), whose existence has been described in so many religious writings of the past, and by those founders of religions who have had direct personal spiritual experience, but also of beings who are unquestionably *evil*, in the sense that they wish to prevent man from attaining the goal willed for him by those higher beings who are truly interested in his welfare. These evil beings are neither human inventions nor hallucinations, but are perceived by the seer as realities, and they do indeed tempt man, as they once tempted the Christ in the wilderness.

Steiner distinguishes two categories of these beings, in particular, and to their leaders he gave the old names of Lucifer and Ahriman—and indeed it is a very important insight that there are at least two different kinds of evil, whether or not, as Steiner held and as most of us can at present only believe or disbelieve, these evils are also the activity of actual beings anxious to hinder man's spiritual development. The two beings say respectively to man: "You shall be as gods," and "you are nothing but men, essentially no different from animals, and you possess neither soul nor spirit, while the world, in essence, is nothing but a machine." Both beings tempt man by offering him different kinds of power and glory. But Lucifer, as his name implies (the light-bearer) offers him many gifts that fill his life of feeling with a glow of warmth, while Ahriman offers him gifts that are used by his intellect and will to give him an apparent understanding (correct, indeed, as far as it goes) of the earthly world, and the power to use for his own ends what is thus revealed to him.

This is all that needs to be said of these beings at this point, but since they are an essential element in Steiner's teaching and world outlook they will have to be referred to again in this book by the names given to them here. As far as Steiner's own inner development is concerned, he tells us—and we may well believe it!—that he was not led into ahrimanic error, that is, into the belief that the world of nature is devoid of spirit. He could not fall into this trap because of his own actual experience of the world of spirit that underlies the physical world perceived by our senses. But in penetrating deeply for the first

84

time into this physical world, as he had been unable to do before his thirty-fifth year, he necessarily came into contact—apparently also for the first time—with powerful ahrimanic beings who "wanted to cause the knowledge of nature to become, not perception of spirit but a mechanistic-materialistic way of thinking." At that time Steiner tells us, "I had to save my spiritual perception by inner battles. These battles were the background of my outer experience."

Although in later years various opponents accused Steiner of having been a materialist because of his defense of Haeckel and other monists, he informs us explicitly that, as we might suppose, for obvious reasons he was never in any danger of succumbing to this particular kind of ahrimanic temptation. Nevertheless in his autobiography he does speak of having experienced what he calls a "state of inner movement which drove into billows and breakers all the forces of my soul," thus making it necessary here to try to recreate as far as possible from what he says, not always with perfect clarity (see especially Chapter 27 of his autobiography) his actual experience of the time.

In his first years in Berlin after leaving Weimar he was compelled to live in disagreeable lodgings and find his meals where he could. He was extremely short of money because the *Magazine for Literature* could afford to pay him very little for his articles, and indeed it was rapidly losing subscriptions under his editorship, partly, as he tells us in a lecture given in Dornach on October 27th, 1918, because of his own insistence on writing articles that were not pleasing to his older subscribers, most of whom were associated with the University of Berlin. So the *Magazine* was always a source of anxiety to him, if only because he had contracted to pay for it by instalments, which were obviously in such circumstances difficult to meet. In time he might hope to attract new readers for the kind of unorthodox articles and reviews that he was writing, but meanwhile he had to live—and, as we have seen, his co-editor Hartleben was of no use to him in this respect and was frequently absent in Italy or elsewhere. The *Magazine* brought him into contact with many unorthodox persons from all ranks of society, especially writers, dramatists and poets, most of them impecunious. Thus Steiner spent much of his time in cafés, as he had in his younger days in Vienna, and the society he frequented was what used to be called "Bohemian." It is true that he was gaining much experience, especially in the world of the theatre, and this experience he evidently enjoyed. But what he was now doing was very far from what had been predicted for him by those who knew him as one of the most promising young scholars of his day, and it seems certain that he had purposely avoided seeking an academic position that he could have had for the asking because he did not wish to commit himself to such a well defined and circumscribed career, while he was still uncertain of what would be asked of him by his spiritual guides. Later, in a lecture given in 1912, he was to speak of the correct attitude that a man should take regarding a work that he recognized needed to be done. He should, Steiner said then, be happy if the work were done by *anyone*, and never come to believe that he alone was capable of doing it or ought to do it in preference to anyone else. But at the turn of the twentieth century it seems extremely doubtful that there was *anyone on earth* who could have performed the task that Steiner undertook from 1900 onwards. In 1896 he was perhaps just as ready as he was in 1900. He had served out his apprenticeship in philosophy and in Goetheanism. But no obvious opportunity presented itself from the side of the external world, and it seems no inner voice told him that the time had come to act. So he was uncertain, even anxious, and it was while he was in this condition that he was tempted to deny one of his convictions.

Already before leaving Weimar Steiner had become acquainted with J. H. Mackay, a Scottish-German or German-Scot, who, with Benjamin Tucker, an American, were proponents of a kind of theoretical anarchism, to be clearly distinguished from that terroristic anarchism which in the late nineteenth and early twentieth centuries was responsible for the assassination of so many eminent political leaders. Unfortunately this distinction was not always understood, with the somewhat amusing consequence that the *Magazine for Literature* was banned in Russia because Rudolf Steiner, its editor, was a friend of the "dangerous" anarchist J. H. Mackay. Mac kay, who had met Steiner at the salon of Gabrielle Reuter in Weimar, took up residence in Berlin in 1898, and the two men now became close friends, Mackay acting as witness when Steiner married Anna Eunike the following year.

Mackay had written a fairly widely circulated novel called *The Anarchist* and had tried his hand at poems which were too didactic for most tastes, though Steiner claimed to like them. According to Steiner, he was at all times a pure idealist, believing that men should be converted to his viewpoint entirely by persuasion. He also was well aware that before a man could act ethically in a free manner and without any coercion he must have undergone a kind of spiritual conversion. He refused to accept any traditional moral precepts just because they had been imposed by some political or religious authority. Mackay was a disciple of Max Stirner, a thinker about whom Steiner said many favorable things, and he had edited some of Stirner's writings, although not in agreement with all of them.

Clearly such "anarchistic" ideas had some similarity with those expressed by Rudolf Steiner in his *Philosophy of Freedom*, but, as was explained in the last chapter, he believed he had shown in that book that thinking was a spiritual activity and that only through a developed thinking could the human spirit imagine for itself free deeds. Probably Mackay no more understood this concept than Steiner's other friends had done, but he seems to have been closer to Steiner in other respects, and the friendship between them was a very warm one. Even after they had become separated in later years Steiner continued to speak of him with great warmth, always praising his "noble and self-reliant" nature. It may have been only for a brief moment, but it does seem that Steiner was tempted by the possibility of using his own philosophy as a basis for Mackay's political dreams, and for a time he did actually engage in promoting his ethical individualism as a political ideal. His way of discussing this episode so many years later in his autobiography makes it clear that he did indeed regard his inclination of that time as a real temptation.

"It was remote from my intention when I formulated this,"

he tells us, "to make it the basis for a political conception. But *the effort was made* [by whom?] to draw my mind, with its purely ethical individualism, into a kind of abyss. *The effort was made* to change this conception from something belonging to the inner being of man into something external. The esoteric was to be diverted into the exoteric."

Two phrases in this statement are worthy of closer examination—the unexplained repetition of the words "the effort was made" and "the esoteric was to be diverted into the exoteric." It seems clear that the effort of which Steiner speaks was made by hindering powers rather than simply by Mackay and his friends, and the temptation was that an earthly rather than a spiritual goal should be pursued. If Mackay, who had his own following and was a man with wide experience of the world, had indeed taken up the ethical individualism that was at the center of *The Philosophy of Freedom*, then not only would that ethical individualism have been cheapened and misunderstood, but it would have been thought of as another moral philosophy derived from purely human thinking, instead of being, as Steiner held it to be, the only philosophy consonant with the free activity of the human spirit and a necessary consequence of man's spiritual nature. In Steiner's view there can be no truly free act without free spiritual activity. Nothing can be more certain than that Mackay, Tucker, and their friends in adopting Steiner's ethical individualism would simply have stated his conclusions. These would then have become the moral principles of the "individualistic anarchism" that they were promoting. These principles, as Steiner said, were noble in themselves, but if they had been preached without relating them to his teachings about spiritual activity, then indeed "the esoteric" would have been "diverted into the exoteric."

For a few years before the end of the century Steiner was thus tempted to speak and think, and did speak and think occasionally, of ethical individualism as if it had been a noble philosophy that could be accepted by ordinary idealistic men and women who had not reached it through spiritual training, and inner development. This period came to an end through an inner experience which can be described only in his own words, an experience which enabled him for the first time to write and talk about Christianity in lectures given to an audience of theosophists. These first lectures which mark the beginning of his real mission were later published under the titles of *Mysticism at the Dawn of the Modern Age,* and *Christianity as Mystical Fact.*

"After the time of testing," he tells us, "had subjected me to stern battles of the soul, I had to submerge myself in Christianity, and, indeed in the world of spirit itself. . . . What is achieved of the knowledge of spirit in *Christianity as Mystical Fact* is brought directly out of the world of spirit itself. . . . The true substance of Christianity began germinally to unfold within me *as an inner phenomenon of knowledge.* About the turn of the century came the *testing* of soul I have described. The *unfolding* of my soul rested upon the fact that I had stood in spirit before the Mystery of Golgotha in most inward, most earnest solemnity of knowledge."[28]

As a result of this experience and of writing these first books on Christianity, he tells us that "ethical individualism again stood, after the test, in its rightful place."

Since the full meaning of these two passages is not self-evident it should be noted that when Steiner speaks of the "Mystery of Golgotha" he usually refers to the entire sequence of events from the baptism to the ascension of Christ Jesus, though sometimes also he appears to mean only the events from the betrayal at Gethsemane to the ascension. In any event what he clearly means here is his direct experience of the Christ, something he had, as he tells us elsewhere, not experienced before, nor had he paid much attention to the truths of Christianity either in his writings or lectures. From 1900 onward, by contrast, he was to refer frequently to the *Philosophy of Freedom* as having been inspired by Christianity and what he calls the "Christ Impulse," and he explains that the human being cannot attain to ethical individualism in the sense in which he uses the words unless he is filled with the Christ Impulse. The clearest expression of the connection between the two is to be found in a series of three lectures given in 1920 on Thomas Aquinas and last published in English in 1956 under the title of *The Redemption of Thinking*. The relevant passage follows (page 110 in this edition published by Hodder and Stoughton):

"Just as we have shown that knowledge is . . . an event related to objective reality, so ethics, moral behaviour, is shown to be something which the individual, as he passes through the events of this real knowledge-process, experiences intuitively through his moral imagination as objectively real. Thus there arises what is presented in the second part of my *Philosophy of Freedom* as "ethical individualism," which is, in reality, founded upon the Christ-impulse in man, although this is not expressed in the book. There, it is based upon the free spiritual activity which man achieves by changing ordinary thinking into what I called in my book "pure thinking." This pure thinking then raises itself to the direct experience of the spiritual world and derives from it the impulses to moral behaviour. This is due to the fact that in the spiritual activity of pure thinking the impulse of love, which otherwise is bound up with man's physical nature, spiritualises itself, and when the moral imagination discovers the ethical ideals as actual realities in the spiritual world, this spiritualised love becomes the power by means of which they express themselves '. . . I have laid special stress upon the "transformation" of the human soul, and upon the necessity of its being really filled with the Christ-impulse, even in its thought-life. The life of knowledge has been shown to be a real factor in world evolution, as I set out in my book *Goethe's World-Outlook*. But this which takes place on the stage of human consciousness is at the same time a *cosmic happening, a real event in world-history*. Moreover, it is just this event that carries forward towards its fulfilment the world and ourselves within it."

Rudolf Steiner tells us in his autobiography that his period of testing lasted from the time of his move from Weimar (1897) until the lectures that he gave to the theosophists on *Christianity as Mystical Fact* (1901). It was during this period that his relationship with Mackay flourished, that he was the editor of the *Magazine for Literature* (1897 to the end of September,

1900), and became a fairly well known figure in the cultural life of Berlin through his weekly articles in the *Magazine* and his reviews of plays presented on the Berlin stage, as well as through his membership in various scientific and philosophic societies. These were the last years of waiting before he felt authorized to begin his public mission as teacher of the science of spirit, and it may not seem too surprising that his work during this time seems to stand apart from the rest of his life, having relatively little relationship to what he was doing before and what he did afterwards. Even the marriage with Anna Eunike in 1899 seems to have fulfilled its purpose in his life by the time he embarked on his public mission, and had to be abandoned, like almost everything else from his past when a new life opened up before him.

For a period after his arrival in Berlin Steiner was acutely unhappy because of the circumstances of his living. When Frau Eunike offered him a home again in Friedenau, a suburb of Berlin, he experienced, to use his own words, "the best of care, after having endured for a time the utter misery of living in an apartment of my own [actually two successive apartments]. Living in the Eunike house made it possible for me to have an undisturbed basis for a life which was both inwardly and outwardly very active." On October 31st, 1899 Frau Eunike became his wife in a civil ceremony. Steiner himself always remained reticent about this marriage of convenience, saying that "private relations are not something to be publicized. They do not concern the public."

It is evident that the situation in Berlin was very different from that in Weimar, where Steiner had lived in the Eunike household as resident tutor of the five children of the newly widowed Anna Eunike. He was then given a part of the house that he could regard as his own where he could entertain his friends. Now that Frau Eunike had moved to Berlin and her daughters would soon be of marriageable age and no longer needed their old tutor, clearly the most suitable solution was for the couple to enter into a civil marriage. A valuable testimony exists which describes how the relationship between the two Steiners appeared to an outsider who later became

91

friends with both of them and was made welcome in their home. This testimony will be given later in the chapter. Here all that needs to be said is that the marriage lasted only for a short time after Steiner had begun his public anthroposophical work. From Herr Rudolph's memoir, of which some extracts will be given later, it is clear that Anna Steiner disapproved from the beginning of his career as leader of the German section of the Theosophical Society which took her husband completely away from her—though she was to tell her daughter, shortly before her death in 1911 in her fifty-eighth year, that her life with Steiner had been the most beautiful epoch in her life.

The *Magazine for Literature* edited by Rudolf Steiner had as its official sponsor the Free Literary Society, founded in the year of Goethe's death, When Steiner took over the magazine it also possessed a recently founded affiliate called the Free Dramatic Society, in which he played an active part, thus becoming involved in the production of experimental plays unlikely to be successful in the commercial theatre. In this work his co-editor Otto Erich Hartleben was associated with him. The theatrical experience of these years was later to be of great benefit to Steiner, helping to make possible the astonishing course in dramatic art that he gave to members of the Anthroposophical Society in Dornach in 1924, during which he showed a remarkable and unexpected familiarity with the drama of the time. He attended the Berlin theatres regularly and wrote reviews of the plays he had seen in the *Magazine*. However, his reviewing method was highly original, and, by his own account, little understood. Unlike most critics, he refrained from passing judgment on the play or its production. It was his opinion that if the review was, as he attempted to make his own reviews, an "artistic painting of ideals," as a result of which the thoughts in the playwright's mind would arise in imaginative form in the minds of his readers, then the judgment would, or ought to, arise of itself at the same time. There would then be no need to tell the reader what to think of the play, nor should their judgment be swayed by the opinions of the reviewer.

The first play that Steiner produced himself was Hartleben's translation of Maurice Maeterlinck's play *The Intruder*, which he felt to be particularly challenging because of its symbolism. Though Steiner did not at all approve of Maeterlinck's use of symbols, characterizing them as "mystical-sentimental," he regarded it as a part of his task to present them effectively on the stage. Still less did he have any sympathy with the Maeterlinck cult of that period, with its pretensions towards "spirit." "The less it was possible to tell distinctly what lay behind the suggestive symbols, the more many people were enraptured by them," he commented caustically. In spite of his distaste he found it fascinating to work at the staging of such a play because, as he said, "the representations of the symbols by appropriate stage means required the managerial function in an unusual degree." Steiner enjoyed exercising this "managerial function," and he liked to make use of and develop his own sense of style. He gave much thought always as to how each play should be staged in accordance with his own understanding of it, while he made full use also of the opportunity he was afforded to give a brief introductory address to the audience when an experimental play was presented. He was able thus, as he tells us, to allow the spirit to permeate his words, even though the audience "otherwise had no ear for the spirit."

The *Magazine for Literature* he used largely as a forum for his own ideas, which he admits were not too well suited for his particular audience, and were not greatly appreciated, even when they were understood. Almost no one could sense what lay behind his words. On one occasion he wrote about the Dreyfus case in France that was dividing public opinion all over Europe, giving "information that I alone could give." (Issues of December 11, 1897 and February 19, 1898) Such information fell on deaf ears, as did his interpretation of Goethe's fairy story *The Green Snake and the Beautiful Lily*, which he published in 1899 under the title of *Goethe's Secret Revelation*. Steiner tells us that his interpretation was only "very slightly esoteric," whereas a later lecture given on the same subject to an audience of theosophists contained much esoteric knowledge. The theosophists were able to accept it fully and asked Steiner to give more talks on similar subjects and in the same vein.

In a lecture given in October, 1918 to an audience of anthroposophists in Dornach, Steiner was to speak very freely of this period of his life and of his experiences in Berlin, much more freely than when he was writing his autobiography at the end of his life. The occasion for this lecture was the appearance of the second edition of *The Philosophy of Freedom*, the first new edition since its original publication in 1894. Some quotations from this lecture are of considerable interest, as are his characterizations of the life in Berlin and his own attitude towards it.

He began by criticizing openly the "philistinism" of his Berlin contemporaries, and especially the leading intellectuals who were associated with the *Magazine*, most of whom were originally subscribers to it, and, in general, the avant-garde of the time. Steiner was more than willing to admit that it was his policies as editor that drove away his original subscribers, making it impossible for the *Magazine* to pay its way and provide him with a living. "I acquired it," he said, "in order to have a platform for ideas which I considered to be timely, in the true sense of the word, ideas that I could advocate publicly." When his correspondence with Mackay was published, numerous professors wondered aloud (not too surprisingly considering the reputation of anarchists at that time, and even since!) "what Steiner was up to," and gradually many of them cancelled their subscriptions. "I must admit," Steiner commented, "that with the publication of the *Magazine* I had the happy knack of offending the readers—the readers and not the Spirit of the Age!"

Others were offended by his defense of Emile Zola in the Dreyfus affair, while a young worker who belonged to a group to which Steiner also belonged wrote a critical article in which, to use Steiner's words, "he tried to show in his pedantic way that I did not fit into this community, and that he looked upon me as an unpaid peripatetic theologian among a group of people who were anything but unpaid peripatetic theologians, but were at least youthful idealists." On another occasion in reviewing a new play Steiner tells us that he "took all the Berlin newspapers to task and told the Berlin critics one and all what I thought of them. This was hardly the way to launch the magazine, but it was a valuable experience for me. Compared with the Weimar days one learned to look at many things from a different angle. But at the back of my mind there always lurked this question: how could the epoch be persuaded to accept the ideas of *The Philosophy of Freedom?* If you are prepared to take the trouble you will find that everything I wrote for the *Magazine* is imbued with the spirit of *The Philosophy of Freedom*. However, the *Magazine* was not written for modern bourgeois philistines. But of course through these different influences I was gradually forced out."[29]

A few years later, when he was writing his autobiography, Steiner said little about such difficulties as these. "In spite of all the difficulties confronting me," he wrote, "it would have been possible to expand the circulation of the weekly if material means had been available to me. But a periodical which could at the utmost afford only the most meager fees, which gave me almost no basis for my own material existence, and for which nothing could be done to make it known, could not thrive upon the limited circulation it had when I took it over,"[30] and, of course, still less on the circulation it had when he gave it up, which was considerably lower than when he took it over. When Steiner later founded his own magazine which was called *Luzifer-Gnosis*, he was able to find a different public which was indeed interested in what he had to say, and this magazine was eventually abandoned only because its editors, Rudolf Steiner and Marie von Sievers, were so deeply involved in other work that they could not find time for it. The *Magazine for Literature* was directed and had always been directed to a quite different public, and this was no more likely to be interested in Steiner's esoteric teachings than were the scientific and literary societies to which he belonged in the Berlin years. Not until after 1900 did he find the audience which was genuinely interested in what he had to say, and by that time he too was better prepared to speak, having passed through his years of trial and won the right to do so.

95

In 1899 another audience presented itself that was always of great interest to Rudolf Steiner, perhaps in part because of his own background as a member of the class to which this audience belonged. Wilhelm Liebnecht, one of the founders of the German Social Democratic party, had organized in the early 1890's a training school for workers in Berlin in which members of the German working class could attend courses on numerous subjects, higher education thus being opened up for them for the first time. Similar educational institutes (such, for example, as the Cooper Union in New York City, and the Workingmen's College in London, where, among others, Ruskin taught) were founded elsewhere for the purpose of giving instruction to the working classes. The Working Men's College in Berlin (as it may best be called in English), founded as it was by a man who was for twenty-six years until his death in 1900 a Social Democratic member of the German Reichstag, was naturally oriented toward Marxism. Wilhelm Liebnecht had worked with Marx in England for a dozen years in his youth, and was completely familiar with his writings. Though he himself disagreed with many of Marx's conclusions the Working Men's College was basically Marxist in orientation, and most of the teachers taught according to the principles of dialectical materialism. However, from 1899 to 1904 the College was still primarily interested in the general higher education of the workers, and only from 1908 onwards did it become rather a training ground for Social Democratic party workers. Nevertheless it was probably inevitable that Rudolf Steiner, simply by agreeing to accept a teaching position in the College, was widely regarded at this time as a materialist and Socialist himself—a view certainly not shared by his audience or by those who knew him well.

Fortunately we possess some precious testimony regarding Steiner's work at the College from two of the students who later published their impressions. One was a young woman, Johanna Muecke, who later became an anthroposophist because of what she had learned from Rudolf Steiner at the College, the other, Alwin Alfred Rudolph, was one of the delegates who first approached Rudolf Steiner with the request to give a course on history at the College. Rudolph did not commit his recollections to paper until forty years later, but his reports of the lectures, as well as his vivid and almost unique account of Steiner in his domestic life at the time of his first marriage, cover the entire period of Steiner's teaching at the College until the lecture on *Monism and Theosophy* given on October 8th, 1902 before the Giordano Bruno Bund. Rudolph tells us that when he first called on Rudolf Steiner to ask him if he would lecture to the workers neither he nor anyone else on the program committee knew Steiner personally. Two men in touch with labor circles had suggested that a poet of their acquaintance should give the history course. The poet proposed Rudolf Steiner and gave them his address, whereupon the delegation called upon him at that address without giving him any advance warning of their visit.

"We were ushered into a large room full of light, which was a living room and study at the same time, with a desk of enormous proportions by the window, laden to overflowing with books and papers. Dr. Rudolf Steiner stood in the middle of the room, straight and slim and dressed in black, with a small untrimmed moustache on his upper lip, and wearing a long broad bow tie. He greeted us in the most kindly manner. There was a most welcoming atmosphere in the room, so much so that we at once felt like good friends, without any shyness or reserve. An older lady in the room was introduced to us, but we could not imagine who she was, though we gathered that the young woman who opened the door to us was her daughter. Actually I ought not to speak of them as "ladies," because they were really two simple women, openminded and many sided. Before we could state our mission we were invited to the great table where a coffee machine was soon put to work. The daughter brought in some tea-things and her mother a plate full of pastries, which Dr. Steiner took and offered to us, saying that we must first refresh ourselves. They were delicious white tartlets, and we were told they were made by a local bakery in accordance with a recipe which was a strictly guarded secret and had been invented by the poet, Steiner's friend Ludwig Jacobowski, [founder of the society *Die Kommenden* of which we shall hear later]. We enjoyed a really delightful coffee hour . . ." When the visit was over and Steiner had agreed in principle to give the history course, "he shook hands with us, telling us that we should come again very soon and tell him what we should like to hear in his lectures. He believed he had taken on a most worth while task, but he forgot altogether to ask about the fees. We were sure that we had found a history teacher, and an extraordinary one. But all we were authorized to pay was eight marks."

When Rudolph and his colleagues returned to the Council responsible for arranging the lectures, they were criticized for not having obtained Steiner's agreement to accept such a small fee. So there was nothing left but to return to his house and clinch the final arrangements including the title of his course. From his account of this second meeting it would appear that Rudolph went by himself, and in his memoirs he declared that never had he received such a friendly reception as he now received from any of the men or women he had enlisted as lecturers, even though so many of the others were fellow-workers in the Social Democratic party; nor, he relates, had any of them had the firm handshake given him by Rudolf Steiner, who advanced to meet him as soon as he was announced and took both his hands in his own. The same openness was shown by mother and daughter, and though Steiner's face looked like that of an ascetic, his smile was always warm and gay. It never seemed to be an inconvenience when anyone visited him even though he might be hard at work at the great desk, which was always so full of papers and books that only enough space remained for a single sheet of paper on which he was writing. What he always desired to hear from his visitors was the impression made on them by a work of literature or something else that had been read, never what it contained, which, indeed, he always seemed to know.

It was not at all clear to Rudolph at first what relationship the two women had to him. In themselves he says they were both open and kind, but they had such an evident feeling of reverence for Dr. Steiner that a matrimonial relationship seemed to be out of the question. Frau Eunike always waited for him to speak and answer any question, although she was willing to engage in conversation with Rudolph when occasion offered. When the coffee machine was again brought in, in order to make conversation Rudolph asked how the water was heated as he could see no fuel. After he had asked if it was charcoal Steiner said that it was not, but that it was spirit (presumably methylated spirit), which led to a joke about spirit, playing on the various meanings of the word. At this Frau Eunike jumped up and showed Rudolph a ragdoll which had been sitting on a little table and told him to look carefully at it. It was a "masterly likeness" of Rudolf Steiner, dressed in the characteristic black coat and black bow. She lifted the seam of the black coat to reveal a bottle of French cognac. "The cognac is a gift of Ludwig Jacobowski," she said, "and its meaning (inside the rag doll) is that 'the whole body is spirit.'"

The remark struck the materialist Rudolph, as he says, most strangely, and he was still pondering it while he was eating the pastries she pressed upon him. Then Steiner began to speak about the lectures he intended to give, just as if everything had been agreed. So Rudolph proposed a course of ten lectures, each lasting two hours including questions and a discussion, preferably on Thursdays. Frau Eunike reminded him that he gave lectures to Ludwig Jacobowski's *Die Kommenden* on that evening, but Steiner replied that Jacobowski would be quite happy if he turned up some time after ten at night. Still he would not give Rudolph the chance to mention fees, but asked when the course was to begin, insisting that it would be quite unnecessary to remind him in writing. He would be there; and if no change was made thereafter—and he made it clear he disliked changes—he would be there at the same time each Thursday for the ten weeks agreed upon.

The evening of the first lecture arrived. The rather small hall was full to overflowing, and more seats and tables had to be brought in, even though Steiner was not at the time very well known in Berlin. At five minutes to eight the Council was fidgeting, wondering whether he would indeed arrive. But promptly at two minutes to eight he stood in the doorway with the two women standing just behind him. He looked very happy at such a large audience of working men. Forms were thrust in front of him to be filled up, and he did this in the two minutes remaining before the lecture hour, beginning on the dot of eight. He had no notes with him. He just gave a brief look at the faces before him and spoke. According to Rudolph everyone present recognized at once that here was a man of all-embracing knowledge that it was his life-task to give out, and everyone had something to learn from him. He spoke with an inner warmth, and his words went straight to the hearts of his listeners, as he showed how spiritual forces were everywhere active influencing the course of historical events. He did not so much convince as awaken the faculty of judgment in the listeners, and even in that first lecture, according to Rudolph, he won them over. To him this was true greatness. Later in his memoir Rudolph spoke of the widespread feeling expressed by one of the party members who attended the lectures: "What a pity Rudolf Steiner was not born a German, so that he could have been elected to the Reichstag." Since the Social Democratic party already possessed a considerable number of seats in that body Steiner's election would certainly have been feasible though it is scarcely possible to imagine what would have been the effect of his particular kind of eloquencé, talent, and spiritual knowledge on the assembled members!

Fraulein Muecke was also present at Steiner's first lecture at the College, and it is interesting to compare her account with that of Rudolph. She was for many years secretary of the Committee of the College that dealt with programs, and she tells us that history, on which Steiner had lectured, was "a special child of sorrow" to her Committee. The history courses ordinarily consisted of ten lectures, but usually the students became rapidly bored with the way the subject was taught, and most of them ceased to attend—whereupon the lecturers usually gave up. Thus a rather small room had been purposely provided for Rudolf Steiner's opening lecture, and it was her recollection that only about fifty students were present—though perhaps Rudolph's remark that the room was full was also correct, since the room may have been very small.

"A slender dark man mounted the platform," she records,

"and a powerful voice rang out. To us North Germans his accent sounded a little foreign, but everyone listened with the greatest attention. At the close of the lecture there was a lively and excited conversation among the students. One of them, a specially active comrade and a very wideawake person, came to me and said with a certain amount of pleasure 'Well, that was not by any means the materialistic view of history, *but it was interesting.*' "

Fraulein Muecke, who later became an anthroposophist, adds the comment: "Probably it was exactly this non materialistic element in Dr. Steiner's lectures, and the suggestion of a living spirituality in them that was soon to make these lectures so valuable for an audience that thought materialistically in accordance with the training received from the Party, but many student members of which at that time had strongly idealistic feelings. For whereas on former occasions the audience tended to dwindle away, now it grew larger and larger, so that a few months later Dr. Steiner's courses already began with about 200 listeners. It was especially new to us how Dr. Steiner led his hearers to ask questions, and to participate actively in what they heard. Formerly we had listened quietly to the lecture and then gone home, more or less satisfied or tired. Now a lively interest rapidly developed, and many questions were asked at the end of the lecture. These were always answered in a most friendly and conscientious manner. All objections were listened to in a kindly way, and received explanations that were always to the point. Very soon the lectures lasted until midnight or even later. But it was partly the lecturer's fault that we were so insatiable because of the lively way in which he entered into everything.

"It was curious to see how two different worlds here came in contact with one another," she goes on. "From Rudolf Steiner everything streamed out of the pure spiritual. By contrast his hearers, although because of their position in life they knew and felt nothing but the mechanism of the industrial age, had within them a human soul born out of the spiritual, and filled with unconscious longings and aspirations." Frl. Muecke then reports how Steiner went on to lecture on German literature, both prose and poetry, on Indian, Persian and Arabic culture, on the history of philosophy, chemistry, and the history of industrialism. He also offered instruction in public speaking, and corrected all papers submitted to him with such care that, according to Frl. Muecke, "many of the students really accomplished things which previously could never have been expected of them."

Steiner tells us in his autobiography how he made it a condition for speaking at the College that he should be allowed to present history "according to my own views of the course of human evolution, and not in the Marxist style in which this was customary in Social Democratic circles." When this condition was accepted he felt it was no longer any concern of his that the College had been founded by the Social Democratic party. What interested him was that he now for the first time had the opportunity to teach adult members of the proletariat, and he felt it a challenge to learn to speak to them, using forms of expression he had never had to employ before. Moreover the men and women in his audience took the materialistic view of history for granted, and could scarcely conceive of the possibility that it was not only economic, but also— perhaps even more decisively—spiritual forces that determined the course of history. According to his own account he succeeded in silencing their objections to his presentation by conceding at once that economic forces had been of very great importance since the sixteenth century but scarcely at all in earlier centuries. This concession enabled him to speak about ancient and medieval history just as he wished, without further objections from his audience.

On October 27, 1918, in a lecture given in Dornach to members he spoke somewhat differently from what he was later to write in his autobiography. Here he tells us that he "could speak on any subject at all except that of *freedom*. To speak of freedom seemed extremely dangerous. I had only one follower who always supported me whenever I delivered my libertarian tirades, as the others were pleased to call them . . . This man (a Pole) always supported me in my defense of

freedom against the totalitarian programme of socialism."
That this insistence on freedom was not acceptable to the
Socialist leaders, who eventually decided to oust him in spite of
the support he had from his actual students, was emphasized
by Steiner in a later passage in the same lecture.

"I had attempted to introduce spiritual ideas and was to a
certain extent successful, but I was gradually driven out. One
day I was defending spiritual values in a meeting attended by
hundreds of my students, and only four members who had
been sent by the party executive to oppose me were present.
Nonetheless they made it impossible for me to continue. I still
vividly recall my words: 'If people wish socialism to play a
part in future evolution then liberty of teaching and liberty of
thought must be permitted.' Thereupon one of the sycophants
sent by the party leadership declared: 'In our party and its
schools there can be no question of freedom, but only of
reasonable constraint.'" To this remark Steiner added the comment: "One must not imagine that the modern proletariat is
not thirsting for spiritual nourishment! In fact it has an
insatiable craving for it. But the nourishment which it is
offered is largely that in which it already firmly believes,
namely positivism, scientific materialism, or else an indigest-
ible pabulum that offers stones instead of bread. *The Philosophy of Freedom* was bound to meet with opposition here too,
because its fundamental impulse, the impulse of freedom, has
no part in this most modern movement (Socialism)."[31]

In this lecture given just at the end of the War, which was
quite certainly delivered extempore, and to a Dornach audience, Steiner was trying to sum up a long period of teaching
in a few minutes, and there is no doubt that in spite of his
views on freedom, and even of his teachings on spiritual
matters which he was already giving as General Secretary of
the German Section of the Theosophical Society, the directors
of the Working Men's College left him ample latitude for
teaching as he wished, and it would seem probable that this
was permitted precisely because of the popularity of his teachings with his students. When, as he says, the hostility of a few

leaders put an end to his contract, he had already been teaching at the College for more than five years, from early in 1899 to late in 1904.

Herr Rudolph remained in touch with Steiner after the latter began his regular lectures on different subjects at the Working Men's College, and even offered to help him in his work on the *Magazine for Literature*. This work brought him into intimate contact with the Steiner-Eunike household. When Steiner married Frau Eunike in October 1899 Rudolph reports that there was no apparent change in their relationship. "She continued to look after him," he tells us, "with motherly attachment and modesty, and retained her reserve." She and one of her daughters used to accompany her husband when he went on excursions with his students into the surrounding countryside. When the day was fine, Rudolph tells us, they would all lie on the grass and Steiner would talk on all kinds of subjects. "He would talk about books and the theatre, about old and new literature, about the Greek poets and philosophers, about the wisdom of Confucius, the Altar of Pergamum, Emile Zola and his defense of Dreyfus. Then suddenly he would switch to talking about the flowers in the grass, explaining to us what they were. He talked about the bracken, and about flying insects. Once when we thought we had found a rare caterpillar Steiner was able to tell us to what family it belonged, and he gave us an exact description of it. He seemed to us to be a silo brimful of knowledge of the world."

Fraulein Muecke also included in her memoir an incident from one of these excursions. "On one occasion," she wrote, "several young people walked by his side and spoke of their lives. One of them cried out impetuously, 'Why do we have so little pleasure in life, and yet everyone would like so much to be happy?' Dr. Steiner replied, 'Yes, but perhaps life is not given us in order that we may be happy.' 'Whatever else can it be for?' said the young man, quite taken aback. 'Well, suppose we had life *in order to fulfil a task*,' Steiner replied. These words were uttered in a very kindly tone, but with such deep emphasis that we all walked on for a while in silence, and even though I did not understand them fully, the words remained

104

firmly fixed in my memory. Already at the time such power lay in his words that they did not fade from one's mind."

On June 17, 1900, Steiner gave a lecture to members of the Typesetters and Printers Union on the five hundredth anniversary of Gutenberg's invention of printing. As far as I have been able to ascertain, this was the largest audience ever addressed by Rudolf Steiner; over 7000 assembled in the Busch circus, the only auditorium able to hold such a huge throng. The lecture, of which only an extended summary exists, was not strikingly original in its observations, but Rudolf Steiner connected the discovery of Gutenberg very effectively with the change in human consciousness which began about the beginning of the fifteenth century to which he later gave the name of "consciousness soul." Gutenberg, he told his audience of workers, placed the book in men's hands just at the time when they had the greatest need for it—not least in that one of the first books to be printed in Germany and distributed on a wide scale was Luther's masterly translation of the Bible, and without the Bible in the vernacular the Reformation would have scarcely been able to take root. With the arrival of the printed book men were given the tool for conceptual thinking. Ideas which would never have occurred to the vast majority of them were revealed to them through the medium of the book—even though falsehood could also be spread, and charlatans could be believed often only because their notions had been printed in books. The tendency to believe what is seen in printed form in books has remained, even though lies can as easily be printed as spoken. When all books had to be written out by hand and copied, most education was given by word of mouth, and there was a natural inclination to accept on the basis of authority what a speaker said. Thus when printing made books accessible to the multitude a man could read for himself and still feel quite free, accepting or rejecting the authority of the writer in accordance with his own judgment. The great pioneers in the new scientific knowledge, men such as Copernicus and Kepler, could make their ideas known to an ever larger public, as could also those who discovered and described new scientific facts. When knowledge of the outer world was not valued, and

105

only what could be thought by the mind of man was considered important, the printed book was not so necessary. The invention of printing favored the development of the individual personality, and it now became possible to acquire a wider and more up to date view of the world, a real world outlook; and here Rudolf Steiner cited the first newspaper, which appeared in 1505. In this newspaper appeared news about Brazil, which had been discovered only in 1500. Men could also now play an active part in world and national affairs, especially with the development of the newspaper, pamphleteering, and the like, and they could arrive at their own judgment through access to more information. Even popes no longer received news only from their envoys, but from the press, while scholars could have their work read by a wider public than their university colleagues when they published their findings in printed books.

The printed word, Dr. Steiner declared, is "a co-creator of modern culture," especially in so far as man becomes for the first time a true individual and wider horizons open up before him. Men from different cultures and different spheres of life can now forge a new unity among themselves because they all have available to them books available equally to the others. The Brethren of the Common Life in Holland, medieval pioneers in education for the lay public, began their work in the fourteenth century before the inventing of printing; but this work took on a new lease of life when they began to print good educational works which could be widely circulated. In the late fifteenth century (1473 onwards) the King of Hungary (Matthias Corvinus) encouraged printing, and as a result there was a great cultural upsurge in Hungary, while his contemporary ruler, the absolutist Turkish sultan Bayazid II, forbade printing on pain of death. In concluding Steiner again emphasized how important printing had proved for the study and understanding of history, and how much more intimately we know modern history than that of earlier times.

This lecture, though not on any subject directly connected with what later was taught by Steiner as Anthroposophy, not only demonstrates the wide range of learning possessed by him at this time, but all through what he said is visible the distinction he was later to make between the "intellectual soul" and the consciousness soul, and the difference in man's consciousness during the medieval period, which marked the end of the age of the intellectual soul, and during the modern age since the fifteenth century. Thus, as always, he wished to emphasize how history is to be understood as a picture of the evolution of human consciousness, and why the student of history should always look for symptoms of this evolution. Gutenberg's invention of printing was just such a symptom, not only occurring in the first century of the consciousness soul, but making possible all its subsequent achievements. In 1900 Steiner had no wish to make these things explicit before an audience of printers; but from the manner in which he spoke and the illustrations he used it is clear that he wished, without being explicit, to lay the foundation for the understanding of the evolution of consciousness in the minds of his hearers.

Rudolf Steiner was also closely associated with two other organizations at the turn of the century, and both of these provided him with audiences for his lectures. One was the Giordano Bruno Bund, founded by Wilhelm Bölsche, a man who was later to be criticized in strong terms by Rudolf Steiner, especially for his "philistinism," and Bruno Wille, author of a philosophical work much admired by Steiner. With the aid of a liberal theologian named Theodore Kappstein these men founded a Free Academy in Berlin. Here Rudolf Steiner gave the history courses, which continued until as late as the beginning of 1905, since he remained acceptable to the Academy long after he had become a theosophist. But almost from the beginning he had his difficulties with the Giordano Bruno Bund, although he was one of its founders. The Bund adopted as its own a philosophy that Steiner characterized as "spiritual-monistic," more in keeping, as it thought, with the ideas of the original Giordano Bruno, martyed by the Catholic Church in 1600, than with the monism of Ernst Haeckel, which it regarded as excessively materialistic. Steiner gave occasional lectures to the Bund, including one on medieval scholasticism that greatly upset its members, as well as the lecture on Theosophy that will be discussed at the end of this chapter.

More in accord with Steiner's developing ideas was a society called *Die Kommenden* (The Coming Age) founded by his intimate friend Ludwig Jacobowski, who died not long afterwards at the early age of 30. The society he founded lived on and Steiner delivered many lectures to it, including his memorial address on the death of Nietzsche. The membership was made up of writers, artists, scientists, and persons interested in the arts. Since *Die Kommenden* did not subscribe to any particular group of ideas it was more tolerant than the Giordano Bruno Bund, and, indeed, was quite willing for Steiner to speak on Christianity, if he wished. At the very moment that he was being installed as General Secretary of the German Section of the Theosophical Society he was engaged in giving a cycle of lectures to *Die Kommenden* on the subject of *From Buddha to Christ*, a topic that would at that time have been unacceptable even to the theosophists. It was only after Steiner had become well known as leader of the theosophists that he ceased to be acceptable as a lecturer to *Die Kommenden*, when, as Steiner puts it in his autobiography, "I appeared to be stamped as a theosophist. It was not really the thing itself; it was the name, and the association with a society, that no one wished to have."

By contrast with this attitude on the part of the intellectual élite of Berlin, Steiner was able to continue with his lectures to the working men in their College until 1904, as we have seen, and it was not his theosophical association that led to their cessation. Of course in his lectures to the working men he never spoke on subjects that were obviously theosophical, even if his spiritual knowledge underlay all that he had to say to them.

Steiner's relationship with the Giordano Bruno Bund was necessarily an awkward one. The Bund opposed the ideas of Haeckel, which Steiner had publicly defended when Haeckel was attacked by theologians. He always said that Haeckel's theory of evolution when rightly understood was entirely

108

compatible with his own teachings regarding the spiritual origins of man. On the other hand Steiner was critical of Haeckel's notions of "spirit." In this respect the ideas of the two men, if we may simplify a little, were almost exact opposites, as Haeckel held that all spirit had a material basis while Steiner regarded matter as an aspect of spirit. Steiner's own ideas of monism, as expressed, in particular, in the last chapter of *The Philosophy of Freedom*, differed essentially from those of the members of the Bund, who with scarcely any exceptions were strongly anticlerical, while in their desire to be modern and up to date they accepted without question most of the scientific theories of the time. Thus, though they did not like to be thought of as thoroughgoing materialists like Haeckel their idea of spirit was extremely vague, and they were inclined to stress their monism while playing down any spiritual ideas they had.

This attitude was found increasingly irritating by Steiner, who purposely tried to stir up the Bund by giving a lecture on Thomas Aquinas, in which he presented the medieval theologian as a true monist. "He obviously saw in the Unity of the Godhead the Monon underlying everything in the universe," he told his audience, a statement that was found extremely shocking by members of the audience and by all the main leaders of the Bund, who had been brought up to believe that the Middle Ages were a period of intellectual darkness, the very reverse of their own enlightened age. They spoke of Steiner's lecture on Thomas as an "attempt to smuggle in Catholocism." "Here we are," Steiner reported them as saying, "taking all possible pains to deal Catholicism its death blow; and now comes a member of this very Giordano Bruno Bund and takes to defending Catholicism" (the same Catholicism that had burned Giordano Bruno as a heretic).[32]

On this occasion some influential members supported Steiner's right to speak as he wished, and he was not expelled from the Bund for his "heresy." But when soon after returning from England where he had attended a Theosophical Congress in July, 1902 he delivered a lecture to the Bund on *Monism and Theosophy*, and defended his theosophical viewpoint, opinion

109

in the Bund ran strongly against him. Even his friend Alwin Rudolph could not follow him along his new path, and soon afterwards he left Berlin to make a new home for himself in Switzerland. Forty years later he recorded his experience of this lecture in a memoir, telling at the same time of his four years' association with Steiner, whom he never saw again. Most of what follows is drawn from this memoir, which may not be accurate in details, based as it is on an old man's memory. Only a short summary of the lecture itself given to an audience of about 250 persons exists, and this also has been used. The lecture and report will conclude this chapter, leaving Steiner's relations with Theosophy and his appointment as the first General Secretary of the Theosophical Society for the next chapter.

As already noted Steiner travelled to London to attend a Congress of the Theosophical Society in July, 1902. He was accompanied by Fraulein Marie von Sievers, who was later to become his second wife, and was from the beginning an active collaborator in the theosophical and later anthroposophical work. In London he met leading members of the Theosophical Society, including Annie Besant, and final decisions were taken as a result of which he took over the leadership of the Theosophical Movement in Germany, Switzerland, and Austria-Hungary. When he returned to Berlin from this Congress, Rudolph found him much changed, even in appearance—he had shaved off his moustache and was wearing a bowler hat!— and he seemed to have placed a distance between himself and his former friends and students. "The intimacy we experienced with him before was never recovered," Rudolph reports, and it cannot have been too great a surprise to him that the long awaited lecture on *Monism and Theosophy* was not at all to his taste and revealed a Rudolf Steiner that he had never known before.

When Steiner entered the hall, contrary to his usual custom he looked straight out into the room and above the heads of his audience. His lecture was a long one, and began with a strong statement dissociating himself from the movement known as "spiritualism." Such a statement was necessary because the

110

founder of Theosophy, H.P. Blavatsky, had been a gifted medium, and many of the most important theosophical books had been written by authors who claimed they had received communications from various so-called "Masters," who were no longer alive if they ever had been. The communications were, as a rule, received while in a condition of trance, or at all events when not fully conscious.

After his opening remarks on spiritualism Steiner declared that he had in no way changed his long held view that any serious philosophy of life—and Theosophy, he insisted, was such a serious philosophy—must be in accord with the findings of natural science, as long as these findings are genuine facts, properly verified by scientific means. However, scientists make a mistake when they adhere to a materialistic philosophy not justified by the scientific facts. By contrast the new philosophy of life that has become vitally necessary should be in accord with idealistic philosophy, as well as with the facts established by science. Haeckel's materialistic theory of evolution was certainly in accordance with the facts so far as they are known, but the theory is unable to explain the existence and development of man. Nor will chemical investigation of the brain ever lead to any information about the life of the spirit. It was clear that the gap between religion and science was growing ever wider. Adolf Harnack, the noted theologian, had even declared himself as happy to find that science could make no contribution to his own specialty while at the same time the English freethinker Robert Ingersoll was insisting that all talk of the spirit was meaningless, and that ideas were nothing but transformed foodstuffs—as were works of genius like the plays of Shakespeare!

By contrast to these men a German philosopher, I.H. Fichte, son of the more famous Johann Gottlieb Fichte, had stated that it was man's true task to transform philosophy into "theosophy," by introducing the idea of God into it, while at the same time giving the word theosophy a respectable German pedigree. It is not man's task, Rudolf Steiner declared with great emphasis, simply to observe the *facts* of nature, but to perceive the divine element *in* nature. New means must be

111

found for investigating the human soul without doing violence to the norms of natural science, and religion must unite itself once more with science as in ancient times. For this purpose it was necessary to develop a true theosophy, entirely separate from hypnotism and somnambulism, phenomena that can be investigated scientifically but have nothing to do with theosophy. In conclusion Steiner referred to a picture he had seen in Brussels, whose meaning he had tried without success to convey to Rudolph and his friends. In his picture the Belgian painter Antoine Wiertz had portrayed a giant who was holding in his hands weapons of war and other "attributes of modern culture," beside whom his wife and children had shrunk to the size of pygmies. The picture was entitled "The Man of the Future," and Steiner, in concluding his lecture, urged his audience to act and think in such a manner that they would not appear to men of the future as pygmies.

It was evident from the reception of this lecture that Steiner had converted very few of his audience to his thesis that the scientific monism of the present should be permeated by religious impulses. According to Rudolph's account, at the end of the lecture not a hand moved, no one clapped or even whispered, no vote of thanks was proposed, while the chairman of the meeting seemed to "have a load on his shoulders." The audience dispersed quietly, and Steiner was never again asked to address the Bund. Rudolph himself broke all relations with Rudolf Steiner, as we have seen, though with "infinite regret." Forty years later he wrote:

"Four decades have passed, but I still treasure the rich experiences of knowledge, the awakening of my faculties of judgment and observation, and the totally new direction given to my life. I still see the tall erect form of Rudolf Steiner, speaking like no other speaker before or since. But he had to follow his new mission, and whatever he did, he did fully. The spiritual world was a reality to him, and he had to live in it; and the literary world in which he had hitherto lived had to be abandoned."

Soon afterwards, Rudolph added, Steiner removed himself altogether from the public life of Berlin, although he did, as we have seen, continue to give lectures at the Workingmen's College and the Free Academy that he had helped to found. "From one day to another" he gave up his apartment and the whole material basis of his life, but according to Rudolph, he didn't care since if necessary he could live on bread and water. In fact it was not until the following year that he gave up his apartment and separated from his wife, who was present at the lecture to the Giordano Bruno Bund but was obviously fundamentally opposed to what her husband was doing, and showed it in her face and attitude.

By contrast to Anna Steiner and Alwin Rudolph, Fraulein Muecke was greatly interested by the lecture, and in this she was far from alone. She described later to Dr. Wachsmuth how the members of the audience stood about in the street afterward until three o'clock in the morning, talking about Theosophy and spiritualism, trying to make sense of what Dr. Steiner had said. Next day when she saw him she asked him outright if Theosophy was spiritualism, to which he replied that he had "never been a materialist and the spiritualists are the worst materialists of all." He then categorically dissociated himself from such bypaths which tend, he said, to lead the spirit into the sphere of the senses instead of releasing it from the chains of materialistic thought. Fraulein Muecke, as we have seen, eventually became a theosophist and then an anthroposophist, playing an important part in the affairs of the society for many years.

A week after the famous lecture of October 8th, 1902 Steiner was present at a small meeting of the Giordano Bruno Bund at which the lecture was discussed, some members of the Bund defending him by declaring that Theosophy should not be condemned by people who knew little or nothing about it. Members, in their view, ought to keep an open mind and at least give Steiner the benefit of the doubt. Steiner intervened several times in the discussion. He explained that even the ancient Vedanta philosophy of India had been a kind of monism, and he insisted that even though some theosophists had had dealings with mediums, thus becoming involved in spiritualism, his own path was totally different. What med-

113

iums said in their seances had no philosophical or scientific value, and it was, in his view unethical, even immoral to pay any attention to them. His leading supporter at the meeting, Otto Lehmann-Russböldt, the second president of the Bund, concluded it by telling Steiner that as far as he himself was concerned, the programme for Theosophy as formulated by him would always be welcome, even though "the Indian vocabulary of traditional Theosophy certainly needed to be sifted to make it comprehensible in the West," as he was sure Steiner intended to do. Even so, the general spirit of the meeting still seemed more against than favorable to him, and it is a fact that he never again did give a lecture to the Giordano Bruno Bund. Thereafter by his own deliberate choice his path lay rather with the Theosophical Society, which, in spite of all its weaknesses, and the difficulties that Steiner almost from the beginning had with it, did provide him with the forum he needed. The answer to the question he had so often asked himself "Must I forever keep silent?" was about to be answered, as we shall see in the next chapter.

Chapter 6.

THEOSOPHY AND THE BEGINNING
OF THE PUBLIC MISSION

CHRISTIANITY VERSUS ORIENTALISM

When Rudolf Steiner decided to become the first General Secretary of the newly formed German Section of the Theosophical Society, thus abandoning all his former scientific pursuits, almost all his friends and associates were unable to understand why such a distinguished scholar should join a semi-religious, pseudo-philosophical group, with few if any pretensions to intellectual respectability. Steiner had never shown any apparent interest in Theosophy before this time, and his relationship with leading theosophists, even while he was leader of the German section, was always a somewhat uneasy one. It therefore becomes necessary at this stage to give some attention to the aims and purposes of the Theosophical Society and consider why Dr. Steiner thought it was possible to work with it, as well as why in the end he could not continue his association with it. Even today there is still much misunderstanding about the relationship between the Anthroposophical Society and the Theosophical Society; while those who are most familiar with the serious practical work that has stemmed from the teachings of Rudolf Steiner, and understand both the Christian orientation of the Anthroposophical Movement and how different it is from any movement based on Oriental teachings, find it difficult to understand how Rudolf Steiner could ever have become associated with the Theosophical Society and Movement.

115

In a series of lectures given in October, 1915, to members of the Anthroposophical Society in Dornach, Rudolf Steiner went into considerable detail in explaining the historical context in which Theosophy appeared, and the role played in the Theosophical Movement by its founder Madame Helena Blavatsky. It is scarcely necessary here to go into much detail on the growth of materialistic ideas in the eighteenth and nineteenth century, nor on the role of science in this period and the gradual disappearance of any true insight into religion, which became so largely, for Christians, simply a matter of observing Sunday and behaving in a conventionally moral manner. Since the work of Darwin and Marx, in particular, man had come to be regarded as a kind of thinking animal, primarily influenced by his animal needs, while the world of spirit was simply denied, since it could not be perceived by the "five" senses. Today, in the last quarter of the twentieth century, scientists are seldom regarded with such awe that their opinions on subjects other than their own specialty are listened to with the respect that was accorded them in the last century, and even scientists themselves are not regarded by their colleagues as idiots if they should happen to believe in some of the teachings of religion, whether Western or Oriental.

Even while science was becoming a kind of substitute religion for Western intellectuals, beneath the surface of Western culture occultists and occult movements were active, as they had always been, even though few people were aware of their existence. They did not communicate their knowledge except to a few chosen pupils and successors. Rudolf Steiner does not seem to have been a member of any occult circle during the years covered in earlier chapters, but, as we have tried to show, he possessed much "occult" knowledge acquired through his own supersensible faculties. These he had developed for himself in such a way that he could actually *see* into the spiritual worlds concealed from almost all the rest of us. So, when he lectured in 1915 on the subject of the occult movements in the nineteenth century, he was not divulging anything that he had acquired from others, whether legitimately or illegitimately, but all his comments stemmed from his own insights into the work done by the nineteenth century occultists.

In these lectures he explained that many leading occultists in the eighteenth and nineteenth centuries had become extremely disturbed by the increasing materialism of the age. Vast numbers of men and women had lost all belief in the spiritual worlds, with the result that the enemy of mankind whom we called Ahriman in the last chapter was carrying all before him. The occultists had been loath to divulge what they themselves knew about the spiritual worlds, but they did think that mankind ought to know at least that the spiritual worlds *do* exist, as men had always known in the past. The decision was then made by a group of occultists that what later came to be called "spiritualism" should be introduced to mankind, with the sole intention of providing in this way a kind of proof that human beings do continue their existence after death and can communicate with the living. Through these efforts men did indeed come to believe that the dead can converse with the living through *mediums*, men and women who were able to slip out of their ordinary waking consciousness, thus supposedly allowing access to the dead; and as a result there grew up a vogue for spiritualistic "séances," in which the dead were supposed to speak through the mediums and answer questions. At these séances other apparently supersensible phenomena took place, including the "materialization" of actual physical objects. Thus the spiritual world was itself materialized in keeping with the spirit of the time, and it appeared to be only another "dimension" of the earthly world. Scientists like the Englishman Sir Oliver Lodge became deeply interested in spiritualism and tried to investigate it by scientific means, offering various explanations for the often remarkably accurate information divulged by mediums during their séances.

The unexpected result of their efforts led to great disappointment among the occultists who had been responsible for introducing spiritualism to mankind, but hope revived when they heard of the existence of a kind of "super-medium" who possessed faculties that had not been seen in the West for

117

centuries. This was Helena Petrovna Blavatsky, usually known to her followers simply as HPB, a half German, half Russian woman, who was born in 1831, and after an early marriage travelled widely in many countries of the world, including India and America. The occultists found it extraordinary that HPB, who claimed to have acquired her own knowledge first hand from Masters who were not living on the earth, should have possessed such accurate knowledge of what they themselves had received from others, and had kept as closely guarded secrets. It was therefore natural that the various occult orders in different parts of the world should have wished to control her and use her for their ends. However, none of these efforts were successful for very long, and eventually Madame Blavatsky started her own movement, which was formally founded in 1875 as the Theosophical Society. Her principal associate in this enterprise was an American, Colonel Henry Steele Olcott, a first rate organizer, who became president of the Society on the death of HPB in 1891, and was still president when the German section of the Society was formed in 1902, with Rudolf Steiner as General Secretary.

Blavatsky throughout her life continued to make numerous revelations, which were incorporated in several books. The most important of these was *Isis Unveiled*, published in 1877, and a huge collection published after her death under the title of *The Secret Doctrine*. Rudolf Steiner on many occasions spoke about the occult gifts of Madame Blavatsky, explaining that she received her information from those she called the "Masters" when she was in a condition of trance, and she could not actually see into higher worlds herself while fully conscious. But, unlike most mediums, she was fully aware afterwards, when she had returned to normal consciousness, of all that had been conveyed through her during her trances. According to Steiner, much of what she received was correct, but she could not check it, nor was she capable of criticizing any of it. As a result many things she wrote down were partly true, and very little was wholly false, but the ideas poured out of her without any logical connection between them. Unlike Steiner, Blavatsky had no claims to be a thinker. Nevertheless a large part of what she gave out was at the time known to no occultist alive, and by whatever means she arrived at her knowledge, it could not be disregarded. In an age which craved for knowledge that went beyond all that the scientists of the day could provide, an age when there was a real longing for something less arid than the materialistic view of the world held as a virtual dogma by the intellectual élite of the world, the revelations of Blavatsky fell on most fertile ground, and after 1875 Theosophical Society branches sprang up everywhere. Other theosophists besides HPB began to write books on Theosophy, some of them clearly the result of a certain degree of clairvoyance, no more under control than Blavatsky's had been and no more conscious, but interesting enough, and often sensational enough to command readers and win new adherents for Theosophy. It was estimated that by the time of HPB's death in 1891 there were at least 100,000 members of the Society throughout the world.

Although HPB herself had spent much of her time in the West, she was strongly attracted by India, and her revelations were much more in accord with what was known in the East than what was publicly known in the West. From the beginning therefore, in spite of the fact that Olcott was an American and the Society was strong in America, most people regarded Theosophy as primarily an Oriental movement, and such religious ideas as it possesses are far closer to those of Buddhism than of either Islam or Christianity. Steiner indeed explains that Blavatsky through her own configuration of soul was herself antagonistic to both Judaism and Christianity; and this was usual in her followers, who often entered the Theosophical Society precisely because of this antagonism to the established religions of the West. After Blavatsky's death in 1891 Colonel Olcott remained head of the Society for the next sixteen years. But the real leader was an Englishwoman, a former freethinker named Annie Besant, who was always a thoroughgoing Orientalist, much more interested in Oriental teachings than in anything that stemmed from the West. She was as opposed to Christianity as HPB had been; and it was through her influence that the world headquarters of the Theosophical Society was moved to Adyar, India. Nevertheless for many years Annie

Besant remained tolerant to ideas other than her own, and she respected the fact that the Society she headed from 1907 onwards was not only world wide in scope but stated in its statutes that one of its tasks was to further the brotherhood of man, and another recognized the absolute equality of all religions.

There had been theosophists in Germany from the 1870's onwards, and many "lodges" had been formed, perhaps as many as 400 by the turn of the century. But there was no organized national society, which by the statutes of the Theosophical Society was known as a "section." The lodges were made up of individuals who wished to associate together for study, and in Colonel Olcott's opinion there was no need in Germany for anything larger and more formal. It was his view that the Germans with their sceptical and materialistic spirit would never take kindly to Theosophy. Mrs. Besant, who was a gifted and dynamic organizer, was far from being as defeatist as the Colonel, and it was she who welcomed Rudolf Steiner as a possible founder of a German section, and she was willing to agree to the terms he proposed, much though she may have regretted it later. An Italian section had been founded only a year previously, and she was willing to make the necessary concessions when a gifted scholar like Steiner who was already fairly well known became available as leader for a new German section.

Steiner had been familiar with Theosophy since his student days in Vienna, and when a German translation appeared in the early 1880's of a book by A.P. Sinnett, an English theosophist, called *Esoteric Buddhism*, he was one of its first purchasers. In later years he criticized this book severely as a medley of bits and pieces put together from many occult sources, and he was not otherwise much attracted by what he saw of theosophists. He regarded Theosophy as a "dilettante" pseudo-occult movement, and many of its members irritated him by trying to fit their occult beliefs into the ordinary scientific ideas of the time, without having any profound notions either of the occult or of science. The first book of Blavatsky's to be published in 1877, *Isis Unveiled*, Steiner was likewise ready to criticize as a compilation of occult teachings, but *The Secret*

Doctrine, published only after her death, fell into a different category. According to Steiner, there was more occult knowledge in this book than was possessed by all the occultists in the world who drew their knowledge from traditional occult sources, even if they had pooled their knowledge. This fact was recognized by the occultists themselves. For this reason those who regarded themselves as the custodians of the ancient wisdom were seriously worried by Blavatsky's "unauthorized" revelations. But by this time there was nothing they could do about them.

Although Steiner acknowledged the truth of so many of Blavatsky's revelations, he never ceased criticizing the manner in which they had been presented in *The Secret Doctrine*, and he deplored the absence of critical spirit among her followers. But after the book's publication he was ready to admit that Theosophy was a genuine occult movement, and from its reception he knew that there were indeed many souls who were truly searching for this kind of knowledge, even though most of it was hitherto derived from Oriental sources and contained Oriental wisdom, neglecting the Western occult tradition. It was reasonable for him to hope that it would be among the theosophists that he might well find his eventual audience, though he certainly had no expectation before the turn of the century of ever becoming a theosophist, much less the head of the movement in Germany. But he did, so to speak, keep an eye on what theosophists were doing. Looking back on the history of the Anthroposophical Society from the vantage point of 1923 Steiner spoke to its members at considerable length on the subject of the Theosophical Society and his work within it, as well as about leading personalities who belonged to the Theosophical Movement at the beginning of the century. In these lectures he spoke of how he had recognized that so many people who were searching for spiritual knowledge had gravitated toward the Theosophical Society and its many lodges precisely because there was nothing else capable of attracting their hungry and thirsty souls.[33] These people he called "homeless" ones, searchers, for whom no home on earth existed. Many of them had left the security of their homes and families and all their accustomed associations in order to seek what they needed.

Such men and women had been greatly attracted by Blavatsky's books and those of other theosophists because of their occult and religious content, so different from anything then being offered by traditional churches and traditional philosophies. Rudolf Steiner knew that he had more to offer them when at last he would be permitted to speak. What he had to give would include a true understanding of Christianity that was notably missing from Theosophy. To use his own word for it, what he had to teach he called *Geisteswissenschaft*, an untranslatable word that we shall here be calling "science of spirit," instead of the more usual older term "spiritual science," which seems to many people to be a contradiction in terms. The entire content of this science of spirit was derived from his own spiritual knowledge and research, and owed nothing at all to any previous occult writings—though of course it could not contradict such writings if they were true.

The opportunity to speak for the first time to a theosophical audience was offered to Steiner through an unexpected set of circumstances. When his time as editor of the *Magazine for Literature* was drawing to a close, he wrote an article for the hundred and fiftieth anniversary of Goethe's birth, to which he gave the title of *Goethe's Secret Revelation*. In this article he offered an interpretation of the little known fairy story by Goethe entitled "The Green Snake and the Beautiful Lily," which formed a part of his novel *Stories of German Emigrants*. This story has as its theme the building of a bridge between the earthly and spiritual world by the Green Snake, who sacrifices herself to create the bridge. Clearly the story is an esoteric one, but the esoteric side of Goethe was not very well known at the time, and Steiner's readers were apparently not at all excited by his interpretation, which, as he said, was only slightly esoteric. He does refer in the article to the "supersensible" world and takes it for granted that it exists, and that Goethe also was well aware of it. The very detailed interpretation given by Steiner therefore was largely disregarded by the subscribers to the

Magazine, who were scarcely the "homeless ones" for whom he was searching.

In spite of this general lack of interest, one reader did become not only interested but excited, and since he was a member of the Berlin Lodge of the Theosophical Society he suggested to the leaders of the Lodge that Steiner be asked to lecture to it. It was evident to this young man that Steiner was able to talk on esoteric matters. The suggestion was taken up by Countess Brockdorff, the secretary of the Lodge, and as a result Steiner gave his first lecture to the theosophists in the library belonging to the Lodge on August 22, 1900. The lecture on the subject of Nietzsche, who had recently died, was well received and he was asked to give another on a subject of his choice. The occasion provided him with the opportunity to meet a theosophical audience for the first time, and he tells us in his autobiography that he was able to recognize that there was a genuine interest in the world of spirit among these theosophists.

For his second lecture he chose again to discuss the Goethe fairy tale. But whereas his article in the *Magazine for Literature* had been, as he says, "only slightly esoteric" this lecture contained much esoteric material and was greatly appreciated by his audience, confirming Steiner in his original impression that it was among the theosophists that he would find his destined audience for the spiritual knowledge he was now ready to give. Indeed, he tells us in his autobiography that it was an important experience for him to be able for the first time to speak directly out of the spirit. From this time onwards he gave lectures regularly to the theosophists, soon afterwards beginning a series on medieval mysticism later published in English under the title *Mysticism at the Dawn of the Modern Age*. In the six months from 1900 to 1901 he gave twenty-seven lectures to the Lodge.

In the same way that he had insisted when lecturing to the Workingmen's College in Berlin that he should be permitted absolute freedom to say what he wished, he demanded a similar freedom from the theosophists. He told them that he proposed to speak entirely from his own spiritual insight, and recognized no right on the part of anyone else to censor anything he wished to say. On one occasion, for example, he was told by a member of the audience that what he was saying was not in accord with what Annie Besant was saying and writing in her books at the time. Steiner replied drily in words that simply said, in effect, Is that so? and paid no attention to the comment. At that time the Theosophical Society, the only Society of its kind that existed anywhere, was entirely free, and local Lodges could invite anyone they wanted and were accustomed to listen to anyone who had anything of a spiritual nature to impart. It is evident that some members of his audiences recognized at once that Rudolf Steiner spoke in a different way from other lecturers, and that his material was drawn from a different source. So it was natural for him to attract personal followers, even though he made no special effort to do so.

In autumn 1900 a young woman began to attend Rudolf Steiner's lectures on mysticism at the Theosophical Lodge in Berlin. She continued to attend regularly and became a member of the Lodge. Both Steiner and Count and Countess Brockdorff remarked on the presence of this new recruit, who was destined to share Rudolf Steiner's life and played an incalculably important part in his work. Marie von Sievers, whose ancestry on her father's side was either Danish or Swedish, had a German mother, and had been born and brought up in Russia. Her conventional family looked upon her wish to study dramatic art with great distaste, but after her education in Russia, she insisted on being allowed to go to Paris. While studying dramatic art there she met Edouard Schuré, a distinguished French writer on esoteric subjects, who had recently become interested in Theosophy. It was he who first suggested to Fraulein von Sievers that she look into Theosophy, but she did nothing about it at the time, and had to return to St. Petersburg at the insistence of her mother who was unalterably opposed to a public career as an actress. Soon afterwards she went to Berlin to take part in further discussions about her future, and it was while there that she heard of Rudolf Steiner's lectures on Theosophy. In his first conversation with her, in anwer to a question by him as to her future career, she told him of her feeling about the living nature of speech, with which he was in profound sympathy.

Early in 1901 Marie von Sievers was asked to go to Italy to help in the founding of a Theosophical Section there, and she was working in Bologna when Dr. Steiner was asked to become first General Secretary of the German Section which the Theosophical Society leaders proposed to found if Steiner would head it. He made two conditions, the first that he should be allowed to speak as he wished, and the second that Marie von Sievers should be invited to return to Germany and become his assistant. So began the fruitful working relationship between these two powerful and determined personalities that ended only with Steiner's death, Marie Steiner, as she had become, continuing the work with the same devotion until her own death in 1948.

On several occasions throughout his life Steiner spoke of an occult law, as he called it, under which no new initiative in occult matters should come from the occultist, or initiate himself. All such initiatives ought to come in response to questions and suggestions put by others, to which the occultist is then in a positon to respond. In the series of lectures given in 1915 on *The Occult Movement in the Nineteenth Century*, to which reference was made earlier in this chapter, Steiner describes how the initiative for the work that was to be called Anthroposophy actually came into existence following a question by Marie von Sievers. She asked him if it was not necessary, urgently necessary, to call into being a "spiritual-scientific" movement in Europe. Steiner reported himself as having answered, "Certainly it is necessary to call such a movement to life. But I will ally myself only with a movement that is connected exclusively with Western occultism and cultivates its development . . . And I also said that such a movement must link on to Plato, to Goethe and so forth. I indicated the whole programme which was then actually carried out."[34]

It is clear enough from the published documents that Steiner at all times made it obvious that he would follow his own path, and he continued to give lectures to other groups than the Theosophical Society. For example, while he was giving his

125

lectures on mysticism to the Theosophical Lodge in Berlin in 1901 he started a series of lectures entitled *From Buddha to Christ* which he gave to *Die Kommenden*, a society that had been founded by Jacobowski, as narrated in the last chapter, a group that was more receptive to his teachings than the Giordano Bruno Bund had been. The full title of the lectures given to *Die Kommenden* was "The History of Mankind's Evolution, as shown in the World Conceptions from the Earliest Oriental Ages down to the Present Time: Or Anthroposophy." The word anthroposophy, later to be appled to the whole movement that he founded, was thus used by him for the first time. Curiously enough, at the very moment when he was being installed as head of the new German Section of the Theosophical Society, he had to leave early in order to speak to *Die Kommenden* on a very Christian subject about which more will be said later—the Raising of Lazarus.

It was never at any time claimed by the theosophists that Rudolf Steiner took the initiative in becoming or asking to become general secretary of the new German Section. It was the theosophists who wanted Steiner because of his position, and Annie Besant was wholly in agreement with the move because she had long desired a Section in Germany, the most important European country in which no Section had as yet been formed. Steiner was thus provided with a forum to express his ideas as often as he wished, and he had no objection to being associated with theosophists at the beginning of the century. As yet there was no "party line," and there was no pressure on him from any quarter. This situation changed when Mrs. Besant wished to put forward an Indian youth as the reincarnated Christ—a plan that was wholly repugnant to Steiner and, according to his own interpretation of Christianity, impossible. In any event it seems unlikely that a single Society could hold two such different personalities as Rudolf Steiner and Annie Besant, and the "marriage of convenience," as it may reasonably be called, between the Orientalism of Annie Besant and the Christianity of Steiner, was likely to survive only for as long as Mrs. Besant, as president of the world-wide Theosophical Society, was prepared to let the German Section under

126

Steiner's leadership follow its own path undisturbed by her. She allowed it to go its own way for several years, during which the membership of the German Section increased with a notable regularity. Almost all its members were followers of Steiner by the time of the split with the Theosophical Society in 1912. Even so, in some German cities his audiences were small, while when he travelled to distant places in Europe to give lectures he might in the end speak to only a handful. But in his mind all the efforts were thoroughly worth while, since lectures even to pitifully small audiences were, as he said, heard by spiritual beings and the dead.

Among the theosophical leaders who were anxious for Steiner to take over the theosophical work and form a section were the Berlin leaders Count and Countess Brockdorff who wished for personal reasons to leave Berlin, but did not wish to abandon their work. They offered Marie von Sievers the apartment in which the Theosophical Library was housed and Rudolf Steiner then gave his consent to becoming General Secretary and permanent teacher of the Lodge. Immediately after these decisions had been made both Steiner and Marie von Sievers were invited to England to attend a Congress where they could meet Annie Besant. This Congress of July 1902 was the first that either of them had attended. Both on this occasion were guests, since the charter for the new Section had not yet been received from Colonel Olcott in Adyar.

The official report of the Theosophical Congress of 1902 includes an account of a speech made by Rudolf Steiner which was translated into English by Marie von Sievers, who was a gifted linguist and possessed a good command of several languages. In this speech Steiner told his audience that there was much latent good will toward Theosophy in Germany, and a strong desire to seek for spiritual knowledge. But as yet there was little knowledge of theosophical teachings, though within the movement there many earnest workers. However, among the educated classes rationalistic philosophy had won a firm foothold, and it might prove very difficult to dislodge it. By contrast, within German *idealistic* philosophy there were several key thinkers who might well be thought of as true theosophists, as, for example, Leibnitz, Schelling, Fichte and Hegel, and Theosophy should now be brought within the framework of the thought of these men. Lastly, Steiner stressed that as General Secretary of the German Section he would always be opposed to the promulgation of any dogmas, and it would be his invariable aim to foster independent spiritual research.

As always when they visited important scientific and artistic centers in the different European cities, Rudolf Steiner and Marie von Sievers used every spare minute to visit museums, art exhibitions, and historical monuments. In most of these centers Marie von Sievers, who had received a very thorough artistic education, was able to be of great help to Rudolf Steiner, who, in turn, could from his own spiritual understanding give her further insights into what they viewed together. Although he scarcely saw Annie Besant during this initial English visit Steiner did make many other contacts within the English Section, and was very favorably impressed by the degree of culture and education of the English members, realizing at first hand why it was that the real center of the Theosophical work in the world was now in England. Many English members were deeply rooted in Western culture, and were not attracted so much by Oriental religions and philosophies as they were later. In his autobiography Steiner speaks very favorably of Bertram Keightley who later translated his lectures on Haeckel, and who had been intimately acquainted with Madame Blavatsky. Keightley shared reminiscences of her with Rudolf Steiner, making her "come alive" for him, while he also became acquainted with G.R.S. Mead, a noted author of works on Gnosticism and Oriental religions. Mr. Leadbeater he did not meet though he heard him speak. Leadbeater "made no special impression on me."

On his return to Germany Steiner found that the members in the many different Lodges were by no means unanimous in their support of the new venture of founding a Section of the Theosophical Society, and there was much overt and covert opposition to him. But now that his decision had been taken and the charter applied for he did not waver, and when it finally arrived Mrs. Besant came over from England to present it to him and to inaugurate the new Section on behalf of the Theosophical Society. The inaugural meeting was held in Berlin on October 18th, 1902, just ten days after the disastrous lecture on *Monism and Theosophy* given to the Giordano Bruno Bund which was described at the end of the last chapter. During the course of this inauguration meeting Annie Besant gave a lecture in English on the purposes of Theosophy, of which Steiner gave a digest in German. She then visited several other towns in Germany where there were scattered members of the Theosophical Society and lectured there. But once Rudolf Steiner had become the leader of the German Section of the Society the vast majority of members tended to gravitate toward the Section, leaving only a few exceptionally persistent devotees of Oriental wisdom to continue on their old paths independently of him. A few of the old leaders also resented his leadership and preferred to remain in charge of their local Lodges. If there had been no break with the Theosophical Society over Mrs. Besant's determination to put forward Krishnamurti as the reincarnated Christ, it might indeed have been possible, as Steiner was later to write in his autobiography, for Theosophy and Anthroposophy to have amalgamated in a peaceful and organic manner, at least in Germany, Switzerland, and Austria-Hungary for which countries he was responsible, and where he lectured tirelessly during the decade following the inauguration of the German Section.

Of crucial importance to this early work was the devotion shown by Marie von Sievers, who threw herself heart and soul into it, and made possible Rudolf Steiner's single-minded devotion to what we shall already call Anthroposophy, although the word was not used as long as Steiner remained within the theosophical fold. When Theosophy is spoken of hereafter, the word will refer to the movement centered in Adyar, India, and headed after the death of Col. Olcott in 1907 by Annie Besant. Frl. von Sievers took care of the entire organization of the material needs of herself and Steiner, and when the magazine *Luzifer*, later *Luzifer-Gnosis*, was founded in order to publish Dr. Steiner's teachings, she performed the work of organizing it, taking care of subscribers and the like. The *Magazine for Literature* had been handed over to more suitable owners and editors on September 29, 1900, and until the new magazine appeared in June, 1903, no Anthroposophical periodical was available.

A casualty of the new task that Steiner had undertaken was his wife Anna, formerly Anna Eunike. She had been able to enter into his previous life most comfortably, making a home for him, going on picnics with him, welcoming the students who visited them. But she had neither interest in, nor understanding of his theosophical path. Hence, although she was present at the lecture to the Giordano Bruno Bund Rudolph describes her as "strangely withdrawn and closed up, speaking very little." The work with Anthroposophy that was to occupy her husband in the future could not be shared with her. And indeed, as we have seen, destiny had provided for Steiner an ideal co-worker, without whom he could not even have begun his public work, and whose question, as we have seen, had to be asked before Steiner felt free to begin his new work. In the spring of 1903 Steiner therefore moved out of the home he had shared with his wife in the Berlin suburb, and moved into a house which was to be the headquarters of the Theosophical Section in Berlin, where the new magazine was written and edited, and where Frl. von Sievers also set up her own working and living quarters. In this house, and working outwards from it into all parts of Germany and neighboring countries, the initial expansion of Anthroposophy took place, and during the course of the next few years all the fundamental anthroposophical books were written and published, Marie von Sievers opening her own publishing house when the need for it became obvious. When Steiner gave his lectures elsewhere than in Berlin, invariably Marie von Sievers made the arrangements and accompanied him, even though the audiences might be made up in the end of only five or six members, and the journey thus represented a serious financial loss. The lectures themselves, however, were usually taken down either in outline or verbatim, and form part today of the anthroposophical corpus of about 6000 lectures.

Interest in Theosophy in the Western world was, at least in part, an aspect of the increasing interest in Oriental art, philosophy and religion that accompanied the growth of scientific materialism in the West in the nineteenth century. Great numbers of men and women whose parents and grandparents had accepted Christianity as a matter of course suddenly began to think that a belief in the teachings of Christianity was no longer scientifically respectable. This attitude was characteristic of such groups as the Giordano Bruno Bund, which adopted Giordano Bruno as its hero because Giordano had been one of the last men to be put to death by the Inquisition because of his heretical (and scientific) views. Almost all Roman Catholic countries also harbored anticlerical movements. Above all it was extremely unfashionable at the end of the century to acknowledge one's faith in Christianity.

However, this was not true of Oriental religions, including both Hinduism and Buddhism. These were *exotic* religions, not traditional ones, and Oriental philosophy, though not easily comprehensible in the West, was at least not based on something that freethinkers regarded as scientifically impossible, namely the Resurrection and Ascension into Heaven of its martyred founder. At most such men might be willing to accept the Incarnation of a very superior kind of human being who could in some respects perhaps be thought of as superhuman. By contrast such a religion as Buddhism in its purest form in no way strained human credulity. Buddha was not a god; even though some of his followers had deified him after his death, it was certainly not an essential part of the Buddhist religion that its founder should be regarded as a god. Hindu philosophical thought was of a very high order, and some Oriental religious practices could be regarded as beneficial, even for health. So it was not at all unnatural that Annie Besant, as a former freethinker, should have found Oriental philosophy, and even Oriental religion much more acceptable than the traditional Christianity that she had abandoned in her youth. Undoubtedly she, and many theosophists who followed her, regarded Oriental wisdom as truly more "spiritual" than Western Christianity at the turn of the century, on which materialism had already laid its hand, and far less "superstitious" than many of the dogmas supposedly believed by Western Christians.

In the second half of 1900 Rudolf Steiner had already given his series of lectures in the Brockdorff Library on eleven leading mystics of the early modern period, all of whom were Christians. In the course of these lectures he did introduce a little of the spiritual knowledge that only he possessed, and the orientation given to the lectures could scarcely have been given by anyone else at the time. Nevertheless the lectures, although they go deeply into the particular experiences of the mystics dealt with, and they are described with the greatest sympathy, do not reveal the Christian viewpoint of Steiner himself. As he dryly comments in one of his introductions to these lectures, he was accused of being a Haeckelian when he described Haeckel's ideas with sympathy, and even of being a Nietzschean when he wrote his book on Nietzsche. When these lectures on mysticism were published in book form the following year many theosophists approved of their content, especially among the English members, and the publication of this book was one of the reasons for the invitation extended to him to visit the Theosophical Congress in London in 1902.

In the second half of 1901 Steiner again gave a series of lectures to the Theosophical Lodge in Berlin which was received favorably by most of the members, and this series was published the following year under the title *Christianity as Mystical Fact.* Here he revealed much esoteric knowledge, especially about the ancient Mysteries, his essential purpose being to show how the Incarnation of Christ Jesus was a fullfillment on the earthly plane of what had previously been enacted symbolically in the Mysteries. To this small private audience Steiner therefore revealed for the first time much that had never been spoken of publicly before. Indeed probably very few of the members possessed any knowledge at all of the Mysteries, of which Steiner was to say so much in the course of the years to come. The culminating moment of the lectures was his explanation of the so-called "miracle" of the raising of Lazarus, which is described only in the John Gospel, as an actual initiation performed by Christ Jesus himself, and not, as is ordinarily supposed, the raising to life of a man who had died in the ordinary course of natural events. As a consequence of this initiation Lazarus was the first person truly to comprehend the new Mystery centered on Christ, called by Steiner the Mystery of Golgotha. It is also made clear from these lectures that Lazarus had been fundamentally changed by his initiation and that because of it he was later able to write the John Gospel. He alone among the Evangelists knew, through his initiation, that Christ was the Logos or Word, which was with God in the Beginning, as the Gospel puts it. Steiner later calls this Evangelist Lazarus-John, since he had received the name of John after his initiation. But he avoided making the matter quite clear in these lectures, so that the members of the audience did not perhaps as yet grasp the full meaning of what he was saying.

However, after these lectures nothing could have been more certain than that Rudolf Steiner had something new and revolutionary to say about Christianity, and that Christ Himself was its Center, a divine being who had indeed become man—as it was also clear from the many lectures he gave about Buddha that Buddha was a man, who through his enlightenment under the bo tree became a Buddha and thus escaped from the Wheel of Rebirth, and never again had to incarnate as a man. Steiner, indeed, always spoke of Buddha with the utmost respect, and in later years he told members of his deeds after death and how from the spiritual worlds he was present at the birth of Jesus on the earth. Buddha had a particular task to perform for mankind during his last incarnation on the earth and he performed it. After his death he passed on to other, purely spiritual tasks, performed from the spiritual world. The task of Christ Jesus was a different one, and it still is being performed today; and Rudolf Steiner undoubtedly regarded it as his principal task on earth to show to mankind the truth of the Deed of Christ and how Christ works on, as He Himself declared when He said: "I am with you to the end of the world ages."

This very brief introduction to Steiner's mission as the

133

inaugurator of Anthroposophy, which included a new Christology, necessarily brings up the question of how it was possible for Steiner to give such new "revelations" to mankind, and whether he was claiming to be another prophet, with a message from God to be proclaimed to men. We have spoken in earlier chapters of his gift of clairvoyance, and how he was able to perceive beings in the world of spirit that are not ordinarily perceptible, and are in any event never perceptible by the five senses recognized by science. This gift he never lost, but he made every effort to acquire the fullest possible knowledge about the teachings of conventional science, while also making a systematic effort that was continued all through his life to put into conceptual form his actual perceptions in the world of spirit. By means of systematic exercises his capacity for perceiving in the spiritual world was enhanced. In a series of essays, first published in *Luzifer-Gnosis*, and later in book form under the title *Knowledge of the Higher Worlds: How is it Attained?* he tells his readers exactly how they can acquire this knowledge for themselves, through the processes he calls Imagination, Inspiration, and Intuition, which constitute distinct stages on the path. At a certain stage along the path it becomes possible for the pupil to perceive into the spiritual worlds, and as he progresses, his perceptions can become ever clearer and fuller, above all more *exact*.

A sceptical reader might be willing to concede that higher powers latent in man can be developed by systematic effort along the lines proposed by Rudolf Steiner. But this is a very long way from conceding that all the knowledge given out by Steiner, including knowledge of what actually happened in Palestine in the time of Christ, could be acquired directly by any kind of spiritual vision, however systematically developed. If one is to be convinced that Steiner could in truth acquire such knowledge, and that the knowledge is in fact in accordance with truth, it seems to me that we have no option but to take it at least as a working hypothesis that Steiner was speaking the truth when he claimed that he had the ability to read what has always been called, in the East and West alike, the Akashic Record, or better, the Akasha Chronicle. There is no way of proving or disproving his claim, but at least Steiner

134

supported it with as much evidence as he could. He stated exactly what the Akasha Chronicle is, and he explained, if in a somewhat guarded manner, how he gradually acquired the ability to read it and how others could follow in the same path and learn to read it themselves. He warned all those who heard him and read his writings that they must accept nothing he said or wrote on blind faith, but must test it in every possible way and especially whether what he said at different times was always internally consistent—a very difficult feat for a liar—as well as consistent with all that is truly *known* from other sources (which of course does not include temporary scientific hypotheses).

Everything that has ever happened on earth, Steiner tells us, and even events that have taken place in the spiritual worlds, are indelibly recorded, not by an earthly or even by a heavenly scribe, but imprinted, *while they are happening*, in what he calls the "astral light." Though few occultists are able to "read" it, they have always been aware of the existence of this Akasha Chronicle, which we may imagine as a kind of infinitely wide memory. Our own memories are mysterious enough, even to ourselves, and we should recognize that they do not exist in space, only in time, and that they are in all respects immaterial. We can conceive that some other human being could "read" in our memories because they are not spatially attached to us; and it should be fairly easy to conceive that their contents might well be able to survive long after our bodies have decayed and been forgotten. Indeed, some well-known mediumistic phenomena are perhaps best explained as resulting from the accessibility of our memories to beings other than ourselves. The sum total of *all* memories, not only our own, but those also of higher beings, constitutes the Akasha Chronicle, and Steiner tells us that at a certain stage of initiation it becomes possible for a man to "read" it. This does not mean that he can necessarily understand what he "sees"; the depth and profundity of a man's vision into the Chronicle depends upon the degree of his development, while his ability to understand depends on many more factors that need not be entered into here.

Steiner tells us a little of his own development in Chapters 32 and 33 of his autobiography. "While carrying out the plans together with Marie von Sievers for the external activity," he writes, "I elaborated the findings of my spiritual vision. On the one hand I stood within the spiritual world in full consciousness. About the year 1902 and in the years following I had imaginations, inspirations, and intuitions regarding many things. But only gradually were these combined into what I then gave out publicly in my writings. . . . During the years from 1901 to approximately 1907 or 1908 I stood with all the forces of my soul under the impression of the facts and Beings of the spiritual world that were drawing near to me. Out of the experience of the spiritual world in general developed specific details of knowledge."

The rest of Chapter 33, which deserves careful study by those who doubt Rudolf Steiner's gifts and capacities, is devoted to the struggle in which he engaged in order to be able to speak in a suitably scientific manner about the knowledge he had won of the spiritual worlds. It seems unthinkable that he should while on his deathbed have devoted some of the little strength that remained to him to a detailed account of the difficulties involved in translating his spiritual experiences into an acceptable scientific form, so that they could be communicated to mankind, *if he had never had the experiences at all.* That he could have *invented* all that he tells us from the Akasha Chronicle, seems equally unthinkable. His judgment may be doubted, as we may also have reasonable doubts about his *understanding* of all that he saw, and even his ability to remember it. The *existence* of the Akasha Chronicle, as we have said, is attested by all occultists before him who have spoken of the matter as well as by Rudolf Steiner himself. Whether Steiner's own vision was blurred, or his understanding and judgment impaired, must be left to the discernment of those who read his books and lectures, to say nothing of his autobiography; and it is also legitimate to take into consideration the practical work inspired by his vision and understanding. In this book all that can be done is to assume that he was speaking the truth as he perceived it, and to report what he did as the result of his vision, leaving to those who read the book the task of judging his deeds, and the vision that inspired them.

During the first years of his work within the Theosophical Society Rudolf Steiner was able to teach and lecture more or less exactly as he wished, probably experiencing less opposition from any source than at any later time. His lecturing activity was enormous. He travelled widely, while Marie von Sievers spent her energies unstintingly in arranging for all the public work so that as little responsibility fell on Steiner himself as possible; at the same time she looked after his material needs. Around her also grew up a devoted band of workers, ready to undertake the multifarious duties concerned with the publication of his books as well as the recording or taking full notes on his lectures, at a period when tape machines had not yet been invented and everything had to be done without mechanical aids. Membership in the Section grew with regularity, including foreign members who asked to join the German Section because they believed that Steiner really had something to say that was not being said by other theosophists. Many accounts are extant telling of the impression he made on his audiences, even on those who were originally sceptical.

Nevertheless all opposition to him within Germany did not disappear. Steiner's insistence on placing the Christ event at the center of all history, and his failure to emphasize what most theosophists had always regarded as the superiority of Oriental philosophy to anything that had come out of the West, offended many old members. Others also objected to the manner in which Steiner taught, "as one having authority," and to his neglect of the published theosophical literature— even though he did occasionally go out of his way to praise some newly published book by a theosophist, when the book merited such recognition.

His greatest personal triumph in these years was surely his success in Paris in the summer of 1906. A Theosophical Congress lasting a few days was held in Paris, and Steiner attended and lectured, as was his custom and duty. But at the same time another conference took shape in a Parisian suburb

(Passy), originally attended almost exclusively by Russians and Germans. It was indeed held on the initiative of several distinguished Russians including the poet Minski, and the novelist Merejkovsky, who had invited Steiner to lecture in Russia itself, a plan which had to be abandoned after the 1905 revolution and the subsequent continued unrest. So the Russians came to Paris instead, and a house was put at their disposal, in which everything was improvised, including a commissariat that was able to feed all the participants. Here Rudolf Steiner gave a course of eighteen introductory lectures, of which an outline has been preserved, written by Edouard Schuré, the distinguished French writer on esoteric subjects. His two major books *The Great Initiates* and *The Genesis of Tragedy* were widely read at the time and have still not lost their interest, while his outline of Rudolf Steiner's lectures at Passy has remained in print in French under the title of *L'esoterisme chrétien*, and was recently published in English under the title of *An Esoteric Cosmology*. Schuré, who thus met Rudolf Steiner for the first time, was evidently tremendously impressed by him, publicly stating in the introduction to one of his books that now at last he had met with a real initiate in life—something he had never expected, though he had devoted so much of his own life to the study of long dead initiates of earlier times.

The lectures at Passy, attended at first by a couple of dozen persons, were later thronged by as many as could be squeezed into the house, until at last the French Section of the Theosophical Society, whose leaders resented Steiner's extracurricular activities, was shamed into offering him an adequate hall where he finished the cycle. The French Section was largely made up of theosophical traditionalists, who regarded Steiner as an upstart German who was trying to steal the limelight by teaching his own brand of Theosophy, so different from what they had known hitherto. That he should have done this in Paris, the center of world culture, and impressed such a man as Edouard Schuré as well as the distinguished Russians who had come to Paris to hear him, and not to attend the Theosophical Congress, was a bitter pill for the traditionalists to swallow.

Nevertheless there were other members who appreciated Steiner, and in later years when he visited Paris he was always assured of an appreciative if not very numerous audience.

It has been noted earlier that in 1903 Rudolf Steiner founded a new magazine as the organ of the German Section of the Theosophical Society. To this magazine he gave the title of *Luzifer*—the light bearer, to be distinguished from the supersensible being of that name—and the following year another magazine called *Gnosis* was acquired, the two amalgamating under the single title of *Luzifer-Gnosis*. Now at last Steiner had at his disposal a periodical which, unlike the *Magazine for Literature,* owed no allegiance to anyone else, and did not have to cater for a group of subscribers who expected something other than they received. The new magazine was a pronounced success from the beginning, and its list of subscribers grew by leaps and bounds. Unfortunately it had to be prepared by a tiny staff, and Rudolf Steiner was almost the sole contributor. He later recalled how he and Marie von Sievers would address all the wrappers themselves as soon as the issues arrived from the printers, and they then carried all the packages to the Post Office in one, and as time went on in several laundry baskets. In the end it was necessary to circulate the magazine through a commercial distributor. But by this time Steiner could not find the time to write the material because of his numerous other commitments, and the magazine began to appear only at very irregular intervals, to the despair of the unfortunate distributor. By 1909 it had to be abandoned altogether, but by this time Marie Steiner had founded her own publishing house in Berlin, which was to publish thereafter the bulk of Rudolf Steiner's books. It was able to pay him a modest royalty, which then and thereafter constituted the sole reliable, and often the only source he had of personal income. This publishing house was transferred to Dornach during the German inflation, and soon afterwards it became the official publishing organization of the General Anthroposophical Society.

Luzifer-Gnosis published Steiner's major book on self development in serial form in 1904 and 1905. When it appeared later as a book in 1909 under the title *Knowledge of the Higher Worlds: How is it Attained?* it was little changed. His first account of Atlantis and Lemuria was also published first in *Luzifer-Gnosis* under the title of *From the Akasha Chronicle*, but the material in this book was enlarged and in some respects modified when the knowledge had become, as Steiner admitted, more "mature" in him. It was then incorporated in the many successive editions of *An Outline of Occult Science* (first edition 1910). The earlier book nevertheless remains in print in English under the title *Cosmic Memory*. An apparent sequel to *Knowledge of the Higher Worlds* also appeared in *Luzifer-Gnosis*, but this publication occurred during the period when the magazine was appearing irregularly, and the book, now published under the title *Stages of Higher Knowledge* (formerly *The Gates of Knowledge*) consists of some valuable information not in the earlier work, but does not constitute a systematic sequel.

It should be noted here that Rudolf Steiner did not write many *books*, and each book that he did write was checked with considerable care. Most of them were revised at least once during his lifetime. The Goethean books and *The Philosophy of Freedom* discussed in earlier chapters, together with the three books of a fundamental nature that will be discussed here, constitute the basic anthroposophic writings, to which perhaps should be added two shorter works on the path of knowledge, published under the titles *A Road to Self-Knowledge* (1912) and *The Threshold of the Spiritual World* (1913). Among Steiner's other books are the Mystery Dramas, which will be discussed briefly in a later chapter, three important books published during the War, entitled *The Riddles of Philosophy*, *The Riddle of Man*, and *Riddles of the Soul*; his fundamental book on the social order, usually published in English under the title *The Threefold Commonwealth* (most recently translated as *Towards Social Renewal*), and the unfinished autobiography from which many extracts have been given, published in German under the title *Mein Lebensgang*, which in one English translation appeared as *The Course of My Life*, while the most recent translation was simply entitled

Rudolf Steiner: an Autobiography. Almost all of his work that is now available in book form was originally given out as lectures, or cycles of lectures, on a single subject. Very few of these lectures were edited for publication by Steiner himself, since in his later life he lacked the time to do any editing or revision. A few of his earlier series of lectures, such as those published under the title of *Christianity as Mystical Fact* he did personally prepare for publication, and even published new editions during his lifetime. But such work became impossible for him while he was lecturing almost every day, sometimes giving more than one lecture within twenty-four hours. It therefore fell to his collaborators, and later his heirs, to publish his lectures which had been taken down more or less accurately, by stenographers. Some of them of an esoteric nature, that had been given originally only to members, were withheld from publication for many years. Then in 1923 with the founding of the General Anthroposophical Society with headquarters at the Goetheanum at Dornach, the decision was taken to make all the lectures public, with a note added by the publishers to the effect that a minimum of prior knowledge was needed before new readers could make up their minds on the subject matter of these lectures, and that criticisms not based on such knowledge would have to be disregarded.

In the present book which is written as a biography of Rudolf Steiner no attempt has been made to present Steiner's writings and lectures in a systematic manner, and the reader is referred to the books and lectures by Steiner himself and by other writers, including a rather detailed study by the present author entitled *Man and World in the Light of Anthroposophy.* However in the present chapter there will be some exceptions to this general rule. During the period when Rudolf Steiner headed the German Section of the Theosophical Society he presented to the membership and to the general public almost all his fundamental teachings, and if his life work is to be understood as a whole, at least an effort should be made by the reader to study the content of the three books in which the greater part of these teachings was embodied. These books are: *Theosophy* (1904); *Knowledge of the Higher Worlds: How is it*

141

Attained? (1904-1909), and *An Outline of Occult Science* (1910).
A few pages will therefore be devoted to these books, with the
warning that the summary treatment which is all that can be
given can in no way do justice to them, and no digest of them
can have any usefulness beyond indicating the nature and
scope of the contents.

Theosophy, that is to say the book of this name, is concerned
above all with *man himself,* his nature, his destiny, his experience between death and rebirth, and—more briefly—how
he can win for himself knowledge of the higher worlds. In
1904 when the book was published, Rudolf Steiner was still in
the process of inventing Western terms for concepts that were
common currency in the East and were familiar enough to
most theosophists. The Oriental concepts were therefore given
in Sanskrit words, for which Rudolf Steiner substituted words
of his own coining in later editions. Only a few Sanskrit words
were retained in Steiner's latest formulations, and his new
terms had usually the advantage of greater precision, at least in
German, though often enough they go only very reluctantly
into English. In any event, in these fundamental books Steiner
is careful to explain exactly what he means by the words he
uses, but no one should pretend they are easy to understand,
nor that they yield their secrets at the first attempt.

The first chapter of *Theosophy*, in particular, is extremely
dense and undoubtedly requires concentrated study, perhaps for
several years. Here man is first discussed as a threefold being, of body, soul, and spirit, as was believed by the Christian Church until the belief was declared heretical in the ninth
century. However, to view the nature of man as threefold is by
no means the only way of viewing him, and these three
elements by no means exhaust his nature. He possesses three
sheaths more or less attached to the earth, three higher principles which are present as yet only in embryo, and in the
center he has the "I," the very core of his being, through which
his lower three are being transformed into his higher three
principles. From this point of view man is therefore a seven-
fold being. Lastly he may be regarded as having already
developed certain soul qualities as the result of the activity of

his I. If one looks upon man from this point of view he becomes a ninefold being. The I as such disappears as a principle, to be substituted by the three differentiated souls, known as the sentient soul, the intellectual soul, and the consciousness soul, important concepts in Anthroposophy which will be mentioned occasionally in this book, but cannot be described further here.

The second chapter of *Theosophy* was revised time and again by Rudolf Steiner as he tried to make ever more precise his teachings on reincarnation and karma, notions on which there was and is so much misunderstanding in the West. The Sanskrit word "karma" Steiner retained throughout his life, never substituting a Western equivalent, for the excellent reason that the concept of karma has hitherto been foreign to Western thinking, and no Western language therefore includes a word for it. Reincarnation, as such, that is the notion that the same individuality returns to the earth in different epochs, is an idea that has been held by many eminent Westerners, including Goethe and Lessing. But the purpose behind reincarnation, its real significance, is generally unknown. What Steiner taught was that a human being brings with him into a subsequent life on earth a framework of destiny that has been determined by previous lives on earth. The human I after death gradually casts off its three bodily sheaths and then passes into the spiritual world, where, with the aid of higher beings, it elaborates for itself its karma for the next life on earth. Man is thus given the opportunity to compensate for his previous evil deeds, while at the same time any spiritual progress that he has made in his earlier incarnations will also be reflected in the karma that he brings with him to his new life on earth. In this new earthly life we do not, except in very rare cases, have any conscious knowledge of our karma, but it is always present in our subconscious, and while we are asleep. It is of course also known to those higher beings who guide us through life.

In the last year of his life Steiner gave several series of lectures on the successive incarnations of a number of individuals, most of whom are known to history in at least one of their incarnations. These lectures contributed immeasurably to the deepening of the concept of karma. But even if Steiner had been able to give out such information in 1904—as he was not—it would have been incomprehensible without the information contained in the earlier work. Indeed, nowhere else are his teachings on reincarnation and karma described as clearly and succinctly as in this second chapter of *Theosophy*.

In the third chapter the style of the book changes in a marked manner, as Steiner proceeds to describe the world after death. During the first stage between death and rebirth man passes through "kamaloca," (another Sanskrit word without and English equivalent), where he experiences within himself all that during his earthly life others have experienced through his deeds. The early Church was aware of this region through which the human soul passes after death, and gave it the name of purgatory, but, once it had lost the idea of reincarnation, purgatory became merely a place where the human being expiated his sins before continuing on to heaven. In Steiner's teachings kamaloca provides man with knowledge essential for him if he is to make the resolution to compensate in his next life for the evil he has committed in this. After kamaloca man is no longer linked to the life he has just lived, and passes through various experiences in the realm of spirit which are described in detail in this third chapter of *Theosophy*.

The fourth and last chapter of *Theosophy* describes *one* of the paths of knowledge available to mankind in this present age. It differs in some respects from the paths given in his other two fundamental books. There is no contradiction between the paths, as each is treated from a different point of view.

Immediately after the publication of *Theosophy, Knowledge of the Higher Worlds, How is it Attained?* began to appear in instalments in *Lucifer-Gnosis*, as noted earlier. This book, fundamental though it is, need not detain us long here. The first half consists of a somewhat informal, even conversational discussion of the nature of the path that leads to higher knowledge, with detailed instructions, given by one who has already followed the path to those who wish to follow in his footsteps. This half was originally published separately and entitled *The Way of Initiation*; the second half was called

Initiation and its Results. These two titles still explain the actual content of the work better than any others. The second half describes the spiritual organs that are awakened and brought into action as the result of initiation, and how when they are active certain spiritual experiences follow, a description of which brings the book to a close.

During the years from 1903 to 1909 Rudolf Steiner began to reveal much from the Akasha Chronicle, as we have already explained. In particular he gave details on Atlantis and Lemuria, earlier prehistoric ages of our earth; and it then began to appear necessary to discuss previous embodiments of the Earth itself (known to occultists as Old Saturn, Old Sun, and Old Moon). During these periods of the scarcely thinkable remote past the germ was laid down by higher beings of what was later to become man. An understanding of these remote epochs therefore becomes necessary if man's antecedents are to be understood, and by what stages he became man—finally on the Earth and during Earth evolution taking on a bodily form and becoming at last visible.

Over these years Steiner spoke much on the subject of human evolution from the time of Old Saturn to now, and he began to work systematically on a fundamental book which should contain all that he had been teaching piece-meal until then. In August, 1906, he began a series of lectures in Stuttgart, in which he gave out much of what was later to be incorporated into *An Outline of Occult Science.* This cycle, at present in print in English under the title *At the Gates of Spiritual Science* is still a good introduction to the subject, but it can scarcely take the place of *An Outline of Occult Science*, which was worked over for three more years before he would allow it to go forward to publication. Every few years after its original publication early in 1910 it was revised again by Steiner, who constantly tried to give it more precision. The first three chapters of the book describe man from a different point of view from that given in *Theosophy*, and the chapter "Sleep and Death" is indeed quite different from anything in the earlier book. Chapters 5 onwards offer still a third path of knowledge different in many essentials from those given in the two earlier works. But the great originality of *Occult Science* consists in the immense Chapter 4 which gives a picture of evolution from Old Saturn to the present time, with its fulcrum the Mystery of Golgotha. Indeed, everything in the book makes clear the central importance of Christ and Christianity, which were not included at all in the earlier books. Nowhere else is all this information enclosed in so restricted a space, and yet the whole remains crystal clear, so that perhaps as many beginners in Anthroposophy start with this book as with any other. It remains absolutely indispensable for anyone wishing to enter Anthroposophy seriously. Even on his deathbed Steiner corrected proofs for the last German edition published in his lifetime, and this edition, like the others, continued to provide further explanations and clarifications.

Since it was Steiner's teachings on Christianity that above all distinguished Anthroposophy from traditional Theosophy and played a major part in his separation from the Theosophical Society, it seems fitting to devote the rest of this chapter on the Theosophical period to a fairly detailed presentation of these teachings, even though this procedure will take us beyond the period of the separation, and on as far as the War. Anthroposophy itself is, of course, unthinkable without Christianity, if only for the reason that the incarnation, life, death, resurection and ascension of Christ Jesus (sometimes collectively called by Rudolf Steiner, the Mystery of Golgotha) alone made human evolution upwards possible on the earth. Up to the time of the Mystery of Golgotha mankind was not only not yet free, but man did not even have as yet the *possibility* of winning freedom for himself. Having originally been directly aware of the existence of the divine spiritual worlds and of the gods as the result of a clairvoyance shared by everyone, men gradually lost this faculty, and in the course of time developed the capacity to think for themselves, while having no direct knowledge of the spiritual worlds nor of the divine beings above man. Until the Mystery of Golgotha men followed a path of *involution*, becoming ever more deeply incarnated in their bodies, and lacking the possibility of learning for themselves the truths of the spiritual worlds because they could no longer develop the necessary faculties. A direct intervention from the spiritual worlds had therefore become necessary if man was to evolve in accordance with the original divine plan. One divine being therefore chose through a deed of sacrifice to incarnate as man for a period of three years. This Being, the Christ, made it possible not only for man to set foot on the path of *evolution* but also for the Earth itself to be redeemed from the same hardening process that had up to this time, as a result of the Fall in Lemurian times, been man's lot.

Theosophists had always held that there was no great difference between religions, and for this reason that the utmost tolerance should be observed toward all of them. According to them, every religion possessed its germ of truth, though some of them were more developed than others. It will be clear from even this inadequate description of Steiner's teachings on Christianity that Christianity is quite different from any other religion. But this does not mean that anthroposophists are expected to be "converted" to Christianity or to any of its branches. For Steiner Christianity was simply a fact, and in the far future it would indeed cease to be a religion at all. Or, as he put it in the title of one of his lectures given a few days before his cycle on the Gospel of St. John: "Christianity began as a Religion but is Greater than all Religions." Meanwhile each of the existing religions was appreciated by him on its own merits as a partial revelation of spiritual truths and characteristic of a particular historical epoch.

The lectures given to the Berlin lodge of the Theosophical Society in 1901 and published under the title *Christianity as Mystical Fact* are still one of the best introductions to Steiner's teachings on Christianity. In them he makes clear how the deed of Christ was a fulfillment on the stage of the world of what had been enacted as a ritual in the ancient Mysteries, and its culmination was, as we have noted earlier, the initiation of Lazarus by Christ Himself. Thereafter Lazarus became John, "the disciple whom Jesus loved," as he is always called in the Gospel that he himself wrote. The first of the great cycles on the Gospels was given a full seven years later, at Hamburg, during the Whitsuntide season of 1908. Fittingly enough, this

147

cycle, which included material already given in individual lectures to different audiences, was concerned with the Gospel of St. John, a Gospel that as we have noted, John was able to write only because of his initiation. As has always been recognized, in many respects this is the most profound of the four Gospels, and its first chapter, in particular, which is quite unique in all Christian literature, identifies Christ with the Logos or Word, which "became flesh and dwelt among us." Much of Steiner's exposition is devoted to the elucidation of this great mystery of the Logos, while another striking section is concerned with the I Am sayings ("I Am the Light of the World"; "I Am the true Vine"; "I am the Resurrection and the Life," and others). The whole cycle, although remaining incomplete for lack of a competent stenographer, remains one of the most inspiring ever given by Steiner, and numerous members of the Anthroposophical Society first came into the movement through reading it.

In later times Rudolf Steiner was to explain that none of the Gospels is written as an ordinary eye-witness account or from oral testimony collected by the Evangelists, least of all from historical documents because, as he says, they do not exist. It is true that some passages in the John Gospel bear the stamp of personal participation, as, for example when John personally asked Christ Jesus a question at the Last Supper and received an answer that only he could have heard. John's account of the Crucifixion is clearly also first hand. By contrast, no human being could possibly have heard with his own ears Christ's prayer to His Father (Chap. 17). Steiner tells us, in fact, that not only John but all the four Evangelists had been initiated, and as a result were able to write directly out of their inner perception of the events they record. This fact explains the presence of four living creatures who in early Christian art so often accompanied the Evangelists. The four creatures are the symbols for the kind of initiation each Evangelist had, the eagle in the case of St. John, the lion of St. Mark, the bull of St. Luke, and the angel man in the case of St. Matthew. The different accounts given of the same events by the different Evangelists are thus explained by their particular kind of

148

perception resulting from their initiation. Friedrich Rittel-meyer reports in his book *Rudolf Steiner Enters my Life* (p. 122) that he himself (a theologian of note, and a pastor) asked Steiner why the Gospel accounts differed and received the answer "The Evangelists were not, of course, giving a historical account. There are no historical records. They tell what was revealed to them as truth after deep contemplation of the events, even when they had not actually witnessed them. And so one word came to one [in connection with the words spoken on the Cross], another to another, each according to his particular preparation." Each account therefore supplements rather than contradicts the others, except in certain cases when two different events are being described although they may appear to be so similar that commentators often suppose they are identical. We should, according to Steiner, usually try to grasp the different viewpoint of each writer, in preference to ascribing the apparent discrepancy to ignorance or error.

Steiner's lecture cycles on the Gospels should never be regarded as systematic commentaries. He does not take each passage and comment on it after the manner of ordinary biblical critics. Indeed he does not even usually indicate the biblical passage he is dealing with until he has already given most of his lecture. His customary procedure was to discuss a particular subject from many angles, and from a profoundly esoteric point of view. Then suddenly he would read out to his audience the passage from the Gospel that deals with that particular topic, usually in a new translation. The passage is immediately flooded with a new light, and understood as it never could have been before.

The twelve-lecture cycle at Hamburg on the John Gospel was followed the next month by an extraordinary exposition of the *Apocalypse (Revelation)* of St. John, in a further twelve lectures given at Nürnberg. The explanations of the visions of St. John have little resemblance to any ever given by anyone else—taking account, as they do, of the most remote ages of the past and looking forward to the most remote ages of the future. In spite of the fact that John's vision encompasses the whole future of mankind, even in future embodiments of the Earth,

149

the cycle can nevertheless, however strange it may seem, be used as an introduction to Anthroposophy. Steiner of course in 1908 was working on his *Outline of Occult Science*, and much of what he was drawing forth from the Akasha Chronicle at the time was very much in the forefront of his consciousness. So, even in a cycle on the Apocalypse the entire evolution of mankind as it appears in that book was woven into his lectures, as it was again, in somewhat more detail, in his second Gospel cycle of fourteen lectures given at Cassel in June and July, 1909 and published under the title of *The Gospel of St. John in Relation to the Other Gospels, Especially the Gospel of St. Luke.*

Other cycles on the Gospels followed, St. Luke later in 1909, St. Matthew in 1910, and an extraordinary cycle in 1911 entitled *From Jesus to Christ*. Meanwhile he had given two background cycles on Matthew and Mark in preparation for the actual cycles. St. Mark was given in Basel in 1912, and in 1913 another totally new revelation was given to members in the form of a cycle called *The Fifth Gospel*, which will be described later. At the turn of the year 1913-14 he gave another deeply esoteric cycle, much of which was concerned with the pre-earthly deeds of Christ (*Christ and the Spiritual World*) and later in 1914 he gave a short but crucially important cycle at Norrköping in Sweden called *Christ and the Human Soul*. When Friedrich Rittelmeyer, a Berlin pastor who later became an anthroposophist and the founder of the Christian Community, asked him why he had given no further Gospel cycles Steiner replied that during the War the spiritual worlds were too deeply disturbed for it to have been possible to draw down material of the profoundly esoteric nature at that time. Then after the War he had had to occupy himself with tasks more directly important for humanity. However, it goes without saying that Christ and Christianity were always a part of the background of his teachings in the postwar period, and he always made the assumption that the members were familiar with his prewar cycles on the Gospels.

It would be out of place here to attempt to give even an outline of the astonishing wealth of information contained in these Gospel cycles. One crucial element in Steiner's teaching about the Christ is, however, essential to grasp—the fundamental distinction he makes between Jesus of Nazareth, the most highly developed human individuality that ever walked the earth, and the Christ who is the highest spiritual Being who takes part in earth evolution. For such a Being to be able to incarnate in a human body, preparation had to be made in the spiritual world over a long period of time, and the Hebrew people had to be set aside and separated from all other peoples so that in the fullness of time as perfect a body as possible could be provided. This body was inhabited by Jesus of Nazareth until his thirtieth year when he yielded up his own ego so that the Ego of the Christ Being could enter it. Thereafter the Christ lived in this body with its three sheaths until the death on the Cross—though, as Rudolf Steiner explains, it was not His suffering nor His relatively short exposure on the Cross that were responsible for His death. The Christ Being after three years on earth had so penetrated the *sheaths* that they were almost destroyed. He should not have died *so soon* solely from what he had physically suffered, as seems to be suggested by two passages in the Mark Gospel. When, as he records, "Jesus cried with a loud voice and gave up the ghost," the Roman centurion who was supervising the Crucifixion was moved to say, "Truly this was the Son of God," while Pilate could not believe that He was dead already and sent to the centurion for confirmation (Mark 15: 39,44).

This and other mysteries, not all of which are usually regarded as such, were cleared up by Rudolf Steiner in these cycles. In particular he emphasizes the importance of the gift of wisdom bestowed on Jesus of Nazareth when he was twelve years old, as it had once been bestowed on the young Solomon (Luke 2: 41-51; I Kings 3:9-12); and he explains the words spoken from heaven at the time of the Baptism and recorded in one of the older manuscripts of the Luke Gospel: "This is my beloved Son, this day have I begotten Thee." In fact, according to Steiner's account this was indeed the first appearance of the Christ upon earth, the moment of the Incarnation, and it should be clearly distinguished from the birth of Jesus thirty years before. The words just quoted here were quoted also by St. Paul, or the writer of the Epistle to the Hebrews if the writer was not Paul (Heb. 1:5), but the editors of the Gospel texts, not understanding what had happened in the Jordan, not unnaturally preferred the reading usually translated into English as "in Whom I am well pleased."

With the great cycle on St Mark, a Gospel that, contrary to general belief, is an exceptionally profound one, dealing as it does only with the Christ after the Baptism leaving aside altogether Jesus of Nazareth, Steiner in 1912 completed his cycles on the four canonical Gospels that appear in the Bible. Late in 1913 he began to reveal the contents of a totally different "Gospel," to which he gave the name of the *Fifth Gospel*. The original cycle was given in the Norwegian capital of Christiania (now Oslo), but the same material was repeated in the following weeks to many different audiences in Germany. In this "Gospel" Steiner filled in at least part of a gap that has always been missing in the canonical Gospels, though various uncanonical "gospels" and legends contain material covering this period. He drew from the Akasha Chronicle a picture of Jesus of Nazareth in the period from his twelfth year to the Baptism in the Jordan, including details, in particular, of his last years before the Baptism. He spoke of Jesus' wanderings over the whole Near East, and he described vividly his inner sufferings, especially when he witnessed the decadence of the ancient Mysteries, and saw how demons had taken the place of the divine beings who had once been active in the Mysteries. Members present at these lectures often spoke of how Steiner seemed to be living through the experiences himself even while he was speaking. Friedrich Rittelmeyer heard the lectures when they were given at Nürnberg, and the following description is drawn from his short biography of Rudolf Steiner entitled *Rudolf Steiner Enters my Life*.

"A hundred or so people had gathered in the narrow premises where the Theosophical Society, as it then was, held its meetings. . . . Rudolf Steiner stood before us and spoke of the boyhood of Jesus. From my seat in the front row I was able to watch every expression. He seemed to be looking away from and beyond the audience, gazing intently at pictures before him. With the greatest delicacy of touch and a most striking alertness and caution, he proceeded to describe these pictures. Occasionally there would be an interpolation of such phrases as: 'I cannot say precisely if the sequence here is correct, but this is how it seems to me.' Or: 'With all my efforts I have not been able to discover the name of the place. The fact that the name itself has been obliterated must have some significance.' He spoke with a reverence in which there was no suggestion of servility, and stood there resolute and firm in the presence of the miraculous. An atmosphere of pure spirituality pervaded the room. It was an atmosphere purged of all feelings not born directly of the spirit—which was there in all its power. He told how the divine revelations contained in the Old Testament had dawned in all their greatness upon the soul of the boy Jesus during the years immediately following his return to Nazareth after the event in the Temple at Jerusalem, how his sorrow grew more and more intense as he realized that any true understanding of the greatness of this former revelation of the Divine was lacking among his contemporaries, how this sorrow lived within him, unexpressed and not understood by those in his environment—'a sorrow in itself far greater than all other sorrows I have known among mankind.' But just because this sorrow was destined to dwell wholly in the inner being of the boy Jesus, he was able to ennoble it beyond all telling . . . .

"Indelible in my memory are the eyes into which we were able to look on these occasions, and how they were gazing into the past. His living spirituality radiated such purity, such convincing integrity and humility that one felt oneself in the presence of a supreme event in human history. . . .I can only be grateful to have had the experience."[35]

Two other important elements of Rudolf Steiner's teachings on Christianity which differ from anything taught in any denomination of Christianity require a brief mention here. In 1910 Steiner gave a short series of lectures on the true nature of the Second Coming. According to him, ever since the Resurrection the Christ has dwelt in the etheric world, the world that is nearest to us of the invisible worlds. While he was on the road to Damascus St. Paul had seen Him there, and at once knew that Jesus had been the Christ, contrary to his belief up to that time, and that He had risen. Thereafter Paul had constantly preached the Resurrection. However, not until our own time has it been possible for men so to develop their supersensible faculties that they can perceive the Christ in the etheric world. As far as men are concerned the possibility has become open to them only since the end of Kali Yuga. But at the same time the Christ Himself has approached nearer to the earthly world than He was immediately after the Resurrection. This approach to our world is, according to Steiner, the Second Coming in the "clouds of heaven," and he interpreted the clouds of heaven as referring to the etheric world. In later years Steiner greatly enlarged this first revelation of the Second Coming, and he spoke about its effects in the earthly world and who would be able to see Him and why at certain times it would be difficult to do so. Perhaps the most important element in this teaching is that the Second Coming is not a once and for all happening, but a progressive revelation of the Being of Christ to men that lasts over a long period of time, during which men on their side learn to see Him, not all at once, but also over a longer or shorter period of time.

The other teaching to be discussed here is what the science of spirit has to say about the Redemption, a subject fraught with great difficulty for many earnest persons who would like to believe in Christianity but find the traditional doctrine in some degree repugnant to their sense of fairness and justice. The difficulty disappears when Steiner's complete teachings on reincarnation and karma are incorporated into the Christian doctrine which holds that Christ is the Redeemer, redeeming men from their sins. Steiner explains the matter most clearly in the last of his Christian cycles given before the War, entitled *Christ and the Human Soul* (Norrköping, 1914). According to Steiner man does indeed suffer for his own sins (as the Church would put it) or, in anthroposophical terminology, man experiences the fruit of his own deeds after death in kamaloca. Then in the spiritual worlds he wills for himself a karma, as a

154

result of which his former deeds will be compensated in a new life on earth. With the aid of higher beings he chooses his parents and a life-framework suited to fulfill this karma. If this is so, one may legitimately ask, where is there a role for Christ, who "takes upon Himself the sins of the world?"

The science of spirit sees no contradiction if the matter is rightly understood. The religious intuition was a true one, but has hitherto not been understood by theologians for lack of the necessary knowledge. Man does indeed bear the consequences of his deeds, the good and the bad, and karma in subsequent lives will compensate for them. Man indeed ought not to wish it otherwise. A courageous human being will wish to make progress through learning from his faults and mistakes. If he never learns the consequences of his acts, a vital experience is missed, and these acts are left unredressed. The last thing in the world he ought to wish is that some divine being should act as a substitute for him, and simply "forgive" his evil deeds without letting him have the chance to compensate for them from his own free will.

However, it is also true that the sins he has committed, the evil he has done, have disturbed the equilibrium of the universe, and delivered over a part of the world to Ahriman, the enemy of mankind, who is trying to take over the earth for himself. Objectively speaking, an evil deed has added to the sum of evil in the world, and the world would suffer from it for all eternity if Christ did not take upon Himself its consequences, thus wresting from Ahriman something that he would otherwise have retained for himself. Christ in this way has made it possible for man to continue to live on the earth, which would otherwise have been overwhelmed by the evil deeds of man. By themselves men, although by their good deeds they do help the earth in a limited way, are not strong enough to vanquish Ahriman, nor can they without divine aid prevent him from taking over the earth for himself. Only a Divine Being can do this, and Christ did indeed undertake to keep Ahriman from the victory by "taking upon Himself the sins of the world." Traditional teachings about the Redemption have always raised questions in the minds of thinking

155

men and women who have felt that men should accept full responsibility for their acts, and that nothing less than this is consistent with man's dignity. But it needed Rudolf Steiner's initiate knowledge before the apparent contradiction could be resolved.

During these years when Rudolf Steiner was giving his many lectures on Christianity his relations with the Theosophical Society were seriously deteriorating. In Paris in 1906 he lectured to the Theosophical Congress on Theosophy throughout the ages, showing how the theosophical spirit had manifested itself in numerous thinkers of the past. This lecture no doubt surprised many members of the Society who associated the word Theosophy only with their particular movement. But as was noted earlier Steiner also gave a series of eighteen lectures on esoteric Christianity both during and after the Congress to an audience few of whose members were theosophists. The following year Germany played host to the Theosophical Congress, and numerous innovations were introduced for the first time at a Theosophical Congress, including the presentation of a play by Edouard Schuré and the decoration of the Congress auditorium with artistic motifs drawn from the *Apocalypse*, as will be discussed in the next chapter. At this Congress Annie Besant was still carefully tolerant of all the innovations, and she had a meeting with Rudolf Steiner in which it was agreed that their differences of opinion, especially on the subject of Christianity, need not lead to an open break.

To hindsight it seems that such a break was ultimately inevitable, but it was certainly precipitated by the decision of Mrs. Besant in 1909 to back an initiative of Charles Leadbeater, who had "discovered" that an Indian boy named Alcyone, later to be known as Krishnamurti, was to be the reincarnated Christ. From that time onward she threw her influence behind the movement to proclaim the new Christ, and she encouraged the establishment of a new order within the Theosophical Society under the name of the Order of the Star of the East. This initiative will be discussed in more detail later in Chapter 8. There can be no doubt that as well as incurring the unalterable hostility of Rudolf Steiner to this movement it also brought the entire Theosophical Society into disrepute and even ridicule. But it may be that Annie Besant intended the movement to be a kind of answer to Steiner's insistence on the Mystery of Golgotha as a unique event, never to be repeated, and that she not only wished to discredit him as a teacher but at the same time to restore the East to its rightful position of supremacy. She might never have undertaken such an initiative if Steiner's teachings on the true nature of Christianity had not been seducing theosophists away from the eastern religions and philosophies that had hitherto been at the heart of Theosophy.

Many leading theosophists may well have doubted Annie Besant's wisdom in thus promoting the Order of the Star of the East, but it was not open to doubt that Steiner's teachings on Christianity contradicted a number of long held theosophical ideas, including some contained in the writings of H.P. Blavtsky. At the same time they were not disposed to believe that Steiner had direct access to the spiritual worlds, and was thus in a position to add to the truths of Christianity as well as providing new interpretations of it. Indeed, many of them regarded Steiner as unbearably presumptuous in making such claims for himself, or allowing his followers to make them for him. Ironically enough, other theosophists did not doubt Steiner's access to spiritual knowledge, but objected to his revelations of deeply occult teachings in books intended for public sale. According to Steiner Annie Besant herself did have a certain grasp of spiritual realities, and when she spoke of the world of spirit, what she said was actually "taken from that world." However, not only was she unable to enter the spiritual world consciously, but she could not even imagine that this possiblity was open to others. So she was totally unable to understand Rudolf Steiner, and as time went on when he publicly opposed her on the subject of Krishnamurti, her former tolerance ceased to be in evidence, and a Theosophical Congress scheduled to be held in Genoa in September, 1911, at which Steiner was to give a lecture on the subject "From Buddha to Christ," was cancelled at her instigation. Clearly she preferred not to give him a platform for a lecture on such a subject.

The final break with the Theosophical Society and the

founding of the Anthroposophical Society will be discussed in Chapter 8, and, as we shall see, most of the German members of his Section stayed with Steiner and became anthroposophists, as did virtually all the foreign members who had been accepted into the German Section, joining it simply because he was its head and it was him they wished to hear.

The formal change made very little practical difference, so independent had the work of the German Section always been. For several years before the break Steiner had been devoting his entire time and effort to this work, and, as he explains in his autobiography, from at least as early as 1907 he had virtually no private life at all. It is in the light of this truth that the sentence that begins the last chapter of his autobiography should surely be understood: "In what is to follow, it will be difficult to separate the account of the course of my life from the history of the Anthroposophical Movement." When he had finished writing this chapter, indeed, he knew that he had reached the end of his life also. This chapter alone is not followed by the words "to be continued." The unfinished autobiography in fact did not need to be finished; the purpose for which it had been started had now been fulfilled, and quite possibly nothing could have been added that would have been significant for posterity.

The autobiography had been started with the aim of explaining the thoughts that lay behind his actions. It had never been his intention to record all his important experiences, to make his life *interesting*. Up to the beginning of his public mission the varied experiences of his life, his human relationships, his contacts with distinguished personalitites, all throw light on his personal development and above all the development of his thought and his spiritual and supersensible faculties. These had now matured in him. With the enormous pressure of work that burdened him after 1903 he could scarcely have had time to cultivate the friendships about which he writes so beautifully in the early part of his autobiography; and it may be wondered also whether he could even have *thought* as much about the work he was doing as he did in earlier years. What was now important for the world to know was what he had *done,* and these things were on the public record, and others could record them. Almost every moment of every day was spent exclusively on the fulfillment of what he regarded as his mission. This seems to have been literally true. When he was not lecturing or preparing lectures or reading or engaged in solitary thought and meditation he was giving advice to all those—and they were numerous—who requested private interviews in which they discussed their problems with him. He seems to have done nothing that was not in some way connected with the work that he had undertaken, and yet he was totally without fanaticism.

Although from time to time we shall offer glimpses of him as seen through the eyes of friends and pupils, the rest of this book cannot fail to be concerned more with his work, and less with his personal life, of which, indeed, we know little except by inference. The remaining chapters will therefore be largely topical, concerned with particular facets of his work. The first of these will deal with some of the new impulses that he gave in the field of art, beginning with the Theosophical Congress held in Munich in 1907, in which he surprised and shocked many of the theosophists who attended it, unaccustomed as they were to the intrusion of art into their religious and philosophical concerns. We shall then continue with a discussion of the beginnings of the new art of eurythmy inaugurated by Rudolf Steiner, and with the staging, also in Munich, of the Mystery Dramas which he wrote in the four years preceding the War. The separation from the Theosophical Society and the founding of the first Anthroposophical Society will then be taken up in Chapter 8, bringing the story to the beginning of World War I.

159

Chapter 7

NEW IMPULSES IN ART

EURYTHMY AND THE MYSTERY DRAMAS

During the years when he was absorbed in philosophy and Goethean science, Rudolf Steiner does not seem to have been especially interested in the arts, or at all events he wrote and spoke relatively little about them—with the exception of the lecture given in 1888 to the Goethe Society in Vienna entitled *Goethe as the Founder of a New Science of Aesthetics.* His association from 1901 onwards with Marie von Sievers, who was thoroughly familiar with art history awakened his latent interest. Once he began to travel with her to the various European capitals, for the first time he had the opportunity to view original paintings, whereas apart from the art treasures in Berlin, Weimar, and Vienna, he had, as he tells us in one of the last chapters of his autobiography, seen little but reproductions. "Her fine and cultivated insight," he comments, "complemented in a beautiful way all that I was able to experience in the sphere of art and culture. She understood how these experiences then flowed into the ideas of Anthroposophy, imbuing them with mobility. For what my soul received as artistic experiences then permeated what had to be brought to active expression in the lectures. . . . I felt it to be a specially favorable stroke of fortune that destiny granted me, in Marie von Sievers, a companion in my work who, out of the deepest disposition of her soul, understood so completely how to foster this artistic element in a way imbued with feeling yet utterly without sentimentality.''[36]

None of this is intended to imply that Steiner took his ideas either from conventional art history or even from Marie von Sievers. She was above all a guide to the art treasures of the places they visited together, while at the same time proving an appreciative listener for all that he was able to reveal from his own spiritual insights in the realm of art. Her own very considerable talents, and especially her organizing abilities, made it possible for her to translate Steiner's ideas into reality, and the arts to be discussed in this chapter owed a great deal to her cooperation even though the original ideas stemmed from him.

Steiner always held that art was a necessary part of life, that man could no more live a full life without participating in art both as spectator and creator, than he could live without religion; and he was fond of repeating that at one time art, religion and science had been inseparable from each other. It was only in relatively recent times that they had become separated. Science no longer felt any relationship with religion; on the contrary religion and science are now only too often opposed to one another. Scientists are inclined to look upon religion as superstition, and faith as a weakness that ought to be outgrown in our modern age. Few scientists look upon art as anything more than a form of enjoyment or entertainment, certainly not as a necessity; though scientists, like other men, are entitled to take up some form of art as a hobby if it pleases them. Most people do not look upon architecture as an art at all. When they call in an architect, it is usually for the purpose of solving some practical problem, such as how to make the most efficient use of a limited space; the same people are likely to prefer naturalistic sculpture or painting—a good likeness—to the experimental work of modern sculptors or painters. They may think that a painted landscape should be an improvement on nature. In our day comparatively few people enjoy poetry; if they do it is likely to be poetry in rhymed verse with meaning and rhythm, as music also should have both melody and rhythm. Drama should be

161

arresting and if possible moving, or it can be entertaining. In any event it should be closely modeled on real life and the characters should be realistically drawn. None of these forms of art can be easily associated with religion, still less with science; nor indeed can they be supposed to rest on a spiritual basis. Yet Steiner proposed to bring new life into all the arts by linking them once more with the world of the spirit, and from his spiritual knowledge to contribute to a renewal of the arts. In this chapter and the following one we shall try to show how he fulfilled this self-imposed task.

When Steiner insisted that in the not so far distant past science, art and religion all formed a single unity, he was, from a historical point of view, on firm ground. In ancient Egypt and Mesopotamia, for example, no separate science existed. Although the Sumerians invented much of the mathematics of the ancient world, their very considerable knowledge was used primarily for the purpose of constructing their ziggurat temples. Their observations of the stars may have formed the basis in later years for a real astronomy, but astronomy at all times was the servant of astrology, which was used primarily for the purpose of predicting the will and intentions of the gods. So also with the dances and music of the Sumerian and Babylonian peoples, which formed part of the temple ritual. Egyptian art was devoted almost if not exclusively to the religious cult of the dead, including the funeral rites for the Pharaohs, who were regarded as gods. So also with the cave-paintings of prehistoric man, which are usually held to have had a magical or religious purpose, and few would claim that this art was created for its own sake. In the case of the Greeks we are on even firmer ground. There can be no doubt that Greek tragedy had its roots in the Greek Mysteries, and it was never presented except at the great religious festivals, for which also most of the Greek odes and lyrics were composed. Even the Olympic Games were celebrated at a religious festival, and the odes composed for the winners by such a poet as Pindar were suffused with religious feeling. The first Greek philosophers, men like Thales and Anaximander, could certainly be thought of as at the same time the first true scientists. But among them they counted such a man as Heraclitus, an initiate and priest

162

of the Mysteries of Ephesus; while the philosophy of Plato, who was likewise an initiate, was based on Mystery knowledge. Such a dialogue as the *Timaeus* is comprehensible only as an example of the old Mystery wisdom. It was not until Aristotle had thoroughly worked through Plato's philosophy that it could be considered as a possible basis for science.

Very little was known about the ancient Mysteries when Steiner began to speak of them from his own spiritual knowledge. One important writer, however, the Alsatian Frenchman Edouard Schuré, who was mentioned briefly in the last chapter as the theosophist who introduced Marie von Sievers to Theosophy, had been writing for some decades about the Mysteries, especially those of Greece, and also about the great initiates of the past. The fact that his books after a slow start had suddenly become bestsellers in many languages shows that there was a latent interest in the subject that could be awakened. But Schuré himself was the first to admit that he did not have any direct knowledge of or access to the spiritual world, contrasting in this respect with Rudolf Steiner who could speak with authority out of his own spiritual experience.

At Christmas, 1906, Steiner gave out for the first time, to a restricted audience in Berlin, a meditative verse, in which he said that "the deepest import of the Christmas Mystery is mirrored," adding significantly that "in all ages these words resounded in the ears of those who were pupils of the Mysteries before they were allowed to participate in the Mysteries themselves." It would seem that this verse, which begins with the words "Behold the Sun at the midnight hour," had therefore been used in the Mysteries of Egypt as well as Greece, and though it was now given for the Christmas festival in a Christian country it could not be considered as a purely Christian meditation. It was at all times Steiner's expressed intention to fill his own work in the field of art with the spiritual content of what had in ancient times been revealed in the sacred Mysteries. His own Mystery Dramas, to be discussed later in this chapter, conceal within them a profound knowledge similar to the knowledge that a great Greek tragedian like Aeschylus had drawn from the Greek Mysteries, though Steiner presented it in a form suited for modern consciousness, and specifically for the age in which we are now living, when what he called the consciousness soul has to be developed. The art of eurythmy, at the heart of which is the new form of speech developed by Rudolf Steiner and Marie von Sievers, is likewise closely linked to the Mysteries, and this first verse from the Mysteries of which we have just spoken was one of the first to be put into a eurythmic form by Steiner himself.*

Steiner once defined "true art" as "an expression of man's search for a relationship with the spiritual" and in numerous lectures throughout his life he enlarged on this theme. He had no use whatever for naturalism in art. Nature, he used to say, must always be a better artist than man, who cannot improve on nature's landscapes when he paints them realistically, while photographically exact portrait painting was for him the lowest form of art, scarcely worthy of the name. But it was not so easy for him to introduce his artistic ideas to most theosophists, who as a rule paid little attention to art, and his efforts to bring an artistic element into a Theosophical Congress attended by foreign theosophists, was found extremely shocking by many of the participants. This effort, which took place in 1907 when the biennial Theosophical Congress was scheduled to take place in Munich, is worth considering in some detail, since, at least in part, it was a factor in the later separation of the Anthroposophical Society from the parent organization.

By way of preparation for the Munich Congress Rudolf Steiner gave several art lectures in different German cities late in 1906, culminating in the Berlin Christmas lecture on *Signs and Symbols of the Christmas Festival*, delivered in front of a

---

*The so-called consciousness soul is discussed in several passages in my book *Man and World in the Light of Anthroposophy*, as is also what is here called the age of the consciousness soul. During this period man should develop the wide-awake consciousness of the scientist who looks upon the external world as a kind of outsider, penetrating the world of nature with his intelligence, while at the same time he should strive to develop another kind of knowledge of it through which he will come to recognize the spiritual element that underlies everything material.

Christmas tree decorated according to his specifications. The lecture concluded with the speaking of the meditative verse from the Mysteries to which we have already alluded. During the early months of 1907 it was decided that a play by Schuré should be presented at the Congress. This was, most appropriately, a dramatic presentation of the ancient Greek Mystery Drama that was performed every five years at the close of the Eleusinian Mysteries, as Schuré had pictured it in his imagination. Called simply *The Sacred Drama of Eleusis*, it included the story of Persephone and her failure to obey her mother Demeter, as a consequence of which she was imprisoned by Pluto in the underworld, from which imprisonment she was eventually rescued by Dionysus. Schuré was later to say of this performance that "the truth of what I had instinctively visualized and represented was recognized by Rudolf Steiner, who justified my creation. He recognized the Eleusinian Mystery to be the point of departure for true drama."

Steiner also commented himself on the play later in the following terms: "This drama reaches up into those ages of European cultural development in which the spiritual currents of humanity which confront us separately as science, art, and religion were not yet sundered from one another but were bound intimately together. Through it we find that our feeling reverts in a certain measure to distant ages of European cultural development, to those ages when a unified culture, born directly out of the deepest spiritual life, imbued souls with religious fervor, in the highest degree of attainment possible for the human soul, so that, in this culture, there pulsed directly a religious life. And it may be said that this culture was religion."[37]

It was of the utmost importance for Steiner that the German words of the Schuré drama should be not only appropriate to the content, but should also, as words, carry with them a spiritual element. When he lectured, and even in ordinary conversations, he spoke words in a different manner from that employed by other men. His auditors often spoke of the spiritual quality he imparted to them, even when they could not fully grasp their content. Even those who could not accept

165

his teachings paid tribute to this quality in his speech. So when he wrote his own dramas, or when he revised Marie von Sievers' translation of Schuré's *Sacred Drama of Eleusis*, as he did for this Congress, supplying just those German words that seemed right to him, he regarded it as vitally important that the words themselves should be capable of being declaimed in a certain manner. It was an extraordinary stroke of destiny, if we wish to call it that, that Marie von Sievers at once intuitively perceived Steiner's intentions, and that her own voice was uniquely suited to the kind of speech required to carry them into effect on the stage. As the only trained actress she herself played the part of Demeter, and it fell to her also to train all the willing and enthusiastic amateurs who played the other parts. A few days before his death Steiner was to explain in his autobiography exactly what was here being attempted.

"The 'Word'," he wrote, "is exposed from two directions to the dangers that may arise from the evolution of the consciousness soul. It serves as means of communication in social life, and it serves for imparting what is logically and intellectually known. On both these sides the Word loses its inherent value. It must fit the 'sense' that it has to express. It must allow us to forget that in the tone itself is the sound, in the modelling of sound, a reality exists. The beauty, the shining quality of the vowel, the characteristics of the consonant, are being lost from speech. The vowel becomes soulless, the consonant void of spirit. Thus speech leaves entirely the sphere in which it originates—the sphere of the spiritual. It becomes the servant of the intellectual-cognitional, and the social life, which shuns the spiritual. It is snatched wholly out of the sphere of art.

"True spiritual vision slips, as if wholly by instinct, into the experience of the Word. It learns through intimate feeling to experience the soul-sustained resounding of the vowel and the spirit-empowered painting of the consonant. It attains to an understanding of the mystery of the evolution of speech. This mystery consists in the fact that divine spiritual Beings could once speak to the soul by means of the Word, whereas now the Word serves only to make oneself understood in the physical world.

166

"An enthusiasm kindled by this *insight into the spirit* is required to lead the Word again into its sphere. Marie von Sievers developed this enthusiasm. So her personality brought to the Anthroposophical Movement the possibility of fostering artistically the Word and the modelling in Words. As an addition to the activity of imparting truth from the spirit world, there developed the fostering of the art of recitation and declamation (*Wortgestaltung*), which now became more and more an important part in the programme of events taking place within the Anthroposophical Society."[38] This statement should be recalled when we discuss later in this chapter the beginnings of eurythmy, an art which, in essence, is the outward manifestation of the Word or the musical tone in the movements of the human body, thus distinguishing it completely from any form of dance. Eurythmy is visible speech and visible song.

For weeks before the Congress preparations were being made by Rudolf Steiner, Marie von Sievers, and by the devoted band of helpers who believed wholeheartedly in what was being done, and who knew that they were pioneers in developing a new approach to the artistic—although they could scarcely have foreseen how, under the successors of Steiner, annual summer conferences would be held in Dornach, at which either Goethe's *Faust*, I & II complete, Steiner's own Mystery Dramas, or other works by anthroposophists, would be presented, as they now are, in accordance with Steiner's own ideas as he first expressed them in 1907. The attempt was made by these pioneers to create, under Rudolf Steiner's direction, "a harmonious concordance of color, space, and the spiritual content of the spoken word," as Marie Savitch, Marie von Sievers' biographer, was later to express it. Workshops were created where some members painted and others sculpted, while others prepared for their roles in the Schuré play. When the participants in the Congress arrived they found the Munich concert hall with its walls and windows draped in dark red and seven carved pillars with capitals corresponding to the seven planets. Seven seals painted by two theosophical artists framed the stage on which the drama was to be presented, while busts of

Fichte, Hegel and Schelling, the masters of German idealist thought, occupied a prominent place. The seven seals were adapted from the seven seals perceived and described by St. John in the Apocalpse.

On the subject of these seals Rudolf Steiner in a lecture given later in the same year to a Stuttgart audience (September 16th) commented as follows: "You can see how the whole world presents itself in such seals, and because the magi and initiates have put the whole cosmos into them, they contain a mighty force. You can continually turn back to these seals and you will find that by meditating on them they will disclose infinite wisdom. They can have a mighty influence on the soul because they have been created out of cosmic secrets. Hang them in a room where such things are discussed as we have been doing here, discussions in which one raises oneself to the holy mysteries of the world, and they will prove enlivening and illuminating in the highest degree, although people will often not be aware of their effect. Because they have this significance, however, they are not to be misused or profaned. Strange as it may seem, when these seals are hung around a room in which nothing spiritual, in which only trivial things are spoken, their effect is such that they cause physical illness. . . . Signs of spiritual things belong where spiritual things are enacted, and become effective."[39]

For the drama itself Steiner directed the staging, designed the costumes, and made suggestions to the actors as to how they should stand, move and gesture—all in such a way as to approximate as closely as possible to the Mystery Plays of antiquity, as Steiner himself had perceived them in spiritual vision. There can be no doubt that the effect of the performance was overwhelming, though opinions were decidedly mixed. Annie Besant's comments were carefully neutral, cordial and tolerant but by no means expressing unstinted approval of the "German innovations." Others were more outspoken in their disapproval. In the last chapter of his autobiography Rudolf Steiner wrote, in particular, of the opposition of many of the Dutch Theosophists, as well as members from France and Great Britain, where Annie Besant's

168

influence was strongest. Very few members, Steiner said, grasped the fact that "in the anthroposophical stream someting of an entirely different inner attitude was introduced from that of the Theosophical Society. In this inner attitude lay the true reason why the Anthroposophical Society could no longer exist as a part of the Theosophical Society."

Although this break did not in fact occur for several years yet, Rudolf Steiner and Annie Besant used the occasion of the Congress to discuss several important questions privately. Undoubtedly these conversations cleared the air, but no compromise was made on either side. It was evident to both leaders that the parting of the ways could not be very far off, but neither as yet wished to take the decisive step that would lead to an open rupture. As it happens, a letter is extant dating from exactly the time of the Munich Congress, in which Annie Besant took pains to reassure an old theosophist named Hübbe-Schleiden that there was no fundamental opposition between her and Steiner. This letter reads in full as follows:

31 St. James's Place
London, S.W.
7/6/07

Dear Dr. Hübbe-Schleiden:

Dr. Steiner's occult training is very different from ours. He does not know the eastern way, so cannot, of course, teach it. He teaches the Christian and Rosicrucian way, and this is very helpful to some, but is different from ours. He has his own School, on his own responsibility. I regard him as a very fine teacher on his own lines, and a man of real knowledge. He and I work in thorough friendship and harmony, but along different lines.

Yours ever sincerely
Annie Besant

There is no reason to suppose that Mrs. Besant was anything other than sincere when she wrote this letter, and its content may well represent her personal opinion at the time. Her attitude was to change radically only when she accepted

Charles Leadbeater's advice and decided to put Krishnamurti forward as the reincarnated Christ.

When the next Theosophical Congress took place in the Hungarian capital of Budapest in 1909 Steiner gave a series of fundamental lectures to the theosophists present, but no attempt was made by the organizers to continue the initiative taken by Rudolf Steiner two years earlier. The Budapest Congress therefore resembled all those held before 1907 which had followed the custom of contemporary learned societies. Papers were read, sometimes followed by discussions, but nothing artistic was included. It was the last time that Steiner was to meet Annie Besant personally, and from their private talks it was evident that the task that had brought them together was almost over. This was understood by both of them.

Disappointed though the Munich members were at the neglect of the artistic work by other theosophists, they themselves remained extremely active, under the leadership of Marie von Sievers, who began to recite poems in the new form of speech that had been used publicly for the first time at the Congress of 1907. These poems were recited by her on the occasion of lectures to the Munich group. A workshop was opened in Munich where preparation was made for a new dramatic presentation by those members who were enthusiastic and anxious to continue the artistic impulse. In this venture they had the wholehearted support of Rudolf Steiner himself, who felt that the time had now come when another play by Schuré, translated seven years previously by Marie von Sievers, could be presented to the members. This play was entitled *The Children of Lucifer*, and it had been written by Schuré at a time when he was an active theosophist. The play itself which portrayed a profound relationship between a Christian woman and a man who had been initiated in the East under the Star of Lucifer and had remained uninfluenced by Christianity, shows clearly the influence of Blavatsky's *Secret Doctrine*. But Steiner believed that a performance of this play might provide an opening into Anthroposophy; and immediately after the first performance in Munich on August 22nd,

170

1909 he linked it to Anthroposophy by giving a remarkable cycle of lectures entitled *The East in the Light of the West*, to which he gave the subtitle *The Children of Lucifer and the Brothers of Christ*. In these lectures he showed how greatly Oriental religion and philosophy now stood in need of the impulse that had been given by Christ, in spite of the profundity of Oriental thought itself, which Rudolf Steiner would have been the last to deny.

Later in 1909 Steiner began to introduce his ideas on art to members in other cities. On October 28th he gave a lecture to the Berlin members, in which he presented an imaginative picture of two sisters who are later identified as human Knowledge and Art. Stranded in a frozen waste Knowledge almost died, but her sister Art, who had found sustenance for her soul even in the frozen landscape, nursed her back to life. The lecture is a most beautiful one, and even today it is moving to read, especially when its purpose is taken into consideration—Steiner's desire to impregnate with art all the knowledge he was imparting to the members of the Theosophical Society, who had hitherto been content with the knowledge, and lacked the realization that they needed art also. On May 10th, 1910 Steiner gave another lecture in Berlin, this time to the public, in which he took his audience through the evolution of poetry, from Homer to Shakespeare and Goethe, for the purpose of illustrating man's changing consciousness from clairvoyant perception of the ancient gods to the development of human individuality in modern times. This lecture was a kind of advance commentary on what he was to present in Munich in the four years from 1910 to 1913 as modern Mystery Dramas, linked in spirit to the ancient Mysteries, but concerned with human beings of our own age who are consciously seeking higher knowledge and a new relationship to the spiritual world.

The second and last performance of Schuré's *Children of Lucifer* was given in Munich on August 14th, 1910. The following day Rudolf Steiner's first Mystery Drama, *The Portal of Initiation* was given to the same audience. It was followed by three more Mystery Dramas in 1911, 1912 and 1913, called

171

respectively *The Soul's Probation* (or, as it was called by a recent translator, *The Ordeal of the Soul*), *The Guardian of the Threshold* and *The Soul's Awakening*. Schuré's *Sacred Drama of Eleusis* preceded the Mystery Dramas in 1911 and 1912. In 1913 the third Mystery Drama, *The Guardian of the Threshold* preceded the new fourth play, which was in turn followed by the first performance in public of the new art of eurythmy, for which Steiner had given the indications earlier in the same year.

It is very difficult to do justice in a short space to these four Mystery Dramas which had been maturing in Rudolf Steiner, as he explained later, for more than twenty years, but which were written down over the course of a few weeks just before the actual production of each play, as he squeezed out the time from his killing schedule of lectures. For the first drama conditions were especially difficult. Many of the parts were quite long and had to be memorized by men and women, very few of whom had had any stage training and who were therefore unaccustomed to memorizing lines. The memorizing also had to be done in a minimum of time, especially for the last scenes, which were handed out only a few days before the dress rehearsal. Each morning new passages of the drama were made available to the players, as they were written down by Rudolf Steiner. All the scenery had to be constructed and painted in accordance with Steiner's instructions in combinations of colors selected by him, and there were many scenes requiring different scenery, some of it representing the ordinary earthly world, some representing various parts of the spiritual or elemental worlds, as well as a final scene called The Sun Temple, a hidden Mystery Center at the surface of the earth. Every costume had to be specially designed also and then assembled by the devoted band of helpers; if an unsuitable costume had been worn the entire effect of the scene might well have been spoiled. In short, the mere physical difficulties to be overcome would have daunted a less dedicated group, and it is truly extraordinary that each time a Mystery Drama was staged there were no outstanding defects, and the general impression seems to have been what Steiner intended. Of course there were

172

no strangers to Anthroposophy among the members of the audience, and at all times Steiner insisted that no one who was not an anthroposophist should play any of the parts.

It may be worth noting here that when the Goetheanum was being built the difficulties to be faced were even more formidable. Yet the construction proceeded as planned, and all the amateur artists were able to do their share of the work side by side with the more experienced professionals. The construction of the first Goetheanum, and indeed the performance of the Mystery Dramas, may properly be compared only with the building of the medieval cathedrals when everyone worked harmoniously together under the direction of the leader in whom all had confidence, no one working for pay or for profit, but all trying to bring to realization the ideal they had consciously accepted as their own.

In the first Mystery Drama, *The Portal of Initiation,* there are two scenes which do not belong to the play itself but nevertheless form an integral part of the performance, curious as they may appear to those who are present at the drama for the first time. In these two scenes, usually called the prelude and the interlude, which are in prose, two cultured modern women are presented, whose views on the theatre, and on life in general, are diametrically opposed, though in a conventional sense they are friends. One of the friends, Estella, tries to persuade the other to come to the theatre with her to see a modern naturalistic drama, evidently of a high quality and concerned with a serious subject, as is evidenced by its title *Disinherited in Body and Soul* (or, more simply, *The Uprooted*). Her friend, Sophia, however, has a prior engagement. The Society of which she is a member is staging its own play, for which it has for a long time been preparing. Estella cannot understand how she could prefer to attend a performance by and for amateurs of a play of which she complains that it is couched in an old-fashioned didactic and allegorical style, with characters who are little better than puppets and types, engaging in symbolical events remote from anything that happens in real life, when she could be watching a play which portrays characters who arouse our compassion and active

173

concern. Sophia defends her point of view in a spirited manner, denying the "didactic" nature of the play in which she is to take part. "Our ideas do not *teach*," she insists. "They pour themselves into our being, enkindling and bestowing life. To the ideas which have become accessible to me I owe everything that gives my life meaning." She then proceeds to criticize the naturalistic drama that so entrances her friend, with the remark that what appears to Estella as genuine art is only a "useless criticism of life. No hunger is stilled, no tears are dried, no source of moral degradation is uncovered, when merely the *outer appearance* of hunger, or tear-stained faces, or degraded characters are shown on the stage."

To this Estella replies that she can understand what Sophia is saying, but it only goes to confirm that she prefers to indulge in fantasy rather than face the truths of life. So she departs alone for the theatre. The following day the two friends meet again in an interlude inserted after Scene 7 of the drama. Estella is full of enthusiasm for "the great artistic power with which the playwright had presented not only the outward misfortunes but also the profound soul sufferings of the characters, which had been portrayed with astonishing insight." She then relates the story of the drama which has many close resemblances with the seven scenes of the Mystery Drama just presented, but of course without the scenes from the spiritual worlds that formed an essential part of the latter. Sophia tells her friend that she does indeed appreciate such plays as the one Estella had seen, but nevertheless, like all naturalistic art, she feels there is a basic untruth in it, concluding her criticism with the revealing sentence. "It is distressing to look at an imperfect representation of sense reality when *even the most imperfect rendering of what lies hidden from external observation* may prove to be a revelation." In other words, the Mystery Drama aims higher, however imperfect it presently is; and without the scenes revealing what is taking place in the invisible worlds, there is no real understanding of what is happening to the characters, even in a supposedly realistic play like the one Estella has just seen. To Sophia the story related by Estella is simply empty and indeed meaningless, in spite of the "outward appearance of hunger and the tear stained faces."

174

It might be thought that these two scenes are attempts by Rudolf Steiner to disarm criticism of his drama by showing that he himself was fully aware of what the critics would say of it. After all, he himself had been a drama critic (see Chapter 5) and was well aware of what was expected of playwrights in the early part of the new century. He was also well aware that his Mystery Drama laid itself open to the charge of being "didactic" and "allegorical," charges which would be levelled by all those who are unwilling to accept the reality of spiritual beings. The fact that these beings are invisible to ordinary sight does not make them any the less real. For Steiner, Lucifer and Ahriman, the Spirit of the Elements, the Guardian of the Threshold, were real spiritual beings, not allegorical figures. The soul powers of Maria, one of the two principal characters of the dramas, are pictured sometimes as persons, her friends, sometimes objectively as soul forces, visible to spiritual sight, and inseparable from Maria herself. The Spirit of Johannes' Youth, and his Double, are also portrayed objectively as beings with whom he can hold converse. The main characters who appear in all the four dramas are not to be thought of as wholly exceptional people. They are presented rather as individuals at different stages of spiritual development, who are subjected to definite trials and temptations simply because they are following this path. But the path itself is open to everyone who wishes to tread it, and the spiritual realities portrayed as personages in the dramas also accompany other human beings, whatever their degree of development. These individual characters are in no way unique; and what Rudolf Steiner shows us in the dramas are the spiritual truths behind their external lives. These had to be shown objectively as beings on the stage, and the characters either are able to perceive them consciously if their spiritual development has made this possible, or they are able to experience them only unconsciously.

For anyone watching the dramas these beings and truths are either real, as they were to Steiner, or illusory (even allegorical) as they must appear to the majority of mankind in our present age. Steiner of course knew this, and there was therefore no need to disarm criticism, especially since the first audiences would be made up of members of the Society, most of whom would surely be in sympathy with his aims. The prelude of *The Portal of Initiation* in fact led directly into another modern scene in which almost all the characters appear. They had just attended a lecture given by their leader, and it is shown how each had reacted to it in a different manner. Johannes, the painter—there was also a painter as hero in the play Estella had seen—experiences the discussion following the lectures as a soul-shattering experience, and in the next scene, which actually represents his inner experience while the first scene was taking place, he remains in deep meditation, and his soul experiences are in effect the entire content of the scene. Thus the prelude, the first scene, and the second scene are all bound together by an inner link; but it is also true that Estella's critical remarks in the prelude are representative of the average person's attitude toward the science of spirit, and her comments on Sophia's fellow members within the Society to which she belongs, are quite penetrating. It says much for Steiner's realism and objectivity that he was entirely aware of how he and his followers were regarded by the "outside" world. But it cannot be supposed that he would have begun his first drama with such a prelude if he had not regarded it as artistically and spiritually necessary, leading the spectator by stages from the world of ordinary reality right into the heart of the drama in the soul world, into which Johannes must enter.

Of course the dramas cannot be judged by Estella's standards, nor is it possible to judge any of Steiner's work in the field of art without taking into consideration how the world of spirit was a reality to him, and accepted as such a reality by his pupils and followers, even when they did not have a direct perception of it. And if, indeed, it is a reality it will necessarily follow that all old ideas in every field must be modified or abandoned to take account of it. So there can be no real meeting of minds between Sophia and Estella, whose very name—"away from the Star"—is intended to suggest she is earthbound by contrast with Sophia whose name means "heavenly wisdom." Within the dramas themselves all the ideas are perfectly consistent. It is true, as has often been remarked, that almost all Rudolf Steiner's teachings about man, his successive incarnations, his pre-earthly and post-earthly life, the destiny that he weaves for himself in successive incarnations and his relationships with other human beings—all these appear in the dramas, as do the spiritual beings who aid and hinder man. It has therefore been said that if the Mystery Dramas are fully understood—and possibly there is no one alive who would make this claim!—all Anthroposophy is contained within them, and there would be no need to study either Steiner's books or his lectures. Moreover this comprehension through feeling as well as thinking would be at a far deeper level than could ever be reached simply through study of his written or spoken works.

The Mystery Dramas are not quite like anything that has ever before been created in Western culture, but the resemblance is perhaps closest to the Greek tragedies, which themselves were derived from the Greek Mysteries. The earlier the tragedy the stronger, in some respects, is the resemblance, in spite of the manifest differences. It will be recalled that Aristotle held that the purpose of Greek tragedy was to arouse pity and awe in the spectators, leading to a catharsis of these and similar emotions, that the theme should possess a certain grandeur, and that it should nevertheless be an "imitation of life." The modern spectator who has witnessed all four dramas in succession as they are given at regular intervals at the Goetheanum at Dornach, or who has studied deeply all the four dramas, may well find that his primary emotion at the end is in fact the "awe" referred to by Aristotle, and that he has indeed experienced something resembling a catharsis. It would be difficult to deny that the dramas possess "a certain grandeur," and yet they are very close to real life—as long as one takes into account the reality of the world of spirit as well as the earthly life, and accepts the fact that the world of spirit is peopled by beings concealed from our ordinary earthly senses. It is doubtful indeed whether the same could be said for any other dramas written in recent times, though some of Shakespeare's tragedies may fulfill several of these criteria.

Steiner's dramas, however, are in no sense tragedies and it is not the "tragic" element, in the sense in which we understand the word, that arouses our sense of awe. We are also not inclined to have pity or even compassion for the characters, such as Aristotle believed the spectators in his time ought to have for them. The reason for this is that we are now living in a different age, when we are called upon to *understand*, not to have pity; and we are enabled to understand because we are shown the spiritual realities behind the events in the lives of the characters. It is these spiritual realities that excite our feelings of awe, when we perceive how at every stage of our life spiritual beings are active, and how beset with obstacles is the path of initiation trodden by those who seek higher development.

It is impossible to exaggerate the virtuosity with which Steiner constructed these dramas, especially when it is realized that they were written with an interval of a year between each drama. Yet events throughout the four dramas dovetail in an astonishing manner. For example, the significance of an event in the first drama or of a few words uttered by one character in the second may become apparent only in the fourth. Many events are understood only in the light of a scene in ancient Egypt which occurs in the fourth drama, in which the earlier incarnations of the leading characters are shown. If Steiner had written a fifth drama, as he had intended, and shown a Greek incarnation, it is probable that even more would have been clarified. Indeed, the intricacies of karma can be appreciated only when it is seen how it works in the lives of human beings, and a few specific examples, such as are given in these Mystery Dramas, are certainly far more enlightening than simple explanations, however valuable these too may be.

There appears to be little action in these Mystery Dramas. Almost everything is conveyed through speeches, sometimes of great length, just as in the older Greek tragedies. Yet the characters evolve throughout the thirty years or so covered by the four dramas, unlike the characters in, for example, the tragedies of Aeschylus, who are usually made to suffer more as the result of the deeds of others, or from outside events, than from their own actions. In Steiner's drama, in which we are enabled to see not only the consequences of former earth lives but also the reflections in the spiritual worlds of the deeds now being enacted on the physical plane, to say nothing of the actions of the adverse powers who are trying to turn the characters from their chosen path, we are given so much more than in the Greek tragic dramas. Nevertheless the similarity with the Greek dramas is evident, and the Greek parentage of Steiner's dramas is unmistakable. In short, it is difficult to disagree with Steiner when he gave them the name of Mystery Dramas, and when he linked them, in particular, to the Mystery Dramas of Greece. When, with the drama of Aeschylus, Greek tragedy first emerged from the Mysteries, only gods, demigods, and partly divine human beings were the protagonists. Only by degrees did this drama become "humanized," culminating in the realistic dramas of Euripides, when ordinary men and women occupied the stage, and even the gods themselves were given strongly human characteristics.

It seems evident, therefore, that Steiner did, quite consciously, return to the origin of the drama in the Mysteries, but inaugurated what we may think of as another line of development than that of Greek tragedy from Aeschylus to Euripides. He too presented spiritual beings on the stage, but at the same time he created also characters in more than one dimension, showing them as they were in earlier lives on earth, and as they were evolving or striving toward goals that belong especially to our age. His characters were aware or unaware of the spiritual beings according to their stage of spiritual development. An achievement of this kind could not even have been attempted in the time of Aeschylus because human consciousness had not yet evolved far enough. The five centuries from Aeschylus to the Mystery of Golgotha, and the nineteen and a half centuries since, have wrought changes in human consciousness that cannot be ignored, while the Mystery of Golgotha itself is always present as a determining event throughout Steiner's dramas. It is therefore perhaps understandable that a small group of fervent admirers of Rudolf Steiner and believers in his mission, should have had the necessary enthusiasm to set to work to overcome all obstacles, and should have been able to present for four years in succession a new Mystery drama, and at least one of the earlier ones in addition. Nor that they should have been so seriously dissatisfied with the conventional theatres available for rent in Munich that they determined to build for themselves a new theatre suitable for the staging of these dramas, as will be discussed in the next chapter.

Although it was Rudolf Steiner who wrote the dramas, designed the scenery and costumes, and chose all the colors for the scenery and costumes, the major work of organization fell upon Marie von Sievers, and it was she who trained the actors, all except three of whom had never performed in public before. This work involved training them in the new kind of speech in which she herself was the pioneer, though always in accord with the indications given her by Rudolf Steiner. She also played the part of Maria while the first Johannes was Mieta Waller, a tall, highly gifted woman, a Dutch painter, who, like Marie von Sievers, was exceptionally endowed for the new art of speech, and was able intuitively to grasp at once and follow all that Marie von Sievers was doing, and could then do the same herself. Several other members of the cast seemed almost destined for the parts they played and continued to play in the later dramas. Thus the performances were far more successful and moving than one could have had the right to expect; and especially the new kind of speech, unfamiliar though it was to members of the audience, seemed, according to them, to have been made part of themselves by the actors, and issued spontaneously from them. Even in the quite unsuitable theatres in which they were played, the mood was such that after the performances of the last two dramas the audience melted away in complete silence, pondering on the truths that had been presented to them through the lives and trials of the characters and the spiritual beings, who could not but remain present in their thoughts after having been experienced on the stage.

The new speech used in the dramas was an integral part of the new art that came into being from 1912 onwards. In order to appreciate any art, but particularly the art of eurythmy, the aphorism of Goethe so often quoted by Rudolf Steiner should be taken very seriously and an attempt should be made to grasp its full significance. "Works of art," Goethe declared, "reveal Nature's secret laws, which, without art, would remain forever concealed." Eurythmy may be defined as visible speech and visible song (or tone). But *how* is speech or song made visible, *how* can they be converted from sound to something that the eyes can perceive? The sounds of speech and music can be made visible as *movement*, and this new art of movement is eurythmy. There is nothing arbitrary in this art, but someone with Rudolf Steiner's spiritual perception was necessary to see that the human larynx as instrument for enunciating the Word is not simply converting thought into speech, saying something that can be *understood* by the hearer once the sound has passed through his ears. Speech does, of course, have a *meaning*; it signifies something to the speaker and the hearer. But it does more than this. Simply as spoken word, it affects the hearer, even if he does not *understand* a word that is spoken— as sound affects him, whether it is the brutal sound of a klaxon or a beautiful melody. What Steiner was able to perceive was that when words are uttered through the medium of the larynx, they are not only carried into the air and as air movements are converted into sounds by the human ear, but these air movements can also be made visible through the medium of the entire human body, which thereby becomes an instrument for making the sounds of speech visible. Though the sounds of music do not pass through the larynx, they do pass through the air and can likewise be made visible as movement. Eurythmy is therefore a totally new art, owing nothing to either music or dance. In Goethe's terms, Steiner perceived the "secret law of nature" concealed in the sounds of speech and music, and made it known to those of his pupils who wished to make use of it. In doing this he created the art of eurythmy, at present taught in almost all schools which follow the curriculum and methods of instruction taught by Rudolf Steiner (see Chapter 10 below), as well as being publicly performed in every country where the anthroposophical movement is established. It became at once an integral part of the Mystery Dramas, and a curative branch was later inaugurated, which will be discussed in due course.

Although eurythmy is visible speech and song, it is *also* an art. But it is by no means a simple one, and the eurythmy course given in the schools of eurythmy now established in most Western countries requires four full years of intensive training. It is not simply a question of *translating* musical sounds or the vowels and consonants of a poem into appropriate movements of the arms and hands. Patterns of movement of the single eurythmist on the stage or the often most intricate movements of the ensembles have also to be designed. Thus a special kind of choreography is needed, and not all eurythmists who are otherwise skilled and experienced are equally proficient in this part of their art. Rudolf Steiner created numerous eurythmy forms and used to delight the eurythmists by suddenly presenting them, for example, at a eurythmy rehearsal. Sometimes in the course of a lecture he would give out a new verse for meditation, and then a short time later create a beautiful eurythmy form for it. For the long meditative verse that he gave to the members at the Christmas Foundation meeting in 1923 when the new General Anthroposophical Society was founded (see Chapter 12) he created a uniquely beautiful and meaningful form which was presented for the first time on the stage at Easter, 1924. These forms given by Rudolf Steiner are quite naturally regarded by eurythmists as scarcely capable of being improved upon by themselves, except perhaps in detail in accordance with the number and quality of the eurythmists available and the circumstances of the presentation. Marie Steiner also in the course of her long life created numerous eurythmy forms which are still used as models. So it is clear that there remains still very much for present-day eurythmists to do, and all feel that it is an art that after more than sixty years is still in its childhood and is still far from having realized all its potentialities.

It was an interesting destiny that led a young German girl of eighteen to become the pioneer eurythmist instead of a somewhat older Russian painter who was, without realizing it at the time, given the opportunity. For many years Rudolf Steiner had carried within him the impulse for creating eurythmy, but the need for it had not yet become so apparent as it was later. So when Margarita Woloschin, after hearing a lecture on the Gospel of St. John, was asked by Steiner if she could dance the Prologue to the Gospel, she replied that "one can dance anything that one feels." Steiner was obviously dissatisfied with the answer, for he commented that today "feeling is not the crucial thing." When Margarita said nothing he repeated his comment. But she still had nothing to say, so he gave up for the time. Several months later, after a lecture about rhythm in the cosmos and man, he told her that the rhythms of the dance go back to the very origin of the world, but that today's dances have degenerated from the ancient temple dances. Again Frl. Woloschin had no comments although Steiner, as she related later, "stood expectantly" in front of her. Only later did she realize that he had been giving her the opportunity—the year was 1908—to ask a question. For example, she might have asked how else than through feeling could one find a way to dance the Prologue to the Gospel of St. John, thus giving him the chance to answer that the very words themselves could be expressed in movement, not necessarily in either Greek or German. Or the second time she could have asked what form the dance could take in modern times that would not be degenerate, giving him the chance to reply that the dance, with its degenerate modern rhythms, should now be replaced by a new art of movement which would express directly man's relationship to the cosmos.

But she asked neither question, so that Rudolf Steiner knew that the time was not yet ripe for speaking of the new art. Either it was not mature enough in himself, or the person to whom it would be given had not yet presented herself—or the times were not yet propitious. In fact it was not until the end of 1911 that the right person did appear, and she was six years younger than Margarita Woloschin had been when he spoke to her. At 17 Lory Smits was too young for him to expect that she could answer such questions as he had put to Frl. Woloschin—and indeed he never put them, nor did Lory herself ever ask such a question as he had been hoping for.

Nevertheless destiny did clearly mark her out as the person to receive the impulse.

Lory's parents had been theosophists for many years, and Steiner used to visit them when he went to Düsseldorf. Then the father suddenly died in November 1911, whereupon Steiner sent his widow a telegram of condolence. Having an un- bounded faith in him she paid a visit to him in Berlin to consult him about the future of her eldest daughter Lory, who would have to support herself soon because the death of her father had left the family in straitened circumstances. When he asked Frau Smits what her daughter was planning to do she told him that Lory was interested in either gymnastics or dancing, whereupon Steiner replied that he could teach her "something of the kind," but based on "theosophical foun- dations," as Lory was to tell the story in later years. Frau Smits then asked him a question regarding the possibility of making rhythmic movements which would have the effect of strength- ening the etheric forces. Thus encouraged, Steiner without more ado gave Frau Smits the first exercise for Lory, but neither she nor her mother had at the time any idea where this would lead. In this case, therefore, it was not the asking of a crucial question that led to a new initiative in Anthroposophy so much as a clear opportunity that presented itself just at the right moment.

During the course of 1912 Lory made very great progress in the numerous preliminary exercises that Steiner gave her at the beginning of the year, and it was clear to him that she was indeed specially gifted for the task he had in mind for her. Often she did everything correctly from instinct, but it was also necessary to teach her to do all the movements consciously so that she could later teach others. All this instruction Steiner had to give to her at odd moments when he was in Düsseldorf or wherever Lory and her mother were available to work with him, but the need for eurythmy became specially visible in August 1912 when the third Mystery Drama, *The Guardian of the Threshold* was to be presented in Munich. In this drama Luciferic and Ahrimanic spirits appear on the stage. Rudolf Steiner had to tell the performers how to make movements in keeping with the character of these beings, but this was not at all the same thing as being able to show in eurythmy the forms that belonged to their speech.

It was therefore almost at once after the August performance of *The Guardian of the Threshold* that Rudolf Steiner gave Lory the first indications for the vowels, and followed this up by asking her and her mother to go to Basel, where he was soon to lecture on the Gospel of St. Mark. There, in September, 1912, in a small suburban room with too much furniture, eurythmy was at last brought fully to birth. During the fourth lesson Marie von Sievers was present, and at the last of the Basel lessons she gave the new art its name. Thereafter she undertook most of the organizing of the performances which began a year later, and she was herself the speaker. Meanwhile Lory worked with a few companions, to whom she taught at once what she had learned from Rudolf Steiner. These few young women constituted the first eurythmy troupe.

The first public performance of eurythmy was given at the close of the 1913 annual summer conference held at Munich, at which the two last Mystery Dramas, *The Guardian of the Threshold* and *The Soul's Awakening*, were presented for the last time in Rudolf Steiner's lifetime. With the coming of the War and the necessary scattering of the few trained eurythmists, Marie Steiner, as she became after her marriage to Rudolf Steiner in December, 1914, gathered together those eurythmists who could live in Dornach, where the new "House of the Word," as Rudolf Steiner called it, was being built. Lory Smits could not be there except for brief periods, though she kept up the work in Germany. But others whom she had taught were able to work with Marie Steiner throughout the War; and when the War at last came to an end eurythmy quickly picked up momentum under the direction of Marie Steiner. Rudolf Steiner constantly made new forms and elaborated his earlier indications. In due course curative eurythmy also was born, and in the last year of his life, as will be discussed in a later chapter, he gave two complete courses on Eurythmy as Visible Speech and Eurythmy as Visible Song, which remain the basis today for all eurythmy throughout the world.

185

Chapter 8.

THE FOUNDING OF THE FIRST ANTHROPOSOPHICAL SOCIETY AND THE BUILDING OF THE FIRST GOETHEANUM

The two events to which this chapter is to be devoted are closely linked. The artistic impulse described in the last chapter, and especially the presentation of the four Mystery Dramas, made the members vividly aware of the need for them to possess a theatre of their own where the dramas could be worthily staged; while the growing divergence of views between the German Section and the central leadership of the Theosophical Society in Adyar, India, made it increasingly clear that those members who chose to follow Rudolf Steiner would soon either be forced, with him, out of the Theosophical Society, or would have to secede from it. If therefore there was to be a new society separate from the Theosophical Society, what more natural than that it should have a center of its own, or even a community centered around a new assembly hall, in which lectures could be given and where artistic performances could be presented?

As we have seen in Chapter 6, the separation of the German Section from the rest of the Theosophical Society appears now to have been inevitable, and it could have been predicted from at least as early as 1907. But members of the Section, including Rudolf Steiner himself, were by no means resigned to the inevitable at such an early date, and it seemed to them that the two branches of the movement could easily have continued to share a common roof, if the principle of tolerance subscribed to by all members of the Theosophical Society had continued to be observed. It was the decision of Annie Besant to support the establishment of the Order of The Star of the East, with the express purpose of welcoming the reincarnation of Christ in the person of a Hindu youth called Krishnamurti, that precipitated the separation, since it was quite impossible for Steiner to do anything but oppose such a plan. But even so, he was unwilling to take the initiative of separating from the Theosophical Society, contenting himself with expressing his opposition to the Krishnamurti venture, and in other respects continuing to cooperate with Adyar. It is interesting to note that Adyar also was still anxious not to break off relations altogether, since it awarded Steiner a prize for the best book on Theosophy to appear during the year. This was *Knowledge of the Higher Worlds: How is it Attained?*, published in book form in 1909. At the Budapest Theosophical Congress held in May, 1909, all was still outwardly friendly and tolerant, and Rudolf Steiner had several meetings with Annie Besant. But later in the same year she finally decided to throw her support to Charles Leadbeater, who had been guarding the young Alcyone, later to be called Krishnamurti, and had been anxious to proclaim him as the reincarnated Christ. The Order of the Star of the East, however, did not begin its official existence until January 11, 1911. A British chapter of the Order was founded in May of the same year.

Now began in earnest the intrigues against Rudolf Steiner within his own Section. As we have seen in Chapter 6, Steiner was always vulnerable to attacks from traditional theosophists because of his insistence on the unique position of the Christ in world evolution, and there was always domestic opposition to his leadership of the German Section because of the very slight attention he gave to the work of other theosophists, including even H.P. Blavatsky. Nevertheless, even among loyal followers of Annie Besant who were willing to follow her leadership in the establishment of the Star of the East there were still some who held fast to the official position taken by the Theosophical Society that every Section was entitled to full

187

autonomy. So frontal attacks on Steiner as leader of the German Section never became the proclaimed policy of the Society, though he did continue to be criticized because he was willing to accept so many foreign theosophists into his Section. Such a willingness was held to be disloyal to the Society as a whole, since ordinarily new members became part of their own national Section. It must certainly have appeared to the Society leaders in Adyar that Steiner was making a bid for leadership of the whole Society when he encouraged membership in his Section by foreign nationals who had wished to join the German Section solely because of his own teachings, which were so often at variance with those of other well known and respected theosophists.

Although he was not attacked officially, even in Germany, indirect attacks increased in number and virulence after the founding of the Star of the East. Steiner was accused of being a Jesuit, or at the very least of having been educated by them, whereupon he included in a lecture cycle given in 1911 (*From Jesus to Christ*) a long passage in which he criticized the Jesuits for their attachment to Jesus and consequent neglect of the Christ. In the same cycle he criticized the *Spiritual Exercises* of Ignatius Loyola the founder of the Jesuit Order, on the ground that they were unsuitable for the present time and led to serious aberrations. Steiner was also accused by theosophists of having intrigued in such a way that the Theosophical Congress of 1911, scheduled to have been held in Genoa, had to be cancelled—though it seems evident that it was Annie Besant herself who instigated the moves that led to the cancellation.

Whether or not it was her intention to drive Rudolf Steiner out of the Theosophical Society, her actions and those of her followers certainly had this effect. It was never at any time Steiner's policy to reply publicly to attacks on him. His policy was rather to take up any points that had been made by the opposition, and refute them, without ever counterattacking. In this difficult period from early 1911 to the exclusion of the German Section from the Theosophical Society in January 1913 he scrupulously observed this policy, although Mrs.

Besant was continually trying to blame him for the impending split. In a letter sent to Lady Lutyens, the president of the British chapter of the Star of the East, later published in Lady Lutyens' autobiographical account of her experiences in the Order, Mrs. Besant wrote: "There is a hail of attack on me from Germany by Dr. Rudolf Steiner and his followers. They are evidently playing for separation and want to throw the blame on me." This letter was dated May 10, 1912, by which time the split was certainly inevitable, but it was more than a little disingenuous to throw the blame for the split on the victim of her own attacks, and attacks by her followers.

By the beginning of 1912 Steiner was fully aware that there would have to be a separation, but he was still averse to making the decision himself, preferring to let destiny decide when the time was ripe. The right moment arrived following the performance of *The Guardian of the Threshold* at Munich in August, 1912, a performance attended by numerous members of other Sections as well as by foreign members of the German Section. Instead of dispersing to their homes, a large number of members met together for a week at the beginning of September, and decided that they wished to form another Society entirely distinct from the Theosophical Society. They then asked Rudolf Steiner if he was in agreement with their decision, and if so, if he would give the new Society a name. Steiner gave his agreement and proposed the name of the Anthroposophical Society, a name which was of course accepted. In December of the same year the executive of the German Section, which did not include Rudolf Steiner himself, decided that membership of the Star of the East was incompatible with membership in the Section led by Rudolf Steiner, and called upon all members to choose. With few exceptions all chose to abandon their membership in the Star of the East, thus virtually cutting themselves off from the leadership of the Theosophical Society based at Adyar. The same executive then sent a telegram to Annie Besant at Adyar, calling upon her to resign as president, to which she replied by cancelling the charter of the German Section, thereby automatically withdrawing recognition of Rudolf Steiner as its

General Secretary. The regular annual meeting of the Section nevertheless took place on schedule in January, 1913, but Steiner informed the members present that it could no longer hold a legal annual meeting, whereupon they constituted themselves the Anthroposophical Society. A month later the new Society held its own annual meeting. All those who preferred to continue as members of the Theosophical Society were free to do so, in which case they would not be members of the new Anthroposophical Society. All the property of the former German Section was legally transferred to the new body, to which Rudolf Steiner did not belong. He was granted the title of Honorary President of the Anthroposophical Society, but never became a member of it, preferring to stay on as teacher and guide.

The relative ease with which the old German Section was converted into a new independent Society demonstrates clearly that the time was indeed ripe for the change, and remarkably few members were lost during the transition. From very small beginnings in 1902 the membership of the Section had grown steadily but not spectacularly, until at the beginning of 1913 it stood at a little over 2500. Among these members there was a small core of very active and enterprising members, who had not only long ago recognized the need for an independent Society, but were very anxious to give it a physical home on earth, especially a building in which the Mystery Dramas could be performed in a worthy setting. Indeed, some of this small core of members were themselves amateur performers in the dramas, even though they were as a rule also fully occupied in their own professions.

The Bavarian capital of Munich, already the most important art center in Germany, where the Mystery Dramas were staged, was naturally regarded as the most suitable city by the Munich members, but Anthroposophy was at least as strong in two other major German cities, Stuttgart and the capital of the German Empire, Berlin. Weimar also was proposed by one influential member. At this time there were more than fifty theosophical groups attached to the German Section. Stuttgart seems to have boasted the largest number of members, and it was there that the first building entirely devoted to theosophical/anthroposophical activities was acquired and opened formally by Rudolf Steiner in October, 1911. But unlike Munich, Stuttgart was not an important art center, and so was not taken quite as seriously as Munich as the possible site for the new theatre where the Mystery Dramas would be performed.

Immediately after the presentation of the first Mystery Drama in Munich in 1910, many members recognized that a theatre of their own would soon become a necessity. The question was therefore raised at the annual meeting of the German Section held the following October. Rudolf Steiner did not as yet favor the project, in part on the grounds that the German Section was not a suitable legal entity for the acquiring of property. However, the proponents of the project did not give up, and after the second drama had been performed the following year opinion was much more favorable. Already tentative plans had been made, money had been contributed, and in September, 1911 the legal position was clarified by the founding of a company with the purpose of bringing the building plans to realization. A piece of property was acquired in Munich, and all other possible sites were abandoned. Architectural plans were drawn up, and Rudolf Steiner himself designed the central building for the project. The plans were then submitted to the municipal authorities for approval, and the authorities asked a number of artists and architects for their opinion before making their decision.

Such, then, was the situation at the beginning of September, 1912. The decision of the Munich authorities was expected any time; much money had been collected and enthusiasm generated. The last steps leading to the separation of the German Section from the Theosophical Society had been taken, and Rudolf Steiner had proposed the name of the new Society that would soon come into existence. The first three Mystery Dramas had just been performed, preceded, for the last time, by the *Sacred Drama of Eleusis* by Edouard Schuré. Never had enthusiasm been higher when Rudolf Steiner undertook the lecture tour that took him to Basel for the cycle he was to give on the Gospel of St. Mark. The moment had also arrived, as we have seen, for the beginning of eurythmy, and Steiner gave Lory Smits her first lessons during the intervals between the St. Mark lectures in Basel. Also during this cycle Steiner was invited by Dr. Grossheintz, an enthusiastic member of the Section, to visit a property he and his wife and a friend had acquired not far from Basel which they wished to be used for some anthroposophical purpose. It was thus that Rudolf Steiner and Marie von Sievers for the first time saw the hill at Dornach, where now stands the second Goetheanum.

After Steiner's death his widow described how she and Rudolf Steiner visited the Grossheintz in their own home, and how delighted she had been with the area with its cherry trees and its vineyards in the bright autumn coloring, expecting the same enthusiasm from Steiner. But the morning after their arrival his mood was inexplicably gloomy, and for once this unaccustomed mood did not quickly disappear. As a rule he could change his moods almost in the twinkling of an eye, so controlled was his life of feeling. In time the mood gave place to one of pleasure and delight which he was able to share with Frl. von Sievers. But she always believed that he had experienced what in other people would have been a simple foreboding, but with him was a definite experience of what was to happen later on this very site when the irreplaceable first Goetheanum, on which so much love, labor, and treasure had been expended was burned to the ground in a single night. If Steiner had indeed known in advance the fate of the building which undoubtedly hastened his own premature end, one may legitimately ask the question, could he not have taken some action to forestall it?

According to the laws of the spiritual world, as others as well as Steiner have explained them, no initiate may ever take any action in the personal realm, least of all an action from which he may draw profit, as the result of such a vision. Everything hitherto planned must be carried out exactly as if there had been no prevision. It can scarcely be doubted, as will be discussed later, that Rudolf Steiner foresaw the Great War, and even knew a long time in advance exactly when it would break

192

out. Yet he and Marie von Sievers and a group of friends paid a visit to Bayreuth to see *Parsifal* just before the War, and only by remarkably good luck was the whole party able to return to Switzerland without trouble at the frontier. Steiner also must have known that a fifth Mystery Drama scheduled for 1914 would never be presented. Yet the theatre had been booked for it as soon as it was known that the building in Dornach could not possibly be ready in time.

Frau Grossheintz in a memoir published some years later was to describe how to everyone's surprise Rudolf Steiner stayed on in Dornach for some time after he had first seen the site and examined the entire area, including even the underground grottos to be found in the neighborhood of Arlesheim. Then he went to see the Grossheintz in Basel and asked them what they proposed to do with the land they had acquired. When they expressed some uncertainty Steiner began to talk about the possibility of a "Bayreuth," and told his hosts of the difficulties being experienced in Munich as a result of the attitude of the municipal authorities. Dr. Grossheintz then told him that no building regulations were in force at Dornach, and offered him the land if he wanted it. Thus when the Munich authorities finally gave the verdict against the building as it had been proposed, an alternative was available and it seems certain that Rudolf Steiner had already made his own decision and he knew that the Dornach hill would be the site chosen.

Much pressure had been put on the municipal authorities in Munich to persuade them to refuse the permit. Neither theosophists, nor anthroposophists, as they were just beginning to be called, were regarded very highly by representatives of Munich culture, nor were either the Catholic or Protestant Churches at all favorably disposed toward them. When anything was known about them at all, they were supposed to be opponents of orthodox religion, or even regarded as a new sect. An important Protestant church was close to the site they had bought, and the pastor did not fancy them as his neighbors. The artists whose opinion had been sought, as well as others who wished their opinion to be taken into account were almost all against the project as it had been presented. Even though

193

the plan was not too unconventional, and had been designed to fit in with its surroundings, it was still not in full harmony with them, including as it did, a building whose external architectural form was relatively conventional, but an interior which would have been in accordance with Steiner's own architectural ideas. The building would not have been visible from a distance since it would have been surrounded by dwelling houses and workshops. Nevertheless in an art- conscious city like Munich, which had been built up as an art center by its nineteenth century monarchs, permission could certainly not be taken for granted, and it was not too much of a surprise when in February, 1913, it was finally refused by the municipality on the ground that it did not fit in with its surroundings.

The news of the refusal was conveyed to Rudolf Steiner at a moment when he was engaged in a lecture tour, and Frau Grossheintz happened to be present. The architect who brought the news proposed to appeal the decision, and Rudolf Steiner did not prevent him, though he believed it was a waste of time. He therefore turned at once to Frau Grossheintz, and told her that he was now ready to accept her offer and build at Dornach. The decision of the Munich authorities, however much it was resented by the anthroposophists at the time, must surely in the light of what has happened since be regarded as most providential. Unending complications would surely have resulted from Germany's involvement in the war. The building could never have been completed by August, 1914, and only German and Austrian nationals could have worked on it thereafter. In the postwar world, especially in the city which saw Hitler's Beer Hall Putsch in 1923, the building might have survived for an even shorter time than did the first Goetheanum in Dornach. Lastly, in Munich the Johannes-Bau, as it was then called, could never have become the international center that the Goetheanum in Dornach became, built as it was by citizens of so many different nations, while the War was raging abroad.

In May, 1913 Steiner again visited the site in Dornach, and within the space of a few minutes he had drawn up in his mind

194

the entire plan for the development of the area, including the main building, the subsidiary buildings as he envisaged them and the connecting roads. It was at once clear to him that on a hill which dominated the entire area, with the city of Basel lying below him in the distance, a hill from which France and Germany as well as Switzerland could be seen, the external architecture must now be given far more importance than had been intended at Munich, since it could now be seen from every direction. Here there would be no question of permission being refused for the building since, as Dr. Grossheintz had already advised him, the cantonal authorities did not control building in the countryside and the site was far from any city.

The disappointment of the German members is understandable, but most of them gave the new project their loyal support, especially since there was at first no intention of making Dornach the main center for anthroposophical activity. Rudolf Steiner at once began to make two models for the building, and these were completed in January, 1914. Meanwhile the fourth Mystery Drama, *The Souls' Awakening*, had been performed for the first time at the summer festival at Munich, and a few days later the first eurythmy performance was given. Amid the enthusiasm engendered by these events, and after considerable sums of money had been collected or pledged, Rudolf Steiner on September 20th, 1913 went to Dornach for the solemn festival of the Laying of the Foundation Stone for the new building, not yet named the Goetheanum.

It is impossible here to do more than give a faint idea of the words spoken by Rudolf Steiner, as the Foundation Stone, composed of a double pentagonal dodecahedron, made of copper and soldered together on one side, was placed in the earth. This "stone," to use Rudolf Steiner's words, represented "the striving human soul immersed as a microcosm in the macrocosm," and the address was rendered even more solemn because the very elements seemed to conspire against this human effort in the year preceding the outbreak of war to achieve something truly spiritual by constructing this unique building. Since only three days advance notice could be given only about forty persons could be present and braved the equinoctial storm that broke on them after sunset on that evening of 20th September, 1913, just as the ceremony was beginning. Torrents of rain fell, and a gale howled around them as Rudolf Steiner's powerful voice sounded out above the noise of the elements. The night had fallen prematurely, but the few members present snatched vine stakes that had been piled nearby and lighted them. These improvised torches provided all the illumination for the ceremony, as Rudolf Steiner called upon the hierarchies to help and protect the undertaking. Then he spoke of the increasing power and malignity of "dark Ahriman clouding vision, who means to spread the darkness of chaos over fully awakened spiritual sight," and how the human soul, symbolized in the Foundation Stone, must find the strength, in spite of the fear of the spirit induced in mankind by Ahriman, to undertake its spiritual task.

As he brought his address to an end he twice entoned, for the first time, the ancient prayer that had once echoed in the soul of the young Jesus when in his early manhood he witnessed the celebration of an ancient Mystery rite long fallen into decadence. This prayer, which Steiner was soon afterwards to incorporate into his lectures on the Fifth Gospel, alluded to in Chapter 6, included as its essential element the recognition of man's falling away from the Divine at the beginning of human evolution. It was at that moment that Jesus of Nazareth for the first time himself experienced the Fall of Man, and the experience had a profound effect on him. But, not having as yet received the Christ into himself as was to happen later at the Baptism in the Jordan, he had to bear within himself all the sorrow that resulted for man from the Fall. Only the Christ could give man the possibility of returning to the heights from which he had fallen, and, according to Steiner, the Lord's Prayer, as given to mankind by the Christ, was in fact the metamorphosis of this ancient prayer. Steiner who conceived it to be his own task to bring to man that true knowledge of the Christ without which there could be no ascent, believed that through this ancient prayer men, or at least some men, could as a first step come to a full recognition of the darkness in which they were enwrapped, and it was for this reason that he gave it to them after he himself had experienced it in 1913. Sounding out on that hill in the torchlight amid the raging elements the ceremony and address must have been almost unbearably impressive, necessarily more so than the explanation given by Steiner a couple of days later to the members assembled in Basel. There he described the circumstances in which the ceremony had taken place, but emphasized with the utmost conviction the necessity to carry the enterprise through to completion, as part of the 'mission of the earth itself.' In so doing he warned that there would be every kind of opposition, saying that the "stone, which for us is a symbol of knowledge, love, and strong courage, will of necessity be for our enemies a stumbling-block and will arouse their anger. We are only at the beginning of our difficulties . . . but let us go forward with a firm confidence in the ultimate victory of the spirit."[40]

The Foundation Stone, having been cemented in, is still there in the earth under the second Goetheanum, though after the fire, at the re-founding of the Anthroposophical Society at Christmas, 1923, Steiner gave another "Foundation-Stone" in the form of a uniquely powerful meditation, which will be discussed in a later chapter.

An address of the kind given by Steiner in 1913 at the Laying of the Foundation Stone, could be given only because of the *kind* of building that was now envisaged, no longer just a theatre or assembly hall in which the Mystery Dramas would be presented, and where other anthroposophical activities take place. An entirely new kind of building had been designed by Rudolf Steiner, truly unlike anything that has ever been erected either before or since, a building that can properly be described as "organic," made up of forms that appear to be living because they were created in the same way that nature creates, using the apparently dead substances of earth to create the living. An extraordinary sentence of Steiner's given in a lecture on the Goetheanum bears thinking about for a long time, whether one agrees with it or not. At all events it does describe what Steiner believed himself to be doing. "If one is able," he said, "to realize how the human body on the one hand is an instrument for thinking and on the other for willing and that both these faculties are held together by the power of feeling; if one understands the whole human structure, the formation of the head, limbs and trunk, with the heart system as center, then *one is able to construct organic forms oneself also.* The Goetheanum is such an organic form."[41]

It has already been noted that Rudolf Steiner first made models of the interior and exterior of the building as he conceived it. It seems certain that it was in this work of modelling that he experienced just how the spiritual could be incorporated into matter, and it was these models that had to be used by the architects with whom he worked, presenting them with numerous problems, some of which appeared at first to be insoluble. Nevertheless, in the end all were solved, in part because of Steiner's insistence that a solution must be possible. Though neither an architect nor an engineer, he had, as we have seen, studied geometry intensively in his youth, and he had a good working knowledge of other branches of mathematics. But it was not as an amateur architect, still less as an engineer, that he won the esteem of so many contemporary and subsequent architects, including, in our own day, some talented Japanese, who are now beginning to use in their own buildings ideas that are taken from both the Goetheanums, and who are even giving lectures in their schools on the work of Steiner the architect! His *designs* for both the first and second Goetheanums, and the models that he made for them, constitute his real claim to fame in this domain, and without the ideas for the buildings that he drew from the spiritual worlds neither building would have come into existence.

The major problem in the construction of the First Goetheanum was how to construct two intersecting domes of different dimensions, one of which was larger than the dome of St. Peter's, Rome, and still have a structurally sound building. The incomplete domes could not be supported, like complete domes, with hidden chains, as were the domes of the cathedral of Florence and St. Peter's in Rome, or with complete "tension rings," such as are used to support modern domes. If tension rings are cut into, they can no longer support the domes, which will necessarily splay. Steiner's architects could not

198

themselves solve the problem which, as Steiner expressed it, was to "construct both domes in one." Indeed the principal architect said the problem was insoluble. Nevertheless they suggested that Steiner take the problem to the leading firm of engineers in Switzerland which happened to be in Basel. Nothing loath, he took his plans to the firm himself, and was sent to discuss his problem with a young Norwegian engineer employed by it. This young genius did indeed solve the problem, not by "constructing both domes in one," as Steiner had suggested, but by designing two structural bands, which thus constituted in effect one single *overall* tension-ring embracing both domes, with two lateral wings going outwards from the domes to give extra support to the bands, in a manner not unlike the use of flying buttresses used by Gothic architects to support the pointed arches of their cathedrals. Without Steiner's persistence and belief that the problem was soluble, it might never had been solved at all. Left to themselves, even the gifted architects who worked on the Goetheanum might have felt themselves compelled to settle for a different design.

It is, of course, possible to study the First Goetheanum now only through photographs and more or less subjective descriptions, as written down by those who knew it personally. It is also possible to study Steiner's intentions when he designed it, in so far as he explained them. To understand these intentions, however, at least a working knowledge of the main principles of Anthroposophy is necessary, and the remarks that follow should not be regarded as an attempt to provide an adequate explanation. They constitute only an introduction to the subject, which could be fleshed out by any student who wishes to undertake for himself the necessary detailed study.

It will be readily appreciated that the members who had been present at the Munich performance of the Mystery Dramas felt very deeply the appalling inadequacies of the theatres in which they had been presented, and large numbers of them were ready to contribute money so that a better one could be built and that Anthroposophy could have a real earthly home. Steiner sympathized with this feeling and shared it. But if he had been merely ready to support the fund-raising and take charge of the project, the next step would have been to call in professional architects and have them design a multi-purpose building and subsidiary buildings as needed, so that full advantage could be taken of the magnificent site. But Steiner did not do this, nor did he even contemplate doing such a thing. For him it was of the utmost importance that the new building should be suitable for the age of the consciousness soul, as virtually no buildings were in 1913. There could be no question of imitating Greek or Roman architecture or any other of the favored contemporary styles.

However, this was by no means all. The architecture of the new building must, in his opinion, be an earthly expression of the science of spirit, since everything in it would be done in accordance with its teachings. Everything in the building, its exterior as well as its interior, must be in conformity with the laws of the spirit, the "hidden laws," in Goethe's phrase, that he as an artist must discover, and bring to realization on earth. The form he chose for the building was not the only one possible. It was one of the many possible forms that would be in conformity with these spiritual laws. The second Goetheanum, which was quite different from the First—extraordinarily different, considering the same "architect" was responsible for both—was another such form; and if Steiner had lived to see the Second through to completion it would doubtless have been in conformity in all its parts with spiritual laws, as the first one was, which was supervised in its entirety by him.

We have said that Steiner thought of the Goetheanum as an "organic," that is to say, living form. Now obviously no building can be actually *alive*, as a plant or animal is alive. But both plant and animals, as well, of course, as man, are moulded, as far as their physical body is concerned, by etheric, form-building invisible *forces*. A stag, for example, or an autumn crocus, do not possess their particular forms by pure chance. They are as they are because forces invisible to human sight have moulded them. A stag without antlers would be no true stag, nor would an autumn crocus be truly itself it it did not secrete certain forces within itself that make it poisonous. Or, to use Steiner's own example, the kernel of a particular nut requires

200

that its shell shall be exactly what it is. A walnut shell could not house a hazel nut or a peanut. It must therefore follow that the science of spirit, being living thought, and not a series of arbitrarily chosen concepts, must have as its earthly dwelling place a building that was not only in conformity with this living thought, but was organically related to it. *In addition* the building must naturally be in accordance with its purpose, namely to provide a thoroughly suitable setting for the presentation of the Mystery Dramas, eurythmy, and such lectures, concerts and other anthroposophical activities as would be desired. This aspect was usually stressed, especially when Steiner was addressing the general public, which could scarcely be expected to understand the true esoteric reason why he designed the building as he did.

For example, in a public lecture given in Liestal, near Basel, on January 11, 1916, he told his audience that "we have striven to make the whole building the right framework for what is to be carried on within it," though he also said that "it is intended to be nothing else but an artistic putting into form of that which is aroused in our perceptions and feelings when we have received into our souls the living essence of spiritual science or Anthroposophy . . . It is a matter of course that it is necessary to live quite in the current of spiritual science in order to understand its art, just as it is necessary to be in the midst of Christianity in order to understand the Sistine Madonna." On other occasions Steiner often used to point out how the Greek temples were designed in order to provide an earthly resting place, when the god to whom it was dedicated wished to descend into it, whereas the Gothic churches expressed the human soul's aspiration toward a transcendent God. For this reason the Greek temple was kept empty, while the Gothic church was only truly itself when it was filled with a congregation singing praises to God. Both required a particular kind of consciousness, which was the consciousness of their age. So also Steiner intended that the Goetheanum should be something altogether new, and suited for the consciousness of the twentieth, and perhaps the twenty-first centuries.

The building that Steiner planned might well not be in

accord with the taste of the members who had asked for it, and indeed many of them might never become accustomed to it, any more than the non-members who lived in the vicinity of Dornach. But the members, at least, possessed an unlimited confidence in him, and as the building began to take shape on its wonderful site most of them grew truly enthusiastic. A considerable number of them found it possible to work on it themselves, as we shall see, and the full cost of construction was met by contributions, with no debt having to be incurred. Nevertheless, it was the unconventional nature of the building that drew so much attention to it, and to some extent to Rudolf Steiner himself. It is, indeed, quite possible that if a conventional building had been constructed simply as a functionally satisfying headquarters for the Anthroposophical Society, its enemies would never have troubled to set fire to it.

Since it would obviously take us too far to attempt any adequate description of the Goetheanum, we shall confine ourselves here to mentioning a few of its more important features. From a distance, as an English architect expressed it, the two domes of unequal size resting on their concrete base gave a "gentle and serene aspect" to the whole area, as distinct from the "rugged defiance" of the present Goetheanum which replaced it after the fire. The wooden domes were roofed with a special slate from Norway that had caught Rudolf Steiner's attention during a visit to that country. This "Vossian" slate was chosen by him because of its unusual capacity for reflecting the light of the Jura landscape. Beneath the domes was the auditorium with seating space for about a thousand persons, and the stage. As might have been expected it was in the interior that the organic nature of the building was most apparent. For example, the seven pillars on each side of the auditorium, each made from a **different wood**—hornbeam, ash, cherry, oak, elm, maple and birch—had carved capitals, which subtly changed from one pillar to the next, from the simple to the complex and then back again to the simple, though this last simple was quite different from the first. This process had been described by Goethe in his book on the metamorphosis of plants. Indeed, it had been his own discovery, the only one for which he is usually given credit by scientists, that plants do grow through a process of metamorphosis, and all the forms of a plant are in fact metamorphoses of the leaf. Steiner did not, of course, take Goethe's idea of the metamorphosis of plants and then apply it to his capitals. But the plants described by Goethe and Steiner's capitals were both organic forms, following the same principle of metamorphosis. The principle was, indeed, used throughout the First Goetheanum, but more sparingly in the Second because the material was unsuited for it. Steiner had, indeed, chosen wood as the material for the First Goetheanum because more than any other material its form, as he expressed it, could be revealed from within. Form did not have to be imposed on it from without, as is necessary when a mineral substance is carved, even one like marble, which was alive in the not so distant past.

It should be noted that in the entire building there was nothing that could be called symbolic, although critics have often asserted that, for example, the capitals were symbolic. Modern symbolism is, as a rule, a product of modern intellectualism; the symbols are *thought out*. This was not true of the Goetheanum. The forms taken by the capitals were the result of Steiner's perception of metamorphosis. Figures that were painted in the cupolas were likewise not symbolic, but real to spiritual sight, as was true also of those beings, half animal, half human, that were actually clairvoyantly perceived by the ancient Egyptians and portrayed by them in their art. Everything in the Goetheanum was *itself*, and not symbolic of anything else. Even Ahriman, as pictured in the smaller cupola, was not a *symbol* of evil, but an evil *being* who, according to Steiner really exists in the supersensible world.

The Goetheanum windows were made of a translucent glass made in sheets by Baccarat, and they were engraved by a process that was known before, but had never previously been used for this purpose. The engraving, as adapted for the Goetheanum by Steiner, made it possible for the light from outside to illuminate the engraved picture, and indeed flood the auditorium with colored light. The engravings were

203

made by a number of artists who worked from some rudimentary sketches made by Steiner, and in a building that still exists today (the glass-house) designed by him. However, he himself was never satisfied fully with these windows. Another artist, Assya Turgenieff, who had worked as a painter and woodcarver in the Goetheanum, was interested in the windows once they were in place, to such an extent that she asked permission from Rudolf Steiner to reproduce one of them in an engraving of her own. Encouraged by him to engrave them all, she first prepared sketches, which she showed to him, whereupon he corrected and simplified them, as well as writing inscriptions for them. It is these sketches that were used to make the much improved windows in the Second Goetheanum, which are the unaided work of Assya Turgenieff, who spent several years in perfecting them.

The cupolas were also painted in accordance with designs made by Steiner. These designs were so unusual, representing spiritual realities, as they did, that few of the artists working on them were able completely to understand his intentions, nor were any of them accustomed to working in the medium used; also their ideas on color, especially those of the professionals, were quite different from those of Rudolf Steiner. One result of their inexperience was that much of the small cupola was in the end painted by Steiner himself, although he did not pretend to be a painter. According to the testimony of those who worked with him, he was, even in this field, a master-teacher, and they learned much from him; and he used to make suggestions in such a way that they knew at once that he had unerringly pointed to what was wrong in their own work, and how it could be changed to produce the effect he desired. Only Steiner, after all, had a complete picture in his imagination of how the finished cupola should look. Margarita Woloschin, who worked on the painting with him for several years, tells of how she discovered that her painting of an angel would impinge on the painting of a fellow-worker, who was working next to her. When she pointed this out to him, Rudolf Steiner told her that it was of no importance. "In the spiritual world things do not stand side by side; they interpenetrate each other.

In painting the forms can interweave." Any scholastic philosopher could have told her that!

For Steiner the coloring was of very great importance, and indeed he devoted many lectures from this time onward to his new theories on color which were brought to expression in the Goetheanum. From his youth he had been interested in Goethe's theory of color, how color arises when light mingles with darkness, how each color gives rise to definite moral perceptions, the active and passive nature of colors. Steiner, however, took the theory much further, speaking of "lustre" and "image" colors, and enlarging on Goethe's perceptions of the moods of the various colors. His theory and practice were at variance with every recognized school of painting in his day. He detested the linear perspective that was the great discovery of the age of the consciousness soul; like the British painter Turner in his last years, he developed a color perspective. But for the kind of painting he wanted, a new technique was necessary. Only with water-colors were his effects possible; and these water-colors were best obtained directly from plants. Such paints derived from plants have a luminosity entirely missing from mineral paints. So there was nothing for it but to start making paints from plants according to Rudolf Steiner's directions, and a group of helpers occupied themselves with this work throughout the building and decorating of the Goetheanum. Colors are still produced by Steiner's methods in Dornach, and have found a ready market. They are sold under the trade name of Anthea.

It is best to explain in Steiner's own words how he looked upon the world of color. The explanation which follows was given by him in 1921 in a lecture at Berne illustrated by slides of the Goetheanum, including the engravings in the windows and the paintings on the cupola. "We have tried," he said, "to realize in a certain degree . . . that form must arise out of the interplay of colors; that is to say, that one must really rouse oneself to experience the world of color for itself. If you contemplate the color world, you will see that it is really a sort of totality, a world in itself; and if you in a living way feel yourself in the color-world, then, I might say, red, blue and yellow, speak to one another. You find something fully alive inside the color world, and at the same time get to know the world of color as a world of being. At this point drawing ceases, and you feel that drawing is something ultimately untrue. What is, after all, the line of the horizon? If I draw it with a pencil, I am really drawing an untruth. Below is the green expanse of the sea, above is the blue expanse of the vault of heaven, and when I put on some color, then form results—the line as boundary of the color.

"And so out of color we can create really everything we want put on canvas. We must not be deluded because there are motifs, all kinds of figures, even cultural-historical figures there. In painting the small cupola I did not try to draw this or that motif on the wall; what I was aiming at was, for example, that here there should be some orange of different shades; out of these shades of color resulted the form of a child. And here I thought that blue should border it; there resulted the figure you will see in a minute. Throughout, the form, the essential, is brought entirely out of color. Here then, there is a flying child in shades of orange; here would be the division between the large and the small cupolas, and this is the first painting in the small cupola. But as you look at this motif you will experience it best if you say to yourselves: There I can really see nothing, I must see it in color. Because it is really experienced and conceived and painted entirely out of color."[42]

After the laying of the Foundation Stone of the Goetheanum in September 1913, work began on the building, but by the following winter relatively little had been accomplished, and it was clear that the money thus far contributed would not be enough. Steiner had always planned to have the building completed by August, 1914, hoping to present a fifth Mystery Drama in the auditorium in that month or the next. Now it became clear that even if the necessary money could be collected something spectacular would have to be done if the building were to be completed by the desired date, and it might never be finished at all if he himself were not present to supervise the work and stimulate the workers. Yet he could not give up everything else he was doing in order to devote himself exclusively to it.

So he undertook a series of lectures to the members, explaining how important the building was, not only for the Anthroposophical Movement but for the progress of spiritual life on the earth. As a result he not only raised enough money to enable work to be continued without any modification of the plans, but he also instilled a new spirit of enterprise into many of the members, so that they now began to regard the building as a communal enterprise in which everyone had his part to play. Professional people ceased to practice their professions for several months, others gave up their paid employment to go to Dornach, many of them camping out on the site. All the householders in the neighborhood were pressed into accepting paying guests. In the end several hundred members took part in the work at considerable cost to themselves, almost all of it being done by workers who had never used a mallet or chisel before. These worked side by side with the few professionals and the skilled paid workmen. A communal canteen was organized, and as early as April, 1914, the framework of the building was in place, and the sheathing of the two wooden domes was ready for the final roofing with the Norwegian slate. According to Swiss custom, when a building had reached this stage a ceremonial celebration was required. A photograph is extant showing the domes covered with their wooden sheathing, and hundreds of workers posing on the scaffolding. Two months later the glass-house, likewise with two domes and designed by Steiner, was ready for occupation, and work began on the windows.

Assya Turgenieff, who was one of the painters on the first Goetheanum as well as engraving the windows for the second, has left us a vivid word-picture of the moment when Steiner first began to carve in the auditorium of the Goetheanum.

"From the network of scaffolding which indicated the outlines of the future building on the hills could be heard the joyful sound of distant hammer-blows. The person seemingly met with most often on this hill was Dr. Steiner, covered with mud. Wearing a working smock and high boots, he hurried from one workshop to another, a model or a sketchbook in his hand; he stopped one on the way with a friendly word or a handshake. . . . In the concrete basement from which the

207

planks had already been removed, workers glued the beautiful wood into colossal blocks. Greenish-bright hornbeam, goldenly shimmering ash, reddish cherry, then warmly brown oak and elm and again the brighter colors of maple and birch. Each wood had its own smell; each felt different under the hand. It was the beginning of March when the carving—at first on the capitals in this room—had to be taken in hand. Dr. Steiner himself began this work. We gathered in a circle around him. Standing high up on two boxes with chisel and mallet in hand, he slowly struck one chip after another from the massive wood, which indicated in its general outlines the motif of a capital. He was completely absorbed in his work, as if he studied inwardly the movements of his hands, as if he would listen to something whispered out of the wood. And so it went on, hour after hour, restfully, uninterrupted. One was already weary from standing; went away; came back . . . He continued to work. And gradually the mass of wood was peeled away from a plastic form . . . The next day all plunged into the work. Everyone received chisel and mallet—but how hard and obstinate the wood was! After half an hour, the hands were utterly sore, and without visible result. It looked as if a mouse had been gnawing at the wood. And still Dr. Steiner had worked yesterday for the first time so many hours and accomplished so much. . . .It took time before the hands learnt to substitute rhythm for force, to make the wood compliant, and most of all until one found the way into the model room in order to study its motif and to measure. . . .

"A few items of advice from Dr. Steiner to those carving: 'In the left hand: the feeling—feel the form with the chisel. In the right: the strength. What matters in this is the work of the two. . . . Your whole feeling must be given consciously to the movement of the surfaces. They must become ensouled. Soul must be in the surfaces. How will the edge between two surfaces come about? That you must not determine beforehand—you must await it with curiosity. . . . Why do you wish symmetrical form? Your nose also is not symmetrical. Just look at the whirl of your hair . . . But in this way inner life comes to expression!

"Thus did he pass from one group to another, encouraging, jesting; yet more and more anxious appeared the expression of the eyes. Much work remained to be done—the carving of the outer wall, motifs over the windows and portals."

A few weeks later the same artist reported on progress as follows: "Still in a crude condition, uncompleted, yet at last the architraves were placed above the columns, and above these the inner dome was arched, and the place was freed from scaffolding. And thus we stood together with Dr. Steiner for the first time inside the Goetheanum. What we had labored at for many months as single fragments we suddenly saw before us blended into a whole, as a space that had never been there before. An impression which will remain forever inextinguishable, overwhelming in spite of everything that was unfinished and defective. And there were plenty of defects.

"And thus we listened to Dr. Steiner's praise and blame—praise which awoke a profound sense of shame in the heart, blame which sounded so hearty and humorous, so encouraging. We listened to him. . . . But just as important was it to look. The expression of his face, his gestures, the movement of his whole body rendered visible and supplemented what had not been expressed. The umbrella helped in the tracing of the movement of the form; and when it became more complicated, the soft felt hat was bent and twisted in order to clarify a plastic curve."[43]

In Steiner's absence Edith Maryon, a professional English sculptress, supervised the work. When he was present Steiner often spent the whole day carving, occasionally stopping work to pay visits to other workshops, especially the largest of all, the building that is always known by its German name, the Schreinerei. Here Steiner gave lectures in the evenings as often as he was able, including his fundamental lecture cycle on architecture, known as *Ways to a New Style in Architecture*, given in June and July, 1914. The Schreinerei was the only large building to survive the disastrous fire on New Year's Eve, 1922-23, and for many years it had to be used as the lecture hall, as well as providing a stage for such dramatic and eurythmy performances as could still be given.

Before the outbreak of war Steiner's lecturing schedule was so charged that he could seldom find time to lecture in Dornach, unless he happened to be there for the purpose of working on the Goetheanum. During the period of dissociation from the Theosophical Society in 1912 and 1913 he gave several important cycles on the general theme of the difference between the Eastern and Western paths to the spirit. On the one hand he emphasized the greatness of the wisdom of the East while on the other he stressed the importance of the Western path for Westerners, showing that there really *was* a Western path, something that was often denied by theosophists. Two cycles were given on the great Indian religious epic the *Bhagavd Gita,* one of them in Helsingfors, the capital of Finland, to which several Russians came. Steiner stressed how St. Paul, as a man of will and force, put his whole being into what he was saying, by contrast with the calm serenity of the *Gita.* He explained this contrast by saying that St. Paul's impulse was new and inspired by the Christ, and for this reason looked toward the future, whereas the *Gita* tells of a world that is mature and ripe, even over-ripe, and thus without a future. A similar theme ran through a cycle called *The Mysteries of the East and of Christianity,* given in Berlin in February, 1913.

Although he made seven journeys abroad during 1913, during all of which he gave lectures to the members who had transferred their allegiance to the new Anthroposophical Society, the bulk of his lectures continued to be given in the various German cities, above all Berlin, where he had been lecturing publicly every autumn and winter in the Architects' House, never missing a single scheduled lecture between 1905 and 1917, even when he was ill, as he was in 1909. Perhaps the most important single cycle was given to Berlin members during the winter season of 1912 to 1913, much of the contents of which was repeated in other German, Austrian, and Swiss cities at the same period. Although he never spoke directly, even to those who were most intimate with him, of the imminence of the war, he suddenly began at this time to give lectures to members which included details of the spiritual world and life between death and rebirth in a manner quite

210

different from hitherto. Contrary to his usual custom, he even explained to his first Berlin audience (*Life Between Death and Rebirth in Relation to Cosmic Facts*, November 5, 1912) that in the last months, that is in the summer and autumn of 1912, he had been specially engaged in spiritual research into the world after death, and he now wished "to present an aspect of the subject which could not previously be dealt with." "It is," he said, "only possible now to consider certain matters which bring home the profound moral significance of the super-sensible truths pertaining to this realm." He then goes on to describe for the first time in detail (if one excepts two lectures given some ten days earlier in Milan on the same subject, and based on the same recent research) the planetary worlds through which the human "I" passes after leaving kamaloca— kamaloca itself having been described in his book *Theosophy*, written in 1904. In this cycle he goes much further, explaining in particular how karma is formed in the life between death and rebirth. He discusses relations between the living and the dead, how the dead can influence us, and how in turn we can help the dead.

In view of the timing of this cycle and his repetition of much of its substance elsewhere, it seems virtually certain that he must have been purposely preparing the members for the imminent war, during which some of them and their friends would enter the spiritual worlds suddenly and unexpectedly. He wished to tell those whose destiny was to survive how they could continue to help their friends when they had passed over the threshold, and in turn how they themselves could receive inspiration from the dead. Although he gave another important lecture on the forming of destiny in Berlin at the end of 1915, the culminating cycle on the subject was given in Vienna shortly before the outbreak of the war. In this cycle entitled *The Inner Life of Man and Life Between Death and Rebirth* (April, 1914) Steiner summed up almost all he had been saying on the subject of the period between death and rebirth, right up to the point when the spirit germ descends at the moment of fecundation before the beginning of a new life on earth. As the war went on, Steiner ever and again reverted to the theme of the necessity for working with the dead. One of the most important cycles on this subject was given to the Berlin members after he had been absent for many months from the German imperial capital. This lecture cycle bears the title *Earthly Death and Cosmic Life* (January to March, 1918).

Nothing has as yet been said about one task that Rudolf Steiner took upon himself, and never until his last illness did he give it up. This was his interviews with individual members and even friends who wished to see him for a personal conversation and personal advice. Many of the meditations that were published after his death were originally given to members who were in need of them because of their personal life-situations. Nearly all the conversations were held at the request of the members concerned, and what he said naturally remained confidential. But there are dozens of statements from such members attesting that what Rudolf Steiner said to them on these occasions had a most profound effect on them, in many cases changing their entire life thereafter.

It remains true, however, that this tremendous activity took a heavy toll of his life forces, especially in the later years of his life. He kept a detailed appointment book in which were inscribed all the interviews to which he had agreed. If someone new appeared and asked to be allowed to see him privately, out would come the appointment book to see if any time were left. Sometimes when no advance appointment had been made he was able to spare a few minutes for an interview, but this was at the expense of the little time he had kept for himself. When he was asked to be a little easier on himself he would answer that this was one of his most important tasks while he was still on earth. Yet from some of the letters to Marie Steiner that have been published, there peeps out a reluctantly voiced wish that members would have a little more consideration for him. Not all the interviews they requested were truly necessary; in some cases they could have solved their problems without his personal spiritual guidance. As Steiner grew older and the life forces at his disposal became weaker, these interviews took ever greater toll of his strength, as we shall see in discussing the last year of his life. In the years covered by this chapter, the matter was not yet too serious. Fewer members attended his lectures, and fewer still were members of the Society—even if a higher percentage of them wished to have a personal discussion with the "Doctor," (as he was almost invariably called by the members). In any event, especially those who worked with him on the Goetheanum saw him often, and sometimes, even without being asked, he would give these co-workers valuable counsel for their personal lives.

There can be no doubt that when he was able and had the strength to talk privately with the members about their lives, he liked to do this, especially if he knew that what he said would be truly taken to heart. His natural goodness of heart, and what he always called himself his "sociable disposition," found here a perfect outlet. How far it must have seemed to him from the days in Vienna, and even in Weimar, when he had tried to talk on spiritual matters to his most intimate friends without striking any responsive chord! Now he was almost overwhelmed by the requests made to him to give answers from his spiritual insight. Quite possibly it was the memory of those days that made him in these years never refuse a request, not even when, as in 1924, his very life depended on his readiness to husband those forces which he was too lavishly and too willingly expending.

To illustrate from actual life how Rudolf Steiner was required to handle this part of his activity, this chapter will close with a few extracts from a book written by Boris Bugayev, a distinguished Russian symbolist poet who wrote under the pen name of Andrei Belyi. His book on Rudolf Steiner was published long after his death in a German translation, but never has appeared in Russian, the language in which it was written in 1928. Belyi, who was married for a few years to Assya Turgenieff, spent four years in Germany from 1912 to 1916, during this time attending as many lectures of Steiner's as he could. After the Russian Revolution he was able to return to the West on a temporary visa, but was required to return home in 1923. Perhaps fortunately for him, he died prematurely in 1934 before the worst of Stalin's purges. Most of the quotations that follow are taken from the account of his first period in

Germany, but the personal interview described here belongs to the 1923 period just before he returned home to the Soviet Union. At the time there had been a slight disagreement between Rudolf Steiner and him, which both were anxious to clear up.

"His apartment in Berlin . . . was like a command post . . . All the inmates of the house, above and below Steiner's apartment, rushed in constant haste from one floor to another with papers and copies, clattered on typewriters and made telephone calls. My impression: Steiner's home is always open; its effect is like that of a cell in a commune where no one places any value on comfort; every minute is already scheduled, and there are tasks, tasks, tasks. Here somebody is editing; there, admission tickets for a lecture are being distributed; here, books are being handed out. . . . Past these involved, restless rooms, and keeping the breathless ladies from their work, there stream—stream and stream all those who have announced themselves for a consultation with Steiner; all of them people who are foreign to this bubbling life. But each comes with a question that is more important to him than anything else in the world. Some of them come for the first time; they arrive as one comes to confession in the greatest state of excitement. And most of them are surprised. Instead of the dignified atmosphere they expected, they are received by loud seething life that may offend their sense of propriety. They ring the doorbell with hearts a-flutter—but the door is open; they are not received by the housemaid; in fact there are no domestics at all. Instead they are received by someone who just happens to be there . . . They are ushered into a small waiting room where every upholstered piece is occupied by waiting people. . . One door leads into the hallway, the other into the corridor . . . directly in front of one's nose a deep voice resounds behind it every so often.

"What, the Doctor is here right behind this wall? One pictures the personal meeting with the "Teacher" within a certain ceremonial framework; but here simplicity rules and an atmosphere of intense everyday work where there is no room for ceremonials, hardly a fitting place for the teacher and the confessing pupil. In one of the back rooms there are probably some open, unpacked suitcases standing about. He returned yesterday from Switzerland and tomorrow he leaves for Hanover—and somebody is readying his luggage for a new journey. Then, suddenly, right in front of your nose, the door of this plain, mystery-filled room is opened, quick as lightning and with a total lack of mystery, and the Doctor appears—a little worn, with a tired pale face; and, the perfect gentleman, ushers a lady out charmingly like a man of the world . . . with his hand raised in greeting from the threshold of the room unless he accompanies her personally into the hallway, where he switches on the light, helps her into her coat and closes the door behind her with his own hands. And then he quickly crosses the corridor leading past the waiting room, pushes his head through the drapes with a smiling 'One moment, please,' and goes on into the dining room, perhaps in order to drink a cup of coffee. His visiting hours last for hours and hours. He gets no opportunity either to eat or drink . . . Sometimes he paces hurriedly through the waiting room even without looking up, with serious, sad, stern eyes, only to return immediately. 'Who is next?' and to withdraw with the next person, sometimes for a very long period, sometimes for five minutes . . . He wears a tight short jacket; a jacket that is no longer new. On occasion he wears slippers; his pince-nez dangle and dance on a little ribbon and sometimes become entangled in the drapes when he rushes through them. And then you find youself in his reception room; a tiny room, black furniture, books, table, an easy chair, everything very modest. . . . When I enter here I immediately lose the ability to perceive anything except him, himself; how he sits down next to me, turning his ear in my direction (he hears less well with one ear). . . . Simplicity remains simplicity, kindness remains kindness, but in the simple interior of this room there occur such dramas of every kind, dreadful and joyous ones. . . But it is of no avail to talk about it. He was, after all, 'Rudolf Steiner' and he has the capacity to transform every situation into an unforgettable moment. . . .

"He had, as it were, a therapeutic smile; the countenance

blossomed . . . one felt that one had nothing *of the kind to* give in return. He had the gift of the smile, the faculty of direct expression from the heart . . . His smile could have had a smothering effect had he not tempered it down when necessary. Many know his sunny smile; we spoke of it. One must speak about it, for not a single photograph of his reflects it. . . . Our last meeting went like this: a long line of persons ahead of me [this was in 1923] and behind me; the car was waiting—Steiner was scheduled to return to Dornach from Stuttgart. He greeted me and led me into the room. We sat down by a small desk. Steiner was pale as death; it isn't easy to listen to such large numbers of people one after the other when each comes with his most urgent problem. His answers were always concrete, but they only unfolded their full nature in the course of the years. All this passed over my mind during our last meeting. He turned his over-tired face with the good-natured eagle nose in my direction with a smile difficult to describe, 'We do not have much time, try to say briefly everything you have on your mind.' This conversation of twenty minutes lives within me as if it had lasted many hours, not because I would have been capable of saying *everything* but because he replied to everything beyond any word. The answer grew out of the facts of the following years of my life. Only he was capable of replying like this, to recognize the leading thought of months and years behind the spoken words and to discern behind this thought the sum of experiences, and to see my will that was not even clear to myself at that time. . . . In his subdued, somewhat deep voice he explained to me in what respect and why I was wrong; and I felt how his atmosphere of warmth and fervor enveloped me too. Everything that I expressed was only three dimensional; but this atmosphere of glowing warmth that purified me from my sins and my pain could not be grasped; this comprehension only developed in the course of years as the best in me.

"A friend also described to me this warmth that seemed to emanate directly from the heart. She had arrived altogether unexpectedly, to leave again soon, and for a long time. She had the absolutely urgent desire to be received by Steiner, but the

Doctor was overburdened; he couldn't suppress the annoyed exclamation, 'Why do you come during the conference? I don't have a free minute!' And my friend replied in the same vein, 'We cannot come whenever we want to, only when we are able to!' She turned around and walked away. She heard a voice calling her name and looked around. Doctor Steiner was running after her with outstretched arms; he took both her hands, was full of warmth. . . .

In his kindness, the demands he made upon himself were unending. "Compassion has its limits," Marie Steiner said to him, but he replied: "No, compassion has no limits." Of love he said: "It is a giving faculty. The more one gives, the more one has to give." Every true love, according to his words, has the quality of infinite extension.

He extended himself."[44]

Chapter 9.

THE WAR YEARS AND
THE THREEFOLD SOCIAL ORDER

It was mentioned briefly in the last chapter that Rudolf Steiner, Marie von Sievers, and a party of friends were returning to Dornach from Germany when the war broke out. Passage over the frontier into Switzerland might have proved embarrassing, or worse, if the frontier had been organized as it was later. Marie von Sievers, as a Russian citizen, might well have been taken into custody by the Germans as an enemy alien before she could cross the border although the Swiss authorities would probably have raised no objection to her entry as long as her papers were in order.

The incident, however, was a serious warning to Steiner that it had become urgently necessary for Marie von Sievers to become an Austrian citizen like himself if he were not to lose the services and indispensable aid of his principal collaborator in the work of Anthroposophy. Thus it came about that after many years during which Marie von Sievers had been looking after Steiner's material needs she became his wife in a civil ceremony on December 24th, 1914. No outward change was visible in their lives. She continued to aid her husband and the anthroposophical work no less devotedly than before, but because of the war more work fell on her shoulders than ever. The after effects of a bad accident sustained in her youth combined with overwork to take such a toll of her strength that she became a cripple. By the end of the war she had had to resort to a wheel chair, and for the remaining thirty years of her life her legs had to be encased in splints. Nevertheless she continued to work as hard as ever, and the postwar development of Anthroposophy, especially its artistic side, would have been impossible without her selfless dedication.

In later years Rudolf Steiner was to explain how the European statesmen without exception had been lulled to sleep in the years immediately preceding the war by the hindering forces, the enemies of mankind, who alone desired it. None of the statesmen involved made conscious efforts to bring about the war, but their actions were such that in time it became impossible to avoid it, thus playing into the hands of the hindering powers. Steiner was greatly saddened by the war, but for at least the first two years he could play no direct part in world events. Although he could no longer travel beyond the borders of Germany, Austria-Hungary and Switzerland he continued to give lectures as before, but it became his custom to open them with a special prayer for those who had recently died and for those who were in danger. He continued to express the hope that something noble and good might yet arise for mankind out of all the suffering and sacrifice. The meditative verse that he also gave soon after the outbreak of the war, and with which he concluded so many of his wartime lectures, expresses this hope:

> From the courage of the fighters,
> From the blood on fields of battle,
> From the grief of the bereaved,
> From the people's sacrifices,
> Will arise the fruit of spirit,
> If souls, spirit-conscious,
> Turn their minds to spirit-realms.

An incident in which Steiner played a part early in the war became rather famous when later it became known. At a time when war seemed imminent but was not yet certain, Colonel-General Helmut von Moltke, chief of the German General Staff, had asked Steiner to pay him a visit as soon as he could, as he was anxious for an intimate talk with him. Although Frau von Moltke had been a theosophist for many years and was a founding member of the new Anthroposophical Society, her husband was not a member, but was an intimate friend of Steiner's, and had often sought his advice. In many ways he was temperamentally unsuited for his position as Supreme Military Commander with full responsiblity for the conduct of the war. Sensitive and introspective, he had been seriously humiliated just before the outbreak of war by the Kaiser, and the incident had badly undermined his self-confidence.

As it turned out no meeting between the two men could be arranged before August 27th, by which time the German offensive was already more than three weeks old. During this period von Moltke had been compelled to make numerous decisions on the basis of insufficient information, and some of these were obviously faulty. As a result his field commanders were already losing confidence in his judgment. On the very day of August 27th when Steiner visited him in the German staff headquarters in the little Rhineland town of Coblenz, he was faced with a particularly agonizing decision, which in fact turned out to be wrong, in that he ordered a general offensive for which the armies he commanded were unsuitably placed.*
It is now generally accepted by historians that the German offensive, in spite of appearances to the contrary, was already by August 27th in deep trouble; and the great decisive victory for the sake of which the offensive had been launched, and the neutrality of Belgium violated, had now become extremely unlikely, if not impossible. The French army, unlike in 1940, had been defeated only in small and unimportant engagements and was still in the field—as was evidenced by its counterattack two weeks later at the Marne.

When Steiner arrived at Coblenz the Kaiser and his court, as well as General von Moltke were in the town, whose atmosphere was not improved by the Kaiser's customary somewhat

---

*For a good modern account of these events and the role played by von Moltke in the German failure, see, for example, Corelli Barnett, *The Swordbearers* (New York: William Morrow and Company, 1964). Barnett's story is endorsed by two of the best British military historians, Major-General J.F.C. Fuller, and Captain B.H. Liddell Hart.

hysterical behavior, including his rapid changes from over-confidence to the depths of pessimism. It is not known what Steiner discussed with von Moltke, or if he was able to give the General any spiritual comfort. In an interview after the war with a Parisian newspaper Steiner told the reporter that only personal matters had been discussed. Even if von Moltke had asked him for military advice—which is in the last degree unlikely—Steiner would never have given it, or if he had, whatever he had advised at that moment could have had no appreciable effect on the eventual failure of the offensive. It was the earlier failure to destroy the Belgian, French and British armies in the field that determined the final outcome; and it is certain that von Moltke himself was at least in some measure responsible for this failure. At 66 he was old and tired and already in poor general health (he died in 1916), and the anthroposophical convictions of his wife and his own inti-macy with Rudolf Steiner cannot be blamed for these things—still less for the loss of the war by Germany.

Nevertheless, when the meeting became known, as it soon was to the French and later to the Germans, Steiner was blamed by nationalistic Germans for the defeat at the battle of the Marne, and he was accused of having used his "magical powers" on General von Moltke. It may be admitted that a visit to the General at this moment lent itself to this kind of charge. But, as we have seen, Steiner never refused a personal appeal of this kind, especially when it concerned a friend whose emo-tional and intellectual difficulties were no doubt known to him. But it remains true that the military decisions made by von Moltke on August 27th and then eight days later, when the decisive mistake was made, did lead to the failure of the great offensive and ultimately to the loss of the war. We cannot know how seriously this charge was really taken by Steiner's adversaries after the war, but it was certainly used by some of them to impugn his patriotism and arouse feeling against him and his work.

His position in other respects was very difficult at this time. He was no doubt grateful to his destiny which had led him to Switzerland, which remained neutral throughout the war,

221

sparing him the necessity to take sides openly in the conflict. But as is usual in such circumstances he was criticized by both sides for his failure to do so. His French friend Edouard Schuré regarded Steiner as too nationalistically German, while the leader of the English anthroposophists, Harry Collison, for a short time took the same position. When they understood Steiner's absolute impartiality as they did later, they both repented of their excessive patriotism. The citizens of seventeen different countries who were engaged all through the war in helping to build the Goetheanum shared a common belief that they were working for the future of humanity. Several of these countries were at war with each other, but the collaborators on the Goetheanum, under the leadership of Rudolf Steiner, remained in almost complete harmony. Any other attitude on Steiner's part than total impartiality would have alienated them. His wartime lectures in Dornach tended to stress world history and human evolution as a whole, and he gave numerous lectures on art in connection with the work being done on the building. The common humanity of the fighters on both sides was emphasized, and all lectures, as we have seen, began or ended with meditations for those who were involved in the fighting. Marie Steiner, meanwhile, was training a small band of eurythmists and preparing actors for performances of *Faust* by Goethe. During the war different scenes from *Faust* were given under her direction while Rudolf Steiner spoke on the significance of the drama at frequent intervals. Indeed *Faust* lent itself excellently to lectures on the nature of evil, a subject most appropriate during these years.

In Germany the situation was more delicate. Steiner did not abandon his lectures in the warring Central European countries. The annual series of public lectures in the Architects' House in Berlin that he had been giving for many years were continued until 1917, when the lecture hall was commandeered by the military. He gave his public lectures then in a different hall, and never thought of abandoning them. By this time, as we shall see, he was becoming rather well known in Germany, attracting more supporters but at the same time more, and more virulent enemies. He occasionally lectured also in Austria during the war years. At all times Rudolf Steiner emphasized that Germany was not alone responsible for the war, as Allied propaganda made out; nor were the Germans exclusively guilty of atrocities. It seems to have been one of his main purposes to give the German people, in so far as he was able to aid in this, a renewed confidence in themselves, and particularly, a recognition of their true mission as a people— something that no one else in Germany was stressing at this time. Only Steiner was in a position as a result of his knowledge derived from the science of spirit to speak impartially of this mission at a time when other Germans and Austrians were totally unable to view the struggle except from a partisan point of view.

Steiner had indeed always been deeply interested in the tasks of the different nations, especially the European nations. When ever he visited a new country in the course of his lecture tours, he made it part of his task to investigate its spiritual background and he often used to explain the esoteric meaning of the country's national legends or epics. In 1910 he gave a detailed cycle on *The Mission of the Folk Souls* in the Norwegian capital of Christiania (Oslo), a cycle that for once he personally revised for publication when Prince Max of Baden, who later became Chancellor of the German Empire, asked him for a copy. In this cycle he explained how each nation was guided from the spiritual worlds by a higher being of the rank of an archangel, who was indeed the folk spirit of that nation. Each nation thus had a mission to fulfill. Immediately after the beginning of the war he took up this subject again in his lectures within Germany, especially the public ones in Berlin, which bear such titles as "The Enduring and Creative Power of the German Spirit," "The Rejuvenating Power of the German Folk-Soul," "German Idealism," "The Evolution of the German Soul," and the like. A lecture available in English, entitled "The Spirit of Fichte in our Midst," shows clearly that he was trying to draw the attention of the German people to their true spiritual mission, as exemplified in the great figures of German idealism, Fichte, Hegel and Schelling, whom he had always admired—to say nothing of Goethe, whose con-

223

nection with idealism he emphasized in a lecture given in Berlin on December 2nd, 1915 to which he gave the title of "Goethe and the Cosmic Conception of German Idealism, in respect of the Sentiment of our Critical Times."

According to Steiner, the German task in world evolution is to develop within man's being the "I" itself, which, as explained in Chapter 6, works through the three different souls, the sentient soul, the intellectual or mind soul, and the consciousness soul. Different European peoples have the task of developing the different souls, for example the Italian and Spanish peoples the sentient soul, the French people the intellectual soul, and the English speaking peoples the consciousness soul. But the I itself could be truly developed in the way it ought to be especially by the German speaking peoples. No other people had showed itself so deeply interested in this development. No other people had developed such a philosophy as German idealism, and philosophers from other nations did not write books such as those of Fichte, with his emphasis on the "absolute ego" which he equated with God, or Max Stirner, with his book *The Self and its Property*, briefly discussed in an earlier chapter. No other people had produced a Goethe, whose *Faust* was scarcely an individual at all but rather an embodiment of the human I as it strives eternally in our striving age.

Within the twentieth century world it was, in Steiner's view, the task of the German speaking nations, Germany and Austria, to maintain the balance between East and West, between Russia on the one side and Great Britain and America on the other. If Germany should be destroyed, then there would be only the two extremes, and nothing to hold the balance. Steiner indeed likened the role of Germany to that of the rhythmic system within the human organism, which holds the balance (as we shall see later in more detail) between the head and senses system and the metabolic and limb system. The rhythmic system belongs in part to each of these, the blood circulation being attached more to the metabolic system and the breathing system to the head. However this may be—and it was and is a most important part of Steiner's teachings, and lies at the basis of anthroposophical medicine—the German role had to be performed by some nation or nations, or, in Steiner's view, chaos would ensue. It is certainly arguable that he was and is right. But he was in his lifetime very careful indeed not to approve any of the policies adopted by the German Reich, and he had no use whatever, as was clear, for the German imperial policy or for the Kaiser, the German warlord. The task laid upon the German people was laid upon it by the spiritual worlds, and it was a great and terrible responsibility, not a cause for self satisfaction or reason for self assertion. As the individual human I when developed onesidedly can lead to all kinds of "selfish" aberrations, so could the egotism of nations lead to all kinds of exaggerated nationalism, even to the German racism of Adolf Hitler and his followers. These things as yet constituted only a potential danger, and as yet there was no need to criticize German nationalism above the nationalism of other warring nations. It was Steiner's endeavor always to place world concerns above those of any nation, and especially when he was at home in Dornach he continued to speak not only about these concerns but about general Anthroposophy, as he had done since the beginning of his public mission in 1900.

Just before the beginning of the war there appeared a new edition of his book *World and Life Conceptions of the Nineteenth Century*, originally published in 1900. When Steiner wrote it, it was his purpose to show what kind of soul-condition had been responsible for the kind of philosophy that appeared in the nineteenth century, and how this philosophy culminated in an entirely materialistic manner of thinking in the later part of the century. Now he renamed the book *The Riddles of Philosophy, Presented in an Outline of its History*, and he added another part, not quite as long as the older book itself, covering the history of philosophy in a brief manner up to the beginning of the nineteenth century. The emphasis now was on philosophy from Greek times to the end of the nineteenth century as a picture of the changes in human consciousness during these centuries. His emphasis was on *how* philosophers had thought, what problems they were dealing with,

225

rather than *what* they had thought, which was of lesser interest to him. The book therefore cannot in any way be regarded as history of philosophy. It would be more accurate to describe it as a history of human consciousness as this is reflected in the history of philosophy.

During the war years Steiner also was able to find the time to write two other major books, *The Riddle of Man* (1916) and *Riddles of the Soul* (1917). It was in the last named book that he presented for the first time his teachings on the three "systems" of the human organism. In addition, for the first time since 1894 and 1897 he was able to bring out new editions of his *Philosophy of Freedom* and *Goethe's Conception of the World*. Both books now could look toward an assured, if limited, public, as could *Knowledge of the Higher Worlds. How is it Attained?* which also appeared in the same year in its second edition, revised by Rudolf Steiner for the first time. It had never been out of print and continued to sell regularly, in view of its special character as a guide to higher development. So its appearance in a newly revised edition was not such an important event as was the new edition of the *Philosophy of Freedom*, which in its original edition had not even sold a thousand copies and had been long out of print, even though Steiner constantly referred to it in his lectures.

While Marie Steiner was working with the eurythmists in preparation for the time when eurythmy could be introduced abroad on a wide scale, Rudolf Steiner when in Dornach continued to work on the Goetheanum and supervise the work of others. Since none of the other artists could fully understand his intentions if he were not there to aid them, it was he who did most of the painting on the cupolas. However, the most taxing of his artistic tasks was the carving of a huge group of figures which was to have been placed at the rear of the space beneath the small dome in the completed Goetheanum. When the building was opened in 1921 this carving was not yet ready, nor was it entirely finished by the time of Steiner's death in 1925. Since it had not yet been removed from the Schreinerei at the time of the fire, it was saved from destruction. In its still slightly unfinished state it is now kept in a special room in the

226

present Goetheanum, and may be seen by anyone who wishes to view it.

The group, which is carved out of elm, is of an enormous size, needing a scaffolding nine meters (about 29 feet) high. The original model, which was the same size as the final sculpture, was largely made by the English sculptress Edith Maryon in accordance with Rudolf Steiner's instructions. Several other sculptors in addition to Miss Maryon worked on the wooden Group itself, once the huge pieces of elm had been glued together and were ready for the mallet and chisel. Steiner sometimes left this original sculpture as they had left it, but more often he added a few essential touches to make the figures conform fully to his intentions. The figure of the Representative of Humanity, or the Christ, the central figure of the Group, was in the end almost entirely his own work, although in this case also Miss Maryon prepared the way. Her own conception of the figure of the Christ, which she carved first, was beautiful in the Greek style, but far from being as Steiner had pictured Him. Teasingly he told her that her Christ was too much of the English gentleman! In the sculpture in its final form the Christ, the central figure in the Group, has one arm raised, while He points downward with the other. By the sheer force of the Christ Being Lucifer, above Him on the left, destroys himself, while below Ahriman is held fast by his own self-knowledge. These two forces, the traditional tempters, are thus held in balance, or rather, hold themselves in balance, not because of the *power* of the Christ, but simply through His *presence*.

It was Steiner's original intention to have only these three carved figures in the Group. In the course of the work he decided otherwise, and added a smaller Lucifer and a smaller Ahriman to the right of the Christ; while at the top left, looking down on the whole sculpture, is a somewhat enigmatic figure, who was called by Rudolf Steiner a "Rock-being." Artistically he balances the entire sculpture, and the viewer may decide that that is a sufficient reason for his presence in the Group. In any event such beings, according to Steiner, do exist and are visible to supersensible perception.

His presence therefore, in the last analysis, does not have to be justified at all any more than it is necessary to justify the presence of the angels in a Renaissance painting, who are just *there*, whether or not they are also *doing* something, and serve a visible purpose in the picture.

By the beginning of 1917 the armies of the warring powers, at least in the West, were close to exhaustion, while the Russian army was openly mutinous. No early decision could be expected in the West, whatever happened in the East; and the only new move the Germans could think of was to institute unlimited submarine warfare in the hope of forcing Britain to her knees, or driving her out of the war—even though the cost was virtually certain to be America's entry into the war on the Allied side. All through 1916 President Woodrow Wilson of the United States had been making somewhat half-hearted attempts, especially through Colonel House, to bring the war to an end by means of mediation, and at the end of the same year he made a series of more definite proposals himself. The Germans showed themselves willing to negotiate and authorized Wilson to enter into contact with the Allies. But their own proposals were too severe for the latter, since they still expected, with the aid of the Americans, to win the war outright. From almost the beginning of his reign in 1916 the new Emperor Karl of Austria tried to make peace, with or without the consent of the Germans. The possibility of a negotiated peace and an end to the fighting seemed to be in the air, but the statesmen seemed to have no idea of what kind of terms they really wanted; and it was difficult to translate Wilson's vague generalities and talk about self-determination of people and the rights of man into concrete proposals. At the same time, after his re-election in November, 1916, it was abundantly clear that when peace came to be made he would be the most powerful political figure in the world, whether or not his country became an active belligerent.

It has sometimes been difficult for anthroposophists, especially American anthroposophists, to understand just why Rudolf Steiner was so antagonistic to Woodrow Wilson. Even before the war while he was a simple peacetime president,

228

Steiner had spoken about Wilson's particular style of thinking, criticizing it unmercifully as typically "professorial" and "schoolmasterly." Though Wilson set himself up as an idealist, his ideals and ideas were dead, abstract and thought-out, lacking any relation to true social realities, as Steiner saw them. His taste for moralizing and preaching little sermons evidently greatly irritated Rudolf Steiner, while his thoughts about nationalism and self-determination were spoiled because of their failure to take into account the actual conditions in the world, all his knowledge of which he had acquired second hand or from books. In a word, Wilson, according to Steiner, in spite of appearances, never at any time thought with his heart, while the thoughts of his head were wholly inspired by Ahriman. None of this might have mattered if his position had not been so powerful and if so many of his hearers had not thought in just the same way and therefore admired him and followed him with abject docility.*

By early 1917 few if any thinkers of any substance, if one excepts the Marxists who were trying to apply the ideas of their master to the situation in their own countries and in Europe as a whole, had given any serious thought to the possibility that major changes in the social order might become necessary after the war if the world were to return to a truly peaceful way of living. No "peace-aims" of this nature seem to have been studied in any of the warring countries, and at this time it seems to have been taken for granted, at least in circles where policy was made, that after the unfortunate aberration of the war peace would be made much as it had been made after previous wars, and the world would settle down as it always had done before. It occurred to very few to suppose that there was anything fundamentally wrong with the social, political and economic structure of the world.

The last two years of the war radically changed this viewpoint, and after the outbreak of the Russian Revolution in

---

*For a more detailed discussion of Woodrow Wilson and his ideas of nationalism and self determination see my *Man and World in the Light of Antrhoposophy* pp. 325-331.

February, 1917, followed by the Bolshevik Revolution of November, more statesmen began to be afraid that other revolutions might break out elsewhere, even in their own countries. Woodrow Wilson's speeches also undoubtedly contributed to the general unrest. His praise of democracy, and his insistence on self-determination for peoples who were at present oppressed by their governments, gave new hope to numerous ethnic minorities in the European national patchwork. These peoples began to organize, and determined that they would not accept a peace that failed to give them satisfaction, even if a revolutionary struggle were necessary before they could attain their ends. Yet, in just the same way as at the beginning of the war, no statesman arose with any new ideas, no one seemed to be able to give leadership to the peace-seeking forces of Europe, with the result that as the nations had drifted toward war they now drifted toward peace.

Count Otto Lerchenfeld, a member of the Bavarian State Council, who was also an anthroposophist, shared Steiner's concern over the European situation in the early months of 1917. He was aware of Steiner's lectures being given at Dornach in which he voiced his apprehensions after the beginning of the Russian Revolution and the entry of the United States into the war. He was especially interested in a cycle called *Truths in the Evolution of Man and Humanity* in which Steiner explained the increasing feebleness of human thinking as the result of certain spiritual changes in man, which had the effect of preventing him from reaching maturity in the same way as in the past. In his memoirs published later, Count Lerchenfeld tells how truly barren of ideas all his contemporaries were showing themselves to be, with the single exception of Rudolf Steiner. As a result of his conclusions he made the decision to approach Steiner to ask him for his thoughts on how it would be possible to build a lasting peace, with the intention of presenting these to his friends and acquaintances in high places. When therefore Steiner paid a visit to Berlin in June 1917, the Count called upon him and explained the gist of his own thought. Steiner, in reply, laid before him the outline of those ideas which were later to be embodied in more detail in what is usually called in English speaking countries the Threefold Commonwealth or Threefold Social Order. Although obviously he had already given very much thought to these ideas, he told Count Lerchenfeld at this first interview that it had been his opinion that not only did the outline need still much elaborating, but also it should have been available for study by all classes of society before it could be presented as a real plan of action by their leaders.

After two days' discussion the Count's entire mood was changed, and from deep despair he became full of enthusiasm. For three weeks, day after day, he and Steiner worked together over the ideas that he had outlined until the entire organic structure for a new social order had been built up, answering every question that could be put by either of them. At this point, on July 10th, Count Lerchenfeld sent a telegram to a close friend of his, also an anthroposophist, whose brother was the chief councillor of the Emperor Karl of Austria. This friend, Count Ludwig Polzer-Hoditz, then came to Berlin and joined in the work for the last week. At the end of that time Count Lerchenfeld asked Rudolf Steiner to incorporate their developed ideas in a memorandum which could then be circulated among the leading statesman of Europe. Later, perhaps, it might be presented to the Allied leaders as the Central European counterproposal to the tired old thoughts of President Wilson.* A few days later Steiner presented the Count with the Memorandum, and the effort began to interest the statesmen of Europe in a new social structure for their countries, for which they had as yet perceived no need. How to win the war or save themselves from losing it was unhappily the first priority in such thinking as they could undertake while in the midst of the turmoil of war. Steiner himself was scarcely optimistic about the results of the effort, but he had done what was asked of him, as usual, and, as Count Lerchenfeld wrote

---

*The Memorandum does not exist in English, but it was published in German as recently as 1961 in a work entitled *Aufsätze über die Dreigliederung des Sozialen Organismus* (Dornach: Rudolf Steiner Verlag.)

later, he was convinced that "everything must be done in order that the idea of the Threefold Social Order should sink into the conceptual consciousness of the time."

As for the Austrian Count Polzer-Hoditz, he returned to his country with the intention of giving the memorandum to his brother, who would then place it before the new Emperor. This brother was not himself an anthroposophist, nor was he particularly in sympathy with either Theosophy or Anthroposophy. But he conscientiously examined the document, and came to the conclusion that it was by far the most interesting series of proposals that he had yet seen. But he did not think the time was opportune to present it to his master, preferring to hold it in reserve until the right moment. In fact, what happened was that some months later he decided, for various reasons, to resign his position as chief councillor to the Emperor. It was only at the moment of his resignation that he at last felt free to present the memorandum that he had received several months previously, to the Emperor Karl. Thereafter nothing further was heard of it, and it is not even certain that Karl ever read it. In any event he did nothing about it, but continued to pursue his own plans for a negotiated peace, which of course came to nothing.

The other statesman of importance who certainly had the Memorandum with him at a crucial moment of history, though how much he had studied it is unknown, was Richard von Kuhlmann, foreign secretary of the German Reich, who bore the chief responsibility for negotiating the peace with the Russians after the success of the Bolshevik Revolution. The Treaty of Brest-Litovsk, which he negotiated in March 1918, was the bitterest possible disappointment to Rudolf Steiner, who believed that the Central Powers by agreeing to a magnanimous peace might well have undermined Lenin's position at home. In accordance with the ideas put forward in the *Threefold Commonwealth* the various European minorities, especially the Ukrainians, whose country became a virtual German protectorate under the treaty, could have enjoyed a limited but real independence. This was an option open to the Germans at that time, and in Steiner's view it would have been a truly positive step toward a lasting peace.

232

Although Rudolf Steiner did not publish his book on the Threefold Social Order until 1919, the ideas on which it was based, namely, the threefold (or, more correctly the three-membered) nature of the *social* organism, were already put forward in their essentials in the summer of 1917 when he prepared the Memorandum for the statesmen of Europe. In the autumn of the same year he published a book in which the threefold nature of the *human* organism was explained by him for the first time—although he was later to tell an audience of anthroposophists that he had been able to grasp the central idea many decades before, adding that only "during the storms of war was I able to bring it to maturity." Since both ideas were first expressed in the period covered by this chapter and they belong together, we shall here give a brief outline of the fundamental idea of the threefold bodily nature of man, as first expressed in Steiner's book *Riddles of the Soul,* following this with a discussion of the threefold, or three-membered, nature of the social organism, as explained in 1919 in his fundamental book entitled *The Threefold Social Order* or *The Threefold Commonwealth.**

In Section VII of *Riddles of the Soul* Steiner almost casually introduces the notion of the threefoldness of man's organism by relating the three essential human soul powers (or faculties) of thinking, feeling and willing, to three separate "systems" in the human organism. The bodily basis of thinking is essentially to be found in what he calls the head and senses, or head and neural system, the feeling or emotional life of man has its bodily basis in what he calls the rhythmic system, which includes the blood circulation, while the metabolic and limb system provides the bodily basis for human willing. As we are most conscious in our nerves and senses, so are we more conscious in our thinking than we are in either our feeling or our willing. In our feeling life we are partly conscious, with a consciousness similar to that of our breathing that continues

---

*For a longer discussion of the threefold bodily nature of man see my *Man and World.* . . pp. 296-301. An excellent little book on the subject has recently been published, Walther Bühler, *Living with your Body* (London: Rudolf Steiner Press, 1979).

in its own rhythm without effort on our part; and in our will we are asleep, as we are asleep in our digestive system which we cannot modify at all by any conscious act of ours. The three-fold system is also to be found *within* each of these systems, as, for example in the head, whose upper part contains our brain, linked to thinking, in the middle is our nose which is our organ for breathing, and below is the mouth which is linked to our digestion. If one system impinges on another, illness results, as when we suffer from a headache as a result of disorder in the digestive system. The three systems in the human organism are separate and distinguishable from one another, but they are all an inseparable part of the human being, who needs to have all functioning effectively together if he is to lead a healthy life. Thus the systems, though *distinguishable*, are not *divisible*. All these ideas were later to form the basis of anthroposophical medicine, which will be discussed briefly in a later chapter, but do not need to be elaborated further here, where our concern is with the threefold nature of the social order, not the bodily organism.

According to Rudolf Steiner the social organism is composed of three separate domains, which he calls the "spiritual-cultural" domain, the political or jural domain, and the economic domain. It was the same kind of thinking and observation that led Steiner to distinguish these three separate domains as led him to distinguish the three domains or systems in the human organism. He always insisted that there was nothing arbitrary in these distinctions. "By means of this cognizing which the human being exercises in connection with this view of the threefold natural human organism," he said, "one arrives also at a true cognition of the social organism in its threefold nature." This kind of cognizing we have elsewhere referred to as Goethean or "living" thinking—that kind of thinking that alone is capable of comprehending the living organism.

In Steiner's view a particular kind of social organism should be striven for in the age of the consciousness soul. It was not to be regarded as a utopia in any sense of the word, nor would it last for all time. It should be striven for, not because it was the will of the spiritual world but because the social order itself was tending toward it of its own accord. "The present crisis," Steiner was to write in 1919, "demands the development of certain faculties of apprenhension . . . From now on it is necessary that the individual should be trained to have a healthy sense of how the forces of the body social must work in order for it to live." The social order would eventually evolve in the long run in the direction he foresaw and urged, because it was demanded by the conditions of the time. Though it could be impeded by men who tried to preserve the old system because it suited them, the old system nevertheless was in fact doomed in the long or the short run. Conversely, when enough people saw the necessity for the kind of changes demanded by the times, their combined activity might succeed in bringing the new order into being. The chaotic conditions that would necessarily come about at the end of the war, and the inability of the responsible statesmen to decide on peace terms in keeping with the needs of the time, made it worthwhile for Steiner to express his ideas, and later, after the war, to make a personal effort to bring them to realization.

According to Steiner, the correct ideas had been, so to speak, "in the air" at the time of the French Revolution. But they had not been really understood by anyone, with the result that in the end very little was changed by the Revolution. However, it had left behind it the slogan "liberty, equality, and fraternity," a slogan that expressed exactly what was needed if only it had been understood. Steiner now explained that the word liberty should have been applied to the spiritual-cultural domain alone, equality to the domain of rights, the political state, and fraternity to the economic realm. If the attempt should be made to apply these ideas in realms inappropriate for them, trouble would immediately ensue. The idea of equality cannot be applied to the realm of human freedom, of thinking, because we all think differently. The attempt to make all men think alike leads to tyranny. In the political domain what is needed is equality of rights, enforceable by a government freely elected by universal suffrage. No other freedom is needed in this domain. In the economic life we must all co-operate like

235

brothers if we are to produce what we all need for our living. Steiner, of course, did not use these ideas as slogans for his own Threefold Order. All he was trying to do at this stage was to point out how beneath the surface the ideas appropriate for the times were already finding expression, but no one had the wisdom to understand them in their true meaning.

In the same way that thinking, feeling, and willing are intermingled in the human being, and each of these three soul powers plays a part in our every act, so do we play a part in each of the three domains of the social order. We partake at all times in the spiritual-cultural life of our country and the world, we expect to have our rights respected by others as we respect theirs, and for this purpose we elect or should elect a body to which we delegate powers sufficient to enable it to enforce these rights; and as consumers and perhaps also as producers we are vitally interested in the production and distribution of those goods which we consume every day of our lives. But there is no need whatsoever, so Steiner held, for the political organization, the state, either to interfere in the production and distribution of goods—a task which belongs properly to the economic and not the political domain—nor in education, which belongs exclusively to the spiritual-cultural realm, and should be provided by those people who are active in this realm and wish to contribute their cultural knowledge and insight to others. In the spiritual-cultural realm we are concerned only with the individual; in the political realm the natural unit is the state, which may be quite small since its tasks are limited; in the economic realm the natural unit is the world, since all goods should circulate freely without any hindrance from any source outside the economic domain itself.

Steiner, as may be imagined, did not content himself simply with making obeservations, and offering ideas regarding the present functioning of the social organism. He also suggested social and institutional changes which would take account of the separateness of each domain. Since all production of goods, for example, belongs to the economic domain it is necessary for this domain to generate a surplus which will be used to finance the activities of those whose work lies primarily in other domains. But it should not create *unneeded* surpluses, goods that can be sold only through mendacious and tendentious advertising; nor goods that will lie unsold in warehouses (as happened so often in the earlier years of the Soviet Union). The organization proper to this domain is therefore an association between producers and consumers, with the latter constantly feeding the necessary information to the former. These associations will be left strictly alone by the political domain, with the single exception of its duty to impose a minimum wage, calculated on the basis of what is needed for human subsistence—this being a right to which all men are entitled. By contrast, the spiritual-cultural domain will be expected to pour new ideas into the ears of the managers of the economic associations, and these ideas will be adopted or rejected on the sole basis of their utility. If production costs are reduced by making use of an idea, and if the consumers agree that the quality of the product is no lower than before, or if they wish to have a new product that can be made with the aid of the idea, then this idea will be regarded as a valuable and productive one, and the inventor will be duly remunerated and encouraged to think up further useful ideas. Thus the spiritual-cultural life will fertilize the economic life directly, as it indirectly fertilizes it by educating the populace in such a way that educated workers are always available to play their part in the economic sector of the social order.

It is certain that if such a Threefold Order were to come into being numerous changes would be required in the existing order. Within the spiritual-cultural domain education would have to be taken out of the hands of the state, and associations of teachers would provide education thereafter. The surplus from the economic realm would have to be channelled directly to them or through the medium of the parents, without the intervention of state bureaucrats who, now just as much as in 1917, use the authority of the government to collect taxes from the economic domain to pay the teachers and school administrators. Parents would choose those schools for their children that pleased them, and associations of teachers who could not attract the parents (let us hope that this means they were bad teachers and not merely exacting ones) would not be able to keep their schools open. Obviously such a scheme would disturb numerous vested interests. In the economic domain joint stock companies would be replaced by associations of producers, distributors and consumers as described above— thereby, among other things, putting an end to the power and influence of financiers, banks and big business, while the associations would no longer look to the state for support or special privileges.

The state, thus losing so many of its current tasks, would find itself reduced in power and authority. Thereafter its task would become solely to maintain and enforce the rights of all citizens of the state. Having no role to play in the management of the economy nor in providing education, it would still have the duty to defend the people against external aggression, and could call upon them for armed aid if so authorized by the parliamentary body elected by all citizens. But it was thought by Rudolf Steiner that the other arrangements of the new order would remove most of the causes of war. In particular, since the economy would be world-wide and national economies would disappear, no impediments to world wide trade would ever be imposed; presumably raw materials would belong to no particular nation but would be used by all for the benefit of all. It follows that the boundaries of the various states would no longer be of vital importance. There would be no rich states and poor states, only "rights-bodies" maintaining the rights of the citizens who had elected them to office. In principle there would be no reason why each ethnic group that desired it should not have its own rights-organization, and thereafter all states could really be too small to think of waging war, even if there were any reason for it. It is perhaps scarcely surprising that politicians and bureaucrats who owed their living to the existing system should have felt themselves personally threatened by even the idea of such a new social order.

Thus powerful opponents could be expected from all three domains, and those who might prefer such an order to the existing one were not those who currently wielded power and authority. The postwar history of the movement for the Threefold Social Order showed that it had indeed many potential supporters, but that these were not to be found in high places. Steiner therefore in 1919 after the founding of the movement was quite right in making his appeal directly to the people, and to enlightened industrialists and other individuals who could be convinced by his ideas, and not so much to the established leaders of postwar Germany. But in 1917, when the memorandum containing his basic ideas was circulated to other influential leaders by Counts Lerchenfeld and Polzer-Hoditz, it was surely too much to expect that it would be heeded. Most of the men who read it found some of its details interesting, even practicable, but rejected the document as a whole—especially, no doubt, those parts that affected them personally and threatened their position.

Yet every item in the memorandum was intimately linked with every other item, and this continued to be the case even after the war. The Threefold Social Order was not a thought-out plan, as the Soviet state system so largely was when it was imposed by Lenin and Stalin. It could not be *imposed* by any authority, however well disposed; and Steiner was at all times totally opposed to making the attempt. It must, he thought, come about more or less by itself, through men and women who understood it and would themselves do what was necessary in their own field of activity. He put forward the ideas in 1917 only because he was asked for them, not because he believed that the leaders of the warring nations could or would accept them, nor that the Threefold Social Order would be brought into being overnight if they did. What he did hope was that the leaders on both sides would give some thought to them, and that when it came to negotiating and making peace they, or some of them, would keep the ultimate goals in mind, and take some steps toward attaining them. His opposition to President Woodrow Wilson, the most powerful and influential of these leaders, thus becomes entirely comprehensible. The most definite and concrete of Wilson's ideas was undoubtedly that of self-determination for minorities. But such self-determination would make matters much worse if each of the new countries were to try to administer a national economy. Only if a world-wide "international" economy were already in operation and were maintained after the peace could the peacemakers afford to grant self-determination to the minorities who would thereafter possess effective self-government in the form of national "rights-bodies," while their economies would form part of the larger world-economy.

Rudolf Steiner was especially shocked by the action of the German military in helping Lenin and his fellow revolutionaries to return to Russia, an action that led directly to the Bolshevik Revolution. Thereafter he began to lose hope that anything constructive would come out of the war. With his spiritual vision he was able to perceive how the forces of evil who were opposed to the goals for mankind willed by the spiritual world were beginning to rage unchecked, and from Michaelmas 1917 he began to give several series of lectures to those members in Dornach who he felt were able to bear the truth. He explained in particular how from 1879 onwards certain Ahrimanic spirits were driven out of the spiritual worlds and began to haunt men, and how certain occult brotherhoods allied themselves with the forces of evil in order to gain power over other men. This was no legend, Steiner insisted, but the actual truth visible to spiritual sight. Moreover, the numerous violent deaths during the war had greatly disturbed relations between the spiritual and earthly worlds, and this increased the power of those occultists who could make use of the dead for their own ends. For this reason early in 1918 Steiner once more gave a key cycle to the Berlin members (*Earthly Death and Cosmic Life*), in which he spoke again about the need to keep in contact with the dead, and how to help them through their own thoughts and feelings toward them. In October and early November he gave another long cycle, this time to Dornach members, with the German title of *Historical Symptomatology*, translated into English under the title *From Symptom to Reality in Modern History*, which is full of insights into the entire age of the consciousness soul, concluding with a discussion of contemporary history.

Immediately after this last cycle was completed Steiner began a series of three separate cycles, of which the first lectures were delivered just before the signing of the Armistice. The titles of these cycles *Foundations for Social Thinking in the Evolution of History, In the Changed Conditions of the Time,* and *The Fundamental Social Demand of our Time,* demonstrate clearly enough that Rudolf Steiner was prepared to educate the members on the realities of the Social Order as he saw them. His social ideas were not altogether unknown to older members. As early as 1905 and 1906 he had published three articles in *Luzifer-Gnosis* entitled "Theosophy and the Social Question," in which may be seen the outlines of the Threefold Social Order. But at that time he was evidently not interested in making his views widely known, and indeed they may well not yet have come to maturity in him. Now, as the war was ending, he was ready to make his ideas known, in spite of the failure of his effort to reach European leaders through Count Lerchenfeld. No other European statesman seemed to have any new ideas. The only leader who was making any real attempt to consider world issues and place them above national interests remained President Woodrow Wilson of the United States, and, as we have seen, Steiner was thoroughly distrustful of his kind of thinking and feared the worst if he were to have his way. The other victorious allied powers, considering that the Central Powers had been decisively defeated, had no intention of taking their wishes into consideration in the making of peace.

By contrast Steiner, as he was to state later in his *Appeal to the German People and the Civilized World,* soon to be discussed, was of the opinion that the German point of view should be put forward to the victorious powers, and that this should be based on spiritual impulses that had hitherto not been able to be heard "above the thunder of cannons." Wilson's Fourteen Points, on the basis of which the Germans claimed they had laid down their arms, had been enunciated, Steiner claimed, from a purely American point of view. "Wilson," he said, "was confronted by a Germany that had nothing to say for itself," and he, for one, was not prepared to let the German case go by default. But, in his view, only a new kind of Germany, with a new social order based on the separation of the three domains of society, could properly negotiate with the winners.

These views by the end of 1918 had not yet been made public by Steiner, but some of his collaborators had come to feel that his ideas were so important that they should be widely known. In particular two anthroposophists, Dr. Roman Boos, a lawyer from Zurich, and Emil Molt, an innovative industrialist from Stuttgart, were anxious not only to make his ideas known but to do something positive themselves, taking advantage if possible of the chaotic conditions of the immediate postwar period to effect some radical changes. Roman Boos, as a Swiss, thought that his fellow-countrymen, even though they had not taken part in the war as belligerents, might be ready for a new social order if the idea were to be placed before them, while Molt was ready to see what could be done among his fellow-industrialists. Others also asked Steiner for his advice and help. As a consequence he decided to issue a special appeal to the Germans and to the entire civilized world, intending that it should, in effect, be the German answer to President Wilson, who, when the Appeal was launched in February, 1919, was already in Europe and engaged in the early stages of peace-making. In order to make the Appeal as representative as possible, Steiner insisted that as many signatures as possible should be collected from representative Germans. When eventually it was published, it contained the signatures of many notable personalities, very few of whom were anthroposophists. The list included Gabrielle Reuter, the authoress whom Rudolf Steiner had met and admired in Weimar, and—no doubt much better known today—the distinguished novelist and later Nobel prizewinner, Hermann Hesse.

The Appeal to the German People and the Civilized World, as prepared by Rudolf Steiner, and signed by so many representative personalities, was the first salvo in the movement to establish the Threefold Social Order, and it was followed two months later by the publication of Steiner's long awaited book, published in three centers simultaneously—Dornach, Stuttgart and Vienna—under the title *The Threefold Commonwealth*,

242

or, more descriptively, "Basic Issues of the Social Question," the subtitle the book bore in German speaking countries.* The world into which it was launched was indeed a rapidly changing and extremely chaotic one, though this fact did not prevent the book from selling over eighty thousand copies in its first year. But from a practical point of view it is scarcely thinkable that its ideas could have been adopted *in toto* anywhere even in the chaotic conditions of 1919. Almost no one was willing to admit as yet that the social order was in need of a thorough overhauling. Even so, if the circumstances had been even slightly different, at least the main idea in the international realm—the separation of the state from the economic organization—might have been applied to the Austrian Empire, with results far better for the world than the actual settlement imposed by the victorious allies. In the economic realm a customs union could have come into being within the entire territory formerly ruled by the Dual Monarchy, allowing free trade within the area, while each minority could have had its own "rights-body" with limited powers, with an equally limited central government made up of representatives from the component bodies, whose task would be to administer the former empire as a whole. The Austrians might then have been ready to look eastward rather than toward the Germans in the west, and truncated Austria might well never have been swallowed up by Hitler's Third Reich in 1938.

In Germany itself during the first half of 1919 a very weak central government under Socialist auspices was trying to function in Berlin, following the abdication of the Kaiser. This

---

*This fundamental book, published in German under the title *Kernpunkte der Sozialen Frage in den Lebensnotwendigkeiten der Gegenwart und Zukunft* has been translated in its three English editions under three different titles, none of them much resembling the sesquipedalian German one. The three titles are *The Threefold Commonwealth*, *The Threefold Social Order*, and the latest one, published in 1977 in a translation by Frank Thomas Smith, bears the simple title *Towards Social Renewal*, with the subtitle coming close to the German, "Basic Issues of the Social Question". Here we shall use the first title as the one most familiar to anthroposophists.

government backed by the army which in this instance was willing to obey it, had already put down a rebellion of left wing Socialists and Communists, while in Bavaria Kurt Eisner, an independent Socialist leader, had proclaimed a republic to replace the former monarchy. A relative moderate, he was assassinated in the same month that Rudolf Steiner launched his Appeal; and at the beginning of April a Soviet Republic was proclaimed in Munich, which lasted for almost a month before being in its turn suppressed bloodily by troops obeying the orders of the Berlin government. All through these months the Allied blockade of Germany, instituted during the war, continued, and was used as an instrument of pressure to persuade the German government to accept the proposed peace treaty on the terms of which it had not been consulted. The treaty of Versailles was finally agreed to after the Socialist Government of Philipp Scheidemann had resigned in preference to accepting it. The blockade was lifted, and German life gradually returned to almost normal until the era of uncontrolled inflation which began in the summer of 1922. In the light of hindsight it seems now clear that it was only during the few months of virtual anarchy while the blockade was still in progress that wide support could have been won for Rudolf Steiner's Threefold Commonwealth movement. Once the peace treaty had been signed on June 28, 1919 the vast majority of Germans accepted docilely the return of the old social order. The Kaiser had gone into exile in Holland, and was not greatly missed, while the always rather feeble republican governments did their best to cope with the problems resulting from the German defeat, within the framework of the institutions they had inherited from the defunct Empire. The Weimar Constitution, adopted on July 31st, 1919, substituted an elected president for the Kaiser, and modified the former system of voting in such a way that it would be virtually impossible to avoid coalition governments. In other respects it changed nothing, and numerous groups of Germans, especially rightwing nationalists, were disgusted with it. But no doubt the vast majority of Germans felt at home with it, at least for the time being, and turned their attention to the problem of making a living, eschewing all revolutionary ideas, including those of Rudolf Steiner.

But in April, 1919, when the *Threefold Commonwealth* was launched, there still seemed to be hopeful signs that the German people were ready for radical change. This seemed to be especially true of the Swabians in the former kingdom of Württemberg, whose capital was Stuttgart. It was in that city that Emil Molt had his tobacco factory, which bore the name of Waldorf-Astoria, and it was above all in Stuttgart that Molt was able to find other industrialists interested, like himself, in the Threefold Order. But neither Molt nor Boos nor, indeed anyone else among the small band of anthroposophists, possessed enough knowledge or authority to lead the Threefold movement. So, if such a movement were to be brought into existence, there was only one possible leader for it, and that was Rudolf Steiner himself, in spite of the enormous demands on his time and energy that such leadership must involve. Whatever his misgivings must have been, he took up the burden, and as soon as he could escape from his pressing commitments in Dornach he paid a visit to Stuttgart, where he delivered a long awaited lecture to the group of enthusiasts who had been discussing for weeks the *Threefold Commonwealth* and its ideas, and were ready to do whatever they could to help bring them to realization. His first public lecture on April 22nd excited a tremendous enthusiasm, and numerous members of the audience asked him to address them and explain his ideas further. He did his best to respond to these requests, and even met with groups of workers in their smoke-filled taverns, apparently to the detriment of his voice, since he himself had long before given up smoking. It is, however, reported that, though he usually started his talk in a somewhat muffled voice which amounted to little more than a croak, he was soon able to overcome his temporary disability, and before the end of his talk he was able to speak with his customary warmth, clarity and strength. For several months he remained in Stuttgart, devoting himself whole-heartedly to his new task, organizing the work and expounding the threefold ideas to individuals and groups, to industrialists and trade unionists, wherever a suitable audience presented itself. He did not return to Dornach until August. The Threefold movement in Germany was given a formal organization in May under the name of the Union for the Threefold Social Order, and at the same time Roman Boos founded a Swiss Union for the Threefold Social Order in Zurich. A new weekly periodical was launched in July under the title of the *Threefold Membering of the Social Order*, to which Steiner contributed over thirty articles, while Boos founded a similar monthly in Switzerland.

The political effectiveness of the Union was perhaps less than it would have been if it had been backed by a political party, or if the Union had itself become such a party. Nevertheless, it will be clear from a study of the principles of the Threefold Order outlined earlier in this chapter that it never was at any time possible—and still is not possible today—to bring about the threefold membering of society through political pressure. When members of the audience spoke, as they often did, of "introducing the Threefold Order" Rudolf Steiner invariably replied that no one could *introduce* the Threefold Order, but individuals could and should work in every possible way to bring some elements of it to birth. If it ever came into being it would be as the result of the untiring efforts of individual men and women. If this seems to be at variance with his Memorandum of 1917 in which he made it clear that the Central Powers ought to adopt the Threefold Social Order through action by their rulers and with his willingness to have the Memorandum submitted to leading statesmen in Central Europe, it must be remembered that it was originally drawn up at the request of Count Lerchenfeld, and Steiner himself had little hope that it would be accepted, much less put into effect by fiat from above. He wished above all to launch the idea, and have men of influence think about it. It might then become part of the peace program of the Central Powers, in this respect forming an answer to the abstract Fourteen Points of President Wilson.

Nevertheless, it remains possible that a political party which accepted the desirability of the Threefold Order and placed it at the center of its programme could indeed have won several

246

seats in the Reichstag in Berlin under the new system of proportional representation, and thereafter used the Reichstag as a platform for spreading Threefold ideas. This was not tried, but the movement did all the same make a marked impact in Germany, where Rudolf Steiner himself became a figure of national importance, an unusual position for a spiritual leader who had sought nothing of the kind. It thus became inevitable that he should also arouse antagonism as well as winning new supporters, and, as we shall see, his new opponents proved to be very serious enemies prepared to stop at nothing to silence him. At the same time many of those who now formed part of the Union and did their best to further his social ideas never had the time or opportunity (and sometimes not even the inclination) to become fully fledged anthroposophists, and were often enough, even when they became members of the Anthroposophical Society, quite imperfectly acquainted with Anthroposophy itself, of which all the Threefold ideas were in fact an integral part. The differences between the new adherents of Anthroposophy who came into the movement because of the Threefold work, and the older members, especially those who had at one time been theosophists, were always latent in the Society, and became accentuated as time went on, never becoming fully resolved even long after the Threefold Movement had become part of history.

Rudolf Steiner during these months in Stuttgart spent himself untiringly. The years during which he had lectured to the Berlin workers in the Liebnecht Working Men's College at the turn of the century had prepared him to speak directly to the workers in a manner uniquely his own, and that no other anthroposophist could match. Time and again he pointed out to them that their real grievance was that their work was bought and sold like any other commodity, and that this was contrary to their dignity as men and women. He told them that it was cultural deprivation from which above all they suffered, because they were forced to enter economic life at about the age of fourteen without ever having received an adequate education capable of preparing them for a full life as adults. He criticized the Marxist solutions unmercifully as irrelevant to the real problems. The state being, as Steiner held, totally incompetent to manage industry, there would be no point in widespread nationalization of private enterprises. If state functionaries were brought into industry as managers they could do nothing except behave like ordinary industrialists. Even the division of profits among the workers would not solve the problem of their cultural deprivation. Least of all would the Bolshevik expedients now being tried in Russia lead to any solution. But if the economic sector ceased to tyrannize over the state and the state ceased to try to regulate industry, then a place would appear for the worker to make his vote effective in a democratic system, in which the state would have but a limited role to play.

It goes without saying that such talk greatly displeased the workers' leaders who belonged to either the Socialist or Communist parties, both of which were Marxist in their ideologies; and after a brief period during which they tolerated Steiner's lectures and discussions with their fellow-members, they began to exercise party discipline and forbade them to attend—an experience similar to that of the early part of the century, when it was the members of the executive of the Social Democratic party who stopped Steiner's popular lectures at the Working Men's College in Berlin. In just the same way as before the union leaders decided that Steiner was a danger to their party aims. Without the full support of the unions as well as the employers it was impossible to bring into being, at least in a unionized company, the economic associations which, according to the Threefold ideas, were to take the place of the ordinary joint stock or privately owned companies that were the norm in the economic domain. Nevertheless Steiner's efforts with the workers were far from fruitless as, at least in some industries in which they had not been deeply indoctrinated with Marxism, the Associations did come into being with the support of both workers and employers. In some workplaces also the dedicated Marxists were heavily outnumbered by those who wished to try something new, and the union leaders were sometimes worsted by Steiner's capacity for laying bare the incongruities and inconsistencies of their arguments.

248

An incident reported by Dr. Friedrich Rittelmeyer, the Protestant pastor whose book on Rudolf Steiner we have quoted earlier, was no doubt typical of many. "In a discussion with workmen at that time," he reports, "I saw Rudolf Steiner from a new angle—amazingly quick and alert as always, but at the same time imposingly active and energetic. His counter-arguments poured down with devastating force on those who were opposing him. One of the lesser leaders, a man not without some knowledge of his own, but who made a conceited little speech, was so flattened by Rudolf Steiner that he left the hall and wept in the vestibule. 'It would not be exactly a pleasure to come up against him here,' I thought to myself. 'But to see him like this is a real joy!'"[45]

It has already been noted that the central idea of the Threefold Social Order was the separation of the three domains, the spiritual-cultural, the domain of the state and human rights, and the economic domain; and that the basis for the economic life in future ought to be an association between producers, distributors and consumers. Since only the economic domain was the actual producer of consumer goods, it was evident that those whose working lives were devoted to the other two domains would have to receive their subsistence from the economic domain, that is to say, from the Associations. In order to enable them to obtain their subsistence the cultural workers and state functionaries would receive money, as they do now. But this money would differ in a marked manner from money as we know it today. Rudolf Steiner had a great deal to say on the subject of money, but most of this lies outside the scope of this book.[46] Here it is necessary to mention only a few important features of his teachings on the subject. To Steiner money itself was not a reality; it was simply a token of value, and showed that some commodity had been produced. It was, therefore, a medium of exchange only, and could not be treated as if it were a commodity itself. Above all it ought not to be accumulated. It should be based on some real commodity (such, for example, as wheat) which would in due course be consumed. The money, so Steiner held, should also be cancelled in the same way. But just before its life-span came to an end it should be given away to the spiritual-cultural realm, which would spend it for the last time. This gift-money, as Steiner called it, should always be used to pay for cultural and not material goods, and the entire cultural realm should be supported by such money, now called profits, since they represent the surplus from the economic domain. Thus the economic Associations, as envisaged by Rudolf Steiner, would always produce a surplus which would not be re-invested in order to produce more—capital for investment would always be new money—or used in ways we today consider productive. The surplus would pay for the relatively few workers in the rights domain, and for the many expenses in the cultural domain, especially education. Once the money had been spent in these areas it would go at once out of existence.

It might be thought that the workers, who had so little to lose, would be more favorable to the Threefold ideas than the employers. But in fact Rudolf Steiner interested a fair number of employers, some of whom, especially in Württemberg, were already anthroposophists, including, of course, Emil Molt, the owner of the Waldorf Astoria tobacco factory. Several leading industrialists in Stuttgart asked Steiner to talk with them and with their workers, including managers of and owners of such businesses as Bosch and Daimler. When it became clear that the Threefold Social Order as such would not come into being in all Germany, the work of the Union for the Threefold Order was mostly concentrated on organizing some Associations in a few industries, whose leaders were willing to convert to this new form of organization. At the same time efforts were made to form cultural councils in the spiritual cultural realm. In the economic realm councils made up of all the newly formed Associations were also brought into being. Anthroposophists themselves organized businesses both in Germany and Switzerland which were expected to function on Threefold principles.

Very few of these pioneer ventures were successful for any length of time, and in due course had to be liquidated, most of the failures being due to the inexperience of the enthusiastic founders, many of whom, as might be expected, came from the ranks of the idealistic young. Emil Molt's factory was in a different category. This was already a going concern, led by a warm-hearted but thoroughly competent industrialist. In his factory at Stuttgart Rudolf Steiner made one of his first major addresses on the Threefold Order, and was asked the crucial question: How can we overcome our cultural deprivation? What can we do so that our children do not suffer as we have suffered? To this Rudolf Steiner answered that it would be possible to have a new kind of school, in which all their children could be educated in a new way.

So as early as April, 1919, the fundamental decision was taken to create such a school, and Emil Molt proposed to devote the surplus of his factory to financing it, thus making this surplus into gift-money for the cultural domain, in accordance with the principles of the Threefold Order that he personally had accepted. So came into existence the first Waldorf School in Stuttgart, the first of more than a hundred and fifty at present operating throughout the world. The story of this school will be considered in the next chapter.

Chapter 10.

THE FOUNDING OF THE WALDORF SCHOOL AND ITS INFLUENCE THROUGHOUT THE WORLD

In earlier chapters of this book it was shown how when quite a young man Rudolf Steiner interested himself in education. While he was still at school he tutored fellow-pupils of his own age and younger; when he was at the Vienna Institute of Technology he eked out his meager scholarship funds by tutoring, and then for several years he was responsible for the education of a severely handicapped boy, who was eventually able to become entirely normal and qualify as a doctor. In view of what has been said in this book about Steiner's extraordinary capacity for observation, and his intuitive grasp of what lies behind the perceptible world, it will be readily appreciated that in all his youthful educational work he was constantly learning from his experience, and observing how human beings develop and change during childhood. It is, therefore, not surprising that as soon as he had a magazine at his disposal in which he could say what he wanted, he began to write educational articles, little though these may perhaps have been appreciated in the last years of the nineteenth century by the rather critical subscribers to the Berlin *Magazine for Literature.* Even at this time he took the position that it was the primary task of the teacher to awaken abilities in his students, and not to stuff them with knowledge, or "transmit to them our own convictions."

When a few years later he founded the magazine *Luzifer-Gnosis* whose subscribers knew that their magazine would be a vehicle for Rudolf Steiner's ideas in every field, it was also natural for him to revert fairly often to social and educational questions in which he was vitally interested. The articles on the social order written for *Luzifer-Gnosis* in 1905 and 1906 necessarily lacked those ideas which he was later to describe in such detail, because, as we have seen, Steiner was not yet ready to speak of the threefold nature of man and so could not speak of the threefold nature of society. But in his fundamental educational lecture first given in 1907 and then personally revised for publication, after having been given in a slightly different form to many different audiences, he was already able to enunciate all the major educational principles later used in his educational work. In this lecture called *The Education of the Child in the Light of Theosophy* (or Anthroposophy) Steiner explains how a child in the first seven years of his life until the change of teeth lives in his will forces and learns by imitation, never by precept; how from the change of teeth to puberty (from the age of 7 to 14) he lives in the element of feeling, making it necessary for his studies to be saturated with artistic feeling, and therefore for him to be guided by a teacher with whom he should develop a relationship of love as well as respect; and how only at puberty can he really begin to think independently as his intellect for the first time becomes free. Human willing, feeling, and thinking thus follow each other in time, as first the physical, then the etheric and astral bodies, are successively developed until the young person at last acquires his own earthly I or ego at the age of about 21.

The entire educational programme of the Waldorf School at Stuttgart and subsequent schools either bearing this name, or called Steiner schools after the name of their originator, or after other personalities or higher beings to whom the school founders feel related, was already implicit in this lecture; and it would almost be possible to deduce an educational programme from it. Everything in Steiner education is based upon the child and his development, and not at all on the supposed needs of society. Thus the word "education," which in Latin means "leading forth" may truly be applied to this form of education, as distinct from the word "learning" which is more properly applied to most educational systems. In this lecture also first appears, most significantly, a passage in which Steiner voices his confident hope that some day he will be asked to take the lead in bringing his educational ideas to realization. "These things," he writes, "can of course only be touched on here, but in future Anthroposophy will be called upon to give the necessary indications, and this it is in a position to do. For it is no empty abstraction but a body of living facts which can give guiding lines for the conduct of life's realities."

Twelve years had passed before Steiner was at last given the opportunity to put his educational ideas into operation. As a result of his first lecture to the workers in Emil Molt's tobacco factory he was asked by them how the next generation could grow up free from the cultural deprivation from which they themselves had suffered. He immediately responded positively to the question and its implied request; and even before a full week had gone by after his lecture, he was already meeting for practical educational discussions with Emil Molt and two other anthroposophists, both of whom were to play a leading part in the school, and one of whom had been very active in the Threefold Movement from the beginning. The discussion, which was very wide-ranging, naturally turned upon the cultural realm of the Threefold Social Order, and on the necessity for new cultural impulses. But Steiner also spoke at length about how necessary it was for industrial workers to become aware of the world outside the field of their own specialized work, and to win back the dignity of which they had been robbed when first they came to be regarded virtually as interchangeable parts in the industrial system.

Up to this time Emil Molt, who was a strongly paternalistic employer, genuinely interested in the welfare of his employees, had been offering extension courses in various subjects to the workers. But they had excited relatively little interest, and he was thinking already of abandoning them for lack of support. But from the beginning the workers were fired with enthusiasm for the idea of a totally different kind of school for their children, and Molt, who was already a leader in the Threefold movement, immediately expressed himself as ready to devote the profits of his enterprise as "gift-money" for this new cultural venture. After numerous discussions Steiner agreed to become what he called the "guide and spiritual adviser" of the school, whereupon Molt bought a downtown restaurant which he proceeded to have remodelled as a school. The prospective student body for the opening, which was planned for September in the same year, consisted of the workers' children, about a hundred and fifty in all, to which were quickly added the children of the Stuttgart anthroposophists, approximately fifty in number, and coming almost entirely from a different class from their new fellow-students. Thus the school was planned from the beginning to include all grades up to the twelfth. A complete educational programme therefore had to be offered, which would include the classes in the various arts that Steiner considered essential, and teachers had to be found for all of them. Perhaps fortunately, a few professional educators, who were also anthroposophists, were available with the necessary teaching experience. But the vast bulk of the teachers were chosen by Steiner himself from volunteers from every walk of life who wished to take part in the epoch-making experiment, and who were already familiar with Anthoroposophy and competent in the subjects they would be teaching. Many of these men and women left their existing employment to work with him in this venture; and it is probable that such a group of dedicated and gifted teachers has never been assembled before or since at the beginning of any school in history.

Obviously, the first task was to train them, both as teachers, and as pioneers in a new form of education. All Steiner schools, including this first one, are run by their faculty. For this reason it would be necessary for the teachers to learn how to work together as a team in a spirit of harmony in spite of the absence of any overall authority. At the beginning, instead of having such an authority over them they possessed a "guide and spiritual adviser" in whom they all had absolute confidence, and he in turn had confidence in them because they had all been handpicked by him. The State authorities of Württemberg had granted him the right to make the experiment over a period of three years, although all he had submitted to them was a memorandum telling them how he proposed to run the school. Thus Steiner was in the unique position for an educator of having no immediate financial worries, no inspector breathing down his neck, and an absolute freedom to select his teachers and his curriculum, with a student body whose parents were willing absolutely to entrust their children to him and those whom he had selected.

It was arranged that Rudolf Steiner should meet with all the teachers in Stuttgart in late August and early September for the purpose of giving them a special training course which would continue almost until the opening of the school. This opening was scheduled for September 7th, 1919, under five months from the day the decision was made to create a new school in Stuttgart run according to principles derived from the anthroposophical view of man. But before giving this course an important task awaited him—to return to Dornach and tell the members there what was being planned at Stuttgart, while at the same time giving encouragement and advice to those who were working on the Gotheanum.

In this series of lectures given to the Dornach members, published under the title of *Education as a Social Problem*, Steiner began by speaking about the necessity for the Threefold Social Order, on which he had been working in Germany for months, insisting in particular on the need for the fundamental transformation of cultural life. He spoke of the great dangers threatening mankind from the one-sided development of the intellect, a faculty that men had only recently acquired for themselves, independent of divine inspiration. They are able now to use this faculty for their own ends, but if it is not to fall into the hands of Ahriman it must in future be permeated by the Christ Impulse. If men do not use their thinking capacity to fulfill the divine purposes it will necessarily be *mis*used, and all kinds of new evils will be allowed entry into the world.

This introduction, on a theme to which he was to revert

often in the last year of his life, was here given mainly as a background for his detailed explanation of the supreme importance of the role played by teachers in the social structure, and the qualities that would be required of them in the new school—how essential it was that they should be thoroughly versed in the science of spirit, so that they could have a true appreciation of the children committed to their charge, as beings of body, soul, and spirit, whose soul faculties would be unfolding beneath their gaze year by year; and how essential it was for these teachers to be able to develop living imaginative thinking in themselves. "The burning question is therefore," he told his audience, "how can teacher training be transformed in future? It can be transformed in only one way, and that is, that the teacher himself absorbs what can come from spiritual science as knowledge of man's true nature. The teacher must be permeated by the reality of man's connection with the supersensible worlds. He must be in the position to see in the growing child evidence that he has descended from the supersensible world through conception and birth, has clothed himself with a body, and wishes to acquire here in the physical world what he cannot acquire in the life between death and a new birth, and in which the teacher has to help, Every child should stand before the soul of the teacher as a question posed by the supersensible world to the sense world. This question cannot be asked in a definite and comprehensive way in regard to every individual child unless one employs the knowledge that comes from spiritual science concerning the nature of man."[47]

As soon as Steiner had given his last lecture in this cycle, a lecture in which he especially stressed the dangers of the development of one-sided intelligence, he betook himself to Stuttgart where his chosen teachers were awaiting him, and here for fourteen consecutive days he gave three separate courses, one in the morning, another in the afternoon, and the third in the evening. The course given in the morning was called *The General Knowledge of Man as a Basis for Pedagogy*, a beautifully exact title for the actual content of the course which has been published in several editions in English under the title of

Study of Man. This course is still regarded as the essential foundation for all work in teacher training programmes for Steiner schools; and indeed it is the most comprehensive course in human psychology as well as in educational theory ever given by Rudolf Steiner. In particular the nature of man as a threefold being is strongly stressed and illustrated in numerous ways. The second course is published under the title *Practical Course for Teachers,* and it contains general and specific information on both the subject matter and methods used for children from different age groups. One of these lectures was also devoted to the arts as they would be taught in the Waldorf School. The third course, never published in English, but made available to teachers, was the so-called Pedagogical Course, or Course on Educational Practice. These courses were completed in the evening of September 5th. The next day, on which no lectures were given, was spent by the teachers in making ready for the next day's ceremonial opening—and perhaps for the beginning of the digestion of the concentrated food of the previous fortnight! The absence of an assembly hall in the remodelled restaurant that was to serve as the school made it necessary for the opening ceremony, attended by parents and children as well as teachers and anthroposophists, to be held elsewhere. The school music teacher opened with a Bach Prelude, which was followed by a recitation by Marie Steiner and a demonstration of eurythmy by some children whom she had instructed. Then came an introductory speech by Emil Molt, followed by Rudolf Steiner's opening address. This, of course was the highlight of the morning's proceedings. In the afternoon, in an atmosphere of general festivity, the teachers and children were introduced to each other, and at night all the teachers were invited to a performance of *The Magic Flute* in the Stuttgart Opera House. There Rudolf Steiner sat by Herr Molt, pointing out to the industrialist where the teachers were all sitting in different parts of the theatre. On such occasions the years fell away from him—he was now 58—and he was as animated and excited as any of the children. School began the next day.

Steiner's address at the opening of the school, important

258

though it was, cannot be considered here in any detail. As he always did during the lifetime of the Threefold social movement, he related the establishment of the school to the need for a new impulse in the cultural life of Germany, an impulse which should from the beginning be drawn from the free cultural realm of the Threefold Social Order. The school was in truth an utterly *free* enterprise in an educational world dominated at the time by the state, and with educational requirements set by the state. Moreover it was a unitary school, and—an extraordinary innovation at that time—a coeducational school, offering only general education, without the specialization that in Germany of that age was thought to be such a great educational advance. The first Waldorf School was, indeed, so unusual at the time, and in many respects Waldorf education is so unusual even in our own age that we shall devote some space to its general features.

It is worth mentioning here that Steiner, even in his opening address, made it clear that the school was not and never would become a school for teaching Anthroposophy. The teachers would work from an anthroposophical impulse and out of the knowledge of Anthroposophy that they had acquired, including knowledge of the threefold nature of the human being. But they would tell the children nothing of what lay behind their teaching. Even in the religious classes that were given in all German schools in the 1920s no anthroposophical concepts were taught. A Catholic priest taught the Catholic children and a Protestant pastor taught the Protestant children. Those parents who were neither Catholic nor Protestants could choose for their children a general nondenominational Christianity course given by one of the regular school teachers, which might of course be somewhat influenced by the anthroposophical orientation of the teacher. In the early years of the school it became, as it turned out, by far the most popular of the three religious courses!

At the center of all anthroposophical thinking in the realm of education is the recognition that a child is not simply a small man or woman, and he should not be treated as such, reasoned with, preached to, filled with intellectual knowledge by adults, and expected to grow up in the image of his parents or teachers. A child is a potentially but not actually mature human being who will develop through the years of childhood at a pace that is virtually the same for all children, since the pace is governed not only by biological laws but by laws of the soul and spirit. At birth a child frees his physical body from his mother's womb, at the change of teeth he frees his etheric body, and at puberty his astral body. Thus for the first seven years of his life, all education should be directed toward enabling him to make proper use of his physical body. With the change of teeth and the freeing of the etheric body, his education is directed primarily to this body for the next seven years until puberty. At the age of fourteen the astral body is usually entirely freed—indeed puberty actually consists of this freeing—and after the young person is able to work with forces not available to him before. With such insights as these provided by Anthroposophy, education ceases to be an arbitrary process of more or less hit-or-miss methods and curricula of study, and becomes a conscious effort to bring out the full potentialities of each individual child as they are inherent at each particular age, by teaching always subjects that belong to that age and in a manner suitable for it, and not for the age he will have reached two or three years later. Not until about the age of 21 does a young person receive his own I which is then freed for his use, as the other "bodies" were freed at birth, 7 and 14.

It is, of course, possible to teach most children to read and write before the change of teeth, but it is not desirable because forces have to be used for reading and writing that have not yet become fully available for their use. It is possible for children of eleven to acquire various mathematical aptitudes before puberty which, according to Waldorf pedagogy, should not be acquired until later. In the long run nothing whatever is gained by trying to make use prematurely of these forces. It is not in the least important at the age of 21 whether one learned to read and write at the age of 5 or at the age of 7. What is important then is one's ability to read and write well and to possess a lively intelligence unmarred by premature senescence. Children in Steiner schools are always kept in the same class as others of their age group, and are never allowed to skip a class because of their precocious intellectual capacities. Many subjects, especially as taught in the Steiner schools, possess relatively little intellectual content in the sense that the children are not expected to *understand* them in the way adults understand them. So it is possible to retain precociously intellectual children in the same class as all others of the same age without boring them; indeed, it is not at all unusual for such children to be relatively backward–in artistic work, and to experience difficulties when they do eurythmy. If they are really good in all these subjects and activities they will certainly be encouraged to help other children who are less gifted than they, thus learning at an early age that it is a privilege to possess such gifts, carrying with it the responsibility to place them at the disposition of others.

In all respects Waldorf education is a *general* education, and at no time during the twelve years or so spent at school do the children specialize in any particular subject. Nor is there any competition within the classes. Marks are not given; the teacher makes his own evaluation of the children which is sent to their parents, who usually discuss the report cards of their children with the teachers and with the children themselves. The evaluation considers them in relation to their own past performances and capacities, as the teacher sees them—never in relation to other children. Parents who wish their children to shine and outshine others so that they may bask in the glory reflected on them by their children, receive no encouragement at Steiner schools; nor are any prizes given. A teacher feels himself most successful if there is a real solidarity among the members of his class and a true social feeling, so that no trace of rivalry or competition shows itself.

Even today all this is very different from what happens in most state schools. In 1919 in Germany it was truly revolutionary, as was also the mingling of children from different class backgrounds. In the first year of the school about 150 children came from the working class, as we have seen, their parents being employees of the tobacco factory, whose fees were paid from the "gift-money" made available by Emil Molt from the

261

factory's profits. The other fifty or sixty children came from the middle or upper class, their parents being anthroposophists, very few of whom at this time were from the working class. As time went on, and the school won a very high reputation in Stuttgart, and even in Germany as a whole, the student body began to increase rapidly. By 1928 there were already more than a thousand children enrolled in the school, and more than fifty teachers. The proportion of children from the working class necessarily dropped with this increased enrollment since fees now had to be charged, and except for the children of the Waldorf Astoria factory workers, it was the parents who paid them. Indeed, little though this was originally intended, wherever Steiner schools have come into being, the student body has never been a true cross-section of society as Steiner would have wished. Scholarships, full or partial, have ensured that some children are enrolled whose parents come from the working class. But they remain a small minority everywhere, and only the original Waldorf School in Stuttgart has ever had the high proportion of children from the working class that it had at its beginning in 1919.

Almost all the innovations that distinguish Waldorf from state schools, and even from so-called "progressive" schools today are based on Steiner's perception of the child as a developing being with different needs at different ages. Most modern Waldorf schools, unlike the first school in Stuttgart at its founding, have kindergartens, and some even have nursery "schools." But no attempt is made in these schools to teach the children anything with an intellectual content, as for example reading and writing, because of the perception that the pre-school child learns almost exclusively through imitation, and *ought* to do so. In kindergarten and nursery school, therefore, the children learn by *doing*, for example singing, dancing, making things with their hands, leaving the development of the intellect to the first year in primary school.

Examples of the adaptation of the school curriculum to the age of the children could be multiplied indefinitely, and the interested reader is referred to the many books on the Steiner schools and the kind of education they offer, including a chapter by the present author in his *Man and World in the Light of Anthroposophy*. Scarcely less interesting to educators is the way the schools are administered in accordance with Steiner's belief that only those who take an active part in teaching should be responsible for the school management. Almost all Steiner schools have therefore established a College of Teachers, which is the decision-making body and includes all fulltime teachers who are employed on a regular basis. The College, at a minimum, will choose all new faculty members, and usually makes itself responsible for all business decisions, including the teachers' salaries, the decision often being made on the basis of the teacher's need and responsibilities. The effort is always made to make it clear to everyone that the salary paid is not regarded as a compensation for work done, thus obeying the fundamental rule enunciated by Rudolf Steiner that labor must never be regarded as a commodity—one of the pillars of the Threefold Order as he explained it. Very few indeed of the schools making use of Steiner's educational principles have ever had to be closed because of bad management or lack of parental support. So perhaps it may be reasonably assumed that the system of faculty management works, and that professional administrators such as are to be found in all state school systems are not an absolute necessity.

Interestingly enough, a report exists in which a state school inspector expressed his impressions of the original Waldorf School in Stuttgart after it had been in operation for seven years, by which time the student body had arisen to over a thousand, and was no longer dependent on the largesse of Emil Molt, who paid only the fees of children of the workers in his factory. This report was not made public, but the inspector, F. Hartlieb, wrote an article based on his report, and had it published in a Württemberg educational journal. It was later translated into English and published. Throughout the article the author, who was not an anthroposophist and had had no knowledge of Anthroposophy before it became part of his official duties to report on the Waldorf School, emphasizes how much the state system could learn from it. Recognizing, as he said, that it was impossible to appreciate the Waldorf

School at its true value without some knowledge of Steiner's educational principles, he devoted much space in his report to a (very accurate) explanation of some basic anthroposophic concepts, and how they are reflected in the educational practice and in the curriculum of the school. Most surprisingly for a professional educator, Hartlieb lavished his praises on the Waldorf School teachers who came to the school from many different walks of life, each contributing his special talents to the whole.

"Without prejudice of any sort," he wrote, "I must put on record the fact that the College of Teachers with its high moral standard and intellectual attainments gives the Waldorf School its peculiar stamp and quality. A staff of teachers in such a close bond of union, working in the same spirit and filled with the same warmth of enthusiasm, cannot but bring their feeling of unity to daily expression. Each one serves the other in love; each one radiates forces, to receive forces into himself in return. . . . Thus they grow together into an exemplary community of life and work, such as deserves the highest recognition . . . The Waldorf School has no Board of Governors empowered to inspect its work. Nor does the time-table subject the individual to any kind of narrowing restrictions. Unity among the teachers is ensured by the teachers' conferences, at which all-important questions are discussed in detail, and which the teachers attend at the School—sometimes several times a week and until late at night. . . . The children are warmly attached to their teachers, both men and women, who, without recourse to corporal punishment, train the soul and spirit of the boys and girls entrusted to them by love, goodness, wisdom and example, more even than by their enlightened methods of instruction. The teacher coming from a State school is struck by the fact that greater freedom of movement is allowed among the children of the Waldorf School than is generally the case. . . . The right behavior of the children in the Waldorf School is not regulated and one-sidedly enforced by an external discipline, but is founded in the inner life, so as to grow spontaneously from within. . . . The friendly spirit in the Waldorf School is beautifully revealed in the monthly

264

festival when all the pupils up to the twelfth form gather with their teachers in the gymnasium, and follow with great interest the musical and eurythmy performances. The presence of the parents, who come in large numbers to all School gatherings, such as concerts, plays and so on, outside the usual school-work, gives the festival a homelike character. It also points clearly to the fact that parents, pupils and teachers are closely associated with one another. Finally, it should be pointed out that, in conformity with the natural family life, boys and girls are taught together. The Waldorf School has established co-education from the first form up to the twelfth and last class, and has contrived to make the differentiation of the sexes in soul and spirit serve the cause of education."[48]

Almost everything that is done in present-day Steiner schools that makes them distinctive originates from Rudolf Steiner himself. During the few years that he was able to supervise the education personally he proved to be a cornucopia of new ideas and suggestions. The school festivals referred to by Herr Hart-lieb remain today one of the distinctive features of Steiner schools, as do the concerts, plays and other performances by the students to which parents are invited. The festivals, as may be supposed, stemmed from Steiner's numerous lectures on their significance, of which something will be said in Chapter 12. For a long time after the founding of the first Waldorf School in Stuttgart he attended in person as many of the faculty meetings as he was able, and though they were held regularly every week he used to make the journey from Dornach to Stuttgart for most of them. The teachers used to call him "the teacher of the teachers," and it was at these meetings that he gave them some of his most fruitful suggestions. To every question he was asked he gave an answer, and he played an active part in all discussions.

Steiner, it appears, was also greatly loved by the children, and during his sojourns in Stuttgart he visited as many classes as he could, always with the consent of their teachers. Such visits were never looked upon as inspections, and he never at any time permitted himself a word of criticism of the teacher in the presence of the class. Sometimes, at the teacher's sugges-

265

tion he would take over the class for the rest of the period, giving an impromptu presentation which often proved of immense benefit to the still not very experienced teacher. When he left the classroom he liked to ask the children if they loved their teachers, always to be met with the enthusiastic "yes" that he quite certainly expected.

Many of the teachers used to make the not very long journey from Stuttgart to Dornach at the weekends for the express purpose of asking Rudolf Steiner yet another set of questions. In Dornach these men and women brought a breath of fresh air to the somewhat hothouse atmosphere. The first group of teachers, being drawn from many professions and coming from all parts of the German-speaking world, included people who had already won distinction elsewhere, though they were new to teaching. They made a considerable impression in Dornach not only with their questions but with their often brilliant talk. The members in Dornach, many of whom had lived there since before the war, were devoted and knowledgeable anthroposophists, but few of them could be considered men and women of the world. Some of them resented the invasion by the Stuttgart teachers and also the enthusiastic bands of young people who were working in one capacity or another for the Threefold Social Order. Some of the teachers and perhaps a majority of the young workers had a relatively slight knowledge of Anthroposophy, which was found somewhat shocking by many older members. Dornach had by this time become the real center of Anthroposophy, but important work continued to be done in other centers such as Stuttgart, Munich and Berlin, whose members were loath to admit the new supremacy of Dornach resulting from the building of the Goetheanum, and the work connected with it.

In addition to his numerous formal and informal talks to the Stuttgart teachers, Rudolf Steiner soon began to give courses on pedagogy elsewhere than in Stuttgart and Dornach. A Christmas educational conference held in the Goetheanum in 1921 was the occasion for visits of many foreign educators to Dornach, leading to further invitations to lecture abroad, in the hope that similar Waldorf Schools could be inaugurated outside Switzerland and Germany. The impulse towards this education proved especially strong in England. Rudolf Steiner was first invited to speak at an educational festival held in April 1922 at Shakespeare's birthplace, Stratford-on-Avon. He took the opportunity not only to see about a dozen plays—he approved of the way the comedies were presented, but had other ideas on the staging of the tragedies—but also to give a lecture on Shakespeare himself and his inspiration, as well as on education. His lectures were well reported in the English press, and he was asked to deliver a whole course of lectures later in the year at Manchester College, Oxford University. These lectures were later published under the title *The Spiritual Ground of Education.* Thus, as early as 1922, Steiner became well known in English educational circles, and the movement to start another school on the lines of the Waldorf School in Stuttgart made some headway. Two further series of lectures on education were given in 1923 (Ilkley) and in 1924 (Torquay). By the time the second cycle was given under the title of *The Kingdom of Childhood* it had been determined that an English school would be founded. This was accomplished the following year when the so-called New School in Streatham, a London suburb, came into being. Later its name was changed to Michael Hall School; it still exists, being located now at Forest Row in Sussex.

In 1923 a young married couple opened a Waldorf School in a private house in the Hague in Holland, with ten pupils. Rudolf Steiner, encouraged by the initiative, paid it a visit later in the year, and the following year, when he visited Arnhem, Holland, for the last series of lectures he was to give in that country, he found time in a very crowded programme to give there a remarkable cycle of ten lectures, published under the English title of *Human Values in Education,* in which he spoke fervently about the future of all anthroposophical work in the world, including education. So many new possibilities existed now, he told his audience, that were not present before, and the spiritual world was waiting to give new inspirations to mankind. The school in the Hague survived and expanded, under a small group of very gifted teachers who remained with it for decades; and though it was closed down by the Nazis during the war, it was reopened immediately after their departure. Several schools in other countries were opened during the next decade, including the first school in the United States, the Rudolf Steiner School in New York, opened in 1929.

Until World War II the Steiner school movement grew rather slowly, in part because of financial stringencies, including the uncontrolled inflation in Germany and Austria in the early 1920s, and the worldwide depression of the 1930s. The National Socialist regime in Germany closed down all the Waldorf schools, including the parent school in Stuttgart, for reasons that do credit to the schools rather than to the Nazis! They claimed that the Waldorf schools were insufficiently nationalistic (as they said also unceasingly about Rudolf Steiner himself whom they regarded as an implacable enemy of their party), and, worse still, the schools had as their aim the development of free individualities. Naturally they could scarcely defend themselves against such charges, of which they were obviously guilty, and proud of the fact. But they had their reward after the Nazi regime was overthrown when the British and United States' military governments did all they could to help them back into operation, for precisely the same reason that they had been suppressed by the Third Reich. In spite of the shortage of materials and bombed out buildings, the schools soon recovered their position as by far the largest private educational system in Germany. The Nazi authorities allowed two of the three Dutch schools to remain open, and of course Switzerland and Sweden as neutrals were unaffected by the Nazi tyranny, except for the financial stringencies engendered by the war itself and the shortages from which they suffered. In Great Britain, curiously enough, all the major schools were founded already before the war and continued to operate during it; and it was not until very recent times that the movement in Britain began to add more schools. The leading school had to be evacuated far from London during the war.

By 1952 there were 65 schools operating throughout the world, though several of these were small and struggling, and not all did in fact survive into the next decade. But with the

1960s the movement began a considerable expansion, the end of which is by no means in sight. It is difficult to state with any accuracy just how many Waldorf and Steiner schools are now in 1980 in operation, in part because some of the more recent schools may not be using all the elements of Steiner education used by the older and better established schools. There is no system of accreditation, and a school that likes to call itself a Steiner school will always be given the benefit of the doubt by its elders. Certainly there are more than 150 Steiner schools now in operation, making it the largest group of private schools in the world following the same educational principles. Indeed, there is no educational movement with a foothold in all five (or six) continents that can be compared with it.

As a consequence, it is mainly because of Rudolf Steiner's contributions to education that he is known to the world today. But probably very few people indeed are aware that the first school in Stuttgart on which all others have been modelled, arose from the positive wish of its founder Emil Molt to make a first step forward toward the Threefold Social Order, by establishing a new kind of school in the spiritual/cultural domain, which would be a free and unitary co-educational school of a kind that was entirely unique in its time. Even today, sixty years later, the same may be said of the network of Steiner schools throughout the world, even though some elements of Steiner education have indeed been taken over by others, usually without acknowledgement. Few, if any, of these schools would deny today that they owe almost everything to the educational impulse given by their original founder, Rudolf Steiner, whose lectures on education remain the basis for every Waldorf teacher training course given anywhere throughout the world.

Chapter 11.

GROWTH OF AND OPPOSITION
TO ANTHROPOSOPHY
IN THE EXTERNAL WORLD: 1919-1922

A very brief reference was made in Chapter 4 to a turning point in history that occurred in the second half of the nineteenth century, and the specific date of 1879 was mentioned. We may now return to this date, since it had great significance for Rudolf Steiner, and was never very far from his thoughts, especially in the last years of his life. He tells us that the spiritual being known as the Archangel Michael took over the leadership of humanity in that year, replacing as guiding spirit of the time the Archangel Gabriel.

Gabriel had taken over the leadership of mankind soon after humanity had entered the age of the consciousness soul, and it had been his principal task to lead men to an understanding of the material aspects of the external world. The result of his work had been the rise of materialistic science, based on what Steiner calls *passive* thinking, a thinking that is conditioned by the facts of the world as they are perceived by men, and which needs no creative effort on man's part. This kind of thinking is admirably equipped to grasp the world of minerals, but a more active, living thinking is needed in order to understand the world of the living, the world of the plants and animals, and above all of man. This active thinking is made possible for us by the work of Michael. In the new age guided by Michael as time-spirit it is no longer sufficient for us simply to perceive the world (passively) by means of the five senses with which we have been endowed at birth, but we must learn by active work on ourselves to perceive how the world, including man, is made up of visible matter and invisible spirit. Such a change has now, especially since the end of Kali Yuga, the Dark Age, in 1899, become urgently necessary because, according to Steiner, we have come to the end of everything that can be understood by the old forms of consciousness. To use his own words in his lectures on the Mission of Michael given in November, 1919, "everything that could have been solved by means of ancient forms of consciousness has been solved; today's demands can be met only by human beings with a new attitude of soul."

It was because the attempt was being made to solve social problems with old forms of thought that, according to Steiner, the war had come about, and no way of building a lasting peace was possible under these old forms. Abstract notions such as the League of Nations would solve nothing, he said, and the problems would continue to grow worse, and ever worse conflagrations would be the result.

This cycle of November, 1919, just referred to, may be thought of as the beginning of the last phase of his life work, in which he made the stupendous attempt to put to practical use all the knowledge of spirit that he had acquired during his life hitherto, while at the same time trying to deepen the essential anthroposophical knowledge which his followers and eventual successors had acquired from him, and were trying to make fruitful within themselves. In this cycle he spoke of the work that had to be accomplished by mankind during the epoch guided by Michael, and in particular he stressed the importance of following what he called the Michael path—"to recognize the supersensible in the immediate sense world, that is, in the world of man, animal and plant, and . . . to find in the world which we ourselves recognize as supersensible, the Christ impulse." In all spheres of activity, therefore, it has become man's task to try to perceive the supersensible at all times behind the material appearance, and to take this supersensible element into account even when men are not yet able

271

to perceive it for themselves. Steiner's work therefore was to give all possible and useful indications regarding this supersensible element, and to encourage his followers to work with it, and through inner effort and inner development to acquire living thinking for themselves, so that they could in due time carry on what he had begun with them.

In Steiner's view, as we have seen in the last two chapters, the Threefold Social Order was willed by the spirit, and was not simply a better form of society, which could be brought into existence by a series of practical measures. The three "domains" of society were not arbitrarily conceived, but were realities, just as much as are the three interlocking "systems" of the human organism. Thus it required spiritual knowledge to *perceive* these social realities, but ordinary people who possessed no direct spiritual knowledge could work to bring the new order into being. By November, 1919, Steiner certainly must have known that the Threefold Order would not come to realization during these immediate postwar years, as he had perhaps thought possible when he launched the movement in April 1919, before the signing of the peace treaties. But for him a new social order based on spiritual understanding was the highest priority for mankind, and he continued to work for it tirelessly, as long as there was any hope that a substantial number of persons would come to believe in it, and would make the effort to bring at least some elements of it to realization on the physical plane. In the end, as we have seen, only the first Waldorf School (and the entire educational movement that stemmed from it) survived as an achievement of the Movement for the Threefold Commonwealth, and many, though not all, present-day Waldorf Schools, have been careful to preserve as part of their internal organization the separate three domains of which Steiner first spoke just after the First World War. If this Threefold movement was, as it has been called, one of the great "prematurities" of history, all the other efforts made by Rudolf Steiner to make use of his spiritual knowledge to transform human thinking in every realm bore some fruit—and in all those realms in which his surviving followers and successors are still working, the admonition repeated so many times in these lectures always to be aware of the spiritual or super-sensible within the material, and thus to think in a Michaelic way, is expected to be at the center of their work, and of their understanding of what they are doing.

Although it was now seven years since the laying of the foundation stone of the Goetheanum, by 1920 the building was by no means finished. Money for its completion remained in short supply, and relatively few persons were available for necessary work on the sculpture and painting. During the course of the war many of the men who had at first worked on the building were called up or had to return to Germany or some other warring country. Most of the remaining workers were therefore women. Nevertheless by 1920 the exterior of the Goetheanum was finished, and the stage was usable, even though all the seats in the auditorium were not yet in place. The great workshop adjoining the Goetheanum, the so-called Schreinerei, was the real center for anthoposophical work at the time, Rudolf Steiner having his own studio here, where, with the help of Edith Maryon, he used to work on the Group sculpture whenever he had a spare moment. One part of the Schreinerei, was also used temporarily for lectures and for rehearsals, where Marie Steiner worked untiringly with the eurythmists or in preparing various scenes from *Faust*. Around the Goetheanum everything else was in a more or less unfinished state, and the building itself was still part of the countryside, surrounded by pasture land and orchards.

Some anthroposophists had erected houses or were planning to erect houses close to the Goetheanum, as might indeed have been expected. As might also have been expected, some difficulties arose because of the excessive "individualism" of the members when it was a question of constructing homes for themselves, in an area which was to become a center for spiritual activity, and with a building like the Goetheanum as its focus. As early as January 19, 1914, Rudolf Steiner felt it necessary to warn members that it would not be feasible for "friends who want to become colonists" to follow their own wishes without thought for the whole complex. Their homes must "together with the Goetheanum and its subsidiary buildings form a connected whole." Members should not even construct too quickly just because they wanted to play an active part in the creation of the Goetheanum, but "should have the patience to wait until the moment arises when it could prove possible to find a good solution for a given dwelling." "Individual colonists should not all go their several ways, but what gets done should be done in harmony." "If, inasmuch as we are colonists, we really manage to carry out our intention and show that a number of us can be filled with a common will and purpose and can guide this will in the direction marked out by our anthroposophical approach, then we will create something exemplary in Dornach."[49]

Lastly, Steiner warned once more that "we do not want to be a sect, some community or other, which asserts this or the other dogma."

In general it must be conceded that his words about the architecture of the area were well heeded, and mistakes that were originally made were in due course rectified. To most people the present area does indeed give the impression of overall harmony that Rudolf Steiner was hoping for and would probably have approved—even if today the famous boiler-house designed by Rudolf Steiner himself and erected in his lifetime still surprises an unwary visitor by its shape which, to quote Steiner again "has not arisen according to utilitarian architecture as conceived hitherto!"

By 1920 the Goetheanum had become usable, but members were becoming impatient to know when Dornach and the Goetheanum would become the real center of anthroposophical work. It was therefore a considerable event when Rudolf Steiner gave his consent to the use of the Goetheanum for a great conference which would last for about three weeks, beginning with Michaelmas, 1920. The consent was given on the understanding that the event would not be regarded as the formal opening of the building; nor should it be thought of as completed and ready for use just because of the holding of this conference. Indeed, the conference was officially known as a "collegiate" course, and hundreds of non-anthroposophists were to be invited to take part in it, especially university students, not only from Germany but from all Western Europe. Rudolf Steiner would personally open and play an active part in it. But the responsibility for the organization of the conference, and decisions on whom to invite, would rest with his assistants and with those who had asked for it, including several of the Waldorf teachers. Lectures would be given by other participants, and discussions would also be led by non-anthroposophists as well as by members. The first public performances of the new art of eurythmy to be given at the Goetheanum would be presented at the conference, under the direction of Marie Steiner.

It will have been realized from the description of the First Goetheanum given in Chapter 8 that this unique building would be likely to present unique problems to those who worked in it, both artists and lecturers. The organic forms, the beautiful lightfilled windows of the interior, including the stage and auditorium, would seem appropriate only if what was spoken from the rostrum and what was presented on the stage were in harmony with the forms. It seems clear from all accounts of this first public conference at the Goetheanum that this harmony was only rarely achieved. Most of the participants brought with them the ordinary materialistic views of their everyday life, and the critical spirit that was natural to them in their work at the universities. The Goetheanum was not hospitable to speeches made for the sake of expressing disagreement, still less for the purpose of showing off the speakers' erudition; and this incongruity between the building itself and so many of the speakers was experienced by older anthroposophists as uneasiness. By contrast, when Rudolf Steiner himself spoke, it was not solely their reverence for him that made them think his words to be acceptable to and in harmony with the building. The eurythmy and music, including the newly installed organ, also belonged there; and this indeed could scarcely have been otherwise since the building was, in part, designed as it was, in order that the art of declamation so devotedly fostered by Marie Steiner, according to indications by Rudolf Steiner, could be presented fittingly in it. Marie Steiner herself was so sensitive to these matters that sometimes she would not permit the whole eurythmy performance that she had rehearsed to be presented in the Goetheanum. Some of the eurythmy numbers she insisted on presenting in the Schreinerei, where they had been rehearsed.

It may well be that the building also kindled among some of those present—more than a thousand persons attended the conference—an opposition to Rudolf Steiner's work of which they had not been conscious before. They felt a kind of hostility to themselves in the very forms of the building, and reacted with hostility to the man who had created it, and to the lofty spirits who stood behind him—as a realization of one's own unworthiness can so easily turn to hatred of those who exemplify the opposite. Steiner himself several years before had spoken of how everything in the Goetheanum should be a "spontaneous affirmation" of what was shown and spoken there. Conversely, what was spoken and shown there ought to have been "spontaneously affirmed" by the forms, and manifestly this was not true of that first public conference, or "collegiate course," in spite of the moving opening address given by Rudolf Steiner himself, and of a poetic last lecture couched in beautiful language by the Swiss poet Albert Steffen, who was ultimately to succeed Rudolf Steiner as president of the General Anthroposophical Society. Only a few of the other lectures came at all close to the standard set by these two leaders.

What became apparent in this conference and in the entire history of the Anthroposophical Movement during these post-war years was that the Movement, even with Rudolf Steiner leading it, was not truly strong enough to spread the new impulse and the new knowledge into an uncaring and largely unprepared world. It did not have within it the inner forces necessary to storm the bastions of religious conservatism and entrenched materialism, especially now that new forces of evil had been let loose in the world by the war. Rudolf Steiner was of course entirely aware of the weaknesses in the movement he led. But there was nothing he could do except what he did; recognizing himself as the servant of Michael and the Christ, he had to try to accomplish Michael's work in the world, to plant the seeds, even if in his lifetime he could not expect to see anything more than a somewhat meager harvest. In the future, near or distant, more healthy fruits might appear and grow ripe. Meanwhile it remained his own task to give out that knowledge that he alone possessed as yet, knowledge that could be used in the external world by his collaborators and successors.

Hitherto Anthroposophy had kindled the spirits and warmed the souls of a few. But in these immediate postwar years there were many who were looking for something new, especially in defeated Germany where conditions were going from bad to worse. Recovery in Germany began only when the currency was stabilized with the help of American loans after the problem of war debts and reparations had been temporarily solved. In Germany, especially, young people were looking for something new, something that would warm their hearts and answer their unspoken questions; and it seemed to many, and not only among the young, that Steiner had the answers for which they were looking. For a few years they flocked to his banner, for a short time swamping the older members who had carried it for so long, some of whom had over the years succeeded in making Anthroposophy truly their own. The newer members were in a hurry. Many of them were distinguished in their own right and had already taken up their careers; others were still studying in colleges and universities, and were increasingly dissatisfied with what they learned. Without having ever embarked on a career, they wished to try something unconventional and different, something responding to their ideals. For every thousand who in despair heeded the call of Adolf Hitler, perhaps one or two turned in hope to Rudolf Steiner. For a time the proportion was much higher than that, when he was filling some of the largest lecture halls in Germany, and crowds thronged outside unable to get in.

Those who joined the Society in these years were often impatient to do something themselves, and it was not uncommon for them to resent the apparent inactivity of the more entrenched and settled members who may have cultivated their inner life, but did not show much interest in doing anything

277

positive in the "outside" world. Thus there were many opportunities for misunderstanding. On the one hand the newer members often lacked knowledge of the core teachings of Anthroposophy, and did not feel the need to acquire it by hard work and persistence. Such persons were content to study what Rudolf Steiner had taught about the particular subject in which they were interested, for example natural science, economics, medicine or even pedagogy. They looked to Steiner to give them new insights into these subjects, and with these they often tried to convert the "outside" world, sometimes in the process covering themselves with ridicule, as when one doctor member tried to convert the entire medical corps of Vienna to anthroposophical medicine, and was howled down by the assembled members. Incapable of answering any questions in depth for lack of profound study of Anthroposophy, they sometimes brought the whole movement into disrepute, to the chagrin of Rudolf Steiner, who had never authorized them to speak on behalf of Anthroposophy. Presenting a strong contrast to these newer members were the numerous older members who did nothing to spread Anthroposophy and were quite content simply to absorb it, never even troubling to defend Steiner against the many attacks made on him during these years of public activity.

With neither side could Rudolf Steiner feel himself in full sympathy. He needed active support, and without supporters the Movement could not survive his death. But if these supporters either could not or would not enter profoundly into the substance of Anthroposophy, Anthroposophy itself could not be preserved by them. The various anthroposophical activities might continue for a time, but if they were to be effective they would have to be nourished constantly from the source. Steiner therefore insisted on the necessity for study and work with the central ideas of Anthroposophy, and for cultivating the inner life, and he warned against severing anthroposophical work in the outside world from all that he had been teaching for so many years as the basic truths of Anthroposophy. So, while he gave out much new knowledge in these postwar years, and provided more information on the basis of which new anthroposophical activities were started, he also tried by every means in his power to deepen the understanding of these basic truths among the members, and especially his lectures on Christianity became ever more esoteric as the years went by. Fortunately for the future of the Movement, at least some gifted collaborators were provided for him by destiny; and it is these men and women and their pupils and successors who have maintained the Anthroposophical Movement in being since that time. In the next chapter we shall consider also the institutional framework given to the Society itself in 1923, a framework that has survived to this day in the form of the General Anthroposophical Society, with its center at the rebuilt Goetheanum in Dornach.

Before coming to the specific details of the work done during these years, some consideration will be given here to Rudolf Steiner as a public figure, which he became at this time. None of his work had, of course, ever been secret, but with the building of the Goetheanum, and especially with his leadership of the Threefold Social Order and the founding of the first Waldorf School in Stuttgart, his activities were for the first time reported by the press, and he was widely regarded as a coming leader on a national, even an international scale. He had in no way sought publicity for himself and his work, but it was impossible for him to avoid it, especially at a time when leaders of renown were scarce, and when millions of people were ready to follow anyone who offered them a way out of the misery of the postwar world. Probably very few people ever fully understood his social ideas, but for a time many thousands wanted to hear about them, and they filled the halls in Germany where he spoke—about the Threefold Social Order, or about other aspects of Anthroposophy. A leading agency, Sachs and Wolff, requested permission to arrange lecture tours for him, and for a time they rented the biggest halls, and filled them with listeners, some of whom, perhaps most, were deeply disappointed by what they heard.

For Rudolf Steiner never at any time made concessions to the desires and expectations of his public audiences. He continued to speak as he had always done, whether he was giving a lecture with the title of *The Essence of the Social Question* or *Anthroposophy and the Riddle of the Soul*, or some other title. Now that he was faced by large public audiences, most of their members hearing him for the first time, he felt that it was his principal task simply to awaken their interest rather than to make new revelations from the spiritual world. Everything that he said he had said many times before in a different form and to different audiences. But each time it had to be brought forth from his inner being, and nothing was ever exactly the same as before. It was far from impossible that members of the audience who had never heard him and knew him only by reputation looked upon him as a kind of latter-day magician, who knew the answers to every question, and who might pull out of his hat some wonderful panacea for all their ills; and because he never gave them one, many no doubt went away disappointed. What he actually did in these public lectures was to speak very seriously and with the utmost clarity about the reality of the spiritual world, and how men might come to know it consciously, as at one time they had known it in a dim primeval clairvoyance. He told them perhaps how to develop their own higher faculties, always making it abundantly clear that the path was a difficult one, that the science of spirit was indeed a science, a knowledge that did not contradict the natural science of the day but complemented it.

Friedrich Rittelmeyer, whose book *Rudolf Steiner Enters my Life* has already been quoted, was present at one of the lectures arranged for Rudolf Steiner by Sachs and Wolff and given in the Berlin Philharmonic Hall early in 1922 before several thousand persons.

"I was present," he reports, "at the gathering in the Berlin Philharmonic Hall—the large auditorium filled to the last seat. Outside people were snatching tickets away from each other and were paying anything up to a hundred marks for them. The hall was full of tense expectation. Unconsciously the people were waiting for the prophet of the age. Rudolf Steiner appeared and spoke for more than an hour to the breathlessly listening mass of three thousand, relentlessly and fundamentally, of Imagination, Inspiration, and Intuition.

280

Again and again I asked myself: Has ever a man let an opportunity for impressing a crowd so absolutely slip by? An officer of higher rank, a respected member of the Wagner circle, was sitting by me in the box. I myself had interested him in Dr. Steiner. He sat there attentively and sympathetically, trying hard to understand. Gradually he lost hope and leant back. Then he shook his head irritably and had disappeared long before the end of the lecture.

"Did Rudolf Steiner know what he was doing—that he was boring this unusual gathering of people who were waiting, openmouthed, for sensationalism? Nobody who knew Rudolf Steiner could doubt that he was fully conscious of what he was doing. Embarrassment before the huge crowd? Inability to speak to the masses? None of this could occur for an instant to those who knew how Rudolf Steiner's speaking could make one tremble with its thunder. For whom was he really speaking? During the lecture I reckoned out how many of the audience were able and willing in some measure to follow it. Apart from anthroposophists, I estimated five to ten. He was speaking to them, quite consciously. Everything that might have made him the sensation of the hour was pitilessly suppressed. Not the faintest breath of a will-to-impress flickered over the assembly. He hoped to awaken interest in spiritual things in those ten or possibly twenty individuals by the essential earnestness and detailed thoroughness with which he spoke of regions utterly foreign to the majority of men.

"I had once heard Johannes Muller say that one must not only be able to 'talk a hall full' but also to 'talk it empty' again. On that particular occasion Rudolf Steiner did this to perfection. Shortly afterwards, when he was again asked to go on a lecturing tour through Germany, the halls were half empty, and the meeting in Munich, where he was threatened with bodily injury and his life endangered as the result of the action of a band of hooligans at the instigation of a newspaper, brought the short period when he was in vogue to a close."[50]

Whether or not Dr. Rittelmeyer was right in his estimate of the reasons for the kind of lecture Steiner gave on this occasion, it is certain that he was following his invariable practice of speaking as he felt the occasion demanded. At this time the Movement for the Threefold Social Order had been virtually abandoned, and he had no wish to arouse the enthusiasm of his audience for any immediate purpose. He could not speak to a public audience, haphazardly assembled through the publicity of a concert agency, of deeply esoteric matters, as he could speak to a small group of members familiar with Anthroposophy. All he could hope to do was to persuade a few members of the audience to take Anthroposophy seriously and perhaps look into it for themselves. Steiner always insisted that, at least in his own time Anthroposophy could never become a mass movement without totally changing its character. He had no wish to attract adherents who enlisted under his banner ready to follow wherever he led them. He was not a leader of this kind.

By 1922 there was already in existence an immense corpus of spiritual knowledge, the content of a dozen or so difficult books and of thousands of lectures delivered to different audiences over a period of twenty-one years. Those men and women who thirsted for this knowledge must necessarily be few in number. But some of them might be in any of his public audiences, and thus for the first time were hearing about Anthroposophy from its founder and teacher. So he spoke to these men and women and these alone; and if members of the audience, like Rittelmayer's friend, left before the end, why then the lecture was not intended for them, but for those in whom a spark of inner recognition was struck by what he said.

In view of the limited nature of his appeal, it may be cause for surprise that Rudolf Steiner excited so much virulent hatred, a word that is by no means too strong for the opposition that he aroused from so many sides. Steiner was an honest man, a man with the courage of a lion, with a vitality and endurance that were almost superhuman, with a personal charm and a never failing sense of humor, and above all an endless patience and love for his fellow-men. Are then these virtues, which are attested to by all who knew him and have never been questioned, such as to excite hatred rather than respect? That Steiner could also be stern when circumstances

282

demanded it, this too is well attested, but it happened rarely, and very seldom indeed was his sternness directed against those who might be thought of as his enemies—only at friends and supporters who were falling short of what he expected of them. Yet it is certain that he was hated, as few men have been hated, and the unique building that he designed, into which for almost ten years he poured his life forces, was burned by, or at the instigation of his enemies. After the fire had done its work, even after he lay prostrate on what was to prove to be his deathbed, the attacks and calumnies persisted. Surely such a hatred deserves an attempt at an explanation, inadequate though such an attempt must be in the absence of any direct knowledge of the hidden forces behind the burning desire to destroy him and discredit his work? It seems to me that the attempt must begin with a listing of those persons and organized groups who felt themselves threatened by his work, as well as those who, for one reason or another, were fundamentally opposed to it. We shall then pass to a discussion of the weapons they had at their disposal and how they used them.

The earliest opponents of his work we have already discussed in earlier chapters. These were the theosophists who stayed with the Theosophical Society, and regarded Steiner as a renegade who had used their Society as a springboard for his own ambitions. He had used pressure on members of his section to persuade them to join his own breakway movement. Many of these theosophists followed H.P. Blavatsky and Annie Besant in their anti-Christian orientation, and disapproved of the way Steiner placed the Christ at the center of earthly evolution, as a divine being who once and for all incarnated in a human body, whereas traditional Theosophy thought of Christ as at best an Adept or Master, even of a very high rank, but still a human being. Well before the war some theosophists were spreading the calumny that Steiner had been educated by Jesuits, perhaps even now was a secret Jesuit—a charge he had no difficulty in refuting, though it continued to be voiced by his opponents.

Both branches of organized Christianity opposed his teachings, and numerous priests and clergymen continued to preach against his ideas to the end of his life. It must be admitted that almost everything he taught about Christianity seemed to conflict with the dogmas to which these men adhered, though it is quite another matter whether they conflict with the Bible when interpreted correctly. The distinction Steiner made between Jesus and Christ, for example, the information given in *The Fifth Gospel* taken from the Akasha Chronicle, his interpretations of the Incarnation, death and Resurrection of Christ—all these things were totally unacceptable to most traditional clergymen. Reincarnation was equally contrary to Christian dogma, especially if one did not study Steiner's teaching about it in depth. It seemed to contradict the doctrine of the Redemption, at the very least. Worst of all, if what Steiner taught were true, there seemed little need for the Church itself, which in any event had no part to play in "salvation"; while the commonly held belief that souls redeemed by Christ would soon pass into a heaven in which they would live forever was given no support by Anthroposophy. In view of the long history of religious fanaticism, which we have no reason to suppose has come to an end, it is not difficult to imagine that some of Steiner's most determined enemies felt it to be their religious duty to discredit him and his work, and prevent it from taking root in human souls. When the Movement for Religious Renewal, to be discussed later in this chapter, was endowed with a renewed Christian ritual through the help of Rudolf Steiner, it takes no great effort to imagine the fury in traditional religious circles, nor how easy it must have been to arouse fanatical hatred against him.

The opposition to Steiner from individual occultists as well as various esoteric groups should neither be overlooked nor underestimated. On the one hand many traditional occultists felt very strongly that the kind of information given out by Steiner, especially to public audiences, should never have been revealed. Some thought that he had revealed truths that he had acquired from traditional occult sources without admitting their origin, and that he was thus "betraying the Mysteries"—a crime in ancient times punishable by death; others recognized that he personally had developed higher faculties. The knowledge he acquired was therefore his own, but the occultists were of the opinion that the world was not yet ready for it. Among these occultists some were certainly theosophists. Both these occult groups, however much they may have admired Steiner, wished him at the very least to exercise more discretion when he spoke; whether they would also have taken overt action to silence him must remain an open question. On the other hand it is certain that the evil secret brotherhoods to which Steiner had devoted three lectures in November, 1917 (*The Right and Wrong Use of Esoteric Knowledge*), and which practiced black magic in the service of the enemies of mankind, would have opposed Steiner on every possible occasion, and it may be taken for granted that some of the numerous lies and slanders which he had to endure spread from such sources as these.

The opposition to Steiner on the part of organized political groups is, up to a point, sufficiently well established. We have spoken of the objections voiced by the labor unions and the political parties of the left to his ideas on the Threefold Social Order, which, if brought to practical realization, would have made their own existence unnecessary. However, these groups were never in any serious danger from him, since it was clear even before the end of 1919 that the Threefold Order at best was postponed until a scarcely foreseeable future. They did not stand to lose much if a limited number of non-unionized workers preferred living in harmony with their more or less enlightened employers to joining a union and accepting the necessity of class struggle. It is true that Steiner minced no words in attacking Bolshevism and its Russian leaders, but this was certainly no novelty, and it is doubtful if an antagonist such as Rudolf Steiner would make them shake in their shoes. Certainly Marxists would disapprove of Steiner's emphasis on human freedom, and no doubt if they had ever come to power they would have suppressed the Waldorf Schools, just as the Nazis did. But the Communists had more important enemies of their own to cope with, in the form of the right wing groups that sprang up everywhere in Germany after the war, and these were armed and militantly anti-Communist—thus far more dangerous to them than Steiner could have been, even if he had won a large popular following.

Immediately after the war, as we have seen, various uncoordinated revolutions broke out in different parts of Germany, at first aided, as had been true in Russia in 1917, by mutinous elements of the army. But Russian history did not repeat itself in Germany, largely because the moderate Socialist leaders preferred a relatively conservative republic and "law and order" to a Bolshevik-style revolution such as the Communists hoped for. They therefore joined forces with the non-revolutionary elements in the army to suppress the various efforts at revolution led by the Communists. Such successes as the latter won were all short-lived, and the repression visited on them by the military with the acquiescence of the moderate Socialists was merciless. The military had no particular sympathy for the Socialists, but they regarded them as at least good patriots who had supported the war, and they were now willing to tolerate them and use them for their own purposes.

However, the traditional military leaders were by no means always in full control of their troops. Relatively junior officers, when they received orders to demobilize, often refused to do so, and formed their troops into independent bands calling themselves Free Corps. Such men refused to accept the Treaty of Versailles, under which the German army was reduced to a fraction of its peacetime strength. They were totally unwilling to join the hordes of unemployed which seemed to be the only future awaiting them. The paramilitary units and the regular army began to claim that the Germans had never been defeated in the war, but had been "stabbed in the back" by Socialists and Communists, in spite of the fact that the Socialist government resigned rather than take responsibility for signing the treaty. Friedrich Ebert, the Socialist president of the new Republic nevertheless accepted the treaty and had to accept that responsibility since without his signature the Allies refused to call off their blockade. When it became known that the Germans had been made to accept entire responsibility for the war, and to pay what seemed to be an astronomical sum as "reparations," a marvellous opportunity was presented to agitators to arouse feelings against the treaty, and against those "enemies" at home who could be made the target of their wrath in the absence of any foreign enemies, who were safely out of reach.

When the attempt to pay reparations led to an ever increasing inflation and later an invasion of the Ruhr by French and Belgian armies in the attempt to collect what was due, it is obvious that those who were losing all they had would turn against those who appeared to be the beneficiaries of the inflation, especially the Jews. It was in these circumstances that a new leader appeared, an ex-corporal named Adolf Hitler who slowly but surely built his German Workers Party into a powerful organization. In this he was supported by other disgruntled veterans, as well as by a number of industrialists who secretly supplied him with money, either as insurance or in hopes of profiting from the movement. Some high ranking officers also cast benevolent eyes upon the rising party, which in time changed its name to the National Socialist Workers' Party, Hitler regarding this title as sufficient protective coloration for his right wing movement.

It is scarcely surprising that Rudolf Steiner became a target for attacks from this quarter, once he had taken the lead in a movement such as that for the Threefold Social Order. Even if he had continued merely to lecture in Germany, as he had always done, and even if neither he nor his pupils had made any effort to demand social changes in the postwar world, it is probable that those among the Nazis who were really informed about his teachings and activities would have considered him a threat to their aims. The Nazi movement was above all anti-Semitic and rabidly nationalistic, owing much to the pan-Germanic movement of prewar days. Though Steiner was regarded as a German nationalist, as we have seen, by British and French anthroposophists, at least for a time, rabid German nationalists would certainly have thought him too lukewarm, even though he did go out of his way to praise the true German spirit. But when he began to proclaim the Threefold Social Order, and attracted large crowds to his speeches, the Nazis and other nationalist groups would surely have noted that he had nothing to say in favor of nationalism, and regarded it indeed as an outmoded concept; that he spoke strongly for the free human being; and that his Waldorf School in Stuttgart sought above all to educate men and women for freedom.

287

Steiner was an Austrian, but was he a true German? Had he not exiled himself to Switzerland during the war and set up his headquarters there, offering hospitality, work, and safety to men and women from so many different nations, including from those which were fighting against Germany? The Goetheanum was certainly called after a famous German, but Goethe was scarcely a German nationalist. Could Steiner, perhaps, even be a Jew? It was known in some German circles that he had had an interview with General Helmut von Moltke during the first weeks of the war, and that a week or two later the Germans had been defeated at the battle of the Marne. Could Steiner have instilled defeatism into von Moltke? In any event a man who could fill the largest halls in Germany when he spoke was worth watching, and it was certain that he was doing nothing to help the nationalist cause. Lastly it was said by German nationalists that eurythmy was un-German. It was not a "German" form of dancing, like the dancing of the idol of the day, Mary Wigman (whose dancing in fact owed much to the Orient). It was very easy, even a pleasure, to hoot and jeer at serious performances like those of the eurythmists; and, as for creating disturbances when Rudolf Steiner spoke, that too was fun for ruffians of whom the Nazi party was never in short supply, even in its early years. In these postwar years also there was no shortgage of assassins among the reactionary right. Kurt Eisner, the Socialist leader of Bavaria, Matthias Erzberger who had received the Armistice terms from Marshal Foch, and Walther Rathenau, foreign minister and industrialist, all fell victims to assassins, and these were only three of the more distinguished victims. Rathenau was the only one of the three who was also a Jew. It had been he who had negotiated the treaty of Rapallo with the Bolsheviks shortly before his death. Though approved of by the German General Staff, to the reactionary right this treaty was a despicable deal with the enemy.

In an introduction to the published version of a lecture Steiner had given in Liestal, near Basel in 1916, Steiner wrote some words which could have been written at almost any time in his life, since at all times he had the same kind of opposition to contend with. "These objections to Anthroposophy", he wrote, "often arise in a very peculiar way. They do not consist in first considering what Spiritual Science asserts, and then attacking it, but they consist in setting up a caricature of what Spiritual Science is supposed to say, and then attacking that. In this way we are frequently assailed, not because of the actual objects we had in view, but because of their very opposite, which we never had in mind. This type of opposition usually has no serious intention of really learning to understand what it condemns. In the face of such attacks as these, there is hardly anything to do save continually to strive to present from various angles the actual methods and aims of Spiritual Science in an anthroposophical setting."[51]

It will be readily recognized from what has been said in this book, especially in Chapter 6, that anthroposophical teachings are not easy to grasp, and that the diligent student of Anthroposophy may have to read many times over the difficult sections in Steiner's books and lectures, before he can pretend to have understood them. Anthroposophy is, indeed, a life-time's study, and with the best will in the world—which is seldom enough present—it is difficult for beginners to make sense of the teachings, certainly to make sense enough to be able to write an objective report on them. It is peculiarly painful, in particular, for journalists, whose employers expect them to be able to make summaries of the most complex world situations in a few well chosen paragraphs, to try to discuss rationally in a similar manner a body of knowledge such as Anthroposophy. Even today, articles about Anthroposophy, in quite respectable encyclopedias, written no doubt, by competent professionals, often go hopelessly astray. It is much easier for a journalist faced with a deadline to pick out a few items that he may (or may not) have heard in a lecture by Steiner and try to write entertainingly about them than it is to write seriously about them. To write seriously about Anthroposophy it is necessary to do some serious homework, and even then it is far from easy to understand enough to be able to write intelligently about it. It is likely to be better for a journalist's reputation if he makes fun of Anthroposophy, especially since anthroposophists are not so powerful that it is dangerous in any way to offend them. Similarly with eurythmy, an offshoot of Anthroposophy. It did not fit into any known category of art. Even if Rudolf or Marie Steiner opened the presentation with a short explanation of what was being attempted on the stage, it was difficult for a journalist who had never seen anything of the kind before to appreciate what he was seeing. The relationship between Marie Steiner as speaker and the movements made on the stage by eurythmists was not so easily grasped, and it was much simpler in this field also to be amusing about the new art, ridiculing it or, at best, damning it with a little faint praise, or perhaps comparing it unfavorably with modern dance which it *ought* to resemble even if it did not. So neither eurythmy nor Rudolf Steiner's own public lectures usually won for themselves a good press, however much the audience itself may have approved of both.

All this should, in fairness, be recognized; and it is quite possible that a very large proportion of the criticisms that Rudolf Steiner and Marie Steiner had to endure were not malevolent, nor part of a purposeful intent to discredit them and their work. Nevertheless, even if one subtracts all those attacks in the press that stemmed from ignorance, or from a wish by their writers to show off how much more clever they were than the benighted audiences who seemed to be taken in by the speaker, there remains a hard core of determined and intentional desire to discredit and destroy him and his work. When Steiner was speaking in various cities in Germany in 1921 and 1922 there were without any doubt organized attempts to break up his meetings. Some younger anthroposophists undertook to be present at all meetings, prepared to defend Steiner if necessary; and on at least one occasion in Munich they did succeed in foiling an armed attempt on his life. Usually Steiner continued to speak, and Marie Steiner continued to recite until the end, refusing to be either intimidated or driven off the stage. But his opponents were able to set fire to the Goetheanum and destroy it, and *that* was not the work simply of uncomprehending critics of his work or even, one would think, of reactionary nationalists, but, more probably, of persons who understood very well the spiritual significance of the Goetheanum and who wished to prevent it from fulfilling its purpose.

Guenther Wachsmuth, in his book *The Life and Work of Rudolf Steiner*, refers in several places to the scurrilous pamphlets and brochures directed against Steiner, pointing out how contradictory the charges against him so often were. According to him, "the falsehoods were constantly spread by many opponents solely because of the endeavor to injure with any means whatever that which he represented. . . . One group of opponents asserted that he was a monistic materialist; others that he was a one-sided spiritualist; one that he was a Jesuit; others that he was an anti-Jesuit; one that he was antichristian, others that he was Christo-centric. One said that he was a Jew, others that he was anti-Semitic; one that he was non-German, others that he was a Pan-Germanist; one that his teaching came from ancient India, others that it was anti-Indian and purely Occidental; one that he preached a "mystical egoism," others that his striving was for the "conscious complete abandonment of the personality"; one that he had "stripped from the conception of reincarnation its moral seriousness," others that: "It is clear that the decisive motives in this idea of reincarnation are moral." Some said that he had not "himself exercised the perception of higher worlds"; others "that Steiner is a seer," a "clairvoyant, an intuitive knower, a person possessing supersensible vision."[52]

Some of these criticisms, such as they were, could certainly have been made in good faith; and the contradictions at least in some instances demonstrate clearly enough the difficulty of Steiner's teachings. No such excuse can be made for a passage quoted by Wachsmuth from a "so-called astrological magazine," in which the writer spoke of "spiritual sparks hissing," against the Goetheanum, and that "Steiner will have need of some of his cleverness, will need to work in a pacifying way, if a real spark of fire is not one day to bring about an end to the magnificence of Dornach." (!) Nor can any excuse be made for an English pamphlet referred to by Rudolf Steiner himself in 1923, entitled *The Secret Machinery of Revolution.* In a lecture

291

given in Dornach on June 16th of that year, less than six months after the burning of the Goetheanum, Steiner quoted a passage from this document which speaks for itself.

"At this stage of my inquiry, I may refer briefly to the existence of an offshoot of the Theosophical Society, known as the Anthroposophical Society. This was formed as the result of a schism in the ranks of the Theosophists by a man of Jewish birth who was connected with one of the modern branches of the Carbonari [an Italian secret society of the early nineteenth century, which worked for Italian independence]. Not only so, but in association with another Theosophist he is engaged in certain singular commercial undertakings not unconnected with Communist propaganda; almost precisely in the manner in which "Count St. Germain" organized his dyeworks and other commercial ventures with a like purpose. And this queer business group has its connections with the Irish Republican movement . . . and also with another mysterious group which was founded by Jewish "Intellectuals" in France about four years ago, and which includes in its membership many well-known politicians, scientists, university professors, and literary men in France, Germany, America and England. It is a secret society, but some of its real aims may be gathered from the fact that it sponsored the "Ligue des Anciens Combattants," whose aim appears to be to undermine the discipline of the armies in the Allied countries. Although nominally a "Right Wing" society, it is in direct touch with members of the Soviet government of Russia; in Britain it is also connected with certain Fabians and with the Union of Democratic Control, which opposes "secret diplomacy."[53]

After reading out this passage, which he translated into German, Steiner pointed out that he was planning a tour in England for two months later, and that the pamphlet demonstrated that the opposition was well organized. It was not enough to say that such a clumsy tissue of lies could not possibly be believed by anyone. As Hitler was later to point out in *Mein Kampf* big and clumsy lies are often believed, more often indeed than more subtle ones, and almost *any* calumny is believed by some people. As a rule Steiner said very little about such attacks, and he firmly pursued the goals he had set himself, not allowing himself to be diverted from them by any lies or calumnies. But on occasion he did draw them to the attention of the members of the Anthroposophical Society, so that they could be aware of what was going on; and it is certain that he suffered deeply from the many slanders directed against him, which could never be compensated by any amount of praise and approval from better intentioned and better informed persons. He believed always that in the end his work would survive and the attacks that he had to sustain in his lifetime would be forgotten. In the end, indeed, he lost the First Goetheanum, but the Second Goetheanum which replaced it has thus far survived; and his work has not been forgotten.

After the first so-called "collegiate course" given at the Goetheanum at Michaelmas, 1920, others were given there regularly as long as the Goetheanum existed. Steiner spoke there regularly, as did other anthroposophical lecturers who gradually became accustomed to the building, and eurythmy performances under the direction of Marie Steiner were a constant feature of the Goetheanum programs. Much attention was now paid to the sciences. Steiner gave a number of public lectures on scientific subjects to various public audiences, and as his contribution to the second collegiate course given in Dornach in 1921 he gave five lectures on the theme "Anthroposophy and the Special Sciences." In July of the same year he was invited to Darmstadt in Germany to give another collegiate course on Anthroposophy and Science. Here he gave several lectures and led numerous discussions with the participants.

It was even more important, from his point of view, that the teachers in the Waldorf School should be able to teach the sciences from an anthroposophical point of view. He therefore gave several lectures and courses at Stuttgart on such subjects as physics, mathematics and astronomy in the light of Anthroposophy. At the same time he gave to the Dornach members more esoteric lectures on such subjects as man and his relation to the cosmos and higher beings, on the true nature of the human senses, and similar topics. It is evident that at this time

Steiner was deeply interested in making clear to all his audiences the spiritual background behind all earthly phenomena, thus attempting to train his hearers to think Michaelically, in the sense indicated at the beginning of this chapter. The emphasis on natural science was in his view especially necessary in a scientific and materialistic age when scientists still had much prestige. He could not ignore also the fact that his pupils would soon be trying to persuade outside scientific experts to take the science of spirit seriously, and this they could not do without much deeper knowledge of the subject than they possessed. Steiner himself could often take on these experts—after all he had studied in his student days at Vienna—but this was not often true of his pupils. In the discussions at Darmstadt Steiner was especially scintillating in his answers to questions, according to responsible accounts of the course.

While he was giving lectures and courses on scientific subjects, new anthroposophical sciences were coming into being as the result of indications given by him, which were followed up by some of his more gifted pupils. Guenther Wachsmuth and Ehrenfried Pfeiffer, two enthusiastic young men who had come to Dornach to be close to Rudolf Steiner, in the summer of 1921 expressed their wish to study intensively the etheric formative forces of which he had often spoken. Imperceptible to men's ordinary senses, they are everywhere present in the world, and the young men thought it ought to be possible to demonstrate their activity in it. Steiner offered them the basement of the "glass-house" for their experiments, and gave them numerous suggestions on how to proceed. Thus came into existence the first anthroposophical "research laboratory," which had neither scientific facilities nor equipment, nothing except gas and running water; also the young men lacked money. Nevertheless this first effort was the beginning of several new scientific ventures. Wachsmuth even before Rudolf Steiner's death had produced, with much help from Steiner himself, a comprehensive book on the etheric formative forces, which remains the best single book on the subject (*The Etheric Formative Forces in Cosmos, Earth and Man*). Pfeiffer occupied himself more with experiments than did Wachsmuth, and was able to demonstrate how the forces may be perceived and interpreted in the crystallization process. These experiments eventually led to a new method of diagnosing disease at an early stage, while it is still in the etheric body and cannot yet be perceived in the physical. Pfeiffer was also one of the most active pioneers in biodynamic farming, as will be discussed in Chapter 13.

Rudolf Steiner also entrusted to a young woman research worker in Stuttgart the task of demonstrating the working of "the smallest entities," that is, the activity of the formative forces in very highly diluted substances. The method devised by Elisabeth (Lili) Kolisko for this purpose is called capillary dynamolysis, and it also is used in the early diagnosis of disease. Greatly interested in the working of moon and planets in earthly substances and with the potentizing of different medicaments used in anthroposophical medicine, she wrote several monographs in this area, and a larger work entitled *Spirit in Matter*. After giving his Agriculture course at Koberwitz in 1924, to be discussed in Chapter 13, Steiner entrusted Lili Kolisko with the task of testing the different preparations that he proposed for use in agriculture. On this subject she and her husband Dr. Eugen Kolisko, a noted physician in the field of anthroposophical medicine who died prematurely in 1939, compiled a huge book called *Agriculture of Tomorrow*, recently republished in English, which is a mine of information and includes hundreds of photographs demonstrating conclusively enough the working of the unseen forces in earthly substances.

These three scientists have been mentioned by name because they were three of the most important pioneers in the work of demonstrating the correctness of Steiner's scientific predictions based not on any experiments done by him, but solely from his spiritual insights. These scientists were succeeded by many others too numerous to list, and today two distinct scientific sections of the School for the Science of Spirit exist at the Goetheanum. Both still engage in research on the basis of Steiner's indications. They have better equipped but still far from sumptuous laboratories, and are headed by two distinguished scientists. The sections are concerned with mathematics and astronomy, and with biology in the widest sense.

Parallel to this work in the natural sciences has been the work in medicine and pharmacy. As long ago as 1911 Steiner gave a cycle in Prague under the title of *Occult Physiology*, which he prefaced by saying that "I myself have only now reached the point where I can at last speak upon this theme as the result of mature reflection covering a long period of time." It will be recalled that when Steiner in 1917 spoke for the first time of the threefold nature of the human being, he also explained that he had been aware of the fact as far back as thirty years before, but not before 1917 had he felt able to speak of it in detail because the perception had not yet matured within him. It was, of course, widely known among anthroposophists that Steiner had very much to give to physicians from the supersensible realms, but he himself was not a medical doctor, and if his knowledge were to become fruitful in the earthly realm qualified physicians would have to take the initiative to make it so. It was not until the spring of 1920 that the opportunity presented itself to give a series of twenty lectures to a group of physicians and medical students who had asked for them, and had, in particular, presented him with lists of questions on which they would like his opinions. This cycle, entitled *Spiritual Science and Medicine*, contains a mass of information and constitutes the fundamental course on anthroposophical medicine. It was followed in later years by several other courses on the subject, culminating at the end of his lecturing life in a course on so-called "Pastoral Medicine," given jointly to physicians and clergymen. In the field of therapy Steiner also gave certain indications for the use of colors in healing, and in 1921 he gave the first course in curative eurythmy, in which the art of eurythmy was modified in such a way that it too could be used for healing. Curative eurythmy is perhaps most in use in the various homes for handicapped children, which will be discussed in Chapter 13. It should not, however, be thought that Steiner's formal lectures represent the sum total of his contributions to the art of medicine. The physicians with whom he worked and who had established clinics for the practice of anthroposophical medicine (especially the clinics in Stuttgart and Arlesheim, close to Dornach) constantly asked him for advice and posed numerous questions, to all of which he replied, thus creating a corpus of medical *obiter dicta* that were then passed on to other physicians and their successors.

Ita Wegman, the woman physician who became the first head of the medical section of the General Anthroposophical Society founded by Steiner in 1923, was also Steiner's personal physician, and together with Dr. Ludwig Noll attended and nursed him during his long illness which ended with his death in March, 1925. Dr. Wegman and Rudolf Steiner worked on a short but uniquely important joint work published just before Steiner's death, entitled *Fundamentals of Therapy*. Dr. Wegman was a Dutch woman born in the Netherlands East Indies, who came to Europe in the early part of the twentieth century, anxious to devote her life, as she put it herself, to the services of mankind. At first she had no intention of studying medicine but took up Swedish massage, followed by hydrotherapy. It was while she was studying the latter that she met Rudolf Steiner in Berlin, where he had recently become the first General Secretary of the German Section of the Theosophical Society. He encouraged her to study medicine, and for this purpose she went to Zurich in Switzerland, where she qualified as a medical doctor in 1911, thereafter working for a few years as assistant and then opening a small private clinic of her own. There seems little doubt that as early as 1907 Rudolf Steiner had spoken to her about the possibility of intimate collaboration with him in the realm of medicine, but she worked on her own until the cycle of *Spiritual Science and Medicine* in 1920 which she attended. Immediately afterwards she made the decision to move her clinic from Zurich to Basel, then, with the aid of a handful of other physicians interested in anthroposophical medicine, she opened a clinic in Arlesheim, soon to be known as the Clinical-Therapeutical Institute. In order to practice anthroposophical medicine effectively it was necessary to have specially prepared and potentized remedies, and with

Dr. Wegman's support a laboratory was established, also in Arlesheim, which was later given the name of Weleda after a legendary Celtic goddess of healing. Parallel events took place also in Stuttgart, where a clinic was opened, led by Dr. Otto Palmer, and in a suburb of Stuttgart (Schwäbisch-Gmünd) another Weleda manufacturing center was established. Both are still active and flourishing today, as are also both clinics. The Arlesheim clinic now has attached to it a Research Institute for the study of cancer (Hiscia Institute) and a small hospital for cancer patients (the Lukas Clinic). Both make use of and engage in research on one of the preparations suggested by Rudolf Steiner for cancer therapy, the mistletoe or *viscum album*, sold under the trade name of Iscador by all branches of the Weleda Company.

It would take us too far to go into any detail regarding anthroposophical medicine, which is discussed in my book *Man and World in the Light of Anthroposophy*, Chapter 13. It is enough to say that it takes full account of the threefold and fourfold nature of man, that it makes use of a very wide range of medicaments not used in the ordinary pharmacopoeia, and makes use of them in special potencies according to the nature of the sickness and its location within the human organism. It also takes account of the unseen etheric and astral forces as they are perceived to work in the human being; and the attempt is made to heal the patient, to help him recover fully from his illness, rather than simply treating his symptoms, which is almost invariably all that is attempted in orthodox medicine. Healing with medicaments used in very high dilution always requires much longer than the customary suppression of symptoms.

Steiner always recognized the advances made in orthodox medicine, and he never contemplated for a moment the idea of creating a competitive medicine. Anyone who wished to practice anthroposophic medicine he insisted must first know all about orthodox medicine and obtain the usual degree. But he wished to contribute to this medicine from his own supersensible knowledge. In a public lecture given in Arnhem, Holland in July 1924, he made his personal attitude abundantly clear: "I do not mean to say," he told his audience, "that medicine has not in recent times made immense progress. Anthroposophy recognizes this progress in medicine to the full. Neither have we any wish to exclude what modern medical science has accomplished; on the contrary we honor it. But when we examine what has been brought out in the way of remedies in recent times we find that they have been arrived at only by way of lengthy experimentation. Anthroposophy supplies a penetrating knowledge which by its survey of human nature has fully proved itself in those spheres where medicine has already been so happily successful. But, in addition to this, Anthroposophy offers a whole series of new remedies also, a fact which is made possible by the same insight applied to both Nature and Man."[54]

It should be added that the anthroposophical diagnosis of disease and knowledge of the right kind of remedies to use necessitate a degree of living and imaginative thinking that is not acquired by the ordinary medical student or practitioner without much hard work upon himself. Dr. Wegman was, through her destiny as well as her own efforts, especially gifted in this respect—surely second only to Rudolf Steiner himself—and in all the work that stems from her pioneer activity in Switzerland and elsewhere, this necessity for self-development is still stressed. Anthroposophical medicine, however, progresses quite slowly, and not necessarily even surely. Today's paternalistic and authoritarian state, laudably anxious to protect the health of its subjects, takes it for granted that modern materialistic medicine is on the right track, and too often makes it ever more difficult for alternative medicines to survive, by sponsoring legislation regarding the practice of medicine and the use of medicaments. So anthroposophical medicine survives, but sometimes has to submit to leonine regulations drawn up for the state by orthodox medical practitioners who continue, in spite of all its deficiencies, to have confidence only in their own form of practicing medicine, and only in the drugs, usually in synthetic form, manufactured by the great pharmaceutical corporations.

We have referred once or twice in this biography to the

Movement for Religious Renewal, which later became the Christian Community and still exists under that name today. Since this movement was given formal existence in 1922 we shall discuss it here in greater detail. This is especially necessary since it is not unusual for it to be said that Rudolf Steiner founded a religion, whereas his true relationship to the Christian Community was always that of an adviser. The actual responsibility for the founding of the Christian Community rests with the group of clergymen who asked Steiner for help, and received the ritual from him. Emil Bock, who was later to succeed Dr. Rittelmeyer as head of the Christian Community, has published a clear account of its beginnings. While still in the army and only twenty-one years of age he met Rudolf Steiner at Easter, 1917, having met Rittelmeyer the previous year.

Rittelmeyer was at that time a man of 44, well established as a minister of the Protestant Evangelical Church, and a popular preacher who had only recently been called to an important charge in Berlin. He had been deeply influenced by Rudolf Steiner and Anthroposophy, having indeed found that Steiner's actual knowledge of Christianity was in all points superior to his own. After long consideration he became a member of the Anthroposophical Society in 1916, but as yet he had no thought of leaving the Evangelical Church, nor did Steiner then or later ever encourage him to do so. The actual initiative which led to the Movement for Religious Renewal in fact came from Bock, who had remained close to Rittelmeyer, and from a number of other young clergymen and theological students, who felt very strongly after the war that some new impulse should be brought into traditional Protestantism. At first they too had no thought of starting their own Movement, but believed that if there should be an influx of young and enthusiastic theologians into the Church, and if these theologians were deeply imbued with Anthroposophy, the Church itself might be reformed from within. Rudolf Steiner also seems at first to have encouraged this hope, and still believed it possible when he gave his first course to theologians at Stuttgart in June, 1921. There were eighteen persons at these lectures, of whom the oldest was only thirty. Rittelmeyer himself was unable to be present either at this course or the other one given in 1921 because of illness, though he studied carefully the transcripts of what Steiner had said.

At the close of this first course Rudolf Steiner promised to give another course later in the year, and this would be given at the Goetheanum. The eighteen theologians then scattered throughout Germany trying to persuade all the young Protestant ministers whom they believed sympathetic to their cause to come to Dornach for the course. As a result about 110 persons were present when the course opened at the end of September, 1921. Steiner eventually gave 29 lectures. At first they were followed by discussions which proved to be similar to those held at the first collegiate course for scientists held at Michaelmas the previous year. The discussions were often led by older theologians and took an intellectual turn which irritated the younger participants. However, before the conference ended Steiner began to speak not only on the theological questions, but on the need for a renewal of the sacraments in a form suitable for Christian worship in the age of the consciousness soul. From this time onwards it became increasingly clear that the religious renewal so much desired by the younger members could not be brought about within the existing Protestant Church, and it would be necessary to form another movement.

For Friedrich Rittelmeyer this decision was necessarily a difficult one. In Berlin in his ministry he was left entirely free to speak and act as he wished. But he also recognized a commitment to Anthroposophy. So he studied with the utmost care the two courses that Steiner had given that he had been unable to attend; and in due course he also received the text for the Act of Consecration of Man, which deeply impressed him. This is the central sacrament of the Christian Community, and it is best to describe Rittelmeyer's reaction to it in his own words.

"I began at once to study it from every side and to meditate on it. When a few trivial difficulties in the language had been overcome, the purity and sublimity of the *Act of Consecration of Man* impressed me very strongly. It dawned upon me that here was the possibility of creating a divine service in which all true Christians could be united, which could be regarded as the central point of a truly Christian communal life, around which a new, manifold, ever-growing religious life unfolds. Slowly it was borne in on me: This *may* not be withheld from mankind! You yourself dare not fail now if you do not want to sin against humanity and the divine revelation! And if it is impossible to bring this to men in the existing forms of the Church, then something new must be ventured! Let it be expressly stated here that Dr. Steiner had been asking for a long time whether it was not possible to do something within the existing organization of the Church, and that, apart from the younger ones, it was I myself who had said emphatically: It cannot be done, if the new is not to be smothered by the old!

"But for me the really decisive factor came unexpectedly and from a different quarter. It was the realization that in the Hallowed Bread, the living Christ actually comes to men. His Presence was there in indescribable purity and brilliance. It was an impression from the spirit itself—one which came, not in the Protestant service of Holy Communion, often as I had celebrated that with a tangible experience of the nearness of the divine world, but in meditation on the *Act of Consecration of Man*. It was an impression so strong and sure that a whole life could have been founded on it. I will try to describe what it seemed to say: Now it is good-bye to your work in the Protestant Church! If what you have found here is truth, it must stand in quite a different sense at the central point of religious life, of thought and of the promulgation of religion than is possible in the Protestant Church as that Church has now become! For if the new impulse is true, it contains the seeds of new divine worship, a new communion, a new Christ impulse, a new Gospel of Christ. . . . From that moment onwards it was clear to me that I must give myself to the service of the reality which had been revealed to me, without the hindrance of other ties. So I came to the new Christian Community from the very innermost core of things. And I am glad I can say this. The final word was spoken, not by Dr. Steiner but by One higher than he."[56]

302

Another year passed during which the young theologians had many interviews with Rudolf Steiner, and had the opportunity to ask all the questions they wished. At last, in September, 1922, the first Act of Consecration of Man was celebrated in the White Room of the Goetheanum, just under the roof. Rudolf Steiner was present, but Dr. Rittelmeyer celebrated. As Steiner reported it in the *Goetheanum Weekly*, a periodical founded the previous year and edited by Albert Steffen until his death in 1963, in the issue of March 18th, 1923: "What I experienced in September, 1922, with those theologians, in the small room in the south wing, where later the fire was first discovered, I must reckon among the festivals of my life."

Present at the ceremony was the entire priests' circle of the time, which was composed of forty-five persons, including three women. Thus from the beginning women have been accepted as priests in the Christian Community, and today there are many women priests enjoying complete equality in all respects with the men. Steiner continued to display a deep interest in everything done in the Christian Community, and to give it further rituals as they were revealed to him from the spiritual world. In 1924 among the last lectures of his lifetime were included important lectures to the priests, as we shall see.

By an unfortunate chance two unauthorized persons were also privileged to witness the first celebration of the Act of, Consecration of Man in October, 1922. Two workmen happened to be repairing the roof of the Goetheanum, and there is no doubt that they were able to see into the White Room, though whether they understood what was going on is an open question. Their story may well have added to the antagonism of traditional Christian leaders to all that took place at the Goetheanum.

Some members of the Anthroposophical Society also misunderstood Steiner's action in providing the Christian Community with a ritual, supposing that since he had given it he was thereby founding an anthroposophical religion, and that the Christian Community was, in effect, an anthroposophical Church. As a consequence Steiner felt obliged to give a very pointed lecture to members on the subject on December 30th,

1922, returning to the subject again a few days later after the fire. In it he explained that both the Christian Community and Anthroposophy were of course derived from the same source, but that the Christian Community was *not* an activity of the Society. Members of the Society could naturally feel free to support the Christian Community as they thought fit, but should not for this reason diminish their support for the Anthroposophical Society. In any event, he insisted, all true anthroposophists could and should find their own relation directly to the Christ through their Anthroposophy. At his death in 1925 there was never any question but that the funeral service would be celebrated according to the ritual he had given, and in view of the special beauty of this ritual numerous anthroposophists in the years since have followed this example. In general they show the utmost friendliness to the Christian Community, but it remains a serious misunderstanding of Steiner's intentions if they join the Christian Community only because they think of it as the religious branch of Anthroposophy. Indeed, on December 31, 1922, in the last lecture he was ever to give in the First Goetheanum, he made his meaning abundantly clear when he said that "Spiritual knowledge is a real communion, the beginning of a *cult* suited to the human being of the present time."

Important though the founding of the Christian Community was in Rudolf Steiner's eyes, it occupied relatively little of his time by comparison with all the other work being done in these years from 1920 to 1922. These were the only years during which the First Goetheanum could be used, since, as has been mentioned several times in this book, it was destroyed by fire in a few hours on New Years Eve, 1922. The building was never quite finished, though the organ had been installed, and artistic and musical programs were regularly presented. Rudolf Steiner gave his own lectures there during these years, as did several of his fellow lecturers. His lectures grew increasingly esoteric, even when he was speaking on various aspects of science and art.

In the years immediately following the war his lecture tours were mostly in the same countries as during the war. In

February 1921 he resumed his lecturing in Holland and later in the year in the Scandinavian countries, these areas having remained neutral during the war. At the same time he took the opportunity to present for the first time in these countries several eurythmy programmes organized by Marie Steiner. But resumption of lectures in England had to wait until 1922 when, as we have seen, he was invited first to Stratford-on-Avon in the spring, and then to Oxford in late summer, both invitations resulting from his work in the field of education; and on both occasions he also gave esoteric lectures on Anthroposophy to members in London. The personal success and the generally favorable and courteous press reports of the public lectures in England provided a striking contrast with what was happening to him in the first half of 1922 in Germany, the country in which he had lived and worked for so long.

Although some opposition showed itself in countries other than Germany, it was in Germany that it reached its climax, especially when he was carrying out the program of lectures arranged for him by the Sachs and Wolff agency. For the first tour the halls were invariably packed, but efforts were constantly made to interrupt him. Marie Steiner in 1926 described the scene at the time of his last Berlin lecture entitled *Anthroposophy and Spiritual Knowledge*. The lecture had been scheduled for May 15, 1922.

"The crowd was enormous," she wrote. "A violent uproar ensued, against which no opposition could be ventured. . . . The Sachs and Wolff agency which had been making enquiries with a view to organizing further lectures to be delivered in Germany, stated that they could not hold themselves responsible for the proposed plans being carried through without personal danger. Thus it was that all in a moment twenty-one years of lecture activity were forcibly brought to an end."[57]

Most of the press reports on Steiner's public lectures in Germany were hostile, sometimes stridently so, and actual attempts on his life were made when he was speaking in Munich and Elberfeld. Thereafter his public lecturing in Germany came to an end for a time, and even his lectures to members were greatly curtailed. Only in Stuttgart, in south

305

Germany, was he able to continue more or less as usual. A course given to young people in that city, usually known now as the Youth Course, is still today scarcely less relevant to the problems of present day youth. In it he showed how young persons must work to achieve their own freedom for themselves in the sense of his 1894 book *The Philosophy of Freedom*, to which he constantly drew their attention, and how they must try through their own enlivened thinking to help provide a "chariot" for Michael himself to enter and work within that earthly world that has become his special concern since 1879.

Steiner's most marked success in the German-speaking world, and perhaps the climax of all his public work, was the so-called East-West Congress held in June, 1922 in Vienna, the city where he had studied so long in his youth and with which he was so familiar. Many reports exist concerning this Congress, which was accompanied by the first really outstanding public success for the eurythmists who performed three times in the Vienna State Opera House. Vienna at this time was plagued more deeply by inflation than even Germany, which suffered a similar fate the following year. As a result there was at the time of the Congress an appalling contrast noted by everyone between the economic position of the native Austrians and the foreigners who thronged to the Congress from abroad. One English pound was valued at 60,000 krone, and for that sum one could rent the finest room in the best luxury hotel in Vienna, modest rooms in lesser hostelries costing a third of an English pound. Even the Swiss franc, not at that time such a desirable currency as now, was worth 3,000 krone. Foreigners also bought out the stocks of the best stores in Vienna, even Germans joining in the legal robbery. It was not surprising that native Austrians tended to present a shabby and down-at-heel appearance, and could not, save in rare cases, attend the State Opera, which presented such a work as *The Legend of Joseph* by Richard Strauss, a production in which no expense was spared for both setting and costumes, but which few Viennese could afford to attend—even if they had wished in the circumstances to do so.

In this atmosphere it was astonishing that Rudolf Steiner

himself, a native Austrian but living and working in Switzerland, seems to have been greeted by the Viennese as one of their own, a long lost son, as well as being the center of attraction for the many anthroposophists who attended the twelve day Congress, in which Steiner gave all the evening lectures. Others were given by leading anthroposophists, and Dr. Rittelmeyer preached a sermon on Whitsunday on *The Spirit of Pentecost and Religious Renewal.* Every evening when Steiner entered the great hall of the Music Association of Vienna (where the Mass in F Minor of Anton Bruckner was performed during the Congress at Steiner's special request), the entire audience rose and applauded, or so it seemed, and on each occasion that audience numbered more than two thousan. Perhaps the foreigners and Viennese, and even the German anthroposophists who were present, wished to show in this way their disapproval of what had happened to him in Germany, and to demonstrate as publicly as possible that Vienna was not in Germany. The first half of the program of lectures was devoted to Anthroposophy and the various sciences, and the second half to the question of how Anthroposophy could be brought to realization in social life. The lectures themselves were serious, even difficult, and in them Steiner appealed directly to the capacity of his auditors for thinking, pointing out to them a new path to the future out of the science of spirit. Though the press was no more favorable than usual, he held his audience, and if any interruptions had been planned, they never took place; while in the daytime when Steiner had no public responsibilities in the program, a constant stream of visitors called upon him in his hotel, bringing their personal and anthroposophical problems to him. Once they had been accorded an interview they received, as usual, his fullest attention.

After the Congress followed the successful journey to Oxford and London, and in September there came the founding of the Christian Community. Contemporary with the latter event Steiner gave an esoteric cycle of great importance entitled *Cosmology, Philosophy and Religion,* resuming a great deal of what he had, from other points of view, been teaching for many years. To be present at this cycle the French members, who had not yet received a postwar visit from Rudolf Steiner, were specially invited, so that the course is called the "French Course." However, it was in no way intended for the French members only, but for all members, and it provided an opportunity for a reconciliation between Steiner and the aged Edouard Schuré, now 81, who had been critical of Steiner's supposed German nationalism during the war. Steiner afterwards spoke of this cycle as one particularly well suited for the kind of work intended to take place at the Goetheanum. His words take on a specially melancholy significance in the light of the events of the following New Year's Eve. "I went to each of my lectures," he said, "and also away from them with an innermost feeling of gratitude toward those who had rendered possible the building of the Goetheanum. For precisely in the case of these lectures, in which I had to lay hold upon an expansive area of knowledge from the anthroposophical point of view, I could sense deeply the benefit of being permitted to utter ideas which had been able to create an artistic framework for themselves in the building."

At the end of the year Dornach was the scene of intensive work, including artistic performances, work on the carving of the Group, and two simultaneous lecture cycles by Rudolf Steiner, one on the origins of natural science and the other, which was given in two separate parts, entitled *Man in Relation to the World of Stars*, and *The Spiritual Communion of Mankind*. The last lecture of the latter course was given in the evening of New Year's Eve, while the scientific course was not yet finished.

The members so recently assembled in the great auditorium of the Goetheanum had scarcely reached their homes when the fire was discovered in the White Room. Though the watchman gave the alarm promptly and firefighting began at once, it was already too late. Not all the efforts of the local fire brigade and the volunteers could save the highly inflammable wooden building, and by morning only the concrete substructure remained intact. The Schreinerei and other adjoining buildings were saved, as well as the unfinished Group sculpture which

308

had not yet been installed in the Goetheanum. But everything else was lost except what could be carried outside by the devoted band of volunteers. A particularly macabre sight was the forms of elemental beings that were being prepared inside the Goetheanum for the Classical Walpurgis Night scene of Goethe's *Faust*. These were rescued from the burning building, and lay around on the lawns surrounding the Goetheanum for the remainder of the night. They survived to be used again in the Second Goetheanum, when at last it was ready and the performances of both parts of *Faust* could be presented, as had been planned for the First Goetheanum.

The consequence of the fire will be discussed in the next chapter.

Chapter 12.

NEW FOUNDATIONS

THE GENERAL ANTHROPOSOPHICAL SOCIETY

It has often been asked why Rudolf Steiner, with his supersensible faculties, was unable to foresee and guard against the burning of the Goetheanum. His answer to this question was categorical: Supersensible faculties, which are a gift from the spiritual worlds, may not be used for personal ends, not even to save one's life; and the safeguarding of a building he himself had so largely created might be thought of as a personal end. Moreover, as Steiner was to explain later, the question shows a misapprehension about the nature of his clairvoyance. It was not a diffuse kind of omniscience as some people apparently believed, but was a *directed* clairvoyance. He would have needed to direct his spiritual gaze upon the Goetheanum as it would appear several years ahead, if he were to have foreseen the fire. If, as Marie Steiner thought was the case (see page 192 above), he did indeed foresee disaster at the moment when he first saw the site on which the Goetheanum would be built, such a prevision would not be the result of consciously exercising his spiritual faculties, but rather, we must suppose, it would consist of a kind of presentiment such as almost all of us sometimes experience. It would not have given him a clear intimation that the Goetheanum, which was not yet built or even designed, would eventually be destroyed by fire. It should always be recognized that Steiner was not a magician, but a seer, and he practiced neither white nor black magic for good or evil ends.

Like all those who had worked on the building with him, and like all anthroposophists who had contributed so selflessly and to whom it had come to mean so much, Steiner was grief stricken beyond words by the fire; and even when he spoke about it on December 31st, 1923, on its anniversary, he remained scarcely less moved than on the day after it. It was clear from the beginning that the fire was the work of one or more incendiaries, and it represented therefore the culmination of the many campaigns of hatred that had been directed against Steiner and the Goetheanum. For the moment his enemies had triumphed; they had succeeded in destroying the fruit of more than ten years' devoted work. A building whose purpose had been not merely to serve as the center of the Anthroposophical Movement, but to help mankind, *all* mankind, to experience the spiritual through art as well as through the acquisition of knowledge, a building through which also beneficent spiritual beings could approach closer to man—this building had overnight been transformed into a still smoking ruin; and those, including Steiner, who had truly *loved* the Goetheanum, were necessarily filled with a sadness from which many of them, perhaps also including Steiner, never fully recovered. All the important newspapers in Europe reported the fire, some objectively, some with compassion. It is scarcely believable today that several newspapers in Germany and Switzerland nevertheless openly gloated over it as though they shared in the "triumph," as perhaps they did. And it is true that it seemed in the weeks and months that followed as if the enemies were closing in for the kill. The attacks never slackened, nor were their authors any more concerned with telling the truth than they had been before. One example Steiner drew to the attention of the members in a lecture at Stuttgart, in case those who had not been present might even believe the calumny. It was said that the anthroposophists during the fire simply watched and meditated in the belief that the fire would put itself out, whereas the truth was that every able-bodied person toiled through the night without stint,

311

constantly entering and reentering the burning building to save as much as could be saved, while others manned the volunteer fire brigades. They did not leave the building to its fate until Steiner gave the order to do so, just before the domes collapsed. He himself and most of the others stayed all night until the entire wooden part of the building had been burned, and the concrete foundations were cracked and blackened. In Dornach there was perfect accord during the fire and immediately afterwards. Only later, and in other places than Dornach did recriminations begin; and though Steiner set himself against recriminations, he did urge all members everywhere to use the opportunity to examine themselves and their personal attitudes toward Anthroposophy and the Society, and towards the Movement, and he himself took the lead in reminding them of their history. As far as the inquest into the causes of the fire was concerned, he insisted that no prosecutions should be started and no effort be undertaken to find the incendiaries and their abettors. Since the authorities came to the definite conclusion that the anthroposophists bore no share of blame for the fire, and that as a consequence full insurance was due to them, Steiner expressed himself as satisfied and turned his attention to the future.

As we have seen in the last chapter, Steiner at the turn of the year was in the middle of a course on the origins of natural science; a performance of a medieval Three Kings Play had also been scheduled for New Years' Day. Never at any moment does Steiner seem to have contemplated abandoning his work, nor even of modifying the immediate programme as scheduled. Since the Goetheanum was no longer available, he gave instructions for the preparation of the Schreinerei for the play, and for the remainder of the lecture cycle; and promptly at 5 p.m., as usual, he entered the Schreinerei with Marie Steiner, ready to give his customary introduction to the play. In this introduction he included some fairly brief remarks on the fire, and on the need for continuing the work in spite of the disaster. Then the play began and it was carried through to the end, although the actress who played the part of the angel and who gave the first speech could hardly utter her lines. In the evening Steiner again gave a short address before continuing the course on the natural sciences.

Thus no alteration in the planned schedule of events was permitted, but everyone who has written about that day has referred to the unusual heaviness in Rudolf Steiner's step which contrasted with his usual light springy tread—though his voice was as deep and strong as ever. In the end not a single item of any program that had been scheduled was dropped.

Looking back now more than fifty years later on that crucial year of 1923 with the benefit of hindsight, it seems clearer than perhaps it seemed at the time that the entire Anthroposophical Movement was gravely endangered by the fire, and that its enemies may indeed have been close to triumph. The members, Rudolf Steiner of course most of all, had made a tremendous material and spiritual investment in the Goetheanum. Although the insurance would cover only a fraction of the costs of rebuilding, the material investment could no doubt be replaced in the course of time, if there were the will to rebuild, and, more important still, if there were in the Society enough human resources to keep the new building going, with enough spiritual substance to fill it when Rudolf Steiner would no longer be there. It should nevertheless be recognized that the problem was not a new one, and that it had existed before the fire. Financial support for Anthroposophy was already falling off, and even if the fire had not occurred, some reorganization of the Society would have been necessary, and some way of obtaining funds would have had to be found.

All this is clear from an urgent appeal made by Rudolf Steiner in the Hague just after he had given a deeply esoteric lecture there to members. He was never at any time an alarmist, but this appeal, made on November 5th, 1922, just eight weeks before the fire, speaks of the Goetheanum as "unfinished," and that "we shall not be able to continue with the building of the Goetheanum unless we receive abundant help on the part of a greater number of our friends, and this Anthroposophical Movement, which has been active these last years at all possible points of the periphery, will then be without a center." After criticising the Society as badly organized, especially by comparison with its opponents, he went on to point out how much could be done at Dornach, in, for example, the field of medicine, if support were forthcoming, but "this depends on the existence of the center in Dornach. The moment the Dornach center breaks down, everything breaks down, and it is this that I want our friends to be conscious of, for it has in many instances disappeared from their consciousness. And I must say, it has really become an extremely heavy burden for me, a crushing burden." Finally: "All can be said in one sentence: Help me to think, my dear friends, how we shall be able to go on with the Dornach Goetheanum; for within a very few weeks we shall have come to the end of our means."[58]

It is entirely understandable that an urgent appeal for funds should in particular be addressed to the Dutch members, since, unlike the German and Austrian currencies, the Dutch guilder was still sound; and Holland had remained neutral during the war, as had Switzerland, thus making it possible for these two countries to contribute more. It is also understandable that after the first great rush of enthusiasm immediately before the war, and the renewal of contributions after it was over, members were no longer as willing to make contributions as before, especially since most of them were inclined to think that the Goetheanum was in all essential respects completed, the organ having been installed, and lectures and eurythmy performances now being given in the great auditorium. After the destruction of the Goetheanum, it must, in January, 1923, have seemed virtually impossible to Steiner even to contemplate rebuilding unless the Society and Movement were placed on an entirely different basis than hitherto. For a man nearing his sixty-second birthday the prospect might well have seemed daunting, and it seems likely enough that the many calls that he made to the members to take stock of their attitudes, and his frequent discussions with members and delegates of the organized groups on the subject of the history of the Movement and Society from 1901 to 1923 were in a sense also addressed to himself. For it was in part his anomalous relationship to the Society that was responsible for its current weaknesses.

When the Movement for Religious Renewal, later the Christian Community, was founded in 1922 Steiner drew attention to the fact that this Movement was in no sense the religious branch of Anthroposophy, and that it should not drain off the limited funds available for the support of Anthroposophy. Nor should support for *any* of the enterprises stemming from Anthroposophy lessen that given to the center without which, Steiner insisted, the periphery could not continue to exist. After the fire he returned to this problem, mentioning specifically the Waldorf School and the various enterprises connected with the movement for the Threefold Social Order. All were in their way admirable, he said, but not if they flourished at the expense of the Anthroposophical Society and its work. He also reserved some criticism for members who initiated a project with enthusiasm, and then failed to see it through to completion. How could members now be persuaded to see a huge new building project through to completion, having already failed to provide enough support to complete the First Goetheanum?

Steiner could, of course, be quite certain of winning the verbal approval of members for the rebuilding, even if a few members, especially from Germany, would prefer to see the new Goetheanum elsewhere. But such a formal approval would be only the first step, and he was unwilling to make a decision until there had been both a thorough heart searching on the part of the members, and a major reorganization of the Society. It seems likely that his decision on the reorganization, indeed a total refounding, was gradually arrived at during the course of 1923, and that the form the new Society was to take was not fully present in his spirit until nearly the end of the year.

The Society at this time (January 1923) was headed by a committee of only three active persons, and its headquarters was Stuttgart, the German city where the Waldorf School was situated, which had in recent years become by far the most active center for Anthroposophy in Germany. In some respects Stuttgart had been spared the great postwar upheavals, the former kingdom of Württemberg of which it had been the capital having quietly dissolved itself at the end of the war. Several of its leading industrialists were anthroposophists, and others were sympathetic to the Movement. But within the Society everything was far from harmonious, and the existing leadership was contested, especially by younger and more active members. Moreover there was some resentment that Dornach had now become the center of the Anthroposophical Movement, in spite of the fact that there were far more members in Germany than in Switzerland or any other country.

The executive committee of three in Stuttgart did not include among its members either Rudolf or Marie Steiner. The latter had been a member of the executive committee until fairly recently but Steiner himself was not even a member of the Anthroposophical Society. Though he could naturally exercise his influence on the Society by addressing the Committee and members, as a rule he preferred to leave them free to make up their own minds without interference from him. Since he lived in Dornach and largely concentrated on his work there, the Committee did as a rule more or less as it pleased, much to the disgust of many of the younger members who felt that the Committee and the Secretariat wasted far too much of their time and energies on what appeared to be unproductive bureaucratic tasks.

During the postwar period there had been a considerable increase in the membership of the Society. Interest in Anthroposophy was also increasing abroad, but all who wished to become members had to submit their applications to the Stuttgart Committee, which had no way of distinguishing among the applicants. The only criterion for membership was readiness to accept the three very general principles inherited from the old Theosophical Society that had remained unchanged when the Anthroposophical Society was formed in 1913. As in the Theosophical Society, members could form local groups, but these had no official status, and could form and dissolve at will. In early 1923 there were as yet no nationwide societies, nor was much anthroposophical literature available either to members or to the public. Steiner's major books were kept in print in German, but lectures, when available at all, were mimeographed, and only members had access to them. Some foreign members had made themselves responsible for publication of the books within their own countries, as, for example, Harry Collison, who later in 1923 became the first General Secretary of the Anthroposophical Society in Great Britain. A company called the Anthroposophical Literature Concern started business in 1922 in Chicago with a list of several books and a couple of brochures by Rudolf Steiner. But, on the whole, it is hard to resist the conclusion that the entire Anthroposophical Movement was underorganized in 1923, and that Steiner was quite right when he came to the conclusion that if a second Goetheanum were to be built, its construction should be approved by as many representative anthroposophists as possible. Above all that the *will* to go ahead with the building should be fortified by a more solid organization, capable of raising funds systematically, and seeing to it that the building was completed and not left to languish half-built for lack of will and funds to complete it.

Such, then, was the material side of the enterprise, and at least one important decision was taken early in the year looking toward the future. Steiner recognized, and mentioned the matter several times in his lectures, that a kind of "federal" system would be a great improvement on the present situation. This would necessarily mean that local societies would have to be organized, which would later be "federated" with the central Society in Dornach. Throughout the year these local "national" societies came into being, usually led by the outstanding personality of the particular country, as long as he or she was prepared to accept the necessary responsibility. This person then assumed the title of General Secretary. By the time of the Christmas Foundation Meeting for the new General Anthroposophical Society there were fifteen national societies, with the title the Anthroposophical Society in Great Britain, Finland, Norway, and the rest, and each had a General Secretary. The only country that had two societies, each recognized by Rudolf Steiner, was Germany, where the breakaway Society, known as the Free Anthroposophical Society, had been unable to reconcile its differences with the older Anthroposophical Society in Germany, with headquarters in Stuttgart, and, with Steiner's acquiescence if not active approval, had been permitted to constitute itself as a Society. Most of the younger members, at least in the Stuttgart area, associated themselves with this new separate Society.

As far as Rudolf Steiner was concerned these arrangements were necessary, but formed in themselves no basis for the founding of a spiritual society. He was concerned with the spiritual substance, and the form was subsidiary. Indeed, if the new Society possessed this substance and it had agreed on its tasks the most suitable form for it might well be expected to reveal itself. At the end of February, 1923 delegates from all over Germany assembled in Stuttgart to form the new Anthroposophical Society in Germany. Steiner used this opportunity to give two important lectures on the subject of unity within the Society. He began by speaking of the fire, emphasizing that the grief and pain of members at the loss of their building "can be turned into strength to support us in everything we are called upon to accomplish for Anthroposophy in the near future," gaining a new unity from the need to face a common disaster. He tried in these two lectures to instill into the delegates the need to experience a feeling of community, of recognition that all anthroposophists were engaged in a common task and were bound together by their karma. He explained with great care why it is that there may well be less, rather than more, brotherliness in a society dedicated to spiritual development. The gist of his explanation was that egotism in the members of such a society will increase if a serious effort is not made to overcome it. Each individual in his search for the spirit must be alone, sunk within his own self. By contrast, if one is engaged in pursuing external aims, a man has necessarily to cooperate with other men, and with some of these at least, he may cultivate a fraternal relationship. The danger for anthroposophists is that they may become isolated and shut up within themselves, convinced that they are right, that their point of view is the only valid one, and that even their fellow-anthroposophists do not understand Anthroposophy as they should. Thus it follows that a view opposed to their own is not only wrong, but *spiritually* wrong, and it becomes a spiritual duty to take issue with it. This attitude is extremely damaging to Anthroposophy, Rudolf Steiner insisted. The most essential quality for an anthroposophist is *tolerance*, to which he must educate himself. As a result of cultivating this quality, Steiner added, no doubt with a humorous glint in his eye, it may even become a pleasure to hear something foolish said, because what at first hearing sounds foolish is often very wise, much wiser than we clever ones are willing to admit. So, he concluded, even if we are tempted to interrupt a speaker, we might bear this possibility in mind and refrain!

Steiner was of course fully aware of the difficulty human beings experience when they strive to unite together in a society, even if it has aims shared by all its members. This is especially true of a society that has spiritual aims. Such societies are particularly vulnerable to the spirit of dissension, and it is not easy to prevent them from falling apart as soon as an important controversy arises. It seems to me that especially in his lectures of 1923, the theme of unity was never very far from him, even though he seldom made it explicit. What seems to have preoccupied him was this question of how the members could learn to work together in confidence in spite of differences, what they could share together that would not serve also to divide them.

I think that the many lectures he gave during this year on the subject of the great festivals, on how to experience the changing of the seasons in such a way as to penetrate to the spiritual reality behind the earthly phenomena, may well have been given so that members could share a common spiritual experience. In April he gave a series of five such lectures, translated under the title of *The Cycle of the Year*, explaining how in earlier ages men, under the guidance of their initiates, were led to .experience the relationship between earth and cosmos at different seasons, recognizing how the earth breathes out during the spring and summer and breathes in again in autumn and winter. In ancient times festivals were held to celebrate each season: the Christians took over Christmas and Easter for their own festivals, and often also celebrated midsummer with a festival in honor of St. John's Day. But the creation of a

319

Michaelmas festival was something that was greatly needed in our time, Steiner said. This should be a festival "of courage of soul, of strength of soul, of activity of soul." Although it would be held at the time of the falling of the autumn leaves, and thus it appeared that there was nothing in outer nature to be celebrated, just for this reason a festival created by man himself was especially necessary.

This theme was taken up again very strongly in Vienna later in the year in a cycle called *Anthroposophy and the Human Gemüt*, and then in Dornach in a deeply esoteric cycle devoted to imaginations of the four leading Archangels, each presiding over one season of the year, Michael in autumn, Gabriel at Christmas, Raphael at Easter and Uriel at midsummer. It is probable that one of Steiner's hopes when he gave this cycle was that members would unite together in spirit at certain times of the year to re-imagine for themselves the work of these Archangels in connection with our planet.

This cycle on the Archangels was followed by one of his most comprehensive and original cycles, translated under the title of *Man as Symphony of the Creative Word*, in which Steiner revealed much about the true relationship between man and the other kingdoms of nature, and with the elemental world, and this was supplemented in a remarkable way by a short cycle given at the Hague on the occasion of the founding of the Anthroposophical Society in Holland, in which he spoke in extraordinary detail about man as he is viewed by supersensible beings living in the spiritual world. This cycle, called simply *Supersensible Man*, places man in his true position as a supersensible being among other supersensible beings—whereas the previous cycle *Man as Symphony* had placed him among the invisible nature beings, as well as among the visible birds, butterflies, and animals, whose true being, like man's, is also invisible because it is supersensible and lives in the spiritual worlds.

By far the longest stay abroad during 1923 was in Great Britain where the Steiners spent almost the whole month of August. The first part was spent in the small resort town of Ilkley in Yorkshire, where he had been asked by some eminent educators to give a course on education preparatory to the founding of a Waldorf School in England, an event that occurred two years later. Here Steiner was extremely well received, as was the eurythmy, presented by Marie Steiner and her pupils. The summer conference which followed the course of lectures at Ilkley, had been scheduled to take place in Penmaenmawr, a Welsh seaside resort. This little town greatly impressed both Steiners, as well as Dr. Ita Wegman, Guenther Wachsmuth, and the eurythmy troupe accompanying them. Many participants in this conference, in which Steiner lectured on *The Evolution of the World and Humanity* (now published under the title *The Evolution of Consciousness*) have published their reminiscences of the lecture hall within earshot of the waves, the rain and the wind and the many leaks in the roof—in short a British summer as it has so often been experienced by natives, but somewhat rarely by continentals.

To compensate, if compensation was necessary, there was the magnificent scenery and the proximity of the Druid circles on Penmaenmawr Mountain. Marie Steiner, determined as ever in spite of her lameness, was drawn up the steep slope in a cart and apparently enjoyed the trip in spite of inclement weather. Steiner himself, accompanied by Wachsmuth, made the climb on foot, Steiner surprising his companion and biographer by his agility and his ability to climb at least as fast as Wachsmuth, and with no visible signs of fatigue at the close. While on the mountain within one of the stone circles, he began to speak about Druids and the ceremonies that had been performed there, about the shadows and the sunlight, evidently from a direct clairvoyance as he was experiencing it again at that moment. The experience made such a deep impression on him that he spoke about it on several occasions, and he included information about the Druids in many subsequent lectures.

It will be clear from the range of Steiner's activity in 1923 that the enemies of Anthroposophy who kept attacking him in brochures and pamphlets, in the hope, as Steiner explained it, that he would be so much occupied in replying to them that he could no longer engage in direct spiritual research, were

321

disappointed. It is true that he lectured scarcely at all in Germany during the year but this was in part due to the enormous difficulties involved in visiting and working in Germany as the result of the uncontrolled inflation. The anthroposophical publishing enterprise had also finally to be moved from Berlin to Dornach in 1923, and Marie Steiner undertook the task, in spite of her infirmity. She has left a vivid account of the difficulties she and the devoted Johanna Mücke, who was responsible for the day to day management of the Press, had in packing up all the books and getting them into Switzerland at a time of such chaos. Steiner gave very few public lectures during the year, usually only one during the course of each foreign visit. There was no regular program of public lectures such as there had formerly been in the German cities, especially Berlin. On the other hand he gave regular lectures to workmen engaged in clearing the site of the Goetheanum preparatory to the new construction, and he continued these lectures until he had to give up lecturing altogether in the autumn of 1924. As a rule he answered questions that he was asked by these workmen, devoting each lecture to one or two questions. He crowned this activity with the workmen with nine lectures on bees which in their way completed the material he had given in his cycle to members, *Man as Symphony of the Creative Word*—though, as might have been expected, the lectures on bees are couched in a colloquial style evidently much appreciated by this special audience.

By July, 1923, Steiner was satisfied that the means would be forthcoming for the rebuilding of the Goetheanum, and a meeting of delegates was held in Dornach from July 20th to 23rd. At this meeting it was unanimously agreed that a new Goetheanum should be built, and Steiner was asked once more to assume the responsibility for designing it. At the Christmas Conference of 1923 he presented a drawing of the proposed new building, and completed a plasticine model of it in the first months of 1924. It was from this model that the architects worked, and the new Goetheanum had already begun to rise over the foundations of the old one before Steiner died. As he lay on his sick bed he often referred to the familiar noises of construction in the Schreinerei and on the building itself. Opened in 1928, it was in most respects a strong contrast to its predecessor. Instead of fitting gently into the landscape, the new building, constructed of reinforced concrete, stands almost defiantly on the earth. It is a building of great dignity and grandeur, and much larger than the old building, as was indeed made necessary by the growth in membership and the many new tasks that would be carried out in it. If it lacks the intimacy of the First Goetheanum, it was also of great interest to architects, especially for the imaginative use it made of its resistant material and the sculptural form of the building as a whole, by contrast with the sculptured interior of the First Goetheanum, which was not repeated in the Second—and indeed could not have been in the quite different circumstances of the 1920s.

Although the decision to rebuild had been taken, the other problems connected with the Society were by no means solved by July, and it seems likely that Rudolf Steiner had not yet come to any definite conclusions himself. But a study of the lectures he gave during the year strongly suggests that he knew that the year's work would reach a climax by Christmas. His own spiritual powers were constantly being enhanced, perhaps even in part as a result of the tremendous testing of his spiritual fortitude represented by the destruction of the Goetheanum. Those who were closest to him at this time have described how sometimes they were awed by him, as they used not to be in earlier years, though in his intervals of relaxation he was as light-hearted and full of good humor and fun as he ever was. We have noted how Wachsmuth was with him on Penmaenmawr Mountain when Steiner spoke directly out of an immediate experience of what had taken place on that spot so many centuries earlier, and this immediacy of experience he had not always possessed. What seems to have been revealed to him fully in 1923 for the first time was his own historical role, the work that he had to do and that still needed to be completed, and the role that would fall in due course to his co-workers. Although there was as yet no outward sign of illness,

323

the experience of the previous New Year's Eve had certainly taken its toll of his forces. He undoubtedly realized that his days were numbered, and that what he had to do must be done quickly or not at all.

The delegates' meetings in Stuttgart early in the year, when the personal weaknesses of the members, and their inability in so many instances to place Anthroposophy always first in their considerations, became so woefully apparent, certainly brought home to him how great was the danger that all his work might eventually come to nothing. In one of his reports to the Dornach members about a Stuttgart meeting, he even told them that at one point in the meeting he had been ready to abandon the Society altogether and find some other way of spreading Anthroposophy. He himself was aware, and had always been aware, of his own responsibility to the spiritual worlds, and to Michael, in whose service he had placed himself. But he knew now, as perhaps he had not fully realized before, that he must do much more than simply acting as a teacher and revealing the results of his own spiritual research. He must also take the responsibility for providing his anthroposophical co-workers with a new and different kind of Society to enable them when he was gone to continue working, and even doing research in those fields which he with his unique capacities had opened up for them.

Several times during the year he drew the attention of the members to the changes in consciousness that men had undergone during the various post-Atlantean epochs, and the role played by higher beings in the process, and how these beings had actually made it *possible* for man to think as he now does, with his present wideawake consciousness. As the year drew to its close he began the last cycle he was to give before the Christmas Foundation Conference; and indeed many of his auditors had already arrived in Dornach for that conference. The subject was *Mystery Knowledge and Mystery Centers*, and in it he spoke in detail about the various ancient Mystery Centers where the initiates had taught, and where under their guidance the neophytes had in turn been initiated into the teachings handed down from antiquity, at a time when direct clairvoyant insight was in the process of disappearing. Then these ancient Mysteries fell into complete decadence and nothing arose to replace them or give them new life. But after Christ had passed through the Mystery of Golgotha, thus in his person fulfilling all the Mystery teachings, human beings acquired the possibility of becoming free, and of achieving a knowledge of the natural world and everything that was in it.

The first new Mysteries which took account of this change of consciousness were the Rosicrucian Mysteries at the beginning of the age of the consciousness soul (fifteenth century onwards). After the Christmas Conference Steiner at once took up again the subject of Rosicrucianism in a cycle entitled *Rosicrucianism and Modern Initiation*, but for the Conference itself he gave a cycle which was a culmination of all he had been teaching during the year, published under the title of *World History in the Light of Anthroposophy*. Here he spoke of the development of humanity as a whole, stressing the different epochs and what they had brought to mankind, showing how, with the loss of all direct knowledge of the spiritual worlds during recent centuries, and the rise of what he called a "God-estranged" civilization, men have now reached the point where it has become a vital need for them to receive new spiritual revelations, which can be proclaimed for all men and not only for initiates. Thus he made it clear to this special audience assembled for the founding of the new Society, that Rosicrucianism had now been brought up to date with the new Mystery knowledge that he himself had given, for which they themselves would in future be responsible. It would be for them to determine the future of the world. Characteristically he did not spell out this message, but left them free to draw the only possible conclusions from what he was telling them.

As late as November, 1923 when he was present at the founding of the Anthroposophical Society in Holland, Rudolf Steiner was still speaking of an "International" Anthroposophical Society which was expected to come into being at Christmastide, and said that the "International Society must arise on the basis of the national societies." It was therefore generally assumed by members that the newly founded Society would be a kind of federation, and that a central executive committee would be chosen by the delegates to the proposed Christmas meeting. This would carry responsibility for the work in Dornach, leaving all the newly founded national societies to manage their work independently. Nothing had as yet been said by Steiner about his decision to become president of the Society himself; and such a move when it came was totally unexpected. When he did present his proposals it was to a small group of collaborators whom he himself had chosen, and who thereupon agreed to become the first Executive Committee (or *Vorstand,* the name by which it is usually known, even by English speaking members). The entire plan for the new Society was presented as a whole to these members, with all necessary explanations, and the discussions that followed were in essence clarifications by Rudolf Steiner of the ideas that had been embodied in this archetype.

This procedure was in full keeping with Steiner's conception of the Society as a body of individuals who wished to join together to carry out a common aim on a completely free basis. Nothing was required of these members except that they should be of the opinion that a true science of spirit exists, and that an organization such as the School for the Science of Spirit at the Goetheanum, a school that was founded at the same time as the new Society, was justified. Initiative, however, rested with Rudolf Steiner and his chosen Vorstand, and it was they who were founding the Society, not the members. No one was elected to office, but the Society would come into existence only if the members accepted Steiner and the Vorstand as their leaders. Only in this way could the freedom of the founders be assured, in Rudolf Steiner's view. The national societies would enjoy the same freedom, except that their statutes must be in accord with those of the General Society. Although they would fix the dues payable by their members, a definite sum of money per member would be sent by them to the Goetheanum to help defray its expenses. Each member of the Vorstand would be in charge of a "section" of the School for the Science of Spirit, and it was in these sections that the actual work of the School would be accomplished. One section was placed in the hands of the sculptress, Edith Maryon, but she was not at the same time a member of the Vorstand. It was assumed that other sections would be formed later in accordance with whatever talent was available; and in fact when Miss Maryon died the following year her section was for the time being discontinued as no one suitable was available to head it. Early in 1924 a new section was formed with the title "Section for the Spiritual Striving of Youth."

As soon as the preliminary discussions with the members who were to comprise the Vorstand had been completed, an invitation was inserted in *Das Goetheanum* to all national societies and *to all members* to come to Dornach for the foundation conference scheduled to begin on December 24th. Such a vast number of members signified their intention of coming that the Schreinerei had to be temporarily enlarged to accommodate as many as possible of them, but those members whose acceptances of the invitation arrived last were urged by the secretariat not to come, as there would be no accommodations available for them. As it was, facilities were strained to the uttermost, and the Schreinerei, (especially its new additions) was often most uncomfortable, as the heating system could not be expanded to meet the need at such short notice. However, the whole Conference must have been a soul-warming experience for everyone present. Even those members who could not be there participated in the event, since Rudolf Steiner laid the new Foundation Stone not in the earth but in the hearts of all the members.

The fundamental purpose of the new foundation was to unify the Society and the Movement, which had hitherto been separate; or, to use Rudolf Steiner's own words, the Anthroposophical Movement was in the future to have its sheath in the Anthroposophical Society. Rudolf Steiner, who had not even been a member of the old Anthroposophical Society, was to be the president of this one, and he thus united his personal destiny with it, while accepting responsibility for everything that went on in it. Entry into the Society was made as easy as possible, and by entering the Society no obligations at all were accepted. But entry into the School for the Science of Spirit with its different sections carried with it certain freely accepted obligations, and members were accepted into it only after they had been approved by the leader of the School—in effect, during Rudolf Steiner's lifetime, by himself. One of the sections of the School had Rudolf Steiner as its head; this was not a specialized section, but a "section for general Anthroposophy," and its members received special esoteric instruction from him. For this reason it was made obligatory for members to have belonged to the society for a certain period of time before they could be accepted into the School.

It was Rudolf Steiner's expectation that there would be a continuous circulation of information and ideas between the Vorstand and the national societies, and that the General Secretaries of these societies would be encouraged to take part in the meetings of the Vorstand whenever they were in Dornach. However, members of the Vorstand itself would necessarily have to be resident in Dornach. During 1924, after returning from his journeys abroad, Rudolf Steiner always reported back orally to the Vorstand and to Dornach members concerning his own activities, and the *Goetheanum News* contained these reports also, so that all members could be kept informed as to what was going on. Such intercommunication had been a conspicuous lack in the old Society. All applicants for membership in the Society would be expected to apply through their national society if one existed, and the application would be forwarded to Dornach by the General Secretary of that Society. However, membership in the national or local society was not obligatory; all members belonged as a matter of course to the General Anthroposophical Society and might or might not belong to a group within it. Rudolf Steiner regarded this aspect of membership as so important that, in spite of the numerous demands made upon his time and energies, he himself as President personally signed all the new membership cards. Since there were at this time some 12,000 members throughout the world, all of whom needed new cards, the task that he thus set himself was no sinecure.

All books and cycles of lectures would be made available in

the future through the Society bookstores. But the cycles of lectures given to members, and never hitherto made available to the public, would in future include a notice to the effect that the cycle in question had been printed for the School for the Science of Spirit and that "no person is held qualified to form a judgement on the contents of these works who has not acquired—through the School itself or in an equivalent manner recognized by the School—the requisite preliminary knowlege." This seemed at the time the best compromise that could be made. The Society in future must be a public one, and it would be out of keeping with its new nature for some cycles to be reserved for members only—especially if these cycles were in any event circulated clandestinely and in garbled and inaccurate form, as had been the case too often in the past. But it should also be possible for Rudolf Steiner and his close collaborators to tell critics who quoted passages out of context, and with little or no previous knowledge of Anthroposophy, that they did not propose to be drawn into futile arguments, which would have been unnecessary if the critic had acquired the relevant knowledge before beginning the argument.

In Chapter 8 we described in some detail how Rudolf Steiner laid the foundation stone of the First Goetheanum in a solemn ceremony on a wildly stormy night in the presence of a mere handful of members. This physical foundation stone was still embedded in the lowest foundations of the building which had survived the fire. The new Goetheanum therefore needed no new physical foundation stone. On Christmas Day, 1923 Rudolf Steiner again laid a foundation stone in the presence of close to eight hundred members in the enlarged Schreinerei. But this Foundation Stone he laid in the hearts of the members, *all* the members, present and future, of the Society, and the ceremony was no less solemn than the earlier one. A week later when he closed the Conference during which the Society had received its new form, he told his audience that "on this Foundation Stone we will erect the building of which the stones will be the individual work done by us severally, in all our groups, as we go out into the wide world."

What then was this Foundation Stone? According to Steiner

329

himself, as he told the members in his address, it was, like the other, the physical stone, a dodecahedron, and he was laying it in the hearts of all those members who were willing to receive it, and to try to make it alive in them. It was, in fact, a meditative verse, but was unlike all the others that had been brought down from the spiritual worlds by Rudolf Steiner, in that it contains within it the deepest secrets of the nature of man and of his relationship with the nine hierarchies and the Holy Trinity. Only through working with this meditation can it come alive, and slowly and gradually reveal ever more of its meaning. Obviously no one present at the Christmas Conference could conceivably grasp this treasure at once, or ever fully realize its manifold nature. But if, as Rudolf Steiner wished, it was received as deeply as possible into the souls of the members, present and future, then from this joint working together the newly founded General Anthroposophical Society might survive as a free society of human beings spiritually united for the same purpose—or, as the last words of the verse read:

> That good may become
> What from our Hearts we would found,
> And from our Heads direct
> With single purpose.

Such, at all events, was Rudolf Steiner's hope, and numerous members subsequently made clear that they too had the same hope after experiencing this most solemn week of their lives. The Conference and the transmitting of the Foundation Stone represented Rudolf Steiner's supreme effort to bring together the disparate streams of the Anthroposophical Movement into a single united Society. During the course of 1924 he was to explain to many different audiences of members in the most profoundly moving lectures of his life what preparations had been made for centuries in the spiritual worlds in order that a Movement such as this could at last come into being—a Movement that had only become possible since Michael had taken over the guidance of mankind in 1879, and since the Age of Light had replaced in 1899 the Age of Darkness, or Kali Yuga, in which the world had slumbered for five thousand years, while all direct knowledge of the spiritual worlds had gradually died away.*

---

*These bald paragraphs represent all that should, in the present author's view, be given here regarding the General Anthroposophical Society as it was founded at Christmas, 1923. They deal, of course, exclusively with the *form* of the Society, and purposely say nothing about the true substance, nor the significance of Rudolf Steiner's deed in uniting himself directly with the Society as its president, an external task that is ordinarily never undertaken by spiritual leaders. It is simply not possible to discuss the esoteric nature of the Society in a book intended for public circulation, nor to attempt to show the historical significance of Rudolf Steiner's act at this particular moment of time—nor even why the form taken by the Society was chosen by Steiner for esoteric reasons rather than because of any external considerations. Least of all can anything meaningful be said here about the Foundation Stone meditation.

It is highly unlikely that any of the members present at the meeting understood at all adequately what was being done, even though they *felt* its tremendous significance, and knew that they had been present and participated in something that was far beyond their capacity to understand. In the years since 1923, however, many members have devoted the most intense thought to the effort to understand the Christmas Foundation and its true significance, and some writings have even been published with the purpose of aiding members to comprehend. Perhaps the most substantial of these is a book by Rudolf Grosse, the present (1980) head of the General Anthroposophical Society, which bears the title *Die Weinachstagung als Zeitenwende (The Christmas Congress—a Turning Point).* In due course no doubt the book will be available in English, but only members who have already done much thinking of their own on the subject are likely to understand, at least at first, much of what Herr Grosse has written. On the Foundation Stone itself a little book published in English as long ago as 1963 will be found most helpful by many. This is F.W. Zeylmans van Emmichoven, *The Foundation Stone* (London: Rudolf Steiner Press, 1963).

Chapter 13.

THE SUMMIT OF ACHIEVEMENT

THE ANNUS MIRABILIS OF 1924

It is difficult for anyone to imagine, and impossible for a biographer to describe with any real hope of being faithful to reality, how Rudolf Steiner was able to sustain the enormous load of work that he undertook in the last nine months of his public career. As early as New Year's Day, 1924, he gave the first recognizable signs of the illness with which he was already afflicted, and that was to prove fatal to him in March, 1925. He had no intention of letting the illness get the better of him while he still had so much work to do, but what the efforts to master it must have cost him, and what prodigious efforts of will it must have required to enable him to carry through his self-imposed programme, while scarcely ever giving any outward visible signs of his sickness, can only dimly be imagined by the rest of us. None of his younger and more healthy collaborators could keep up with the sixty-three year old Steiner, suffering, as he was, from a terminal illness, one consequence of which was that all food acted on him like a poison, until in his last months of life he could hardly eat at all.

Steiner must certainly have been sustained by spiritual forces that most of us are unable to tap, and this alone can account for the prodigious amount of work he was able to do in the fifteen remaining months of his life. For the illness constantly gained upon him, if gradually, and in the end he was forced to yield to it, at least to the extent of no longer being able to appear in public. He had then to remain in his sickroom, almost always in bed, and unable to stand. Yet even in these conditions he continued to write his autobiography, and spent every unoccupied minute in reading. He created forms for eurythmy, gave instructions to Marie Steiner on the arranging of the eurythmy tours she and her troupe were undertaking, he handled all of his correspondence, dictating letters daily to his tireless secretary Guenther Wachsmuth; and as a crowning work he produced a series of letters to the members of the Society that are the most spiritually concentrated writings of his entire life. These became for those members perhaps the most widely studied of all his teachings, containing, as they do, the very essence of all that he had tried to give forth during his lifetime. As if these were not enough in themselves, he also appended to each letter a "guide-line," or "leading thought," for meditation on the subject of the letter, which took its content still further than he had been able to do when he wrote the slightly less concentrated sentences of the letter itself. These letters, collectively known as *The Michael Mystery*, constituted his last legacy to the members, and the circumstances of their writing are seldom if ever forgotten by those of his legatees who, more than fifty years after his death, continue to work with them.[59]

Even if we take into account the tremendous productivity of some of his earlier years, 1924 stands out as the most productive of all, culminating in September with an extraordinary three week period after his return from his last journey abroad, which was to England. During that period he gave no fewer than seventy lectures, usually at least four per day, as well as granting countless private interviews. Steiner spoke later of these private interviews as if they were the most serious of all the threats to his health; and Marie Steiner did not mince her words as she tried to persuade him to cut down on the number he accorded, insisting that at least some of them were unnecessary, and all were cutting into the slender reserves of strength that he still possessed. When he lectured, even if a few minutes earlier he had appeared so ill that he would never be able to give the lecture, he seemed suddenly to spring to life as he reached the podium and began to speak. When he lectured he naturally knew in advance just what strength would be needed for the task, and he could open himself to whatever new force might flow to him from the spiritual worlds while he was speaking. But when he conversed with people who had asked to speak with him privately, he could not know in advance just how much would be asked of him, and so could not make preparations to husband his strength; and though all who spoke with him were unanimous in recording that his understanding and counsel had never before been so sure and so immediate, it remains true that these members occupied the time that he might have used between his lectures to recuperate in quiet solitude—a solitude that he could find now only when everyone else had retired to bed. But until the very end of his public appearances it continued to be his expressed wish that those who felt a need to present their problems to him should be allowed to do so; and when Marie Steiner once asked him if it was not possible for him to spare himself and do at least a little less than he was doing, he replied: "Do less? But I *should* be doing four times as much!"

From the work accomplished by Steiner during the nine months following the Christmas Conference, it is clear that he had certain aims in mind, though to the best of my knowledge he never spelled them out to anyone. Two of them appear to have been crucially important to him. On the one hand he wished to provide those who wished to engage in practical anthroposophical work with as many potentially fruitful impulses as he could, while on the other he wished to deepen the understanding of the members, and as far as possible help them in their inner development, fitting them, as far as he could fit them, to carry on the anthroposophical impulse when he was gone. Almost certainly from the apparently inexhaustible spiritual knowledge available to him he could have given much more than he did, but what he gave was dependent necessarily on the numbers and quality of those who received. Those who asked for his help and were prepared to work with what he gave them received in ample measure. Numerous suggestions made by him for the first time in 1924 were put to practical use only after many years. Some have not yet been used at all for lack of the qualified researchers able to make use of them.

During the nine months following the Christmas Conference Steiner gave no fewer than twelve complete courses on subjects for which workers were already available. Three were in the educational field, a Section having been reserved in the newly founded School for the Science of Spirit for this subject. This Section Steiner had reserved for himself. The three courses were given in three different countries: in Stuttgart, Germany he gave *The Essentials of Education*; in Berne, Switzerland *The Roots of Education*; and in Torquay, England *The Kingdom of Childhood*. These courses were of special value because Steiner was able to include in them the conclusions he had drawn from the five year experience at Stuttgart.

In Marie Steiner's Section for Speech and Music, he also gave three courses. The two courses in eurythmy, *Eurythmy as Visible Song* (February) and *Eurythmy as Visible Speech* (July) brought together at one time all the separate indications he had given over the years since 1912 when he had first brought this new art into being, and he added more that would be of immense value for the future. The third course in *Speech and Drama* (September 5th to 23rd), a series of nineteen lectures illustrated by Steiner himself and Marie Steiner, was in all essential respects a new course as far as its auditors were concerned, though some of the material was known since it had been developed over the years by Marie Steiner from indications given by Rudolf Steiner. It is a veritable treasure-house of ideas and insights, which, under the direction of Marie Steiner and her successors, have been responsible for dozens of initiatives both at the Goetheanum and elsewhere during the last fifty years.

In Dr. Ita Wegman's Section three courses were also given, the first of which began immediately after the Christmas Conference. This course was given in response to a request from a number of young physicians and medical students, who were looking for a kind of medicine very different from the medicine then in vogue, based as it was on the materialistic and mechanized science of the day. In reply to this request Steiner gave them a full course lasting a week on the subject of *Ethics and Practice of Medicine*, which succeeded in arousing among his young hearers a passionate interest, showing itself in endless discussions in the Sonnenhof after the course was over. All those who could stay on in Dornach and did not have to return to their work continued the discussions for an entire day and half the following night, trying to clarify for themselves and to draw forth the full consequences for their profession of what Steiner had said. In later life these young people constituted the nucleus of the anthroposophical medical profession, not only in Central Europe, but wherever they took the impulse, not least in England.

The second course given in Dornach to practicing physicians (April 13th to 17th) deepened and widened the information already imparted in earlier years, while the third course was in some ways the most original, and in all respects one of the most extraordinary in Steiner's life, given at the same time as the equally extraordinary course on Speech and Drama (to say nothing of the concurrent course on the Apocalypse for theologians). This third September course, given not only to physicians, but to priests of the Christian Community, is entitled *Pastoral Medicine*, a subject that is scarcely ever regarded as worthy of serious consideration in the training of physicians, though some clergymen, perhaps especially in the Roman Catholic Church, do make some effort to help the sick and even give some advice on matters of health, apart from their more widely accepted duty to provide as much spiritual consolation as they can. Usually clergymen suffer from an almost total ignorance of medicine, as a result of which they leave so much of their task to doctors, who may be equally ignorant of the teachings of religion. In this course Steiner spoke of the fact that both professions, though separate, are devoted to the service of God, and their practitioners should always work together and be aware of what members of the other profession are trying to accomplish. For a pastoral medicine of the future a knowledge of reincarnation and the biological and psychological development of human beings at

336

different ages is, as Steiner emphasized, essential; physicians and clergymen should also know in what respects the human being is free, at what epoch in his life, indeed, he is capable of making truly free choices, and when, as with young children, he is too young to accept real responsibility. Materialists, he said, cannot comprehend the true nature of man, and so the medicine based on materialism is bound to be one-sided and often very harmful. Physicians and clergymen, even if they lack direct spiritual knowledge, should be aware that illnesses may come from previous karma, or may be paving the way for a next life of great importance for mankind. In concluding Steiner spoke of the Christ as the Healer and Helper of men, and compared the physician, who must know the path that is to be traversed through illness to possible death, with the priest, who must know what comes afterwards.[60]

This course, it is worth remembering, was given at a time when Rudolf Steiner himself was facing death, and suffering from an illness which proved to be terminal; only ten days after completing this course he gave the last lecture he was ever able to deliver (September 28th), that he did not have the strength to complete. It is also worth noting as an illustration of the mastery Steiner had acquired over his physical organism that a young physician who had noticed earlier in the year that Steiner was ill although no one spoke about it, was present at this course on pastoral medicine, and after observing Steiner closely, came to the conclusion that he must have entirely recovered from his illness! "He was fresh and apparently quite unburdened," he reported. "There was nothing unusual to be noticed. The question seemed rather to be: How can *we* endure all that is offered us? In unfathomable fulness the Spirit streamed forth. Every domain which Rudolf Steiner touched became fresh as dew. Every aspect was completely new; there was no repetition, either in the formulating or in the train of thought. An overflowing spring poured out its blessings for us. We drank, and did not guess that we were seeing our Teacher for the last time in his earthly body."[61]

Of the other three courses one was given to the theologians of the Christian Community and so did not come within the

337

framework of any Section of the School for the Science of Spirit. The other two courses require a rather more detailed description. They represent the beginning of two of the most fruitful of all the anthroposophical fields of practical work— Curative Education, which has found a considerable following in all the countries where Anthroposophy is established, and Biodynamic Agriculture, which has spread far beyond the still restricted circles of anthroposophists, perhaps too far, since for a truly effective practice of biodynamic farming a much more accurate knowledge of the relationship between the physical and etheric worlds is needed than the ordinary working farmer possesses!

It is, or should be, clear to everyone that physically or mentally handicapped children, especially those who have been handicapped since birth, present certain problems to mankind that cannot be resolved without some knowledge beyond the ordinary conventional and materialistic scientific knowledge available in our day, and equally beyond the conventional teachings of religion. Among these problems is the question of why children should be *born* with abnormalities, especially the Mongol child who can never "recover" from his Mongolism; what purpose, if any, these abnormal children serve in the world (and indeed why they should not be quietly "put away" as a burden to their parents and society), and what should be done for them in this life by the vast majority of men and women who are clinically normal. If reincarnation is a true teaching, then it must follow that in this realm, more than in any other, any answer that does not take reincarnation into account is bound to be inadequate. The child who never becomes fully conscious in this life and often dies prematurely cannot be understood in terms of this single life. According to anthroposophical teaching he comes into this present life bearing a karma from his former one, and he will be born again with a karma modified through the fact that he has undergone one life as an abnormal child. Few of those who look after children and adults in the homes and villages which have come into existence as a result of the pioneer work done by pupils of Rudolf Steiner, can perceive the previous or future lives of their charges, and can have little inkling of their karma. But they always have to be *aware* of their karma. For this reason their moral attitude is and must be different from that of others, and it is surely because of this attitude that Homes run by anthroposophists are looked on with some favor by authorities almost everywhere. The beautiful name chosen by Rudolf Steiner for these children expresses perfectly the attitude that he hoped anthroposophical curative teachers would achieve in relation to their charges—"Children in need of special care of the soul" (*Seelenpflegebedürftig*). Though the physical organism of these children is often weak also—and Steiner had numerous suggestions as to how this could be helped by special treatments and medicaments—it is indeed essentially the *soul* that is in need of special care. Treatment should therefore, in Steiner's view, be directed especially towards the feeling and willing, since the thinking capacity so often cannot be reached.

In Chapter 11 we discussed briefly the founding of the Clinical Therapeutical Institute in Arlesheim by Dr. Ita Wagman in 1921. Some of the first patients sent there for treatment were children, and among these some were in need of special care or quite severely handicapped. Dr. Wegman and her colleagues nevertheless undertook to treat them, following in each case advice given by Rudolf Steiner. In due course a building was acquired which later was given the name it still bears—the Sonnenhof—but as late as 1924 this work was regarded as part of the regular medical practice of the Clinic, and Steiner had not as yet given a systematic course on curative education, each case being treated on an *ad hoc* basis.

Late in 1923 a few young anthroposophists, none of whom was a medical doctor (two were teachers in a state home for backward children and the third was a university student in psychology), decided that they would like to devote their lives to working with abnormal or handicapped children. As all were anthroposophists they decided to call upon Rudolf Steiner for aid, since they were agreed that no one in the state Home seemed really to know very much about the proper treatment that the children should receive. Nor did the psychology of the day contain much that appealed to them. After listening to what they had to say Rudolf Steiner proceeded to test their patience and persistence for a while. Then he invited them, in spite of their ignorance of medicine, to be present at his course for young medical doctors, after which he encouraged them to ask their own questions. As a result of this first discussion the enthusiasm of the three young men reached close to boiling point, but they still had no money—it was just after the stabilization of the German currency which left millions of Germans without any financial resources—nor was the time propitious for obtaining loans or gifts. But they did hear of a large house in Lauenstein which had suddenly become vacant, whose owner was willing to let it on a long lease. It now became a question therefore of raising the money for a rental rather than a purchase so, with Steiner's warm support and encouragement, they went forth on a fund-raising expedition, which was moderately successful. At all events they were able to find a few months' rent, and were able to buy enough second hand furniture, much of which they repaired themselves, so that by May 1924 they were prepared to accept their first children.

A month later, immediately following the Agriculture Course given at Koberwitz Rudolf Steiner, accompanied by two members of the Vorstand, paid a private visit to the new Home to see what the three friends, and another who joined them with no more experience than they, were doing. By this time they had five children and knew of others who wished to come. Rudolf Steiner met them all and spent the entire day (June 18th) with them, giving advice on each child, and, as one of the friends expressed it afterwards, on that day Steiner gave the tone to the entire curative work. As he left he promised them that he would give them a full course on curative education as soon as he could find time for it. The course was eventually given in Dornach from June 25th to July 7th to about twenty persons, including the doctors from the Clinic and the members of the Vorstand. From this course, which is worthy of careful study if only as an example of the kind of living, imaginative, thinking and close observation that Steiner had now developed to a peak of perfection, have stemmed the more than a hundred Homes for backward, handicapped, and delinquent children managed by anthroposophists in all countries where Anthroposophy has taken root. The well-known Camphill Movement, with its many homes, schools, and "villages" was founded just before World War II by Dr. Karl König and was likewise inspired by Rudolf Steiner.

Perhaps the most surprising of all the activities that have their roots in Anthroposophy is the Biodynamic Movement. From 1920 onwards Rudolf Steiner had given indications to several of his pupils on how to work with the etheric formative forces. These have been briefly discussed in Chapter 11. In the course of 1922 and 1923 several farmers who were also anthroposophists approached Rudolf Steiner with questions regarding the increasing sickness of the land as they themselves were experiencing it, and in particular regarding the apparent degeneracy of modern· seeds. Others asked him for medical advice on animal diseases, while Count Karl von Keyserlingk, who had a large estate at Koberwitz, near Breslau, in Eastern Germany, asked him about plant diseases. The answers he gave whetted their appetite, as it seemed clear that he had as much knowledge of the invisible world in this sphere as he had in others, and his advice invariably was practical and proved to be efficacious. In 1923 he told Dr. Wachsmuth and Ehrenfried Pfeiffer how to produce a preparation that would help to "dynamize" the soil. They followed his instructions to the letter, and the precious material was ready just in time to be exhibited during the Koberwitz course. Time for this course was finally found in June, 1924, and it was given to about sixty persons gathered together on Count Keyserlingk's estate. This number included, to the surprise of many, the eurythmy troupe from Dornach, whose members were also concerned, if in a different way, with the etheric formative forces, and who perhaps, in Steiner's opinion, ought to learn something about the earth to balance the preoccupation with the celestial inherent in their art!

The course consisted of only eight lectures, plus the answers given by Steiner to a number of key questions from his audience, most of whom were practical farmers or landowners. But in these eight lectures are to be found the seeds of everything that has since come to be known as "biodynamic" agriculture (the name was not given by Rudolf Steiner). They contain at the same time a wealth of esoteric information about the relation between man and the cosmos and how this relationship must be taken into consideration by the farmer. However, most of the information in these lectures was eminently practical, dealing with such subjects as how to make a truly dynamic compost, how to "dynamize" farmyard manure, how to control noxious weeds and insect pests, although Steiner also had much to say on the utility of many other plants regarded today as weeds. Human nutrition was incidentally touched upon, since in his view much human malnutrition is due to the consumption of plants that lack the proper cosmic forces. In drawing special attention to the relationship between man and the plant world, Steiner explained how the plant, as he put it, is like a man standing upside down, with its "head" system in the earth (the roots), its "rhythmic system" in the stalk and leaves, and its "metabolic system" in the flower and seed. This remarkable observation, according to Steiner, is the key to correct nutrition, since each of our "systems" is nourished by the corresponding part of the plant.

Every word in these lectures has been worked over, and there have been countless experiments carried out, not least by Lily Kolisko, who was entrusted by Steiner with the task of proving in a scientifically acceptable manner the correctness of the practical indications given by him in this course. A circle of experimental farmers and gardeners was formed in Germany immediately after the course, and in the years since 1924 similar circles have been formed in almost all Western countries. E. Pfeiffer, after working with biodynamic farming in Europe for many years, and undertaking numerous experiments, eventually moved to the United States, where he became the pioneer teacher of most of the American biodynamic farmers, and where in the later years of his life he also established a research laboratory. His advice was very much sought after, and even industrialists in the United States listened to him respectfully, men who would never have anything to do with Anthroposophy and who knew no other anthroposophists. Pfeiffer, who had been a personal pupil of Rudolf Steiner in his youth—Steiner even directed his choice of studies while he was at the university—received official recognition from the Hahnemann Medical College in Philadelphia when it granted him an honorary doctorate, a degree that he had never found the time to earn.

During 1924 Rudolf Steiner took very seriously his role as president of the newly formed Society, and made a special effort to maintain liaison with all the national Societies, though his schedule was too tight to enable him to visit more than a few of them. When he made his visits he always spent a part of his time in explaining to members just what was going on at Dornach, and how he envisaged the new Society. Often also he gave lectures and classes similar to those he was giving at the same time in Dornach, so that members would feel that they really had a share in what was being done there. Conversely, he reported not only to the Vorstand, but also whenever possible, to the Dornach members, telling them of his experiences during his foreign lecture tours. He also published his reports in the Newsletters of the Society, which were distributed in all the countries where Societies or groups were established. It was possible from these reports to appreciate the particular atmosphere of these foreign centers as Rudolf Stiener himself experienced them, and this too helped to bring the scattered members together in spirit. His first foreign tour of the year to the Czech capital of Prague he reported in a specially warm and enthusiastic manner, while after his August visit to England he shared his experiences at King Arthur's Castle near Tintagel in Cornwall with the Dornach members on his return. From December, 1923, he was also, as we have noted in an earlier chapter, writing his autobiography which was published week by week in *Das Goetheanum*, seventy instalments in all.

On January 30th, and thereafter for every week's issue for some months, he wrote a letter to the members giving advice on how to conduct group meetings, the kind of atmosphere that should, if possible, be created in them, and many related questions. These letters originally published in the Society Newsletter have been collected together in a volume with the title *The Living Being of Anthroposophy and its Fostering*, translated into English under the simplified title of *The Life, Nature, and Cultivation of Anthroposophy*. These letters demonstrate in a remarkable manner Steiner's constant care for even the smallest details of anthroposophical work.

Before the end of January he embarked on a cycle which may be thought of as introductory, and indeed it was called *Anthroposophy, an Introduction*. But this title does not mean that the cycle was intended for beginners, nor even for the ordinary public, however well informed in a superficial way. It was given in Dornach to the members and intended as a kind of summing up of the essential elements of Anthroposophy as Steiner now viewed them from the vantage point of his sixty-three years of life, and as he expected members to understand them. Described with the utmost precision and economy, these fundamental teachings are nowhere else presented in such a luminous manner, either in his books or his lectures—and it was evidently Steiner's intention to persuade members to begin their life in the newly formed Society with a re-thinking of all they had studied hitherto. At Easter and Pentecost Steiner also tried to give to the Dornach members a deeper insight into these two Christian festivals. Indeed, at Easter he gave no fewer than four lectures, linking this festival to the Mysteries of antiquity, especially those of Ephesus, once more showing clearly how Christianity fulfills the ancient Mysteries and supersedes them, while the single Pentecost lecture, *The Whitsuntide Festival: its Place in the Study of Karma*, draws together in one mighty Imagination all the three great festivals, Christmas, Easter and Pentecost, showing how the Father, Son and Holy Spirit work together in human life, thus illuminating, as he indeed told his auditors, what he was simultaneously teaching them on the subject of karma.

These lectures that Steiner gave on karma to the members at intervals throughout 1924 constitute his principal work for the members, aside from the specialized courses not intended for all of them. At this time in his life it first became possible for him to penetrate into spiritual mysteries which, as he informed his listeners, had been partially closed to him in earlier years. After a few lectures intended to deepen their understanding of karma itself and its many nuances, into none of which had he entered so profoundly before, he began to speak in February and March, and then again all through the spring, about individual personalities whose lives through several incarnations he had now investigated. Most of these personalities are well known in history in at least one incarnation, but some of the sequences of these lives are most unexpected. Certainly none would have been likely to have been predicted by persons without Steiner's supersensible faculties; but his concise descriptions of the most striking features of these lives make clear indeed how karma worked in these particular cases. This kind of information would of course be utterly useless, and conveying it to members would have been gratuitous, if it had not been that it illustrates certain general principles of metamorphosis from one life to another, and these principles are of the profoundest interest and importance. Steiner's grave and measured presentation of these facts of human destiny was totally devoid of sensationalism, but the significance of what he said cannot be grasped at one hearing or one reading, and perhaps not for a very long time. The different civilizations into which one individuality incarnates, and why these civilizations should have been chosen by that individuality in order to fulfill his tasks, always supplementing in a different way what had been begun before—such material must be pondered over long and carefully, and other information must usually be brought to meet it from one's ordinary knowledge, if the full meaning of these revelations is to be fathomed.

Most of these lectures on *Karmic Relationships* were given in Dornach, but some of them were repeated in slightly different form elsewhere, occasionally with supplementary information. Four lectures, for example, were given on Steiner's visit to Prague at the end of March, three in Paris in May (his first visit to that city since the war), nine were given in Breslau during the agricultural course held on the neighboring estate

345

at Koberwitz, and six were given in England (Torquay and London). Three were given on the occasion of three separate visits to Stuttgart, and three more were given in various Swiss cities. Although it was certain that transcripts of the Dornach lectures would soon become available for members in other cities, Steiner nevertheless thought it important to give virtually the same lectures in other areas whenever opportunity presented itself and he had the strength to give them. The English lectures, as we shall see when we discuss Steiner's last journey to England, were of a different character from the others. So also were three outstanding lectures that he gave in July in the small Rhineland resort town of Arnhem in Holland at a moment in his life when he was so ill that Marie Steiner begged the local group leader, the young physician, F. Zeylmans van Emmichoven, to cancel the lecture on the day of his arrival. Steiner too expressed himself as willing to abide by Zeylmans' decision, but made it clear that he believed he was physically able to give it. Zeylmans, bearing in mind his responsibility also toward the audience which had assembled from all over Holland and from abroad, decided against his medical judgment that Steiner should give it, and the result was three of the most crucially important lectures that he delivered that year, totally different from anything he had yet given on the subject of karma except the lectures he had just begun to give in Dornach. These Arnhem lectures, indeed, supplemented and clarified in several respects those he had already given in Dornach.

At the beginning of July Steiner had embarked on something entirely new, even for him, by speaking of the spiritual background of the Anthroposophical Movement and Society. He explained how preparations had to be made in the spiritual world long in advance if it were to be possible for certain individualities to incarnate at the same time as others, as was necessary, for example, when such a spiritual movement as Anthroposophy had to be introduced into the world. Obviously the content of these lectures cannot be discussed here, but they are mentioned only to illustrate Steiner's apparently limitless sense of responsibility for the Society and his determination to do everything in his power, while he still had the strength, to impress his own sense of responsibility on the members. Aware as they became through his lectures of this year from what different karmic streams they had come, and of how spiritual beings, especially Michael, stood behind their work, they could not help but feel that they must devote all that they had in them to the furtherance of this work. If, after Steiner's death, when he was no longer there to hold together so many varied individualities, with such different pasts behind them in previous lives, they did in fact find it difficult to hold together, this failure can scarcely be laid at Steiner's door, so mightily did he strive to prevent it as long as he was alive.

The three lectures on karma given by Steiner at Arnhem in July, 1924, were by no means the only lectures he gave in Holland on that occasion. Indeed if Dr. Zeylmans had not arranged for two series of public lectures on education and medicine, he would surely not have given his consent to his lecturing at all, but would have insisted that he go to bed. As it turned out the two public lectures were among Steiner's best on both topics. But, according to Zeylmans, it was only while he was lecturing that he sprang to life. Then, as he put it, he was "as always, sparkling with fire, full of life and vitality. One could hardly realize this was the same man." At other times he could not conceal his weariness, and to a doctor's eye he appeared emaciated as well as utterly exhausted. When he went to England, again to a resort town where a full conference had been scheduled (Torquay), a further few weeks had passed, and the illness had taken a further toll of his dwindling physical resources. But he carried the long programme, both in Torquay and London, through to its end, and insisted on making the trip also to Tintagel, which in a sense completed his experience of Celtic Britain begun the previous year at Penmaenmawr.

Dr. Wachsmuth reports in his biography that Rudolf Steiner was already seriously ill while he was in England, and was never able to take more than a very little food. But he was insistent that no one except the members of the Vorstand who accompanied him should be allowed to know, and that no

347

public attention should be paid to his illness. Wachsmuth and Dr. Ita Wegman tried to help as much as they could by giving him various medicaments in the intervals between his lectures and during mealtimes; and it seems that none of the audience noticed anything amiss.

The packed programme at Torquay would have taxed a man in perfect health and in the prime of life. Steiner had been asked to speak on truth and error in spiritual research, and how this kind of research differs from the search for knowledge in ordinary science. No doubt the English members were especially anxious to hear Steiner talk on such a subject because of the widespread interest in spiritualism in England, the efforts to bring supersensible knowledge within the framework of ordinary external science through the medium of such organizations as the uniquely English Society for Psychical Research, and the known existence in England of secret brotherhoods devoted to occult pursuits. Steiner responded to this request with a tremendous cycle of eleven lectures, published in England under the title of *True and False Paths in Spiritual Investigation*, and in America under the title *Initiate Consciousness*. Both these titles are appropriate enough, since Steiner devoted much of his time in the early days of the course to giving a detailed account, scarcely to be found anywhere else in his published lectures, of how the modern initiate acquires supersensible knowledge. He then devoted almost two full lectures to spiritualism, explaining exactly what supersensible perception reveals as taking place during spiritualistic seances, and how mediums damage themselves by allowing their ego to slip out, thus permitting the entrance of an Ahrimanic elemental being who takes the place of the medium's own "I". Then this being, supremely clever as all such beings are, is able to deceive the listeners. Amid much else in this important cycle Steiner drew special attention to the possibilities inherent in the use of supersensible knowledge in the practice of medicine. He and Dr. Ita Wegman, he told his audience, were in the process of collaborating in a book which should draw the attention of the world to these possibilities and what had been achieved thus far. The book, which had been begun in mid

348

1923, was finally published after Steiner's death, but he had the opportunity to correct its proofs just before his death, and to know that the work, entitled in English *Fundamentals of Therapy*, would soon be appearing. In her preface to the first edition (September, 1925), Dr. Wegman wrote that it had been their intention to write several collaborative works on the medicine of the future. This one would therefore have been only the first of many.

While he was giving his cycle on True and False Paths Steiner also gave on the same days seven lectures to a newly formed college of teachers which was planning to open a Waldorf School in London (*The Kingdom of Childhood*). Wishing also to keep the English members informed on everything that he had been doing for the last months he lectured to members the day after his arrival in Torquay on the significance of the Christmas Foundation of the Society, following this with the first of three lectures on karma. In this first lecture he spoke about the character of the present age from the time that Michael became the time-spirit in 1879, explaining at the same time why he had hitherto spoken so little about Michael in spite of his transcendent importance. Certain Ahrimanic beings, he told his audience, had been able to seal his lips, thus preventing the knowledge of Michael from becoming known. But his lips were now unsealed and he was able to speak as freely as he wished without any hindrance from them. The letters of the last six months of his life are an eloquent testimony to his new freedom.

The third lecture in this series, given on August 21st, bears an altogether different character from the others, the result of a visit to Tintagel on the north coast of Cornwall, the traditional site of King Arthur's Castle. As had happened the previous year at Penmaenmawr, Steiner had a direct clairvoyant experience of what had in the far distant past taken place at the Castle, and he related it to his enthralled listeners, among whom was Dr. Guenther Wachsmuth, who includes it in his biography. He was able to describe exactly where the Castle had stood, even the layout of the rooms, and the inner experiences of the Knights of the Round Table as they sat, each with a symbol of

349

one of the signs of the Zodiac above him. He spoke also of Merlin and his teachings and his knowledge of the cosmic deed of Christ, and he explained why it was that such places as this were chosen for the kind of initiation necessary for King Arthur and his Knights. When he gave his lecture on August 21st Steiner was still full of the Tintagel experience of the previous Sunday, and here his actual words characterizing the natural setting of the castle should be quoted directly:

"There, in a comparatively short time, one can perceive a wonderful interplay between the light and the air, and also between the elemental spirits living in light and air. One can see spirit-beings streaming to the earth in the rays of the Sun, one can see them mirrored in the glittering raindrops, one can see that which comes under the sway of earthly gravity appearing in the air as the denser spirit-beings of the air. Again, when the rain ceases and the rays of the Sun stream through the clear air, one perceived the elemental spirits mingling in quite a different way. There one witnesses how the Sun works in earthly substance—and seeing it all from such a place as this, one is filled with a kind of pagan "piety," not Christian but pagan piety, which is something altogether different. Pagan piety is a surrender of heart and feeling to the manifold spiritual beings working in the processes of nature.

"Amid the conditions of modern social life it is not, generally speaking, possible for men to give effect to the processes coming to expression in the play of nature forces. These things can be penetrated only by Initiation-knowledge. But you must understand that every spiritual attainment is dependent upon some essential and fundamental condition . . . In the days of King Arthur and those around him, special conditions were required in order that the spirituality so wondrously revealed and borne in by the sea might flow into their mission and their tasks."[62]

Steiner then went on to speak of the mission of King Arthur and his Knights and contrasted it with the mission of the Knights of the Grail, whose task lay in southern Europe, making clear how each group was aware of the Christ and sought him in its own way. At King Arthur's Court, he said, a

350

"pre-Christian Christianity" prevailed. He returned to this subject once more when on August 27th he gave his last lecture to the English members, the third of three lectures on the subject of karma, similar to those he was giving at the same period in Dornach. This lecture he concluded with the following words of farewell: "We know too that we remain united even when divided in physical space. We shall remain united in the signs that can reveal themselves to the eye of spirit and to the ears of soul, if what I have said in these lectures has been received in full earnestness and has been understood."[63]

After this last lecture to members Steiner still had some public engagements to fulfill before he left London, including two on education and two to physicians on the new anthroposophical impulse in medicine. When at last he was free to leave England, however, he did not at once return to Dornach, where more than a thousand members had assembled, eagerly awaiting the series of courses and lectures that had been promised, a larger assemblage even than had been present for the already overcrowded Christmas Foundation Meeting. Steiner's physical condition was such that he agreed at last to accept Dr. Ita Wegman's advice, and went to Stuttgart for a few day's rest. As a result he was able for the last time to recuperate enough to carry through his enormous program, described earlier in this chapter. Since he arrived later in Dornach than had been expected Marie Steiner had to work for a few days by herself with the many students who had come to Dornach to be present at his promised course on Speech and Drama. This course had originally been intended for professionals only, but after a few exceptions had been permitted, the floodgates were opened, and dozens more were eventually allowed to attend.

On the day of his return, September 5th, Steiner gave his introductory lecture to this course, as well as the first of his lectures to the theologians of the Christian Community on the Apocalypse. The same evening he resumed his lectures to the members on karma that had been interrupted by his journey to England. Thus, starting with a mere three lectures, during the course of the next three weeks he progressed on some days to four, and even five, if we count the talks he gave to those working on the new Goetheanum. Of the three courses given to restricted audiences, those on the Apocalypse and on Pastoral Medicine have not been made publicly available. But it is possible from the published Speech and Drama course to detect without difficulty how much Steiner must have enjoyed himself as he was giving it, even going so far as to recite whole scenes from various dramas, playing every part himself, strongly and without apparent hesitation. He kept this up right until September 23rd, giving a lecture each day as part of this course, as well as all his others. How much of his dwindling strength the course used up we can only imagine— according to himself none at all, as he could *receive* power while speaking to these audiences, *losing* it only in his private interviews.

There can be no doubt at all that in these last weeks of his lecturing life he attained the culmination of his powers, and that all the knowledge he had won for himself over the last decades was now at his free disposal, so that he was more truly *eloquent* than at any previous time in his career. All those who were present have spoken not only of the unfailing flow of his inspiration but of the goodness, the kindliness, that shone from his eyes during these last courses of his life. Dr. Zeylmans van Emmichoven, from whom we have quoted before, was present at the course on Pastoral Medicine, and he painted an unforgettable picture of what it was like to be present at the course especially when he knew as a medical doctor how ill Steiner was, in spite of his ability to triumph over his illness when he was lecturing.

"All of us who went to Dornach to attend the new courses in September 1924," he wrote, "felt that we were lifted into other spheres, high above our ordinary consciousness; our very faces changed, we were seeing and hearing beyond the range of our own capacities. As we looked at one another we asked ourselves inwardly: Is that really so-and-so? It was something quite unbelievable and indescribable. We were already living in a spiritual world that was by no means within our grasp. There were moments during the last lectures of the course on Pastoral

Medicine when only love and spirit radiated from Rudolf Steiner—with such intensity that it was almost difficult to listen to what he was saying. But the audience was, of course, one to which he could allow his whole being to speak. . . .

"That same afternoon, one or two doctors among us, together with Frau Dr. Wegman, had been with him. He lay on his couch with a rug over him and gave us a last injunction. I had then to return to my work in Holland. On 30th March, 1925, his death summoned us to Dornach."[64]

The lectures and courses all came to an end on September 23rd—the last lecture on karma dealing, with an appropriateness that can scarcely have been accidental, with the destiny and former lives of Steiner's first and favorite teacher of German literature in Vienna, Karl Julius Schröer, who for reasons connected with his personal karma, had devoted so much of his life to Goethe, but had been unable "to carry Goetheanism forward into Anthroposophy," thereby leaving this task to be performed by his pupil, Rudolf Steiner. In letters written to Marie Steiner after his collapse Rudolf Steiner told her that he could now see that it might have been wiser to forego these intensive weeks of September, as Dr. Wegman had constantly urged him. "From a purely personal point of view," he wrote, "it would have been more sensible to listen to Wegman earlier; she wanted me to take a rest but, as you know, I had a feeling that I owed it to higher powers to hold those September courses." It is also true, as these letters show and as will be discussed briefly in the next chapter, that Steiner did not believe he was as ill as he proved to be, nor as yet did Dr. Wegman believe he was in any real danger of death. She thought only that it was absolutely necessary as a matter of urgency that he take the rest he had so long refused.

At last, on September 27th, she was able to persuade him not to give the lecture to members that had been scheduled, and a notice was posted to this effect on the bulletin board of the Schreinerei. The members who had climbed up the hill read the notice with stupefaction. No one could remember any occasion in the past when Rudolf Steiner had cancelled a lecture, not even when he had pleurisy! Most of them had not even known that he was ill, though many knew he was on a strict diet. The doctors at the Arlesheim Clinic had been anxious, and their anxiety was naturally shared by its head, Dr. Ita Wegman, who was so often with him. So the crowd of members milled around, reluctant to go home, talking about this unexpected end to the wonderful September feast of Anthroposophy. But few indeed could even imagine that there was anything seriously amiss—least of all that his lecturing days were almost over. So it was with great relief that they heard the next day that Rudolf Steiner would begin the Michaelmas Festival with his lecture, as scheduled.

He arrived, as always, perfectly on time, but many afterwards spoke of their perception that he was indeed suffering, and mentioned that his voice was softer and slightly less resonant than usual. At a moment when he would ordinarily have been about half way through his lecture, when he had in fact spoken about a deeply esoteric subject in a manner that cried out for further elucidation (perhaps wishing to let the members think further about it for themselves), he led his auditors over to Michael and the Michael stream, on which he had spoken briefly at the beginning of his lecture, telling them how important it was that "the Michael activity will be shed abroad in the future among mankind."

"Because this is so," he went on "I have made the effort today to rise up and speak to you, if only in these short words. My strength is not sufficient for more today," and after a few more sentences he concluded his lecture with a four verse meditation on Michael, which provided a kind of keynote for the remaining work which he was still to do on earth—as will be discussed in the next and concluding chapter. Almost the last form Steiner ever gave in eurythmy, shortly before his death, was the eurythmy form for these meditative verses.

As the words died away, Rudolf Steiner left the podium, and walked slowly from the improvised lecture hall to the room in the same building that had been fitted out as his studio and bedroom, in which stood the still unfinished carved Group, with the Christ, the Representative of Mankind, holding in balance the powers of Lucifer and Ahriman.

354

Everyone in the hall stood up and watched in silence as their teacher, who would never again be seen in his earthly life by the vast majority of them, passed from the hall. His steps died away as he entered his studio bedroom which he would never again leave in his lifetime.

Chapter 14.

THE CROSSING OF THE THRESHOLD

The last six months and two days of Rudolf Steiner's life were passed in full awareness of everything that was going on around him, including the first steps toward the building of the new Goetheanum. But only a few of his closest fellow-workers were permitted to see him—Marie Steiner, of course, when she was in Dornach, Guenther Wachsmuth, his secretary and the treasurer of the Society, his personal physician, Dr. Ita Wegman, and Dr. Ludwig Noll, who at her request came to Dornach to share responsibility with her, and Albert Steffen, vice-president of the Society. A few other members visited him from time to time, including a eurythmist who had been given a poem to work out and whose efforts he wished to see for himself. He corrected the distribution of her colored veil with his own hands. However, such visits were very rare and always by personal invitation. We must therefore rely on the accounts of these close friends and helpers for all that is known of his external life at this time. Since almost all his writings for the period have been published his actual work is well known to us.

At first he was able to sit in an easy chair, but soon the movement from bed to chair became too difficult for him, and he lay on the bed, or half sat up, with his papers and books around him. Until the end of 1924 he seems to have thought that his health was improving, however slowly and almost imperceptibly. This opinion was at the time shared by his doctors. It was a great disappointment to him that a series of lectures scheduled to take place in Berlin in October had to be cancelled, and he sent a special message to the members on October 19th, explaining the reasons for this necessary decision. Conditions in Germany, and especially in Berlin, had not in recent years been propitious for lecturing. But by late 1924 the currency had been stabilized and the country was at last beginning to recover. Hitler was still in prison after the fiasco of the Beer Hall Putsch in 1923. This improvement was reflected in the reception given to Marie Steiner and her eurythmy troupe, who performed without further organized interruption in leading German cities, including Berlin, often to crowded houses. Even after his condition had begun to deteriorate further the eurythmy continued, so that Marie Steiner herself was rarely in Dornach during this period.

Rudolf Steiner himself seems to have been aware of the nature of his illness, and on the basis of his knowledge of the medicaments necessary to help him to overcome it, he proposed various new remedies to Dr. Wegman, who took the steps that were needed to procure them. But no real improvement resulted; and though at first he did not grow noticeably weaker, it remained certain that if he could not succeed in assimilating enough food to keep him alive, the illness must necessarily have a fatal termination. It can scarcely be a coincidence that it was on New Year's Eve, the second anniversary of the Goetheanum fire, that his health took a definite turn for the worse. It will be remembered that it was on New Year's Day, 1924 that he first gave an outward sign of his illness when he had to withdraw suddenly from a social ceremony that he was attending. It may be equally significant that his closest collaborator of all in the work on the First Goetheanum, the English sculptress Edith Maryon who had likewise used up so much of her own strength in the sculpture of the building, also died prematurely in the course of 1924 at the age of only 52. On the last day of 1924 Dr. Wegman for the first time became truly anxious, and largely lost the optimism that had sustained her for so long.

Even in the last months of his illness Steiner could write to his wife in terms such as he would scarcely have used if he had believed he was in grave danger. He would use such expressions as "my progress is very slow, but I must soon be able to work again." Later still he wrote: "My progress is slow, but I trust I shall be able to return to work on the model of our building." He planned to give a course of lectures for those who wished to take up nursing as a profession. This course was planned for May, 1925, and was never officially cancelled, as Steiner always thought he would be well enough to give it. Even in March 1925 his death did not seem to be imminent, and Marie Steiner, who acted as his representative in Society matters as well as directing the eurythmy, was in the end not summoned until it was too late, and she arrived in Dornach only after he had died.

Dr. Wachsmuth tells how Rudolf Steiner expected all his correspondence to be brought to him every morning at 11 o'clock, and how he at once dictated replies to almost all of it. He continued to read with the same interest he had always shown. Dr. Wachsmuth was given the task of selecting and bringing to him books that might be of interest to him. When he entered the studio-sick-room with the books Steiner looked at them all and made his decision immediately as to whether to keep them or not, stacking the ones he wanted on the right of the bed and the others on the left. Dr. Wachsmuth could scarcely believe that he actually read the books, but by the next visit Steiner had at least familiarized himself with the contents!

Two important tasks were carried out in February, 1925, the formal constitution of the General Anthroposophical Society in accordance with the requirements of Swiss law, a task to which Steiner devoted himself with his usual careful attention, and the gift of a special ritual for the installation of the head of the Christian Community. This was given to Dr. Emil Bock who had come to Dornach for the purpose of receiving it. Steiner had earlier agreed to be present at the ceremony when Dr. Friedrich Rittelmeyer was to be installed, and the ceremony itself was postponed several times, always with the hope that he could after all attend. Not wishing to postpone it any longer he wrote out the ritual for Dr. Bock, and urged that the ceremony be held at the earliest feasible moment. It took place on February 24th in the presence of Dr. Wachsmuth and Marie Steiner.

Such, then, was the external life of Rudolf Steiner as it could be seen and reported by his friends, and as is shown also in the many personal letters he sent during this period, especially to Marie Steiner. But, as we have already noted, these last months were truly made fruitful for the future by the two great works which occupied him, the letters to the members, each accompanied by "guide-lines" or "leading thoughts," and the instalments of his autobiography. Both were written entirely by hand, never dictated, and were invariably ready for the weekly issues of *Das Goetheanum* (the Autobiography), and the News-sheet for members (*What is Happening in the Anthroposophical Society?*) which printed the Leading Thoughts. Both the autobiography and the Leading Thoughts were started while Steiner was still leading an active life, the autobiography just before the Christmas Foundation meeting, and the Leading Thoughts afterwards. The first Leading Thoughts appeared immediately after the completion of the cycle called *Anthroposophy: an Introduction*, and were a kind of distilled essence of Anthroposophy, as was, in a certain sense, the cycle also. The first Leading Thought begins with the best known of all definitions of Anthroposophy, and it is worth quoting in full as Steiner's last word on the subject that he intended not only for his own time but for posterity. It is also notable in this "thought" how clearly he shows why no one can or should be "converted" to Anthroposophy, but can only, through his own need, come to acknowledge it.

"Anthroposophy is a path of knowledge, to guide the Spiritual in the human being to the Spiritual in the universe. It arises in man as a need of the heart, of the life of feeling; and it can be justified only in as much as it can satisfy this inner need. He alone can acknowledge Anthroposophy, who finds in it what he himself in his own inner life feels impelled to seek. Hence only they can be anthroposophists who feel certain questions on the nature of man and the universe as an elemental need of life, just as one feels hunger and thirst."

When Steiner reached the 102nd thought there is a marked

change which must surely be linked to the abandonment of his active life as a lecturer and his confinement to his sickroom. From this time onwards the Leading Thoughts, which had hitherto consisted of a distillation of the main ideas of Anthroposophy, intended especially to be used for study purposes by the Groups, now become a distillation of the letters that accompany them, though in a slightly different form. The first letters of this new last phase of his work were written to the members just before the onset of his last illness. On August 17th and August 31st he began to speak especially of the age in which mankind had been living since the beginning of the era of the consciousness soul in the fifteenth century, and of the changes that ensued when Michael in 1879 became the ruling archangel. With the issues of October Steiner set out to describe in words of the utmost clarity and conciseness the whole mission of mankind on the earth, and his task of attaining freedom and building love into the world. He spoke of how men in earlier ages harbored only divine thoughts, then step by step they began to think for themselves, and assumed for themselves the task of ruling the earth without interference from the divine world. But as man moved in this direction and absorbed into himself the Intelligence that had formerly been cosmic, and was in any event cosmic in origin, he became subject to ever more temptations from Lucifer and Ahriman, though the Mystery of Golgotha has made it possible for him to choose instead to take the Christ Impulse into himself, and follow the path indicated by Michael. Deeper and deeper the letters go into the secrets of human evolution, and ever more difficult to grasp are the concepts unless the previous letters and their guiding lines have first been mastered.

So at the last, as February drew into March, we may picture to ourselves Steiner on his deathbed working out each thought, putting it in the most perfect possible form, while the chapters in the autobiography also grow shorter and more compact as he thinks out and expresses, still with the utmost precision and clarity, just what he wishes to say for posterity. Then comes the day when he does not write on the manuscript of the autobiography "To be continued," and the installments then come to an end.

The last letter, published only after his death, concerns the danger that mankind will sink into subnature, the realm of the Ahrimanic and even more evil powers, unless he can rise as high with his consciousness into the spiritual world as he sinks below it with his technical civilization.

"He must find the strength," Rudolf Steiner writes in his last message, "the inner force of knowledge, in order not to be overcome by Ahriman in his technical civilization. He must understand Sub-Nature for what it really is. This he can do only if he rises, in spiritual knowledge, at least as far into extra-earthly Super-Nature as he has descended, in technical Sciences, into Sub-Nature. The age requires a knowledge transcending Nature, because in its inner life it must come to grips with a life-content which has sunk far beneath Nature— a life-content whose influence is perilous. Needless to say, there can be no question here of advocating a return to earlier stages of civilization. The point is that man shall find the way to bring the conditions of modern civilization into their true relationship—to himself and to the Cosmos. There are very few as yet who even feel the greatness of the spiritual tasks approaching man in this direction. . . . In the Science of the Spirit, we now create another sphere in which there is no Ahrimanic element. It is just by receiving in knowledge this spirituality to which the Ahrimanic powers have no access, that man is strengthened to confront Ahriman *within the world*."[66]

On March 29th in the evening a deterioration in Steiner's condition was noticeable, and a message was sent to Marie Steiner in Stuttgart, telling her the news, but adding that there were as yet no grounds for special anxiety. In the early hours of the following morning she received a message telling her that his condition had again worsened and that she must return at once to Dornach. She began the journey immediately, but it was too late. In his studio sickroom Dr. Wegman asked him if he had any last message to send to the members. Faithful to the last to his unwillingness to impinge on the freedom of others, knowing that any such last message would become a binding injunction on the members, he looked for the last time into the eyes of this friend who, as both knew so well, had shared his destiny in so many earlier earth lives, and who now anxiously awaited his answer. But he made no reply, a few moments later folding his hands across his breast, and closing his eyes. Without any sign of even a moment's struggle he soon afterwards passed peacefully across the threshold into the spiritual world.

* * *

Often during his lifetime Rudolf Steiner had explained to members that when an important step forward had to be taken in human evolution, an individuality had to be prepared specially in the spiritual world who would later embody in himself those new capacities that would soon belong to all mankind. Such an individuality would necessarily be out of the ordinary, even, in his time, unique. It would never be possible for his contemporaries to understand him fully, because of his very strangeness and only a few would become his pupils and followers.

Rudolf Steiner never spoke of himself openly in this way, although the gift of clairvoyance that he possessed from his youth onwards is not known to have been shared in such measure by any of his contemporaries. He did not declare himself to be a forerunner; he did not even call himself a messenger of the spirit, as some of his pupils and biographers have called him. He simply lived and worked at all times and always as if it was his life mission to perform the task of revealing to such of mankind as would listen, the reality of the spiritual worlds as he perceived them in direct vision, and what the spiritual beings whom he perceived expected of man. To do this was to make the fullest possible use of those gifts with which he had been endowed. As he grew older and his powers matured he perceived ever more clearly the obstacles to be overcome and the magnitude of the work that lay before him still to be done, while the time allotted to him on earth became ever shorter—so much to do and so little time!

When his last illness fastened itself upon his physical organism and could not be shaken off he refused to yield to it and continued his productive work until death took him, almost suddenly. He would never have agreed that his work was done, nor that he had fulfilled all his obligations to the spiritual beings who were his guides—never at any time in his life did he take credit for anything he had done, nor was he ever at any moment in it complacent.

If indeed it is true that Rudolf Steiner embodied in himself capacities that will one day belong to all mankind, and in this sense he is the first example of a new kind of man, in another and different sense he was surely exemplary. He wished to use his capacities for the benefit of all mankind, and in so using them he never spared himself. So, when on March 30th, 1925 he crossed the threshold into the spiritual world, he had earned the right to die at the foot of the Christ statue that would now forever remain unfinished.

Notes on Earlier Biographies of Rudolf Steiner

The main source used for the first six chapters of the book was Steiner's own autobiography, published under the title of *The Course of my Life*, an exact translation of *Mein Lebensgang*. This book, translated by Olin D. Wannamaker, appeared in a second edition in 1951 (New York: Anthroposophic Press). More recently a new translation by Rita Stebbing was published in an edition that appeared in 1977 from Rudolf Steiner Publications, Blauvelt, New York. This edition contained over six hundred footnotes written by Paul Marshall Allen, many of which were of considerable use to me in writing this biography. The title of this version was simply *Rudolf Steiner, an Autobiography*. Of almost equal importance to a student of Steiner's life is Guenther Wachsmuth, *The Life and Work of Rudolf Steiner* (New York: Whittier Press, 1955) translated by Olin D. Wannamaker and Reginald E. Raab. This book gives a year by year account of Steiner's life and work from 1900 to his death, and thus supplements the autobiography in an exemplary manner. Wachsmuth acted as Steiner's secretary for the last years of his life and much of his book is based on first hand knowledge.

Other biographies in English are A.P. Shepherd, *A Scientist of the Invisible*, of which only about a quarter is devoted to Steiner's life, the remainder being concerned with his teachings (London: Hodder and Stoughton, 1954, many times reprinted). Frans Carlgren, *Rudolf Steiner, 1861-1925* is a rather slight but very valuable work, constituting a more or less official biography directed to the general public (Dornach: School of Spiritual Science, Second Edition, 1964). Johannes

Hemleben, *Rudolf Steiner, a Documentary Biography* (East Grinstead: Henry Goulden Ltd, 1975) is a translation (by Leo Twyman) of a book which was extremely successful in its original German edition published by Rowohlt of Hamburg in 1963. The book is much stronger in the first part, that part of Steiner's life covered by his autobiography, than it is in the later chapters which are somewhat sketchy. The author is a Christian Community priest and as might be expected it is particularly strong on the material concerned with Christianity.

Another book by a Christian Community priest, the founder of the Christian Community, is Friedrich Rittelmeyer, *Rudolf Steiner Enters my Life* (London Christian Community Press, 1954). The book is a first hand and often very vivid account of Rittelmeyer's association with Rudolf Steiner.

Perhaps the most complete of the biographies to which I have had access is Simone Rihouët-Coroze, *Biographie de Rudolf Steiner* (Paris: Triades, 1973), a well documented account of Steiner's life in 393 pages. Again the first half of the life is handled much more fully than the second. But both parts are dealt with effectively and the documentation is far from being confined to the autobiography.

Notes

Abbreviations

CL The Course of My Life, by Rudolf Steiner (N.Y., 1951)
R.   Friedrich Rittelmeyer, Rudolf Steiner Enters my Life
     (Christian Community Press, London. 3rd edition, 1954)
N.Y. Anthroposophic Press, New York, or Spring Valley.
London. Rudolf Steiner Press, London, or it predecessors.

1. CL chapter 3
2. CL chapter 3
3. CL chapter 1
4. CL chapter 1
5. CL chapter 2
6. Karmic Relationships, London, 1976. Vol. VIII
7. CL chapter 4
8. Letter of October 26, 1890, quoted by J. Hemleben in *Rudolf Steiner*. English edition, Henry Goulden Ltd, East Grinstead, 1975.
9. CL chapter 7
10. CL chapter 6
11. CL chapter 3
12. CL chapter 5
13. From Symptom to Reality, London, 1976. Lecture 7
14. CL chapter 17
15. Published by Rudolf Steiner Publications (Englewood, N.J., 1960) under the title *Friedrich Nietzsche: Fighter for Freedom*. The book contains also the memorial lecture given by Rudolf Steiner in 1900.
16. CL chapter 18
17. Riddles of Philosophy (N.Y. 1973), p. xvi
18. See note 15. The address is pp 201-212, the quotation p. 212

19. CL chapter 21
20. "Haeckel and his Opponents" in *Three Essays on Haeckel and Karma*, (London, Theosophical Publishing Co, 1914) pp. 85-87
21. Riddles of Philosophy, p. 307. This book is an enlargement, published in 1914, of *Conceptions of World and Life in the Nineteenth Century*, published in German in 1900.
22. Philosophy of Freedom chapter 12
23. CL chapter 30
24. CL chapter 30
25. See note 20. The essay referred to is the third in the book *Three Essays on Haeckel and Karma*, and is entitled "Haeckel, the Riddle of the Universe, and Theosophy." Reprinted in *Two Essays on Haeckel*, London, 1935.
26. CL chapter 27
27. CL chapter 22
28. CL chapter 26
29. From Symptom to Reality, Lecture 6. See note 13
30. CL chapter 27
31. From Symptom to Reality, Lecture 6
32. Anthroposophical Movement, lectures given in Dornach in 1923. (London: H. Collison), Lecture 3
33. Anthroposophical Movement, lecture 1
34. Occult Movement in the Nineteenth Century, London, 1973 Lecture 2
35. R. pp 56-57
36. CL chapter 37
37. Guenther Wachsmuth, The Life and Writings of Rudolf Steiner, (New York. Whittier Press, 1955.) This book recounts Steiner's life year by year from 1900 onwards. References will be therefore to years. This first reference is 1907.
38. CL chapter 34
39. Occult Seals and Columns, (N.Y., 1972) pp. 59-60
40. The address is printed in *Guidance in Esoteric Training* (London. 1972), page 88 ff. The quotation from the Basel address of September 22, 1913 was translated from S.R. Coroze, *Biographie de Rudolf Steiner*, p. 265.
41. Quoted in Arild Rosenkrantz, *The Goetheanum as a New Impulse in Art*. Privately printed, no date. Chapter 2
42. Lecture entitled "The Architectural Conception of the Goetheanum," Berne, June 21st, 1921, privately printed, available as supplement to German edition of *Der Baugedanke des Goetheanum*, (Stuttgart: Verlag Freies Geistesleben, 1958).

43. This translation has been adapted from that appearing in Wachsmuth, op. cit, note 37, under the year 1914

44. These extracts are taken from a section of Belyi's book which appeared in Number 25 and 26 of the *Journal for Anthroposophy*, Spring and Autumn, 1977 (New York, Anthroposophical Society in America). German version was translated from the Russian original by Svetlana Geier (Basel: Zbinden Verlag).

45. R. page 112

46. See especially the course given in July and August, 1922 entitled *World Economy*, 3rd edit. London, 1972.

47. Education as a Social Problem, N.Y. 1969, Lecture 4

48. F. Hartlieb, The Free Waldorf School at Stuttgart, London, 1928

49. Unpublished lecture given at the Annual Meeting of the Anthroposophical Society held in Berlin 19 January 1914

50. R. page 134

51. Human Life in the Light of Spiritual Science, Liestal, Oct. 16, 1916, N.Y. 1938

52. See note 37. Wachsmuth, 1921

53. See note 32. Anthroposophical Movement, Lecture 7

54. Spiritual Science and the Art of Healing, London, 1950, Lecture 1.

55. Golden Blade, 1958. Article entitled "Religious Renewal."

56. R. pp. 137-38

57. Introduction to a collection of prewar Berlin lectures published in German in 1926. English edition (London, 1934) bears title *Turning Points in Spiritual History.*

58. Printed as appendix to lecture given at the Hague November 5, 1922, under title "Concealed Aspects of Human Existence and the Christ Impulse" (N.Y. 1941).

59. These letters are incorporated in a book entitled in its most recent edtion (London, 1973) *Anthroposophical Leading Thoughts.*

60. This very brief summary is taken from the slightly less brief summary by Albert Steffen who, as a member of the Vorstand, was permitted to be present. The summary appears in his book *Meetings with Rudolf Steiner* (Dornach: Verlag Für Schöne Wissenschaften, 1961).

61. Golden Blade, 1958. Article by Kurt Magerstädt.

62. Karmic Relationships, London, 1975, Volume VII, Lecture 3

63. Karmic Relationships, Vol. VIII, Lecture 6

64. Golden Blade, 1958. Article "Rudolf Steiner in Holland."

65. The Last Address, London, 1967

66. See Note 59. Letter # 29, March, 1925

Index

Redemption, doctrine of, 154-155, 284
Redemption of Thinking, The, 90
reincarnation, 143-144, 154
  and Christianity, 284
  and medicine, 336-338
Reuter, Gabrielle, 34, 54, 87, 242
Riddle of Man, The, 140, 226
Riddles of Philosophy, The (Conceptions of the World and of Life in the Nineteenth Century), 3, 68, 72, 74, 140, 225-226
Riddles of the Soul, The, 140, 226, 233
Right and Wrong Use of Esoteric Knowledge, The, 285
"rights-bodies," 238-240
Rittelmeyer, Friedrich, 148-150, 152-153 249, 280-282, 300-303, 307, 358
Road to Self-Knowledge, A, 140
Roots of Education, The, 334
Rosicrucianism and Modern Initiation, 325
Rostock, University of, 49, 55-56
Rudolph, A. A., 92, 96-100, 104, 110, 112-113, 130
Russian Revolution of February, 1917 229-230

Sachs and Wolff agency, 279-280, 305
Sacred Drama of Eleusis (Schuré), *See under* Eleusis
Sanskrit, use of by Steiner, 142-144
Savitch, Marie, 167
Scheidemann, Philipp, 244
Schelling, F. W. J., 39, 128, 167-168, 223
Schiller, Friedrich, 43
School for the Science of Spirit, 295-296, 326-329, 335, and Chapter 13, *passim*
Schopenhauer, Artur, 1, 60, 65
Schramm. Heinrich, 22-23
Schreinerei, 209, 226, 273, 276, 312, 327, 329
Schröer, Karl Julius, 41-42, 50, 54, 353
Schuré, Edouard, 124, 138, 156, 163 165-167, 170-172, 191, 222, 307
Second Coming, 153-154
Secret Brotherhoods, 285, 348
Secret Doctrine, The, 118, 121, 170
sentient soul, 143, 224
Serbia, 15
Shakespeare, William, 177, 267
Sievers, Marie von (Marie Steiner), as actress, 166, 180
  and eurythmy, 163, 185
  first visit to Dornach of, 192
  and *Luzifer-Gnosis,* 95
  marriage to Rudolf Steiner, 218-219
  as organizer, 129, 136, 167
  publishing work of, 130, 139

and speech, 167
  as theosophist, 124-125, 127-128
  at Theosophical Congress, London, 110
  translator of Schuré, 166
  See also Steiner, Marie
Sinnett, A.P., 120
Smits, Lory, 183-185, 192
Social Democratic Party (Germany), 96, 98, 100, 102
Social Order, Steiner's conceptions of, 229, 234-240
Solomon, 151
Sonnenhof, 336, 339
Sophia, in Steiner's drama, 173-174, 176
Specht, Frau, 74
Specht, Ladislas, 37
Specht, Otto, 37-39, 51
Speech and Drama Course, 92, 335-336, 351-352
Speech, anthroposophical development of, 166-167, 180-181
Spirit of Fichte Present in our Midst, The, 223
Spiritual Communion of Mankind, The, 308
Spiritual Ground of Education, The, 267
Spiritual Science and Medicine, 296-297
spiritualism, 110-111, 113
  in England, 348
  as materialism, 117-118
Stages of Higher Knowledge, 140
Star of the East, Order of, 156-157, 187-188
Steffen, Albert, 276, 303, 356
Stein, Heinrich von, 55
Steiner, Johann, 14, 16
Steiner, Marie (Marie von Sievers), on compassion, 217
  and eurythmy, 226, 290, 293, 321, 333, 358
  after Goetheanum fire, 312
  during last days of Rudolf Steiner, 356, 358, 361
  letters of Rudolf Steiner to, 353
  member of executive committee, 316
  at Penmaenmawr, 321
  on private interviews, 333-334
  and publishing, 322
  as Section leader, 335
  and speech, 258, 275-276, 290, 335, 351
  as writer, 305
  See also Sievers, Marie von
Steiner, Rudolf, *passim*
  clairvoyance of, *See under* clairvoyance
  postwar opposition to, 282-293
Stirner, Max, 60, 87, 224
Stratford-on-Avon, 267, 305

374